D1256888

Scuds

A Teenage Jewish Refugee
In Nazi-Occupied Holland

HANNA KALTER WEISS

DE VORA
PUBLISHING
JERUSALEM ◆ NEW YORK

Also by Hanna Kalter Weiss:
Archetypal Images in Surrealist Prose (1988).
'Myten om Människoma': The Myth of Modern Man in
Pär Lagerquist's Novels, SCANDINAVICA, vol. 26, 1.
"Die Einsamkeit des Genies: Das Goethebild Thomas Manns,"
Language Quarterly, vol. V, 3–4.

Translations:
Cinnamoncandy (1990). *Swedish author*
Lars Ahlin's novel Kanelbiten

Jac the Clown (1995). *Swedish author and playwright*
Hjalmar Bergman's novel Clownen Jac

Four Poems, Vox Benedictina, vol. 3, 3.
(Four poems by Ella Hillbäck)

Scuds
Published by Devora Publishing Company
Text Copyright © 2006 by Hanna Kalter Weiss

COVER DESIGN: Zippy Thumim
TYPESETTING & BOOK DESIGN: Jerusalem Typesetting

ISBN: 1-932687-68-8 *Hard Cover*

E-MAIL: sales@devorapublishing.com
WEB SITE: www.devorapublishing.com

Printed in Israel

Contents

Chapter 1

Glass. Crashing. Clattering. Clinking. Glass shards come alive. Spreading. Glass splinters glisten, bounce across cobblestones, cut into sidewalks. Blanket streets. Cover pavements. Break up. Separate. Twist.

Disowned, dismembered, destroyed. Violent visions wander, drift through Hanne's dizzying whorls of dreams. Tumble. Dissolve. Return. Expand. Take hold, envelop her. The street is alive. The mob noisy, hammer-wielding, full of fury. Vents centuries of carefully ministered hatred. Her world erodes in gloatful spasms.

*

Drowsy, she opens her eyes, just a slit, unwilling to wake up in the darkness that threatens around her. She lies still, every fiber alert. Far away, someone knocks at the door. She doesn't want to hear. It must be close to midnight. Another knock. Insistent. She trembles, hesitates, rises. Moves, an automaton, stands behind the entrance door. Watches the slight shadow on the other side of the door shift, grow large in the etched milk glass, rise, recede. She feels Ruth close behind her.

The male voice outside repeats softly, "Your parents want you to come with me. Get dressed. Quickly."

His shadow expands, a huge shape in the milky glass. She unlatches the entrance door, chain on, peeps through the crack. It's a boy, come to take them to a place where they can hide. Be safe. For the moment. They hope.

"The Nazis are rounding up Jewish men," he whispers.

"What's the noise?"

"An angry mob on the loose, smashing the large street windows of Jewish stores. Looting. The synagogue is on fire."

Hanne squints at him, sleepy, trying to comprehend. Thoughts race through her head. Merely a boy. Sixteen, seventeen perhaps. Certainly not much older than she.

Her parents had left earlier that afternoon. Convinced that no one would hurt children. There were rumors of danger. A Nazi killed in France. A Jew did it. She is alone in the house with her younger sister. She hopes that he knows what he is doing.

"Hurry up, get dressed!" Ruth calls from the bedroom.

"Oh, shut up," she growls at her sister. Goody two-shoes, as usual.

"Coming. It won't take a minute," she tells him.

Yes, they have to go with him. There's no time to think. Trust fate. She shivers, unprepared for the enormity of her situation. Shoves dread down her throat. Encases it way down in her guts. His name is Walter. Nephew visiting the Wirths. Close friends.

Outside, the world is in convulsions. Ablaze. A madhouse gone berserk. The walk in the cold night is a nightmare come alive.

November 9th, 1939. *Kristallnacht*. The streets scream, gorged with swarming hordes. Mob in a frenzy. Men, SA, SS, Hitlerjugend heave axes, hurl sledgehammers. Vent their bigotry on Jewish store fronts. On Jews. Glass sheets bend in submission before they splinter off in all directions, crash in disgust at the unwarranted wrath. Eerie, frightening, surreal nightmare. Specters forged alive grimace into her face.

The scene a compound repeat of the Nazi boycott on Jewish stores, years ago. Hanne remembers. 1933 was the year it all started. Booted, uniformed robots had stood in Jewish store entrances for weeks, watching, recording the names of all who entered. Dire threats. Until no one had wanted to buy from Jews any longer. People were intimidated. Afraid. Scornful. Suspicious of Jews. It's been going on for six years now. Is this current outrage the finale?

The thoughts scramble through Hanne's head. She turns, grabs Ruth's sleeve. Drags her forward. They have to stick together. The boy ahead, the three of them sidle through shadowy, dark alleys, carefully avoiding the main streets, shunning the lights. Walk around Kuhlenwall Street, near the synagogue and the community building that has served as their school these past years after the Nazis confiscated the Jewish public school on Am Buchenbaum Street.

A vision from Dante's inferno. Hell on the loose. Boots trampling. People running, gaping, gloat into the rising fire tongues that lick the inky velvet sky. Bleeding fire prongs, red-hot fingers tear at blind, unconcerned, dumbstruck heavens. Ash pillars arch in slow curves downward, glimmer, float momentarily, spread out, then light up for the fiery finale before they dissolve and die into black anonymity over the rooftops. Inflamed pyre beaks exhale hot fumes, spread cascading heatwaves, dire exhalations that dance around street corners, drive acrid smells of burning books, and bits of inflamed parchment through dimly lit sidestreets. Fireworks for the crowd. Emanations from the nether world. Satan's Sabbath revelry.

*

It is an eternity before they reach their destination in the outskirts of the city, the home of the Wirths, close friends of their parents. Walter is just visiting from Düsseldorf. Which is why he could walk the streets. No one around here knows him to be a Jew. Being blond helps. The Wirths themselves are new to the area. Their house should be safe for the time being.

They enter quietly. Shiver with long ingrained dread. A group of twenty some friends has already gathered there, anxiously waiting for the Kalter girls to arrive. Fearful, they wait. Is there a tomorrow? A future?

*

Hanne sees their faces light up when they arrive. Thank goodness, the children. Or are they still children? Hanne can feel her parents sigh with relief, watches the lines of fear on their faces melt into some far more universal dread common to all. The Prostaks, the Nussbaums, the Goldsteins, the Franks, all friends for years, social friends used to meet for bridge, rummy, gossip behind cups of coffee and cake, now turned close brothers in suffering. Gathered in silence. Only the radio, turned low, talks. Reports the latest news.

"Come here," Mutti pulls her two girls down beside her on the sofa. Dad sits next to her. Numb. Hanne feels their body warmth after the cold street. Mutti pulls at their dresses, off-handish, as if wanting to straighten things out. She takes her comb out of her purse, starts to comb Hanne's hair.

Hanne can't figure her out. She tries to remember when Mutti last showed any concern about her. She can't. Probably never. It's always been Ruth, the pretty one, Ruth with the curly dark hair. Whom is she kidding? The others?

Hanne straightens up.

"Leave me alone. I'm not a baby!"

*

They make do with their cramped quarters, share what food they have, tell tired jokes, quarrel about bathrooms, chafe at each other, keep each other alive. Wait. Hope for the mob to calm down. The radio blares its usual hate. The BBC is out of reach. Too dangerous, even if you have a shortwave receiver. Spies are everywhere. Do they know the outrage over there, on the other side of the Channel?

*

4

Outside, the worst seems to be over after two days. Walter scouts and reports the latest news from the streets. Many of the prominent Jewish men have been taken, paraded through the streets, sent off to concentration camps. Strange names – Sachsenhausen, Dachau – become household words, everyday vocabulary, added to previous concepts like *Rassenschande, foreign elements, perverting the blond native stock.*

The friends hesitate, don't know what to do.

But life meanders on. When nothing extraordinary happens, they decide to call it quits. Five days cooped up in tight quarters is more than enough. Life has to continue.

No one talks about the future. But everyone knows that there is no future unless you get out of the country. The question is, how? Each individual must find his own way. The problem is, the world is padlocked. Closed shut. Sealed. Jews are not welcome. Anywhere.

*

Thinking back, Hanne can't remember much of that week. It's a gray-black fog in her memory. Only glimpses remain. Short snatches of recall. Funny, why can't I remember those five days properly? she wonders. Especially how we got home? She wracks her brain. Her mind draws a blank. Only bits and pieces emerge, drawn from deep inner resources. She remembers walking past the burned-out synagogue on Junkernstrasse, the gold dome a sooty black globe, humanity's black stain atop an empty ruin of carved holy stones.

She thinks of the many Saturday mornings she had climbed the flight of stone stairs to the women's section. She would turn left to the front where Gottfried Israel played the organ and she sang with the choir. Ordinarily the schoolchildren sang on Saturdays. Only on the high holidays the grown-ups took over. Then the children stood behind and supported the adults in singing the high holiday melodies.

She has a fleeting picture of herself in a procession around the synagogue with the other children, carrying their home-made flags on Simchat Torah.

The community building next door, the Jewish school the only source of Jewish learning left to the community after their public Jewish school was thrown out of the Am Buchenbaum building. It stood there still, outwardly intact. She is not certain she saw it on her way home that day. Perhaps it is a memory from a later date. The only clear memory etched into her brain is walking up the flight of stairs to their house. The four of them silent. Mutti pushing the unhinged entrance door open. The upper half, a solid square of etched milk glass only a few days ago, suddenly an unfamiliar gaping hole. They step carefully around the glass shards.

*

When Hanne looks up she sees that Dad has tears in his eyes.

"Fifty-two years of my life," she hears him mumble. She has never seen her father cry. She feels like touching him. Wants to comfort him. But what can she do? If anything, she is even more helpless than he.

"Dad, these are mere things. Lifeless furniture."

"Don't talk nonsense," Mutti cuts into the mayhem, her voice shriller than usual when upset. "Get the broom!"

Hanne can see that these dead pieces mean more to her parents than she realizes. Are they worth it?

"If I can find it," Hanne mumbles, unwilling, resentful. She doesn't feel like sweeping. The whole thing is useless.

"It's right there, behind the cabinet in the corner, next to the pantry." Ruth points to the kitchen.

"Of course, Miss Proper. Why d'you always have to meddle in my affairs?" Hanne explodes. That brat is really getting on her nerves.

The table is hanging aloft from the kitchen lamp. Hanne

watches Mutti and Dad getting busy to disconnect the table from its lofty perch before it crashes down on anyone's head.

The house is a mess. Mutti's cherished family pictures, snapshots gathered over a lifetime of family unity, dinner gatherings, grandparents, aunts, uncles, cousins, spa remembrances, lovingly collected in the center drawer of the huge oak credenza in the dining room, made homeless, strewn all over the place. Cabinet doors hang open, unhinged, bent, drawers all over the place, upside down, their contents willy nilly thrown everywhere, odd remnants of silverware in between, bent out of shape, much of it gone. Mutti's pride, the set of cut crystal wine goblets from the vitrine a hodgepodge of colorful shards covering the carpets along with smashed bits of the other cut crystal pieces and the treasured Rosenthal china.

"That's what you get for saving it for your precious company," Hanne mimics under her breath. That dumb, old-fashioned floweret pattern went out of style ages ago, anyway!

Hanne throws her defiance at her mother. Bristles with stashed anger. She glowers back into her mother's black cherry gaze that pierces her brain, cuts open, lays bare her innermost thoughts.

"You'd better wash out your mouth." Mutti glowers.

The words remain hanging in the air. Hanne waits in vain for the follow-up, the usual punishment. She shrugs. Turns to the mess around her.

"They must have come prepared, with hammers and axes," she thinks aloud. How else could they have hacked all this heavy furniture to pieces? Made the kitchen an unholy mess of flour, macaroni, rice, stuff from the pantry.

Hanne wonders who did this. The neighbors? Which ones? The Hohensteins who live to their right? Or the Frickes to their left? What were their motives? What on earth were they after?

"Someone better sweep this up." Dad takes charge from the kitchen.

Hanne takes the broom. Starts sweeping. They have to make this a human habitat again, as best they can. Life goes on.

*   *   *

Unsettling recall.

She wakes with a start, enmeshed in impenetrable darkness. Disoriented, wanting her sleep, she wonders where she is. Snores in all octaves and decibels enfold her, comforting, familiar. Her fingers tap about, slowly aware of the strawsack underneath her, the original bulge still shifting, away from the center where her body wants support. Her spine grates against the wooden plank. Bone on wood. Her fingers hit the wooden Red Cross bed frame. The four slats that support her sack of straw mattress creak their noisy complaint under her thrashing.

The faint nightlight in the distance glimmers through her half-closed eyelids and illuminates the contours of the twenty clunky, solid Red-Cross beds of her fellow refugees. She feels like a prisoner, naked, wounded, and raw inside. Reality hits her square in the face in the darkness. Unforgiving.

"Red Cross beds," she mutters crankily.

Her bones ache. She turns onto her stomach to relieve the pressure on her back. Rearranges her dislocated aching bones. Give her stomach a chance.

Kindertransport. It shoots through her mind. Holland. She is in a home for Jewish refugee children from Germany. In a strange land. With a strange language she does not understand. Too many kids. No privacy. Her inside weeps in silence. Her stomach cringes. Somersaults out of place.

Worry? Fear? Panic? Whatever it is, it has woken her up for the third night in a row.

Her bladder is full. She debates with herself whether to climb out from under her woolen blanket to walk the long hall to the bathroom at the end. Too cold. They don't heat bedrooms in this

8

country. She'll hold it until morning. Hanne crawls deeper into the warmth under her covers.

*   *   *

Kindertransport had been a lifeline after Kristallnacht. An escape. The only escape for Jews trapped like sitting ducks in the country that used to be their home. No longer. Foolish, anyone who had ever thought that the Nazi threat would blow over soon! In the six years since the Nazi takeover their hate has taken on immense proportions; an octopus still growing tentacles to spread them all over Europe and devour everything in its path. Closing in for the kill.

But no one had prepared her for refugee life. *As long as you get out.* Back then you hadn't thought beyond getting out. Perhaps rightly so. Only there is a beyond now. That's the idea. The *Before* no longer counts. What will the transition be like? Her new existence? She wonders under her covers.

Uncertainty is their fate. Children at the mercy of strangers. She comes from somewhere else. A demiurge has bent her former life of middle-class comfort out of shape into a strange question mark. It feels like the loopy limit of life. Understatement of the year. No, it's a million times worse than that. She is like a football. Kicked around wholesale. Unwanted. Unrecognized. A nobody afloat in a subterranean world of restricted human existence. She remembers once, long ago, watching a mole burrowing its way through the end of the garden patch behind her house. She could see the trail from her window above. Now she is a mole herself, burrowing in deep personal tunnels. It's just that evolution has conditioned moles to their way of life. Real moles have inner sensors that tell them where to dig. She can't breathe in this subterranean world. She feels lost.

Above ground, life lies suspended, forked into shape by the necessity to conform to forces far beyond her control. For moles like her, the motto must be *Survive Today.* Tomorrow is a shroud, tiredly afloat in a dense fog. Who may think ahead? Today you breathe. For all you know, tomorrow might never come. Unlike the moles, she is new to this game for survival. So are all the other refugees.

"I'm getting used to being a refugee," Hanne tells the darkness. Full of defiance.

"That's not true," her mind rebels. No, she'll never get used to it. Not in a million years.

Home. A place where she belongs. She longs for Dad. Even Mutti, although she had always played favorites with Ruth.

Hanne remembers the Sabbath afternoons when Dad would read the Torah portion of the week for his girls, the stories of Creation, Noah, Abraham, Sarah, Isaac and Jacob, Joseph and Egyptian slavery, the Exodus. Ancient, tribal memories. An orchestra of mountain flutes and cymbals cascading in rivulets down rocky hills, across stony plateaus into coastal sands, their echo reverberating through the ages, as alive as ever. Dad's arm around her, she learns to read the square foreign characters from his treasured leather-bound books. Makes them her own.

Argues with him about his religion. How stupid it is not to turn on a mere switch on the Sabbath. A mere switch! Instead of going through all that silly rigmarole of asking a stranger to do it? Why not do without? Better yet, get rid of all these old-fashioned, outdated laws. Dad, this is the twentieth century! They crack peanuts together, the three of them at the large dining-room table. Dad sips his tea, so sweet that the sugar draws white lines in the hot yellow-brown liquid, lightened with lots of lemon.

She misses home. Order. Privacy. Even her spats with Mutti and having to help her with the hated house drudgery are better than refugee life.

"I hate housework," Hanne mumbles, "and Mutti making me do it only made it worse." It's a crime, really, the terrible fate of being a girl – the oldest girl.

That kind of life had ended with the train leaving Krefeld. The changing of the guards one cold morning when Frau Hildegard, the leader of the Kindertransport, had stepped off the train with her list. Mutti had stepped forward with her two girls.

"Here is Hanne. And this is Ruth. Do take good care of them." Mutti's words ring in her ears.

Frau Hildegard searches her list, then reads off, "Hanne Kalter. Age fourteen. From Duisburg. Ruth Kalter. Age twelve."

Hanne watches Frau Hildegard check their names off on the long list of refugee children from Germany now in her care.

A kiss. A hug.

"Now be good, girls." Another kiss, wet as usual.

Mutti stands on the platform, shrinks into a dot as they chug away in acrid puffs of steam toward another life. She sees the other children through a hazy fog of traumatic separation.

The Dutch people at the border with their strange language welcoming the poor refugee children to their country with hot cocoa and wheat rolls on the border.

And now she is in Bergen aan Zee, a summer camp by the North Sea turned refugee shelter with nurses trained to take care of poor city children for the summer. Bergen aan Zee. Memories of routine walks to the shore, lunch, naptime, afternoon walks, dinner, playtime, bedtime. Lights off. Like a prison. Naptime? She cries hot tears into her pillow as she watches winter clouds scudding by up high outside the window over her bed. She envies the seagulls, sailing, gliding their unrestricted path through the wide-open sky outside. How free they are! She feels locked up. Chained to an uncaring, outdated authority that brooks no contradiction.

Desperate, Hanne tries to get sick. She wants to stay in bed just to break the routine. Perhaps get some extra attention. Some sympathy. She sneaks upstairs after dinner, climbs through the window onto the roof ledge outside, stands in the icy January wind, hoping to catch cold. At least get enough of a fever to raise her body temperature a few notches above normal. The wind hits her full force, driving heavy salt sprays up from the nearby raging sea nearby against her body. She stands her ground, holds on to the ledge for dear life. The wind dances in her hair, grips her light skirt, chills her bare skin, swings down her spine, bounces off her legs, her ears. Her skin puckers into goosepimples around her belly button right up into her stomach region. She breathes the salt spray, inhales deeply. How long will she have to stand out here to get sick?

It's useless. Her body refuses to cooperate. Her temperature remains normal. She is unhappy. But not sick.

From her ledge, Hanne watches a flock of seagulls swooping down and settling on the next ledge, chattering, fighting. Some carry small fish in their beaks, others try to snatch the food away. A noisy invasion. Hanne watches, fascinated. One of the gulls stands on one leg. Hanne looks again. Yes, indeed. Her second foot is missing. Hanne feels a warm flow of pity for the bird. How can this handicapped animal survive? She watches the bird carry on, just like the rest. Scolding. Fighting for bits of food.

A sudden wind gust drives around the ledge. Without mercy. One after another, the birds scud upward in its wake. Sail off into heavy gray clouds. Onward. The one-legged bird included.

"Hanne! Hanne!" The voice calling her name reaches her as she withstands the biting wind out on the ledge. "Hanne! Hanne!" The voice is impatient.

What do they want from her?

She searches her memory for something she has done wrong. Imagine they find her out here! No one is allowed upstairs until bedtime. They're not supposed to be in the bedrooms during the day.

"Rules!" she scoffs. "I'm here," she shouts into the room, climbing back onto the windowsill. Her bad conscience makes her stomach shrink.

"Where on earth were you? We've been looking for you all over the place!" Ilse stands in the door to their bedroom.

"What d'you want?"

"You're supposed to be in English class now. Mrs. Dekker wants to return our stories. The whole class is waiting for you."

"Oh. I forgot the time. Does my head feel warm? I think I'm running a fever," Hanne declares from her perch on the sill.

She hopes Ilse won't mention where she found her – they're not allowed in the bedrooms during the day. But Hanne doesn't like to plead. Better leave it to chance. Ilse won't squeal on her.

How could she forget Mrs. Dekker's English lesson on Wednesdays? It's the highlight of her refugee life. Mrs. Dekker, a retired English professor, has volunteered to teach the refugees. Last week she had assigned them to write an essay on a topic of their own choice. At first Hanne had been at a loss for a theme. There's so much to write about! Not until last Wednesday morning had she known what her topic would be. But then the brainstorm had hit. Of course! A room. Not just any room. A room of her own! Private space. *My Room.* The subject had been there all along. All her life, really. Even at home, where she had to share with Ruth. Feverishly she had written all day. Finished just in time to hand it in. No time for revisions.

Ilse stretches her hand out to feel Hanne's forehead.

"I don't think you're too warm," she says. "Why don't you go to ask Nurse and have her take your temperature after class?" Ilse's hand feels cool over Hanne's eyes, soothing contact with a fellow human being.

Hanne grabs her pad and pencil, and goes downstairs with Ilse.

"Fat chance I'll get a prize," Ilse says.

Hanne thinks of her English, which is far from perfect. "I doubt my paper's going to cut it either," she says.

All eyes turn to the two as they enter the room. Mrs. Dekker smiles from behind her stack of papers. Hanne likes her a lot. At least someone who shows interest in her.

Hanne feels her teacher's searching gaze. Or is that just her vivid imagination playing tricks? The icy wind may have scattered her brain. To think that she can fool others. They find two empty chairs and settle down. Hanne watches Mrs. Dekker shuffle her papers, slowly, deliberately as if to raise the general excitement.

The class grows silent. Mrs. Dekker looks at the papers, then at the class. Finally she picks up the top sheet.

"First prize," she says slowly, looking out at the children before her, creating tension, raising expectations. Hanne feels an electrical shock. Did her teacher's eyes graze Hanne's just now? Or is she going totally wacky? Her insides click. It can't be.

"First prize… Hanne Kalter!" Mrs. Dekker announces from her desk.

Thunderstruck, Hanne rises to get her paper. This is far more than she ever expected. To win. First prize at that. Her shoulders straighten up. Her stomach takes a leap. She must keep calm. It's unbelievable! First prize. Yippee! Her stomach turns a somersault. She walks forward, slowly. A picture of composure. She receives her paper from Mrs. Dekker. She can't help blushing.

"There are quite a few language mistakes in your story. But you write with sincerity and great feeling. That's why we thought you deserve the prize."

All smiles, Mrs. Dekker hands her the paper.

Hanne watches her bend down again and pick up a small box from the table.

"First prize gets a little extra recognition," Mrs. Dekker says and hands Hanne the small narrow box.

Hanne gazes at the box in her palm. A little silver teaspoon with the local emblem nestles inside. *Bergen aan Zee*, it says. One of those mementos people buy when visiting at the shore.

"Thank you," Hanne says, her insides shaky. She heaves a deep sigh out of nowhere and returns to her seat in a mental cloud. This is far better than getting sick.

"I didn't expect that," she mumbles, more to herself and the spoon than to Ilse. She feels her face flush. Sure, she is an expert on private space. That's from back home where she had to share with Ruth. They fought about every centimeter of space in their room. Since Holland, the need for privacy overwhelms her. Reassured,

CHAPTER 1

Hanne looks up. Some of her long lost self-esteem flickers in her. Spreads through her trunk, arms, legs. She straightens up. Out.

*

A few weeks later the ladies of the refugee committee decide that Hanne would be better off if they move her to where her sister is. *Huis Cromvliet* is in Ryswyk, a suburb of The Hague. She wonders whether her story in Mrs. Dekker's class has anything to do with that decision. Or the nurse who watched her silent crying during their afternoon nap hours. Hanne can still feel her gaze. Strange, she never asked why. She should have, really.

*

Hanne listens to Ruth's regular slight snore in the next bed. No, she hadn't been that anxious to be with her younger sister. Why should she be? The brat hasn't changed much since home. Still as irritating and pushy as ever. Trying to push her older sister aside. Get ahead of her. Push, push, push. Ever since she had come into Hanne's life.

No, Cromvliet is no answer to Hanne's problems. It is a home for refugee kids run by another set of distant wealthy committee ladies who do not know her. Surely don't care much about her beyond providing food and shelter for *these poor refugees*. She hates being a refugee. She hates being poor.

Still, life at Cromvliet is decidedly better than life in the converted summer camp in Bergen aan Zee. Nurse Haverkort, the director, is strict, but fair and decent. A friend. Hanne likes her. She and Nurse Zindel run a well organized home. Nurse Zindel is half Indonesian. Jokingly calls herself a *halfbreed*. The Dutch consider the halfbreeds untrustworthy and devious.

But that's none of Hanne's concern. What matters to her is that the home is smaller and most children are closer to Hanne's age. There are a few smaller fry. Even a baby, Yvonne. They have their own bedroom. Yvonne's mother is in some grown-up camp nearby and comes to see her baby almost daily. No more of those stupid childish walks here. The older girls have their assigned household chores before and after school. They keep the building clean. Help in the kitchen. Assist in the care of the small fry.

Mevrouw deGroot, a retired opera singer, is another plus. Round, soft, perfumed, big-bosomed in black décolletage, she rolls in on padded feet every week to teach them Dutch songs. *Kinderen van een vader* is the latest. Hanne loves to sing. The idea of everyone being created by one Father surely hits a chord. But why teach it to refugee children? Why not teach the world? Starting with the Nazi crowd in Germany.

Then there is stern Miss Kahn who lectures in world history twice a week.

Hanne stops crying. No use crying by yourself.

Julie Arendt is another benefit, newly hired to keep the kitchen kosher. Hanne's job is to help her. Not that kitchen work will ever be Hanne's cup of tea. Far from it. But Hanne knows about kashruth. And being with Julie is fun. They are friends. Julie teaches her Dutch and makes sure that Hanne pronounces the language correctly.

"Cup is *kop*; milk *is melk*; cinnamon is *kanel*; onions are *uien*."

"*Euen*," Hanne repeats with her German accent.

"No, *uien*," Julie says.

"Euen," Hanne repeats.

"No," Julie corrects, "it's *Uien, Uien, Uien, Uien!!!* not *Eu-en*." Julie almost shouts, trying to imitate Hanne's wrong pronunciation. "Look at me, *Ui-en!* Push your jaw forward. Like this."

"*Uien*."

Hanne tries, again and again. All night long.

"You're getting on our nerves," Ruth complains, and the others agree.

"I want to pronounce it right. Can you?"

"*Uien*," Hanne says when Julie arrives in the morning.

"Great. Practice. That's all it is. Let's move on to Scheveningen, *S-cheveningen*. That's where Germans usually fail."

"*S-cheveningen*," Hanne repeats. Julie looks at her, mouth wide open. All surprise.

"Say that again."

"*Scheveningen*," Hanne says.

"You're beginning to sound like a Dutch native."

"No problem," Hanne says. "If you know Hebrew, the *s-che* is a cinch. Guttural. There's *l'chaim, Chanukah, challe*. Anyway, it's the idea. *Scheveningen, Scheveningen, uien, uien, uien*. I want to lose my German identity. They've thrown me out. I'm an outcast. Being Dutch is just fine with me."

A few times Julie invites her and Ruth to spend Sabbath after services at the house of her parents. A real Orthodox Sabbath. It isn't the religion she enjoys so much as the homey atmosphere around the meal. Away from the collective straightjacket of noisy institutional life. A set table. A clean table cloth. Napkins. Intelligent talk without excessive background screaming that makes every conversation a shouting match. Individuality a luxury. To be recognized as a person. It's almost heaven. A.l.m.o.s.t.

Other invitations follow when they start walking to the youth synagogue in downtown The Hague on Saturday mornings. A group of high school Agudah boys impress Hanne with their knowledge. They conduct services there like pros. Read the Torah portion flawlessly every week. Then their parents invite the refugees for the Sabbath meal afterward. Hanne knows these invitations are well intentioned. But they make her keenly aware of her status. An outsider. A poor refugee invited to a meal in the home of the newly rich. Their questions, their behavior ooze pity. Like insults. For her poverty. For being a refugee.

Hanne hurts inside. She takes it in stride. It's better than staying home. She sweeps her wounds down into her guts like buried sores, forever festering. Hopes they'll dissolve eventually if she ignores them long enough. It's a truce of sorts. They settle like a dark shadow over her being. Her former life, her home, her parents descend farther down in her memory.

The cries wake her up. Midnight stands velvet black in the windowpanes. Hanne crawls deeper under her blanket. Pulls her pillow over her head. Tries to shut out the noise.

"Must be Yvonne," says Ruth Pestachowsky, a few beds down the aisle. Hanne hears her bed creak, sees Ruth's dark, substantial silhouette rise out of her bed. "Let's see what the kid wants." All self-assurance, Ruth stomps off toward the smaller adjoining nursery where the little ones sleep. The wooden floor squeaks angrily under her weight.

At night the older girls look after the small fry before the staff has time to get down.

"This is the third night in a row," Hanne complains and crawls out of her covers.

"You talk in your sleep," Ruth retorts from the next bed, her nose barely sticking out from under her blanket. The room is icy.

"What of it? I had a nightmare. Besides, I heard you sawing airspace like a woodcutter just a minute ago," Hanne hisses.

"You wave your arms. Make stupid noises. Like the nut you are," Ruth continues.

"Who's asking you anyway?" Hanne shoots back on her way to the nursery. Busybody. No, the brat hasn't changed a bit since home. Unforgiving perfectionist to her fingertips. Hanne shrugs in the dark. Who wants to start a fight in the middle of the night?

Little Yvonne stands by the rail of her crib, tears streaming down her round baby face. Hanne looks into those huge gold-flecked brown eyes full of tears. Her diapers are down. Poop all over the crib. Smeared over her tiny hands, across that soft round face.

"Phew! What a stink! Do you think she wanted to eat it?" Hanne shrinks back.

"We'll have to clean her up. And change the sheets," Ruth directs from the faucet, where she is filling the pail.

"Hush, Yvonne," Hanne says, fully awake now. "Hush, baby." She takes the child out of the crib, undresses her, and holds her soft body, rocking and soothing her, while Ruth washes off her rump.

"Good girls," Nurse Haverkort says from the door, still tying her gown. Her hair sticks out like a halo. The girls relax.

"Little Yvonne misses her mother," Nurse Haverkort says, cooing reassuringly as she sits down and takes the baby onto her lap.

Yvonne's mother's camp can't be too far away. As often as she comes by, Hanne muses. Together they finish cleaning, change sheets, wrap the baby in clean pajamas. All the other kids are wide awake by now. It's mayhem. They have to soothe and reassure the rest.

"Thanks, girls, for your help. Clean up and get yourselves back to bed now so we can turn the lights off," Nurse Haverkort takes final command of the situation.

They feel the cold water on hands and face. The chill in the unheated room. Goosebumps crawl down their spines. They towel dry. Then crawl back under their blankets. Happy to be back. Of course, everybody is awake now. Who can think of sleep? They hear Nurse Haverkort move about next door in the dark, a guardian angel watching the small ones go back to sleep. Hanne snuggles under for warmth. Everything goes quiet.

"Goodnight."

They hear Nurse Haverkort tap back upstairs. The dark is quiet once again. Hanne waits for the dawning day.

*

It's a beautiful day in early spring when Hanne and Ruth have a surprise visitor.

"Uncle Henry!"

His muscular body sits square in the large hall. Hanne runs over to him. They hug.

"I bring regards from your parents in Gothenburg. We just

left them. Our visas finally came through. We're on our way from Sweden to the United States."

Hanne looks at the familiar face. Her mother's brother. The same black cherry eyes under folded eyelids look down at her, the distinctly Bindefeld eyes she herself has inherited.

"How is Aunt Jean? Sue?"

"They're fine. Our boat anchored in Rotterdam this morning. Just for the day. I got permission to visit you in The Hague for a few hours."

"I'm glad you did," Ruth says. They hug. Sadness in delight. Family members on the move in all directions these days.

"I couldn't pass up the chance to visit. And give you the good news. Now that we've gone, Uncle Adolf and Aunt Regi in Sweden have enough room in their house for your parents. They arrived there a few days ago."

"Great! They're out of Germany," Hanne says. "The best news we've had in a long time. Their letter must be on its way here."

What a relief to have Mutti and Vati out of Germany. She sees Ruth and herself joining them already.

"Too bad that is has to be such a short visit," Ruth says.

"Yes. But the boat won't wait. Here, this is for you." Uncle Henry gives them each a five guilders coin. Rises heavily. Then he leaves. Hanne looks after him, a heavy-set man, his balding forehead ending in a round polished crown, his body slightly forward bent as he lopes onward to another life in another country with another language, other mores.

It feels good to be part of a large family. Help each other in need. She longs to be with her parents. Wherever they are. Might even overlook the old lady's habit of making her drag that kid sister along whenever she wants to meet with her girl friends. Or both her parents insisting that she give in to that conniving brat whenever they get into a fight.

"You're older. You have to be smarter," she mimics their unfairness with a shrug. Memories. She hopes for their visa to the United States to come soon. It's the basis for their permission to stay in Sweden. Once the visa comes through they'll all emigrate together to the United States. A family once again.

"I can't wait for our visa to come," Hanne informs the heavy silver coin in her hand. She has not seen this much money in a long time.

"It won't be a day too soon," Ruth says.

"Five guilders. We're rich," Hanne says. She tries to figure out what she'll do with her sudden wealth. It's a lot of loot, all right. Only not nearly enough for what she wants.

Chapter 2

"We're leaving tomorrow," Liesel says, all smiles. Her body exudes happiness from every pore.

Hanne looks at the two letters Liesel waves in front of her. "So soon? I'll miss you."

Hanne squints at her current best friend. At the official letters she has just gotten. One from her parents that tells her of the family's immediate emigration to Brazil, the other from the authorities releasing her and her brother David for departure to Rotterdam where they'll meet with their parents to board the M/S Vespucci, bound for Brazil.

Hanne is jealous. Boundlessly jealous. She can't help it. The vibes coming from her friend's body hurt. Drive her insane.

"I wish our visa would come too," she mumbles.

"It'll soon come, you'll see," Liesel tries to comfort her friend. "I'll miss you too."

Hanne suspects that Liesel's father, a former judge in Berlin, knew how to rattle the right connections to get out.

"I shouldn't be jealous," Hanne says. "After all, my parents are out. But you're getting out of *here*. How I wish I could too."

She looks at the pretty face before her, the rosy cheeks, the black hair that contrasts so well with the stark violet-blue eyes.

"Promise you'll write? Let's keep in touch."

They exchange snapshots.

"I hate living in this dump," Hanne says.

The dump is Huis ten Vijver, where the refugee committee has moved the children during the summer, consolidating several refugee homes under one roof to cut costs. Ten Vijver lies in the Scheveningen Woods, one of the ritziest sections of The Hague. It is the largest among the large estates in the neighborhood. The owner, a government official in the Dutch West Indies, has put it at the disposal of the homeless refugee children from Germany.

The estate is huge. It's named for the large pond at the end of the grounds. Awed, Hanne marvels at the opulence of her new home. Gaudy, right out of the fairy tales. Or Hollywood movies. She gapes at the Rococo-style paintings on the vaulted ceilings in the dining and living rooms of the mansion. Rose-tinted shepherds and shepherdesses survey, from their lofty heights, the strange creatures that now occupy their gaudy territory. Smile in dainty unconcern down on the stateroom, suddenly degraded to sleeping quarters for German refugee children, where clunky wooden Red Cross beds have replaced the original, delicately curved period furniture. Wooden squares, covered with straw filled hemp sacks as mattresses, on which suitcases and small personal belongings of all kinds and shapes give themselves airs. Wet towels hung out to dry on the top part of the wooden frame.

Chubby cherubs and cupids float on pink-edged clouds on ceiling and walls, indifferent to the dank smell of fresh straw that permeates their building these days. At night from her shifting, settling straw sack Hanne stares at the images from an era far removed from her drab, musty reality, wonders about the owners of the mansion and the people who built it, marvels at their world, their life, their concerns. More than ever she shrinks into herself. Not that she dislikes the individual kids around her. She resents them as a crowd, hates to be one of the many. They encroach on her life, cramp her breathing space, interfere with her need to have a quiet place of her own, to be by herself. A space from which she can reach out to others when she is ready. Without interference.

She closes her eyes. With the exception of Liesel. But she is about to leave. There is no escape. There is no space. No peace.

"Wish I could leave. Away from here," Hanne mumbles longingly into space.

Her sleep is filled with ruminations. Unfulfilled desires.

Hanne thinks back to when they first heard of the great big move from Ryswyk to the other side of the city. Ryswyk to Scheveningen. The day Nurse Havercort announced, "Next week we'll go and stuff mattresses – fill jute sacks with straw."

"Do we need new mattresses?"

"Yes. Cromvliet's owner is back from Jakarta and wants it back. There'll be a new place in Scheveningen. It's bigger, for a lot more children."

"It's cheaper to run that way," Nurse Zindel added. Hanne heard an undertone of dissatisfaction. Or jealousy? Or was it anger?

"Are you coming with us?" she asks.

"No. There'll be other people there. No more nurses."

Actually, it had been fun to stuff the sacks. For several days in a row Nurse Haverkort had packed lunch and gone with the older of *her children*. Like a picnic outing. The smelly straw itched and left red marks on their skin. They got acquainted with Ten Vijver, the new place.

"Wow, what a fancy neighborhood," Erna Faktor says.

"Have you seen the house? It's a mansion," Greta says.

"Inlaid oak flooring, all waxed and shiny," Arnold says.

"Who's going to keep all this in tip-top shape?" they wonder together.

They walk through. Awed. Hardly dare to step on the polished oak floor, buffed to a shine.

"La-di-da! My mother should see this!" That was Ruth Pesta-chowsky, of course, trampling ahead.

"Just look at the garden. You can get lost in it. And this pond!" Hanne is fascinated.

After that they had settled down in the garden to the mundane task of filling straw mattresses for two hundred beds.

"Phew. The straw stinks," Sonya Bronstein sniffs into the giant heap in the corner.

"Be careful. It'll scratch your skin bloody if you hold it close. Don't take too much at once," Nurse Haverkort warns.

They had lunch and got used to the straw smell. In the fresh air it wasn't so bad. And the scratches will heal soon, they had comforted themselves. After all, it was for the common good. Too bad they would lose Nurse Haverkort. Even Nurse Zindel.

Hanne had found it hard to separate from Julie. They had promised to keep in touch. But never did.

Change had becomes an integral part of their unsettled lives.

* * *

"Hanne, can you come in a minute? I want to talk to you." Battist, the co-director at Ten Vijver, asking her into her office.

Hanne scrutinizes her director's round face with the broad, flat nose, the blond braids peasant fashion wound around her head and held in place with hairpins. The hairdo looks like a basket. Several loose hairpins stick out, releasing ends of blond fluff.

"Sure," Hanne says and enters. Lampe, the male half of the directorial team, is in the back, tinkering with his broken typewriter. Loud, upset grunts fill the air around him.

"Did you know that we moved the Flesh sisters into one of the maid's rooms on the third floor?" Battist asks, motioning Hanne to sit down by her desk. Trying to get confidential. Hanne is on guard.

"Yes."

Of course she knows. She envies Mathilde and Sidy Flesh their own little room up in the attic. They're the oldest *children* in the home, if you can call them that. As far as committee rules are concerned, Mathilde at 26 and Sidy at 19 are far too old to qualify for the children's compound. People their age belong in the grown-up refugee camps. How they ever managed to get included in a Kindertransport is a puzzle. Their rabbi father must have helped. It's so-called *special pull*. The whole world runs on special privileges.

Because of her age, Mathilde holds a special position, somewhere between staff and kids. Mathilde runs the sewing room in the attic with Sidy's help. They take care of all the sewing and mending needed for the home. A real cushiony job, as far as Hanne can see. While the rest of them go to school. The two spread an aura of studied privilege. They don't scrub or get their hands dirty on cleaning bathrooms after school. Or sorting dirty laundry. Or breathe damp washing machine vapors in the basement laundry. The older girls hate them. Avoid them, their self-conceit, their pompous arrogance, their acting special.

Hanne takes a deep breath. Swallows her mixed feelings. Waits intently for what Battist has to say.

"There's room for a third bed. We thought that you might like to move in with them."

Battist's words hang heavily in the stale smoke of the office air. Hanne glances over to where Lampe's broad athletic back bends over his typewriter, absorbing their conversation. Thoughts race through her mind. Room with these two fanny lickers? Would that make her *special* too? She doesn't want to think. She has to accept. Quiet. Privacy.

"I'd love to."

"All right. We thought you would. When you're done with your chores today, you can pack your stuff and move upstairs. Take fresh sheets for your bed."

"Thanks, Battist." Hanne is all smiles. To get out of the noisy communal bedroom? Supergreat. Her head sings. Her feet itch to leap. Enough staring at dumb peach-skinned, curly-haired blond cherubs floating in curlicue clouds. Their lofty smiles remain forever vacuous, empty, unmoved. They provide no clues! Her roommates are nice kids, but twenty-five all at once is way too much. To exchange them for two! Any old day! Even for pompous elitists!

"I'm moving upstairs. With the Flesh girls," Hanne tells Ruth, who watches her older sister pack her gear.

"Oh?"

Hanne feels envy float from Ruth's bed to her own, fill the air between the two beds. Time to put some distance between her and that pushy sister of hers. The brat has cramped her style long enough. Now let her squeal on her to Mom and Dad!

"Yeah. Battist told me this afternoon," Hanne says and snaps her suitcase shut with decisive finality. Ready to lug it upstairs. Mustn't forget my towels. They're too damp to pack with the rest.

*   *   *

Hanne is lying in her new bed, absorbed in the adventures of the *Daddy Longlegs* orphan when her roommates come in.

"In bed already? It's barely nine o'clock," Mathilde says from above.

Hanne's mind leaps from the story world of the lucky, freckled teenager to current reality.

"I want to finish the book before the lights go off at ten," Hanne explains. "It's due back tomorrow."

"Hmmm."

Hanne hears the two tussle in their corner by the window. She tries not to mind. Secretive as usual. Now they start crunching again. Where on earth do they get all the money for snacks and cookies?

These two never share. Either snacks. Or secrets. She senses keenly that she's the third wheel in their little attic. An intruder. Tolerated necessity to fill available space. Oh, well. You can't change people. The situation even less. She tried when she first moved in to make friends with them. The glass wall around these two stops her.

Okay, have it your way. There's always the park. The pond. Above all, her books. From behind her book she glances at the slanted rafters over the window. Whitewashed walls. A typical, plain attic for maids. Hanne likes it just fine. It beats having to share the master quarters downstairs with a noisy crowd. Fancy decorations make no sense in this environment. It would be nice to have a secretive Daddy Longlegs turn up. With enough money to send her to boarding school where they clean up after you!

She hears their whispers, their crunching.

"So different from Ruth and me," shoots through her head. For as long as Hanne can remember, she and Ruth have always fought. Who gets more dessert? The bigger piece of cake? Mutti had to count out the cherries, the grapes so no one got more.

Mutti had dressed them alike for the longest time. But Hanne had put a stop to that when she was in second grade.

"Why do you always give us the same things to wear?"

"I think it looks cute for sisters to look alike."

"But we don't look alike. My hair is straight, hers curls. Mine is light brown, hers is black. People always stop to look at her. 'Oh, look at that. Like a doll. Cute as a button,'" she mimics. "As if I didn't exist." Hanne drills her eyes right back into Mutti's flashing black gaze. "Did Grandma make you wear things to match Aunt Marie, or Aunt Frieda?"

"All right. Starting tomorrow you may choose what you want to wear for the day."

Hanne had stared at her mother, unbelieving. That was the first time she had ever won an argument with her mother. That at least had settled the matter. From then on she could wear what she wanted. Be herself. Not part of a team, or whatever you could call it. She took a deep breath. It wasn't easy to win arguments against Mutti. She should have spoken up more often.

Through her indignation she can hear the faint murmur of

the two in their corner by the window. She'll extend *Daddy Long-legs* tomorrow for another day. She turns her light off.

"Good night," she says into the semi-darkness before she settles on her straw mattress and goes off to sleep.

*   *   *

It's Saturday afternoon. No chores today. Hanne sits by the pond, resting up from the long walk to the youth synagogue in the morning. She loves to daydream by the still waters. Listen to the throaty croaks of lovesick toads, their bloated carmine throats undulating, blown into huge, swelling red balloons, declaring their readiness to mate. Heat-flushed pairs glued to each other crowd the dark-green lily pads. Hanne marvels at the dragonflies, wings fluttering atop a narrow grass blade, delicate, translucent, shimmering in all rainbow colors. The poplars extend to double their height in the prone water below, sleek guardians between earth and sky. A slight breeze ripples their mirror surface into a million ruffles. Hanne watches two swallows quarrel over a worm in the grass. The bigger one wins.

The pond is Hanne's private world. She would like to stay here, forever, bound up in her private reality. It's like an inner fight every time she has to return to face reality. Without mercy.

"The Agudah boys are here," Käte Neuberger shouts from the gate.

The Agudah group has made it a habit to visit the refugees at Ten Vijver every so often instead of inviting the refugees home for the Sabbath meal. Nine boys, dressed in their Sabbath suits, wearing the customary hats, even in this heat. Religious to the hilt.

"It's a long walk. Why do you make the effort?" Hanne once asked Aron, the leader by sheer size. At seventeen, he is taller than the rest. Rather good-looking, Hanne thinks, flattered by the attention he's given her lately.

"It's a mitzva," Aron says. Hanne could see his eyes light up with pride for what he is doing.

"The group has decided to invite the refugees to a summer

camp in the country," Benji joins in. "Aron and I are working out the plans."

"That's awfully nice of you," Hanne says. Of course it's good to have outside contact with the normal world when you're locked up in a refugee home.

Hanne remembers the conversation. And the week of camping out with the group. Fun all right. Tents, sleeping bags, kitchen duty, on a site near a barnyard close to mooing, cud-chewing cows. Holland is a beautiful country, easygoing, small, lots of heavy clouds and rain, sea, ocean, lakes, canals. Water, water everywhere.

Reluctant to leave her peaceful hideout, Hanne saunters back to the circle behind the building where they always meet. She wipes her brow. It's hot. Sticky. She wonders about the Agudah boys. Their dedication to teach their brand of Jewish heritage to the refugees. It must have been a grueling, long hot walk out here today. In their heavy clothing. Do they expect an extra seat in heaven?

"All right. We better stop with whatever we're doing and entertain them," Lilly says.

"They come here to teach *us*," Hanne says.

"There isn't much to do in this August heat anyway," Ruth says. They look at the heavy thunderclouds gathering on the horizon.

"It might blow over. If it starts to rain we can always go inside," Ruth says.

They watch the boys enter through the gate.

"Shabbat Shalom."

They sit down in the grass, listen to stories by Sholom Aleichem, then sing Hebrew songs.

Battist comes out with lemonade and cookies.

"My joints are getting stiff," Lilly complains.

"Let's dance a hora," Käte suggests.

"Good idea."

Several girls get up. Stretch their stiff joints. The rest of the refugees and the Agudah leaders keep on singing.

Happy to move, Hanne, Ruth, Erna, Käte, Lilly and Gerda interlock arms and dance a hora to the tune of the singers.

Shouts. Suddenly Aron stands in front of them.

"It's the Sabbath. You're not supposed to dance on the Sabbath," he screams, furious, like an insulted godhead. A few of the girls stop their dancing. The fun of the afternoon has suddenly evaporated.

"What's the matter with you? We're just dancing. Enjoying the Sabbath!" Hanne shoots back. Dares him. No one has ever forbidden her to dance on the Sabbath. Not even her father.

"You better stop. It's sacrilege," Aron declares.

"Who makes those rules?"

Hanne gathers the girls. They keep on singing, dancing.

"You're crazy. A real killjoy. If your religion demands idiotic things like not dancing on the Sabbath, you can keep it," Hanne tells him, and she means it. They continue. Defiance in action. Stupid Agudah.

Aron shrugs. Returns to his group of singers. They are all angry. Bits of conversation hit them in the heat, like *ingratitude, shameful, goyim.*

"He's nuts," Hanne fumes. "I'm not going to let him tell me what I can and cannot do! He has no right to order us around."

"Who's he to make up new laws?" Lilly agrees. The friends nod agreement. The others mill around the Agudah boys. The afternoon is ruined. The boys leave soon afterward.

"Far as I'm concerned, they don't have to come back," Hanne declares to the others. "I don't owe them anything. I didn't ask them to spend money on us *poor refugees.* What do they think? That I'll become a Chasid out of gratitude? That'll be the day!"

* * *

The sudden roar awakens her. It's overhead. Deafening. Roars past, diminishes gradually, disappears. Returns in a new wave. Startled out of her sleep, Hanne squints, opens her eyes slowly into the gray-rose dawn. There's a faint strip of light in the lower section of the small attic window. Suddenly wide awake.

"What is that?"

She runs to the window, horror in her limbs. Sidy gets there with her. Mathilde is slower, still getting out of her bed. They stare into the dawning morning.

"What on earth is going on?"

There it is again. Worse. Louder still. Like thunder descending on them, enveloping them, drowning them, a huge black monster, buffed to a shine by the first rays of the sun just tearing loose from the horizon. The monster dives out of the sky, right above their heads. Hanne ducks in automatic reflex, expects it to crash on her. But it zooms past in a deafening roar, barely misses the roof gable overhead before it disappears behind the house in a cloud of black smoke. There are more of them, shiny black vultures that grow huge out of the horizon, boom past overhead in short succession.

Speechless, Hanne watches thousands of balloons unfolding in the widening strip of light over the North Sea, glistening golden red in the rising sunlight. Float inland. Fill the sky over the woods. She stares in utter disbelief. The sky grows full of them – parachutes, opening wider and wider, crowd the heavens. Ominous helmeted messengers dangle in their strings, evil agents boding no good. Her mouth goes dry. Her stomach turns. Her limbs weaken.

Volleys of anti-aircraft from the nearby beaches rend the air, fiery flares dart across the heavens hung with live cargo. Deafening mayhem. It hardly matters whether some parachutes arch downward, fold, sink. Get stuck in trees. Millions of others take their place. The heavens remain clouded over with these strange apparitions that block the sun. Malevolence incarnate, bent on destroying the civilized world. Hanne shivers in her pajamas. Her spine tingles with dread well remembered. Fear absorbed in a long ago.

"Germans," Sidy mumbles next to her.

"They've caught up with us," Mathilde says behind them.

A hollow feeling spreads in Hanne's stomach. She feels weak. Exhausted. Unwilling to register what is plainly before her. The facts are clear enough. The shooting. The flares. The roaring airplanes. Worst of all, the helmeted creatures that hang in these glittering balloons. Prehistoric Grendel, resurrected in Nazi garb, spewing its fire breath from its fen, its hornwebbed, beastly tentacles in a wide westward sweep gluttonous for the kill. They are trapped. For a second time. Sitting ducks in a mudcake pond, earmarked to bake to a crisp.

"The Nazis are here."

* * *

They dress in a hurry. Run downstairs. The others are already assembled in the dining hall. Pastoral shepherds smile their vacuous smiles in their curlicue clouds. Only two staff members remain to pass out breakfast. Battist and Lampe are gone. *Needed to be with their families*, the staffers say.

"Sure... who wants to be found with Jewish children on a day like this?" Hanne is full of sarcasm. Sidy nods.

Hanne looks for Ruth. Takes her tray over to where she sits with her chums.

"Let's sit together," she tells her younger sister.

"If you want to," Ruth says with a nonchalant shrug. She moves closer. Hanne feels her body warmth against her.

Somewhere in her brain her mother's voice drones, "You're the older one. You ought to know better. You should give in."

"Does that mean that I've got to take care of her too?" Hanne used to argue vehemently. Still does. She has a bad conscience. Outside, the planes thunder past, their noise mingles with anti aircraft flak clatter. Rat. tat. tat. tattak. The solid building shakes in fever convulsions.

It's May 10, 1940.

"Let's sing Happy Birthday to Lilly," the staffer says up front and steps behind fat Lilly Rosen from Berlin. Lilly is twelve years old this tenth day in the beautiful spring month of May. How lucky can you get?

"*Happy birthday, dear Lilly, happy birthday to you,*" they sing. Loud. Defiant.

"Can't blame the staffers for leaving," Mathilde meditates across the table. "Who wants to get caught minding us? We'll have to do our best caring for the small ones."

"What does the radio say?"

*

Radio Nederland screams with war. The Germans have invaded Belgium too. And in France, they simply walked around the "impenetrable" Maginot line while the French slept in front of it.

"Funny, I always wondered what war looks like," Hanne ruminates amidst the mayhem. She had always pictured the streets littered helter-skelter with wounded and dead. Who was there to ask? Certainly not her parents.

The girl she played marbles with on Fulda Street years ago had warned her of the coming war. "They'll use gas next time."

"How would you know?"

"Oh, my parents get a trade journal. It has pictures of people with gas masks. They show how to use a gas mask."

Hanne absorbs it, frightened. Her parents never talked about such matters. The girl's parents sound like Communists. Something inside her warns her. These people are odd. Not at all like her parents. Or their friends. Mutti and Dad aren't interested in any wars! War is in the past. Something older folks talk about. Like they talk about the inflation, when a loaf of bread cost a bagful of money. Imagine. No. Hanne shrugs. We know better than to do the stupid things they did in the past. We are the future.

That's what she had thought, then, with childish superiority.

Hanne shrugs, gets back into the present. What a simple-minded fool she had been. War does not depend on those who want peace! The bully decides that. And you'd better be prepared to stand up to him. Better yet, carry a big club so he won't attack you in the first place. With guns and tanks to back you up.

I don't think they'll use gas now, she argues with herself. It would endanger the paratroopers if they did. As for the corpses, so far there are none in the woods here, as far as she can see. She listens to the rat-tat-tat-tat of the anti-aircraft from the coast nearby.

"War is a lot worse than I ever imagined," Ruth breaks into her train of thought.

"You better believe it," Hanne looks at her little sister. The brat who's no longer little!

A sudden stabbing pain cuts through her abdomen. Makes her double up. She feels a warm stream trickle down between her legs. It won't stop. Funny, she had forgotten all about menses for over two years. Ever since she left home her period had stopped. Not that she ever missed it. Now it's back with a vengeance. *Ausgerechnet Bananen*! What an utter nuisance!

"My period. That's all I need today. I better get some napkins," she tells Ruth and heads for the bathroom. She feels bloated. Tired. Everything hurts, inside and out.

*

"Look at the sky over there," someone shouts later that day.

They watch the northwestern sky flame crimson, then turn a bloody red. Fiery black smoke pillars rise into the evening sky. Stretch for help from an impotent universe gone berserk. Rotterdam and its harbor are burning. Going up in flames.

*

Five days of utter confusion. The radio news keeps getting worse. The Queen has left the country. Her government with her. The Queen is safe. Good for her. But we are here. The air remains alive with planes, rockets, flares, anti-aircraft clatter, booms. Searchlights rotate, scan the nightly heavens, turn night into an eerie coruscation. Army trucks, jeeps, cars keep rolling on the highways. A hushed noise invades the woods surrounding their estate.

Five interminably long days in May. Hanne can't stay inside. The house chokes her. The tension is unbearable. She does her chores. Then escapes to her favorite spot in the park. Numb, she listens to the branches rustle in the gentle breeze, watches their bare bark sprout tiny green leaves. Buds peep into a world full of wonder. The birds sing their eternal love songs overhead. Tiny creatures feather their nests. Procreation in progress. Life.

*

Nothing here has changed. Nature is as serene, as lovely, as bustling as ever. The sun shines. The rays vibrate, scintillate. Warm. Invigorate the trembling earth. The damp grass smells growth. Verdure. Spring has come. She finds it impossible to fathom that outside a warped world is rising, that slaughter and horror are marching to a ghastly drumbeat outside their gates. She feels the soil under her feet lose its invigorating touch. The pond holds its pearl breath with an inaudible sigh. The sun's golden sparks dance tormented jigs in emerald ripples. The poplars stand as erect as ever, unmoved, stark green regal guards on the far side of the pond. Yet, imperceptibly they lose their protective stolidity in the wavy water mirror below. The world is rotting away at its core. Nothing is solid.

Hanne wants to scream out loud. Her heart begs for protection. But her screams get stuck inside her throat, throttle somewhere in her stomach region. All she can manage is a groan. She feels terribly old. Tired. All the world's sorrow has settled on her shoulders. What is to become of us? Her. Ruth. She is responsible for her younger sister. That's what her parents always told her.

"You're the older one. You ought to give in."

Hanne cringes, remembering the unfairness of it all. The brat knew it. Knew how to take advantage. Liberties. Knew she could get away with it.

Hanne has a fleeting memory of revenge. Once. Mutti had given the maid some of her beautiful dresses. Slinky, silky, gorgeous georgette affairs Hanne had suddenly detected hanging in

Alwine's closet. She remembers taking a lead pencil and drawing circles and lines across those sheer things. Just for fun. Really, just for fun. She reels in memory on her bench. What else could have prompted her to do it? She recalls shouts. Mutti's cutting voice, demanding. She remembers being frightened. Vividly. Most of all, that she kept mum when Alwine fussed and Mutti called for the culprit. She had kept her mouth shut when they accused the kid of doing it. Ruth crying. Ruth taking a licking. Protesting. Screaming. Hanne can still feel the slaps. They hurt her as much as the kid.

She never owned up to what she had done. Kept quiet. Mutti had a hard slap. The kid's screams still bother her. She had been afraid to admit the truth. Afraid of Mutti. Her dark gaze that pierced your heart. Her hard hand, with its shiny, long dark-red manicured fingernails hitting the kid's butt. Oh well. Hanne shrugs off her memory. Served the brat right for always taking advantage of being the younger one. The pretty one with the curly black hair. The one everybody liked.

"You're older. You ought to have better sense."

She can hear them still. The words are carved into her brain. They infuriate her. She gnashes her teeth. It isn't right. It's unfair.

"Why do I always have to give in? It's not my fault that I'm older than she!"

*

Five endless days. An eternity. A warped world outside. A world without mercy. The shooting stops. Boots trample the roads. In fiendish formations. Companies. Battalions. *Radio Nederland* informs the listeners that the Queen, her family, her government are safe in England. Then Canada. Suddenly it goes silent. A while later the radio broadcast resumes with a German slant. We are the masters of the *blitzkrieg*. In addition to the eastern countries, we now rule Holland, Belgium, and most of France. Supreme conquerors of the western European coast.

"The irony of it all," Mathilde says. "Last year we fled the Germans. Now we're right back where we were."

"Yes, right back in German hands. And refugees on top of it," Hanne says. Her period is waning. The stabbing pains settle into dull constancy, then disappear altogether. An unavoidable nuisance. Mutti said it goes on for life.

"Who's next?" Sidy says.

England across the Channel is next. Then the United States. But no one dares to even voice these thoughts out loud.

"I wonder how Mutti and Vati are doing? Do they know about this war?" Ruth wonders.

"Well, for one thing, Sweden is free. They are safe. I'm sure they know what's going on here."

"It's about time they send for us," Ruth complains.

"It's hard to imagine being home again. I mean as a family," Hanne spins on the dream. Something in her brain concludes that being in conquered German territory makes that dream an impossibility. But she can't give in. Does not want to give in. Debates with herself. Informs Ruth, "Even if it's impossible. You have to keep on believing in it".

Hanne can't stand the tension any longer. Somewhere in her stomach area something tightens, cramps, hurts. Without a word she gets up, walks out into the garden to her favorite spot. Lies down in the cool grass and meditates into the heavy, loaded, cloudfilled sky. Scuds. Mountains. Valleys. Lighter, darker, endless, the clouds dissolve, regroup, take on shape, scatter, spread, dissipate. Grow heavy. A flash of lightning zigzags between them. When is too much too much?

Chapter 3

Shortly after the take-over, ten Vijver is dissolved. The original committee gone, the Jewish Council assumes the care of the Jewish refugee children. The children are parceled out among the Jewish families in The Hague.

Is it resentment she feels for the Goldbergs? Loathing? Hate? Hanne tries to find the proper word for her feelings, in German, in Dutch, whatever. Fatso hypocrites, that's what they are. All three of them – husband, wife, son. Do-gooders who use her as a maid without pay.

Hanne is in revolt. It's a silent revolt. Can't show it. They'd call it ungrateful. That's the problem. Another problem is her birthday. August fourth is coming up. Should she remind them? They have seen her papers. Know she'll turn fifteen soon. They tell everyone of their new houseguest. Member of the family. Ha!

She crawls out of bed. Stretches.

"I'm fifteen today," she says out loud, feeling grown up. Lonely. Gets dressed, full of secret expectations. It's her special day, after all. No matter what. Deliberate, determined, she enters the kitchen to prepare breakfast for her new family. Grinds coffee beans, boils water, drips it through the filter. She hears them stir in the bedrooms upstairs. Sonny flushes the toilet. Mr. Goldberg gargles in the bathroom. She sets the table in the overstuffed dining room – white bread, brown bread, rusks, butter. Strawberry jam for Mr. Goldberg. Sonny likes chocolate sprinkles on his rusk. She puts the glass jar next to his plate. Funny taste buds. And these ridiculous, cheap lace doilies under those horrid porcelain knick-knacks and Czech cut glass on mantel and furniture. The sun glides through the heavy, partly drawn draperies that give the room, actually the whole house, a dour smell.

"Thank goodness for the sunshine," she tells herself. Its rays paint pale spots between the flowers on the moss-green wallpaper, tingle in silver reflections from the heavy silver candelabra. Hanne gazes at the Jewish calendar with an angry Moses holding his tablets on the mountaintop, his bearded head ringed with a yellow halo. Stares at the square with the big number four. Her day.

The Keren Kayemet box stands light blue and prominent on the tea table underneath. Mrs. Goldberg stuffs it with pennies every Friday evening before lighting the Sabbath candles. Hurries back to the kitchen to see to the black brew. Tastes it. She loves coffee. Strong coffee. She hears them trample down the stairs. Waddle into the dining room.

"Good morning," Mrs. Goldberg sticks her head into the kitchen.

"Good morning. Breakfast is ready," Hanne says. She fills the porcelain coffee pot decorated with those god-awful tiny flowerets.

"Roses," she mumbles. No taste at all. Remember, old lady, this is my birthday. Hanne whistles a tune under her breath to cheer herself up. Ready. She walks with her black brew behind Mrs. Goldberg into the dining room.

"Good morning." She places the pot next to the mistress of the house. Seats herself. *Member of the family!* they call it.

"Good morning." The men continue chewing. No one thinks of her birthday. Hanne thinks of home. Her birthday has always been a problem.

"Too bad it's in the middle of summer vacation," Mutti used to say. "There's no one here to invite." Or they were themselves in some spa.

Right. She never had a real birthday party. Only those stupid family gatherings with a cake. But never a party with lots of kids, surprise presents, ice cream, games. After all, presents are an important part of birthdays. Hanne sighs. That was then.

No letter from her parents, either. Probably held up at the border. The Nazis check every piece of mail coming in and going out of the country. No use to remind the fatsoes of her birthday. Downright foolish. They only care for themselves. Their convenience. Their money. Oh yes, above all, their food. She eats her hot cereal.

"I'll be late for dinner tonight," Sonny says into the silence. "The group is meeting to discuss the finances of the camp for the refugees. It set us back quite a lot." He shoves his plate back on the table, ready to leave.

Hanne can feel his sly gaze in her direction as he heaves himself out of the chair. Is he holding her responsible for the shortfall? She looks at him. Their eyes meet for a second. Then he walks out. She gives an invisible shrug. All right, blame it on us. Didn't you know beforehand that doing good costs money? She hears the front door slam shut behind him.

Hanne takes note. It means serving dinner twice tonight.

"They are such a well-meaning, devoted group," Mrs. Goldberg reflects with a sigh between chews. Her eyes beam with pride. Sonny. She looks full at Hanne. Beady eyes inside folds of flesh in a moon face. An overripe melon with reddish perm frizz on top.

"What they are doing for the German refugees!!"

A long silence.

"There's such a big difference between Belgian and German girls," Moonface suddenly spins on, her eyes on Hanne.

Hanne sits rigid between spoonfuls. The cereal gets stuck in her mouth. What's that the woman is saying? It's clearly directed at her.

"Oh? What *is* the difference?" Hanne doesn't know what else to say.

"Yes. Belgian girls are much more graceful, more feminine," Fatso lectures, like a challenge to a disappointing adversary.

Hanne is stunned. The stab cuts right into her gut. Suppresses a nasty retort, like *Look who's talking?*

She has met their daughter-in-law, married to Sonny's older brother. A Belgian by birth, though her parents came from Poland. Stringy, greasy curls down her neck. Waiting to be washed. Long, blood-red fingernails. Wobbling on high heels that bend under her ankles with every step. Make her tush wiggle in unison.

Hanne thinks of last night's disastrous pot roast. Sure, she put the roast on the gas stove in good time. It sputtered. Smelled terrific throughout the house. She added some water once. Perhaps even a second time. But then it had slipped her mind when she got engrossed in her book, Max Brod's *Reubeni*. What a book! One of those written by those great Jewish writers the Nazis had outlawed and whose books they had burned long ago – Brod, Wasserman, Feuchtwanger, Tucholsky. She had found it in the synagogue library. What a fantastic story about a Jewish messiah! A Messiah! Of course, the people trusted him. Did they have a choice? She stops to think about it again now. *Deliver the Jewish People.* Nah, these things happened only in the past. She sighs. In the end they recognized that he wasn't a real Messiah after all. Imagine, someone like that coming today. Wouldn't it be wonderful? NOW. A leader. A Moses. To take them out of German territory in droves.

She shivers. Looks into Mrs. Goldberg's flesh folds, beady black sparklers on either side of fleshy nose. Tries to follow her trail of words.

She had completely forgotten the roast. Remembered it only when she heard the keys turn in the lock. Couldn't help remembering it; the house was full of blue burnt smoke. Their store is just down the road and they decided to come home early. She has a fleeting memory of Mrs. Goldberg waddling past her, a steam engine headed for the kitchen. Suddenly she could smell it too. Full of dread she ran after her. Saw her lift the lid, watched her hand disappear in the smelly, greasy smoke spiral rising out of the pot like an evil jinni. The meat had shrunk to a square of crisp, dark brown shoeleather. Her bad conscience as she watched Mrs. Goldberg add water in tiny spurts, trying to rescue a small end of last night's dinner.

Hanne scans the inscrutable face opposite her. The woman is mad. Mad at her. Mr. Goldberg gets up, goes for his coat in the hall.

"German girls just don't have the knack," she hears the end of Mrs. Goldberg's tirade. She glances at Mr. Goldberg in the door holding his wife's coat. He must be used to these outbursts.

"Come on. It's time," he says. His face inscrutable.

"I'm going to prepare today's roast when we come home for lunch. You'll have to learn to mind it. Set the clock to remind you every half hour or so to add some water. Meat is expensive these days," Mrs. Goldberg concludes.

How did the woman ever get from German girls to roasts?

Crushed, she watches both waddle out of the room. Relieved to hear the door fall shut behind them.

The house is quiet. No one here to stir up trouble. Hanne eyes her image in the hall mirror. Does she really look that dumpy? She steps on a stool to get a full view. Her figure is not bad. Actually pretty good. Her thighs may be a bit too fleshy, but no one sees them. She hasn't worn a bathing suit for years. Sure, her face could stand some improvements. They don't leave her much time to fuss about her looks with all the work they want from her. And who cares anyway? That conceited son of theirs? Or his buddies? Orthodox boys are unbearable. Trained to be overbearing. Mothers' favorites. Fathers' pride, to carry on the name. She fiddles with her hair. Perhaps she should change her hairstyle.

"I'll go down to the Woolworth's after lunch," she tells her mirror image. Watches her face talk. It's just a few blocks away. Get some lipstick and rouge. A present for my birthday. They might even have *Mouson*, the facial cream Mutti uses. The large tube, as a special treat. It'll smell like a whiff from home.

She steps off the stool. Looks at her hands. Shrugs. Nothing she can do about them. The skin is red and rough from washing dishes. Wind and weather make them worse, despite all the creams and lotions she rubs on. And the nails break at a certain length. No matter how hard she tries to grow them long. Oh well.

She spends the morning in silence. Washes dishes, makes the beds, fixes lunch, sets the table, grieves about her lot. When she gets home with her purchases that afternoon, she minds the roast carefully. Almost too nervous to get engrossed in what *Reubeni* does at the end. He converts. For crying out loud. The traitor! She puts on lipstick before dinner. The roast is tender. A success at dinnertime.

"It's my birthday today," Hanne announces between slices, unable to keep it to herself any longer.

"Oh, that's why the roast tastes so terrific today," Mr. Goldberg tries a corny joke. Jovial, obviously satisfied with his food. "Happy birthday."

No, he isn't half bad. It's that stupid wife of his who's nasty. Cruel.

"Happy birthday," Mrs. Goldberg chimes in..

"I'm fifteen today," Hanne boasts, almost against her will.

After dinner Hanne helps Mrs. Goldberg put away a case of fancy soap from the black market. Spanish Gold.

"Soap is getting scarce. Better put some away while it's still available. This is soap from Spain," Mrs. Goldberg chats. "I remember how scarce it was at the end of the last war, even here. In Germany soap was impossible to get. We used to send a few bars every so often to our friends in Cologne. And they were ever so grateful. It's getting terribly expensive nowadays."

The woman acts as if she had saved their lives, single-handedly! Hanne thinks.

They stack the hoarded soap cartons above the shelf where the bottles of prepared butter stand lined up like fatty yellow grenadiers. Liquid butter they had prepared from sticks. Hanne thinks it tastes awful. Greasy yellow liquid. Nothing you can spread on a sandwich. But Mrs. Goldberg says that this will be better than nothing when the Germans take everything else. Good for cooking. She may be right. But who cares?

Mrs. Goldberg holds out a bar of soap under Hanne's nose. She smells the perfume through the wrapping.

"Here. Take it. It's for your birthday."

Hanne looks at the fleshy round hand, holding the bar of Spanish Gold wrapped in its colorful red and black paper with the flamenco dancer. At the moonface with the piercing dark beads, the flesh folds on either side, staring at her. She takes the bar.

"Thank you. Thank you very much."

*

It is not long after her birthday that the Germans order all foreigners to leave the strategically important coastal areas. Hanne reads it in the *Haagsche Courant*. Wonders about all the refugees, including the children. They discuss it at dinner. Mrs. Goldberg is sure that the Jewish Council will take charge of the refugees. All the refugees.

The letter from the Jewish Council arrives within a few weeks. All the refugee children are to gather next Monday morning at the train station. To be sent farther inland. Mrs. Goldberg gives Hanne another bar of her precious flamenco dancer soap as a good-bye gift. Hanne puts both bars in the bottom of her suitcase. Packs her clothes on top, shuts the case. She is ready to say goodbye. Good riddance is a better term, she thinks quietly. I'll never make it as a maid. She has hated housework all her life. Perhaps it's because Mutti made me help her ever since Jews were not permitted to hire Gentile maids.

She is not sure. But now she hates it more than ever. No. She wants to be a movie star. Betty Grable. Jeanette McDonald. Norma Shearer. Greta Garbo. Glitter. Fame. Play opposite Clark Gable. Take over *The Bounty* with him and his crew in the mutiny against

Captain Bligh. Escape with them to Tahiti or some other island in the South Seas. Live under breezy palm trees and eat coconuts and pineapples the rest of her life. No. She is not cut out to be buried inside the four walls of a kitchen. Or even a house. No way. She needs a wider area of interests. Excitement! Splendor! Position!

* * *

Again, Hanne sits on a train. Reunited with Ruth and about ten other girls. Some of them she knows from Huis Cromvliet or Ten Vijver. Others are new. They watch the flat Dutch landscape speed past in the window. Homeless. Wanting shelter. They talk about their homes. Parents. About their most recent experiences. Many had similar encounters like Hanne with her Goldbergs.

"Where are we going?" Hanne asks Mr. Felsenheld, the leader of the group. A refugee himself, he is new to the girls.

"We're going to Arnhem, a city in the province of Gelderland."

"That's in the south. Close to the German border," Gerda says.

"Yes. But borders don't count any longer, remember."

"A large group of boys from Rotterdam is already in Arnhem. Younger kids go to Driebergen."

Hanne looks forward to the boys. She hopes for boys her age. Older perhaps. No babies, please! She remembers Yvonne. Wonders what happened to her. Her mother.

"Are we going to live in a home?" Ruth asks the burning question on all their minds.

"Don't think so. Far as I know, you're going to private families. The boys are together in a home. But there are no facilities for girls."

Hanne looks at their suitcases crowded into the nets of the train. Shaking to the rhythm of the train. Rat-tat-tat-tat, rat-tat-tat-tat. She feels like a suitcase. A package shipped from here to there. Like extra baggage no one knows what to do with.

Better not think ahead. Stay with the present. Perhaps not

think at all. But how can you do that? Turn your mind off. Look at the landscape. Study the new faces traveling with you. It's a comfort to know that you're not alone. Plenty of fellow refugees are riding with her on the train into an uncertain future. What a relief not to have to make up Sonny's crumpled bed any longer. Get lost in his many books instead of minding the Goldberg roasts, with disastrous results! No more being alone, abandoned in their house. She wonders what her new family will be like. Prays for a goodhearted family. With lots of love to spare. She wonders about all the years of school she has missed. Lost. She will have to learn a trade to be able to take care of herself. Get a place of her own.

*

They stand on the platform in the cool evening air, a group of girls, tired, each one holding on to a well-worn suitcase. A cool sun peeps through the cloud-soaked sky, dips the tips of the sky's gray mountain ridges in blush rose. Lined up on the opposite side are the grown-ups, mostly ladies, respected citizens of the Arnhem Jewish community, waiting for their new charges. Drafted volunteers in obligatory goodwill. Cream of the crop to do their civic duty. They all know each other. The head of the community reads from a list, compares the names on his list with the names on the list Mr. Felsenheld has given him. He checks off the names each time he matches a family with their new charge.

"DeHartogh," he calls. A well-groomed woman steps forward, dragging an unwilling little boy behind her.

"Hanne Kalter." Their eyes search the group of refugees before them.

"So long. I'll get in touch with you as soon as I can," Hanne taps Ruth on the shoulder and steps forward. Pushes the suitcase slowly ahead of her on the platform. Her insides are a fervent prayer. She shivers. Pulls herself together. Stands up straight. Shakes hands with her new mistress. Politely. Stands still, her head tilted slightly backward under the measuring gaze of the woman before her. Tries to accomplish a slight smile. She wonders what fate has in store for her this time.

"This is Flipje." The woman pulls the boy forward by way of introduction.

"Hi, Flipje." Hanne bends down to shake the kid's unwilling hand. She smiles dutifully.

The boy disappears behind his mother's sturdy legs. Hanne is uncomfortable under the woman's evaluating stare. Like a piece of meat in the meat market. Musters courage from somewhere, meets the woman's eyes while her hand instinctively grabs the suitcase, like seeking refuge in holding on to the only familiar thing left. Her identification from home that no longer exists.

When everyone is signed out, she waves goodbyes. Walks leisurely toward a new home. Next to a new mistress. A new family.

The pavement along Park Sonsbeek is still slightly wet after the rain. The sun streaks through the heavy hanging clouds in the late afternoon. The windows sparkle by the wayside, the town is quiet, peaceful, washed clean, at ease with itself and its burghers. She feels slightly out of place. Anxious. Waiting for a new beginning. Yet another in her short life.

"Where are you from?" the woman inquires.

"From Duisburg," Hanne says. "But my parents are no longer there. They are with my uncle in Sweden. Arrived there just two weeks before the war with Poland."

Hanne thinks of Duisburg as the city where she was born and raised, where she went to grade school, the city whose language she speaks. The city that no longer wants her. It's no longer *hers*. She thinks of the Stadstheater, the local theater, the big building and the court house on *Königsplatz*, the plaza she walked every day on her way to school. She remembers the inscription on the theater, visualizes it on the triangle above the Greek-inspired columns of the theater. Recites it in her mind:

Mit allen seinen Tiefen, seinen Höhen,

Rollt sich das Leben ab vor Deinem Blick,
Wenn Du das grosse Spiel der Welt gesehen,
So kehrst Du reicher in Dich selbst zurück.

The poet was right. The plays shown inside this building will enrich and expand a person's consciousness of the world around him. A few times Hanne herself had been with Mutti and Dad to see a play. Highlights in her past. Funny to think that she no longer belongs there. No one she knows lives there any longer. Her friends, her parents, her relatives – gone. Cut off from everything she has known all her life.

"My grandmother used to live close by," Hanne reminisces aloud. "We used to spend the Sabbath and holidays with her. But she moved to live with my Aunt Mali and her family in Krefeld a few years ago. I don't know where they are now," she mumbles, like an afterthought. Hanne swallows any possible sighs. "My other grandmother used to live in Leipzig. She and Grandpa moved to Paris to live with another uncle a few years ago. Gramps died last year in Paris. My Mom's whole family used to live in Leipzig. We went there every summer to visit."

She falls quiet. Thinks of her father's store on Steinschegasse, the warehouse nearby on old Venusgasse with the cat, the smell of textiles in her nose. Where are all the employees that treated her as someone special whenever she went there?

"Do you hear from your parents now?" Mrs. deHartogh wants to know.

Hanne watches Flipje skip across the flagstones ahead of them, obviously bored with their chitchat.

"Yes. But the mail takes weeks. They're fine. I don't know about the rest of my family."

"No one knows these days," Mrs. deHartogh says, offhandedly. She seems far removed from such concerns.

"Flipje, be careful. Come back here. Hold on to my hand," she orders and bends down to slap the boy slightly on his rump. "You better mind."

The woman chats over past and present. Tries to find out about her new houseguest. Mr. deHartogh is a prominent lawyer in town, like his father. Flipje is their only child. Four years old. The local Jewish Council had asked for volunteers to shelter refugee children from the coastal areas. Girls. The boys, about fifty, are going to a home called Jongenshuis, Boys' House. The deHartoghs feel it their duty to help. So did the others who volunteered. Hanne reads the street signs. *Van Miereveldstraat.*

"We turn here. It's the fifth house on the right," Mrs. deHartogh says.

The woman opens the iron gate to Number Ten, a whitewashed row house in the quiet, middle class neighborhood with the typical miniature grass square of a front yard inside an iron fence. Hanne drags her suitcase behind Mrs. deHartogh and Flipje, past geraniums, a rosebush, poppies, marigolds, through the white entrance door into a typical Dutch home. Living and dining rooms downstairs, the kitchen in the back leading to the backyard. Hanne looks up the narrow, carpeted staircase. Bedrooms upstairs. Overstuffed. Closed in. Full of stupid knick-knacks all over. Like under wraps. Not much breathing space. Hanne has the feeling of being trapped in a cage. The smell of roast beef permeates the house. It's like all other Dutch houses. Not much individuality here.

"Miep, this is Hanne," Mrs. deHartogh introduces. Hanne shakes hands with Miep, the maid, who wipes her hands on her apron before reaching for Hanne's hand.

"Dinner is on the stove," Miep says. "The potatoes are peeled, ready to cook when Mr. DeHartogh arrives."

"Fine. There's plenty of time then for you to show Hanne the guest room upstairs. "You may want to wash up and start unpacking before dinner," she says, turning to Hanne.

Hanne lugs her possessions behind Miep up the narrow stairs.

"This is it," Miep says. "I sleep in the maid's room on the third floor."

Miep is a young girl, blond, sturdy, not much older than Hanne. The two smile at each other.

"I'm glad I can speak Dutch with you. That makes it so much easier," Hanne reflects aloud. The memory of being deaf and dumb when she first arrived in the country is fresh in her mind. To hear everyone else talk a blue streak in another language had made her feel stupid. Lost in another culture, another vocabulary. No longer, Hanne thinks with pride. She may not speak perfectly, but she can make herself understood. She may not always know every word that is said, but she knows what people are talking about.

"This is the bathroom. This is the master bedroom. Over there is Flipje's room." Miep points to the different doors. Hanne smiles back at her. She is full of questions she cannot ask. Miep smiles back, shrugs her shoulders.

"I better get back to my kitchen and mind the roast."

*

Hanne sits down on the bed. She is dead tired. Her bed? She strokes the cover. She'll sleep in it. "Nowhere else to go," she mumbles. She has the distinct feeling that Mrs. deHartogh does not like her. Would she have liked someone else better? Hardly. Common sense tells Hanne that she would not. Sure, Mrs. deHartogh is polite. But her heart is somewhere else. Heart?

"I'll do my best," Hanne decides. Question is, how? She climbs off the bed to unpack most of her stuff. Whatever does not fit in the wardrobe or the chest of drawers she must leave in the suitcase. As always. She snaps it closed and shoves it under the bed. As in all the homes she has inhabited since becoming a refugee. She hears Mr. deHartogh come home. Voices from the living room, his, hers, Flipje's high pitch.

"Hanne, dinner is ready." Mrs. deHartogh claps her hands at the bottom of the staircase. Apprehensive, weary, Hanne walks downstairs to meet her new family. To start another life. Again.

*

Things go smoothly for a few days. Everyone is polite. Perhaps a little too polite, Hanne thinks, after the first night's second interrogation into her background, this one at the dinner table. She feels that somehow her status is precarious. It's as if things are on hold. She tries to help Miep with the household chores. But Mrs. deHartogh frowns on that. Usually she has other plans. She wants Hanne to go shopping with her, to the market, the butcher, the corner grocery. She sleeps in the guest room. Unlike Miep who eats in the kitchen, she eats with the family in the dining room.

But there remains a sense of distance. Hanne cannot figure it out. She tries hard to please. But how? Is it a matter of language? When her lady friends come for morning coffee, or tea, Mrs. deHartogh wants Hanne to be in the parlor. Part of the *family*. Hanne feels looked-over. Discussed. She watches Miep come in with the teapot under the embroidered tea cozy. Cross-stitch. Hanne had a hard time with cross-stitch way back in second grade with old Mrs. Rader, who used to stick her extra knitting needles through her white hair bun. Mrs. deHartogh lifts the cozy, carefully pours the steaming brown beverage into delicate porcelain cups. Tiny flowers, almost like Mutti's Rosenthal pattern. The ladies hold their teacups daintily with crooked little pinkies. They take small, careful bites with exposed front teeth from the sweet sugar and cream pastries, carefully arranged on the shining silver tray with its lace doilies. Hollow calories of the upper crust.

Hanne tries to follow the discussion. She doesn't understand all they are saying, but she knows that they are talking about her. About *The Refugees*. Hanne feels exposed. Naked. She tries even harder to please. Problem is, she does not know how. These ladies' teas are like Mutti's *koffee klatsche*s. Hanne remembers them vividly. With extreme contempt.

"What d'you do all afternoon with your ladies?" she had once asked Mutti.

"What's wrong with my coffees?" Mutti asked.

"Gosh! Don't you have anything better to do than to sit and gab, gossip about flighty nonsense, exchange recipes, or the latest

52

knitting pattern!" Hanne chides with an air of extreme filial supe-riority. Catches her breath at her daring. Mutti's black penetrating gaze in the heavily loaded silence that follows!

"Well, I can't see anything wrong with meeting my friends. What do you talk about with your friends?" Mutti's black eyes burrow further into Hanne's with a counter challenge.

Hanne often thought about the differences between her and her mother. She liked nothing better than to list them. Right then and there.

"What do you do in the house? Alwine is here to clean it. She prepares the vegetables and peels the potatoes for dinner. Then you go out to meet your friends for coffee because you worked so hard shopping for food. Now, I and my friends like to think for ourselves. We use our brains. Discuss literature. Great literature. Writers and their work. Like Lion Feuchtwanger, Max Brod, Jakob Wassermann, perhaps even Thomas Mann, though he is dull to read. Schiller, Goethe. Bet you have never looked at serious novels. Not even one."

But that's long ago. In another life. When there had still been maids. She is a refugee now. She can't help that. Isn't she the same person any longer? What do these ladies think is wrong with her? She lies awake at night. Wonders. Life is on hold. A strange past. Where is her future? What is she doing here?

*

This whole deHartogh volunteerism comes to a head a week later. On Thursday morning Mrs. deHartogh sends her on an errand. Pastries. When she returns Hanne decides to go upstairs to change into something more comfortable. She is surprised to find her suitcase open, its contents in disarray. Who on earth would want to search her clothes? What are they looking for?

"Hanne, come down. I'm in the living room."

The harsh tone disconcerts her. Frightens her.

"Yes, ma'am."

Downstairs, she faces Mrs. deHartogh. Like a shark, with

her pointed chin, ready to bite. Overwhelming, huge, she stands beside her teacart with the dainty cups and saucers, the stuffed tea cozy upright, guarding the precious china. She is flapping her arm, a bar of soap in her hand.

Hanne recognizes the black and red wrapper with the flamenco dancer. *Spanish Gold.*

"Where did you get this?"

"Why, it's mine. Mrs. Goldberg gave it to me as a going-away present."

"That's an outright lie. That bar is missing from the provisions I laid up when the war started. You took it. I found it among your things."

"Honestly, Mrs. deHartogh. It's mine. I did not take it from you. I had it when I came here. I'll write to the Goldbergs. They'll confirm what I'm saying."

"Don't bother. It's no use. I already called the Refugee Committee. You pack your things. You're moving to the Jongenshuis. That's where you belong."

"I assure you, Mrs. deHartogh. I did *not* take your soap."

Hanne looks at the woman standing before her, waving the black-and-red-wrapped bar of soap. She retreats back up the stairs to pack her suitcase, minus *her* bar of soap. Her insides are in an uproar. Hot tears flush her face, tears of long withheld hatred, anger, frustration, fury. Terror come alive. People pretending to help. She feels like throwing up. People are mean. She can't rely on anyone. No, she is not going to make an exhibition of herself here. She swallows hard. Looks around for anything she might have forgotten to pack, overlooked perhaps. Nothing. She flips her suitcase shut. Lugs it down the stairs.

Mrs. deHartogh stands by the door, all her sharkey self. What's she looking at with her nasty eyes? Whether I'm lugging her house away?

"Goodbye," Hanne mumbles, strides past the woman, her luggage in tow. The woman has to give way to make room for her.

"Goodbye."

Hanne doesn't want anyone to see her blood-shot, swollen eyes. Without looking at the woman, her head high, Hanne pulls the door shut behind her.

"Good riddance."

Hanne grabs her suitcase. Off to another place in life. Jongenshuis. Amsterdamsche Weg 1, her new address. She cries all the way there. The unfairness of it all. People are untrustworthy. Liars. Hypocrites. They don't like strangers. People who are poor. They tell lies for convenience. Pretend to help. But it's all a sham. Hanne's whole body is a raging revolt. It's like rattling a cage. Tough to be a refugee.

No, she does not dislike moving in with the boys. Actually pretty neat to be with her own kind. But refugee kids should have rights too! And justice! That Goldberg letter, if it ever comes, will be far too late to do any good.

*

"Nurse van Gelder?"

"Yes, dear?"

"Did they tell you why they moved me here?"

"Why, Hanne?"

"The deHartoghs accused me of stealing a bar of soap. 'Their soap,' they say. Honestly, I didn't do it. It was mine. The soap was a going-away present from the Goldbergs in The Hague."

Hanne feels the presence of the woman in the heavily starched nurse's uniform on the side of her bed. Her round blue eyes protruding out of their sockets look like loose marbles.

"I believe you," Nurse van Gelder says softly and strokes Hanne's head.

Hanne feels her gentle touch. It makes her feel warm inside. It's so long ago… she dares not to think the thought to its finish.

"Why did they accuse me? I don't understand."

"Good question. There are so many things that can't be solved. Hush. Don't cry anymore."

Her hand feels so good as it strokes across Hanne's head.

So cool on her forehead. Like a long-lost blessing from the past. Hanne sighs, an involuntary whiff of breath escaping from inside, like a welcome relief.

"I wrote to the Goldbergs. They'll confirm that what I'm saying is true. It's so unfair of the deHartoghs to accuse me! I didn't steal!" There is that rage again.

Nurse van Gelder shakes her head above Hanne.

"Don't dwell on it. You might like it better here than with them, who knows? Here you'll be with children your own age. There's another girl coming tomorrow, so you won't be alone with fifty boys. I'm sure there are more girls your age to come eventually."

Van Gelder pulls out a voluminous handkerchief and dries Hanne's tears. It smells of starch, ironing. Hanne has the faint feeling that van Gelder knows far more about the matter than she lets on. She sighs.

"Well, at least I don't have to look at their false faces any longer. For that alone I'm glad that I'm here."

Silence.

"Do you think they wanted to get rid of me?"

She sees Nurse van Gelder shrug ever so slightly, watches her heave her round body from the side of Hanne's bed, taking with her the expanse of white starch. She pats Hanne's head.

"Call me if you need me."

The words come quietly, like solace. Then she leaves the room.

Hanne is alone. She stares at the white door.

Deliberately she undresses and goes to bed. Lies down under the Dutch woolen blankets, so different from the huge down covers they had at home. She folds her hands under her head. Alone at last. Free to think. It isn't half bad to be rid of the tea cozy people.

She takes a deep breath. Looks around in the spacious room. There is a wonderful breeze coming in through the large open window. The high ceiling gives enough breathing space. She listens to the noises outside. Boys. Voices. Calls. Footsteps. Laughter. She will leave them to think about tomorrow. She is angry, smarts at her impotence in the face of injustice. She balls her fists, lashes out at the bed, hurts her knuckles, realizes the futility of her rage. She tries to hold back her tears, tears of repressed fury. But they well up in spite of her and she gives in. Drip, drip, drip, the tears roll across her cheeks. Her chin gets wet. It's good that no one sees them. No one laughs at her here.

Darkness floats slowly through the room, envelops her. The darkness of a warm summer night. The moon comes up. Round glitter. Its silver sheen throws comforting patterns on the white walls opposite her. Her parents are far away. But Nurse van Gelder is nice. Hanne sobs quietly. Tries to sleep. She'll look at the boys tomorrow. Investigate. Can't be worse than the deHartoghs. May actually be fun to be with. She hears their footsteps trample heavily up the wooden staircase to their bedrooms. Doors open and shut mysteriously in the growing darkness. Muffled voices. Sounds from afar. Full of exciting expectation. Promises of life yet unlived. She stretches between the sheets. She must try to get back to school. Convince the Committee, whoever that is, that she needs to learn something to be able to stand on her own feet. Grow up, become independent of the whims of others. She does not want to be hemmed in.

Chapter 4

Hanne, Eddie and Werner huddle around Werner's sketch, spread before them on the long table in the huge living room. The three are deep in thought, contemplating the design. The two boys attend the local arts and crafts academy on stipends. Hanne feels a twinge of jealousy because that's what she wants to do too. Be an artist. Ever since she came to Jongenshuis, she has watched the two boys doing their homework after school. She hopes to get a stipend herself before long.

"It's my anniversary. Exactly a week that I've been here," she says.

"One week too long already." Their teasing is merciless.

"Ought to appreciate having an expert around to critique your designs," she tells them.

"Well, what do you think of it?" Werner asks. "It's supposed to be an ad for a seed company."

They gaze at the oversized single flower balancing on a long, thin green stem stretching out of a tiny flowerpot underneath.

"Isn't the stem too long and slender, out of proportion? I mean…" she hesitates. Takes a deep breath. Collects her courage. Take the bull by the horns!

"I mean..." she draws another breath. "Isn't it... too fragile a stalk to hold that big a flower?" She faces the artist.

"But that's just the point. I want to show the effect of the fertilizer. That's the ad," Werner shoots back at her.

The silence is pregnant with dissonance.

"I can see the symbolism here," Hanne says slowly. "But you need something to make it more appealing. Break the uniformity. It's too stern. That stem's too delicate and fragile."

She looks up at him, straight into his eyes. She feels uncomfortable as a critic. Doesn't want to hurt his feelings. Doesn't need any enemies here. Not for anything in the world.

"You could give it a face. Put some humor in it," Eddie suggests.

"Yeah..." Werner contemplates, "like this?"

Werner takes Eddie's idea and sketches away.

Hanne looks on. Envies them their sincerity. Their dedication. Werner enrolled in advertising. Eddie, the jeweler's son from Pforzheim, an apprentice goldsmith back home, takes a related subject available here: silver- and metalsmithing with Zwollo, the famous Dutch artist. Art, that's what she wants to study too. She is certain that she is going to make a great artist, if they'd just give her the chance. She wants that stipend badly. Girls too need an education. Outside the kitchen. To support themselves. She does not want to be locked up in a house. Housework. Her whole being revolts at the very thought. If she hadn't known it back home already, her Goldberg experience has made the matter so much more urgent. She is not cut out to be a house drudge.

"Oh, before I forget, I brought you the application for next semester," Werner cuts into her thoughts. He pulls the sheets out of his schoolbag. "Good luck with it."

He hands them over.

Hanne flattens the sheets on the table, straightens the wrinkled edges, and scans the questions.

"Thanks. I'll fill it in today. And see Dr. Wolf in the morning for his signature. Above all, his support."

She sends a fervent plea for success to whoever is up there to receive prayers. God? It's urgent!

*

Gradually her interest in Werner extends beyond art. Watching him work in the afternoon is one way of getting his attention. Does she have a crush on him? Ruth thinks so. Hanne's feelings are muddled. She can't draw the line where one interest intersects with the other.

Other girls have joined the Jongenshuis during the week. There are now six in the bedroom. Van Gelder says there are more to come.

*

Hanne's eyes wander around the huge living room. Dark and somber. But now the late August sun splashes the room with gold accents. Even the dark brown wainscoting looks grand, stately in the afternoon glow. Some doctor built this home when he arrived in town at the turn of the century. He had lived in it with his family on what was then the edge of town until he died a few years ago. After that the building had stood empty. Then someone remembered the Jewish refugees and let them move in.

Now the building is full of life. Much more than originally intended for it. The wooden tables and benches are more recent acquisitions. Tacky hand-me-downs for the refugees that don't match the building at all. But they serve their purpose. Her eyes follow the bright yellow sun spots that make them look more cheerful. She gazes at Eddie opposite her. Werner on the other side. She feels content in the company of the boys. The house is becoming a home. Sort of. As much as a refugee home can be a *home*.

"How did your teach like your seed ad?" Eddie asks Werner.

"Oh. So so."

"Obviously his idea wasn't so great after all," Hanne thinks quietly.

"How're you doing?" Eddie turns to her.

Werner has told her to paint a bunch of wildflowers. She has started sketching the outlines.

"You better get cracking so you don't look like an idiot on your first tries at school," he advises sagely.

They obviously feel an urgent need to train her. They crane their necks to see what she has accomplished. She lets them, hesitant, insecure. She has always drawn pictures, even at home. Her parents considered it a nice hobby. Doodling. A childish preoccupation. Nothing serious. Certainly nothing with which to earn a living.

"Not bad," Werner says into her ruminations. She returns to the present from being back home. Mumbles something, she doesn't know what. Werner's praise feels good.

"Dr. Wolf signed my application. I sent it off with the mail this afternoon. Let's keep our fingers crossed that I get in," she reports, anxiously dreaming of future greatness.

She looks at Werner. His wavy brown hair with the cowlick on the left side, the long curled eyelashes over light brown eyes with green specks. There's a hint of dimples in his cheeks. She swallows the flutter between stomach and intestines. Makes sure to keep it from floating up into her throat while sitting next to him. It feels great to have his attention. Working with him in the afternoons tickles, spiked with longing. That stipend. She crushes her thumb knuckles between her fingers for good luck. Everything hinges on it at the moment.

Werner looks at his watch.

"Almost five o'clock. Time to pack up. The kitchen folks will be here any minute." He gathers his brushes and paint box slowly. Meditates over Lord knows what.

"Tell you a secret... I'm starved," he grates in his nasal voice.

"That shouldn't be a secret. We're always hungry. At least I am," Hanne counters. She gathers her paraphernalia.

"True. My stomach growls constantly," Eddie agrees.

"Time sure flies when you're having fun," Hanne singsongs.

Hanne puts her stuff aside. She hates to stop right when ideas come flowing. She may not remember them later. Grudgingly she pushes her stuff into a heap beside her.

Then the boys from the kitchen move in on them, at their usual high noise level. Like it or not, the three have to make way for the crew who needs to move the diagonally slanted tables into horseshoe formation for dinner. Six long tables, one after another. Dark brown. No match for the fancy wainscoting on the wall. Well-worn wood, scrubbed, nicked, scratched. Ugly lines and spots of dirty white as if rodents had nibbled on the tables in tiny bites for decades. Benches on either side of each table. Same gnawed condition. The wood could stand a decent coat of stain. For every meal the kitchen crew pushes the tables into position to make feeding sixty starving youngsters easier on the staff. After the meal, same process in reverse.

*   *   *

Fifty boys, ten girls. Sixty in total. Boys are a new item in Hanne's life. Her heart flutters at odd intervals these days. Excited about no one in particular. Except, perhaps, Werner could be a prime candidate. She is not certain. It would be nice to have someone to confide in. It's always been as though she lives in a world apart from others. Afloat in some different dimension. She shakes her head. Her stomach rumbles in bass.

"Wonder what color the food is tonight," she thinks out loud.

"That's a secret," Freda winks wistfully from the kitchen door. The wooden, long-handled scoop in her hand signals the significance of her position. Freda, the kitchen chef. From Frankfurt, an emigrant like her charges, tall, blond, welldressed under her starchy apron. A real knockout in her free time. The boys whisper. Wonder about her dates. For whom is she getting all dolled up? But Freda keeps them guessing with her surreptitious smile.

As far as Hanne is concerned, Freda is a dress-freak. Much like Mutti. Only younger. In contrast to plain, dumpy Dutch van

Gelder with the golden heart. Right now the two staffers stand side by side in the kitchen door, a united front in white solid starch, on their watch that food distribution runs smoothly. Pat and Patachon. Tall-and-skinny versus short-and-round. A great team. Hanne prefers the short-and-round one. She's more loving. Warmhearted. Easier to approach and talk to. A rarity in Hanne's life.

"Secret? *Stamppot*, either green or red!" Werner pipes up. His voice grates in melodramatic timbre when he spreads sarcasm as wisdom.

"We better get out of here," Eddie says, stepping out of the way of the four kitchen boys who push and shove their way through the room like minor dictators. An immense explosion of forces that ignore the three *artists* like mere nuisances.

"I have a feeling we're not wanted here," Hanne steps out of the way. Sighs with a mocking grunt.

"Better get out of our way if you don't want to be pushed."

"You'd better wash up. The gong's about to ring," Nurse van Gelder advises from the kitchen door. Trampling, shoving, shouting, joking, the boys lug the heavy dinner plates and flatware around her into the dining room. Then roll the huge, steaming pots from the kitchen to the center of the horseshoe in the dining room. King Food. Majesty of the hour. The clatter is deafening.

Hanne shakes her head. Why can't boys do things at a normal sound level? Always in high gear. Unbearable in multiples. She runs upstairs to put her painting stuff under her bed, away from prying eyes and sarcastic comments.

"My art matters," she mutters defiantly. Wizened by experience. It's the same all over. Back home her art was never more than a nice diversion. Something to show friends for admiration, but unimportant in the scheme of everyday life. Hanne shrugs. Present reality is even worse. Refugees need to consider financial ramifications. But she loves to create. Needs it like air to breathe. Like food to digest. To be accepted at art school is the only way left to reach her goal. Train for artistic crafts. In spite of them all.

Time will take care of the rest, she thinks defiantly. She catches a glimpse of herself in the mirror. Better hurry. Dinner is important in the daily routine here. It's the time to catch up on what's going on in their circumscribed refugee world. Beside the all-important, life-sustaining nourishment.

She is still washing her hands when the dinner gong blasts through the building. The building comes alive with a million feet. The sturdy turn-of-the-century stone walls shake and shiver as all feet trample in direction dining hall. Hanne turns, runs in lockstep with the others, wipes her wet fingers dry along the way on the underside of her sleeves. Down the stairs, two steps at a time. Past Dicky Strauss who gingerly bangs away at his gong, the polished round brass plate in the hallway. The noise is deafening. Her eardrums revolt. She wonders where they found the ancient gadget. Some fleamarket probably. It looks like a vestige from a long-ago past doing its old trick under Dicky's modern hands.

"Enough already," van Gelder shouts. Holds her ears. Laughs out loud.

Together Nurse van Gelder and Freda move to their steaming pots in the center, ready for the onslaught. The building smells of food. Potatoes of some sort. In color. As usual.

"Come on, slowpokes, hurry up. Dinner's getting cold."

Nurse van Gelder dispenses good-natured backslaps on the rumps passing her, right and left. Like most warmhearted people, she loves to eat and loves to feed her charges. As if anyone around here needed encouragement to eat. It's a marvel she still finds enough food, despite the growing scarcity. Hanne suspects that she has some pull with neighborhood farmers who have a soft spot for refugees and sell their stuff at a decent price. The meals are not so great. The staff prepares what they get. Their main course, potato mush, is anything but original. Downright dull. But what's there to do with spuds for a crowd other than mash them with the vegetable of the day and mix snippets of gristly meat into the potato glue on the rare occasions when it's available. But van Gelder and Freda have a thousand ways to fix desserts. Van Gelder's old

Dutch recipes. Their rice pudding makes the two kitchen gods *the* favorite staff members.

Hanne finds her seat, steps over the bench from behind between Werner and Eddie. Her stomach growls while Dr. Wolf, director and administrator of Jongenshuis, arrives with his usual entourage. Peter Marcuse is Wolf's favorite. Behind them trips diminutive Miss Sussmann, secretary, bookkeeper, confidant, and whatever else the boys mumble she is. Funny, both are hunchbacks. His hump is pretty solid, front and back. Hers doesn't show as readily. Only her size and her curved spinal column near the shoulder regions give her away. Wolf climbs laboriously onto his cushioned seat at the head of the table. Miss Sussmann presides at the other end. The boys think they're a terrific pair in the truest sense of the word. Stress the point with a meaningfully knowing glint in their eyes.

Boys have a fertile imagination when it comes to gender relationships. Downright vile. Girls think differently. Less graphic. Less violent. Gentler? More romantic? Hard to pinpoint the difference exactly. Though it's there. What is love anyhow? Love? Sex? Hanne has a hard time to figuring these fellows out. She has known boys only from school. Never from up close. From a distance, where they hold a different place in society

Actually, qualify that. Long ago. In another life Edith Goldmann, her best friend back home, had an older brother. About sixteen. Gymnasium junior. Victor could leave the house whenever he wanted. Come home whenever he liked. Unlike Edith, the girl. And in her own case there was Mutti with her stupid, disgusting curfew. Ten *SHARP*. Needed to know every minor detail even before she'd leave home – where, when, how, with whom? Mutti's voice still drones in her head. A penny for every slap I got for the smallest fraction of a second I was late. I'd be rich.

Take Monday evenings, when Emil Wollheim used to walk her home after gym club. They used to stand inside the entrance to her house, on the right side to avoid the street lamp that shone right into the other corner. Kissed. There was so much to gab about, up to the kiss. Even if you didn't gab, just stood near each other, call it soulful or some such thing. Yes, stand they did. Close. The feeling begins long before you kiss and melt. Starts somewhere from the toes, creeps up the legs, up, upward, diffuses somewhere between chest and thighs. Then settles below the stomach, with an exciting sting in the groin region when you felt the warm moist lips. Moist.

Emil, her schoolchum. Hard to tear yourself loose when you stand that close. To remember Mutti. And going upstairs.

Wonder where he's now? She heard that he got out. Supposedly to Holland. He might have come with some other children's transport. Be in another home. Far? Near? Who knows what became of him. Of the other children in her class? Is she lonesome for the old crowd?

"Hi, what's new?"

She wants to keep things casual as she slides into her place between Werner and Eddie at the dinner table. Ever since her arrival the three of them have gradually evolved into a generally recognized threesome. *The artists.* Their common interests make for closer understanding. Set them apart from the rest. Eddie, the pipsqueak, agile, nervous, always fidgeting with those three horsehairs growing out of that huge mole on his right cheek. From Pforzheim. He talks with that typically soft southern accent. It's *Gel?* at the end of every sentence. Metalsmithing with Mr. Zwollo was his logical choice at *Kunstoefening*. Hanne thinks it's an intriguing craft. She would like to join that class – if she's accepted, of course. Hanne crosses her fingers in a silent prayer to someone up there. Please, send me that stipend… Who's up there to talk to? Her fingers stay crossed while the others file in.

Across from her on the inside of the table sits Gerd Perl. Next to him Horsey, who got his name because of his huge front teeth. Hanne likes his slow, easygoing, almost meditative way of talking.

"It's spinach. Green's the color for tonight," Horsey spreads his expert information. His large hands drum the beat of some self-made melody against the edge of the table. His body shakes in rhythm. He almost shouts to make himself heard above the general din. His dental equipment glitters white in his wide smile, prominent and distinct. Sure looks like a horse. She smiles back at him across the table.

"Green, eh?"

Out of the corner of her eyes she follows Ruth coming through the door with Atze Natt, her newest beau. From Berlin he too. Many of the children in the home are from Berlin. The rest are from Vienna. Ruth sits at the far end on the other side of the horseshoe set-up. Close to Miss Sussmann. Far away from her older sister. During the day Ruth attends middle school. The sisters have very little in common these days. They stay away from each other as much as possible as if by mutual silent agreement. Ruth has her own friends and that's fine with Hanne. It's enough to meet her at night in the bedroom. They sleep next to each other, probably out of sheer old habit. They grate on each other. Talk, when they must, about home or parents. There's plenty of time at night upstairs to do that.

Sussmann is a sort of mousy looking little person. Must have been to the hairdresser. Freshly set fingerwave.

"Yuck, I hate spinach," Gerd voices his distaste, written all over his swarthy face. He has a real beard already. Must have been too lazy to shave in the morning. Strange, cocky fellow. The typical conceited Berliner. No, *Balinnaa*. Hanne tries to imitate the way they talk. Gerd's the silent type. Jet black hair, black cherry eyes. Hanne looks at him. He'd be good-looking if his right eyelid were not halfway shut, hiding half his right eye in a permanent droop. When looking at the world he tilts his head backward, chin forward and out. Gives him a kind of slightly dangerous, if not downright shifty look. Funny, how looks do affect a person. He reminds Hanne of the Flying Dutchman, or some such insidious character. For all that, his odd exterior might even disguise a nice fellow. Who knows?

"Pulpy mush, as always," Werner grunts next to her.

"What d'you expect? Roast beef every day for refugees?" Eddie pipes up.

The din in the dining room is deafening. There's so much to catch up on and tell after a whole day's worth of events.

"The noise is getting out of hand," Dr. Wolf calls.

He tinkles with his spoon against his empty glass, his habitual call for silence. He does not have to wait long. The crowd is hungry. They know that Dr. Wolf will wait, patiently. All night if necessary. Those who keep on talking get poked in their ribs. "Shut up. We want to eat. The food's getting cold."

Dr. Wolf gazes at the crowd before him with an expectant smirk.

The chatter subsides slowly. Two talkers. Then one. Stops. Obviously embarrassed. Then silence. You can hear a pin drop. Dr. Wolf smiles, all satisfaction.

"Peter, the prayer please," he says.

Saying grace before meals is usually Peter's job. Entertaining Dr. Wolf is another. Peter. The born clown and practical joker. Sure knows how to handle the old man. Gabs. Tells stories. Dr. Wolf likes that. Hanne hates people in charge when they have favorites. Should be outlawed! The practitioners with it!

"It's downright criminal. Don't they realize that they hurt all the others with their favoritism?" she grumbles under her breath. She should know. Lots of experience makes her an expert on the subject.

No, she doesn't like Dr. Wolf much. For other reasons too. He upsets her. Her current life depends on his likes and dislikes. A repeat of home and Mutti. Is it dislike, or hate? Or bad experience? Whatever it is, it's mutual. The creepy way he looks at her. Makes her feel uncomfortable. Keeps talking while his gaze moves upward. Beginning with her legs. Grown-ups don't look up when they talk to youngsters.

It bothers her that she can't figure out what he has against her. Has she done something to upset him? If so, she'd like to know what. She can't believe that she has. Surely not on purpose. As much as she likes to please strangers. She wants them to like her in return. Particularly those in charge of her life. Oh, well! People are hard to read. Some people get along. Others don't. Like she and Ruth. Add Dr. Wolf. Plus hump. Dislike for Hanne must sit inside that hump of his, she mumbles. Shrugs. Unable to figure this out.

Peter recites the short Hebrew prayer over food.

"Enjoy your meal," Dr. Wolf says. That's the cue. Forks and knives start to clatter.

The din moves in waves, ebbs and flows. Freda and van Gelder dish out the food, first Miss Sussmann, then Dr. Wolf. Dicky pulls the big pots behind the two kitchen gods. They proceed from youngster to youngster, fill each plate with mush and hand the plate across the table. Hanne can't for the world understand why the Dutch mix all kinds of vegetables with potatoes into an indefinable, sticky mass they call *stamppot*. It's downright criminal to ruin perfectly good food like that. Why not leave the potatoes whole and serve the spinach on the side?

"If you fish long enough you'll even find meat in it today," Werner says with his usual sarcastic undertone.

"It's called gristle, Mr. Sarcasm," Hanne chuckles, all agreement.

Institutional food stinks. But there's nothing else to eat.

Food is getting scarce because the Germans take it from the farmers to feed their soldiers at the various fronts all over Europe. The rest is for the occupation forces, who skim off the best for themselves before they pass the leftovers on to ordinary folk. If the war lasts much longer, people in Holland will starve. Some of them, especially the poor in the cities, already do. Sure, the farmers aren't stupid either. They cheat. Hide whatever they can. That's why it's good to be friends with a farmer these days. Those who have enough money can find enough stuff on the Black Market. But that's out of reach for German refugee kids.

"We could bike to the farm on Sunday for strawberries. I found a farmer who sold us strawberries the other day. He'll have apples later in the fall," Werner suggests.

"Great idea," Hanne says. She glances at Werner. Good-looking fellow. His cowlick hangs in a thick brown strand across his forehead. Too bad he has such a mean streak under his good-looking exterior. Still, she feels drawn to him.

"The other day Peter got up enough nerve to complain to Wolf about the stamppot," Eddie says.

"Yeah, you should have heard him," Horsey confirms. "I was there. Wolf called it *chutzpa*. The height of ingratitude! Then he snitched our complaint to the board of the Jewish Council. Imagine!" Horsey drawls each syllable into an eternity. You need patience to hear him out.

"That was just before you girls descended on us. The entire board appeared for dinner one day. Wanted to verify."

"But Freda knew they were coming. She spruced up the stamppot with big chunks of meat and gravy and all kinds of yummy stuff that night. *They* thought the food was great. End of complaints." Horsey shrugs with the impossibility of complaining against the board, or any authority.

"The spinach stamppot is delicious. Very tasty, Nurse van Gelder," Dr. Wolf declares pointedly from his elevated front-seat.

"Thhhhhhhh," Hanne blows air through her front teeth as she looks at the white-haired head of the institution in disgust.

"Thank you. I like spinach," van Gelder smiles back, really loud. Even in this sixty-person cacophony everybody can hear her. Her round face shines. A full-moon flashbulb.

"Of course. She's Dutch. She likes stamppot," Horsey mumbles, defiance under his breath.

"No one give a darn whether *we* like it."

"No."

They nod silent agreement across the table.

"Lucky she loves desserts," Eddie says.

"Her rice with raisins is decent, you must admit."

Joking, talking, the two kitchen chefs have come to the end of the other table. Dicky pulls the huge kettles, halfway empty by now, over to where Gerd sits.

"Here you are," van Gelder holds out the plate with Eddie's dinner across the table.

"Thanks."

"Not too much, please," Hanne says, offering her empty plate with her usual nightly request. It's not only that she has a weight problem with the starchy, greasy food served in this place. She craves some individual attention in all this impersonal equality of institutional life.

"Save some room for dessert? We're having rice pudding," van Gelder teases. Full-bosomed, heavy, she recognizes no weight problem. Considers girls silly for even thinking about it. There's a war on! Hunger everywhere out there. Of course, her mind is not set on Hollywood, or any other movies anywhere.

"Want some meat?" Eddie has speared a thick piece of grayish gristle on his fork and waves it under Hanne's nose."

"Yuck! No, thanks a lot."

"Wolf has chutzpa to call it chutzpa," Horsey mutters on.

"Ouch." Hanne feels Werner poke into her flank.

"For crying out loud, take all the rice pudding you can get. I'll eat it," he orders in a whisper.

Van Gelder's rice is the favorite dessert at Jongenshuis, thick, with sugar, cinnamon, and raisins. Hanne is a popular dinner neighbor at rice time. The boys around her appreciate her weight consciousness. What else can she do? She wants to be slim like her movie idols – Greta Garbo, Marlene Dietrich, Betty Grable, Lana Turner, Gitta Alpar. The lot.

"I might want to eat it myself," she threatens.

"You'll get fat and ugly."

Hanne has good reasons for being careful about her eating. Most of the other girls have gained a lot of weight since coming here, tubby Ditta as much as twenty pounds. Ditta drags her old snapshots from Vienna around to show how slim she used to be. Oblivious to whether one cares to look at them or not. Even though, it's hard to believe that the two Ditta's are the same person.

Hanne is used to being careful about her weight. She's has had to mind her figure ever since she was overweight in third grade. Mutti never stopped reminding her not to eat so much. Dad too.

"Careful, Hanne. You're getting too fat."

She was the family laughing stock at dinnertime back then. Ruth was the worst. Made her feel ashamed for eating. No, she has learned to be careful with the food. It's hard. A nagging nuisance in her mind. Why don't boys have to watch their weight? It's unfair, like everything else. No justice in this world! She wonders how her movie idols manage to stay slim.

"How about some rice pudding?" Nurse van Gelder stands behind Gerd and Horsey on her second round. Hanne feels Werner's poke in the ribs area again. Ouch!

"Thanks," Hanne says out loud and takes the full dish. It breaks her heart to look at the plate with the heap of creamy white kernels, chock full of raisins. The cinnamon smell wafts tempting odors up her nose. Hanne feels greedy eyes bore into her dish. Deliberately she sticks her spoon into the food. Stirs, then carefully selects a small mound with raisins. Spoons it into her mouth, ever so slowly. Chews carefully. Her conscience reproachful. Brain and stomach fighting the ancient battle of the righteous. She wants to be a movie star. Another Betty Grable. Not a tub.

She munches. Savors her bite ever so slowly. Then, resolutely, she takes her knife and cuts across the mound of rice pudding and slides the greater part over onto Werner's plate. Her heart hurts. Silent. Proud. Stoicism in action.

"Here, for you."

Of course she can do it. She radiates an inward smile at her victory.

"Thanks," Werner says. Hanne feels envious eyes watch what she is doing. Her brain leaps with a sigh of relief. Werner is happy. The few spoonfuls of rice pudding left on her plate better not make her fat. What price beauty?!

*　　*　　*

CHAPTER 4

Food is in control. The talk dies down while the clatter of sixty busy forks and knives takes over. Hanne looks at Wolf on his throne up front, shaking with laughter at one of Peter's sick jokes. His head sort of bobs between his front and back mounds in typical hunchback fashion. Actually, he has a good-looking head of silky, silver-gray hair. It just sits on the wrong body. She marvels at his hands with their long, sensitive fingers. Head and hands seem grossly at odds with his misshapen body. His intelligent eyes bore deep-blue rays into her face every time he looks at her. Give her the feeling that he can read her mind. Like Mutti at home.

He was a pediatrician in Berlin. Ran his own clinic. Quite famous, they say. A real Prussian, terribly bossy. Too bad that he resents her so much. Hanne wants other people to like her. Everyone. Those in command of her life most of all. Especially he. She shrugs. It's useless. She has tried her level best to get closer to him. But the hate in his eyes is unmistakable. She'll have to resign herself to the situation. Go on to the more pressing things of her daily routine. Like getting a stipend to the art academy. Gripe about the lousy food. Get along with the boys and girls around her.

"Werner Strauss heard their door creak during the night," Gerd whispers across the table. His eye under the half-closed lid has that shrewish gleam.

"Oh, you're making it up," she shrugs it off.

"No, I heard it too last night, loud and clear," Werner nods with a smirk. Horsey nods too.

"So? So they visit in the evening after office hours. They probably talk business."

"Come on. Use your brain."

"They'd be foolish not to take the two best rooms in the house for themselves," Hanne defends them, much against her better judgment.

The boys' bedrooms are on the first floor, the same floor as the offices. With the growing number of residents, six girls now sleep in a small room carved out in the attic, Hanne and Ruth among them.

"Why worry what they do at night?" Hanne shrugs. The boys look at her as if she had a screw loose. The rising noise all around makes it hard to keep up this conversation – any conversation. Dr. Wolf taps on his glass again for attention. For a change his smile bodes good news.

"Silence. We have decided to give you an extra hour of freedom starting next Sunday afternoon. From now on, supper will be at eight PM on Sundays. And… self-service."

The howl of thanks from the crowd is deafening. Dr. Wolf smiles from ear to ear. His head bobs between his humps like a newly filled silver helium balloon. Hanne feels an urge to touch his hump. Strange desires. Wonders what it feels like. Looks like. Bony? Soft? Little Miss Sussmann, overwhelmed with the noise, holds her ears. Smiling.

"How old do you think he is?" Hanne asks her neighbors.

"Hard to say. Forty at least. Ancient, at any rate. Out of tune with our reality."

"The administration has come to its senses," Peter jokes up front, all beaming appreciation.

Wolf exudes benevolence. Everyone else agrees with the decision. From two o'clock until seven was far too short for outings on Sunday afternoons. Supper will now consist of cold sandwiches, coleslaw, dessert, laid out on the table for everyone to take. Self-service. No extra work for the kitchen an hour later. The staff members grin, pleased with the result. In an unusually good mood, Dr. Wolf taps his glass.

"I'm happy that you approve." He waits quite a while for the noise to subside.

"All right. Peter, let's say grace. The kitchen people want to get their well-deserved evening rest."

*   *   *

"We can ride out next Sunday and get strawberries. It's not too far," Werner repeats his earlier suggestion..

"Fine. I'm all for it. I love strawberries," Hanne says.

"Karel promised me his bike. You can get van Gelder's, I'm sure."

"I'll ask her."

* * *

Early summer. Sunshine. An ideal Sunday morning for a bike ride into the countryside. Yesterday Dr. Wolf called her to his office and gave her the good news. The art academy had accepted her request for a stipend starting with the fall term. She is happy. Extremely happy. Life will have meaning.

Werner waits on the street with the bike.

"You ready?"

"Let me get my sweater. Be right back."

They pedal off.

It's one of those rare warm, sunny, lazy early summer Sunday mornings. Arnhem minds its public Sunday routine: morning walk and coffee, gossip with friends. Women prepare Sunday dinner. Roast beef smells fill the houses, waft along the tidy, gleaming streets. Then afternoon teatime. So far the war is a distant reality reserved for newspaper articles, radio news, general food shortages that no one in the provinces need to worry about. Yet. The war is a threat no one cares to examine from up close. Nazis are visible on the streets, their guttural yells audible, their brown, black, green and blue uniforms a hated fact no one wants to tackle. Not yet. Not until it intrudes on your own life. Some things are getting scarce. There's a Black Market. Rumors abound. There's an Eastern Front. So far, Arnhem has kept the occupation at bay. People go about their business of living and the weather obliges.

Hanne and Werner ride through the fertile, lush, green countryside of Gelderland, leisurely enjoying the calm, stolid atmosphere of the landed population. Natives. Farmers wave greetings as they ride past. A day of rest. Smells of cows, horses, dung, hay. Songbirds fill the air. A soft wind crackles gently around their ears. Rye, wheat, potato fields flutter by the wayside.

Werner's farmer is glad to sell them his extra produce. Two

baskets each. Happy to help the refugees. Better than to let the *moffen* have it. His weather-beaten face expresses contempt when he utters the Dutch derogatory term for the Germans.

They pedal home in the lazy humid summer afternoon heat.

"It's hot. I'll have to take my sweater off," Hanne says, wiping the sweat from her forehead. She swipes a few strawberries from the nearest basket behind her seat and stuffs her face.

"Wasn't it a great idea?" Werner says, beaming with pride.

"The farmer was even nicer. When he heard we belong to those *vluchtelingetjes* he let us have two for the price of one. Mighty nice, I'd say. Though I hate to get special treatment for being one of those refugee creatures." Hanne reaches backward into her basket. The red, ripe berries are tempting. "Mmm. Did I tell you that my stipend came through? Wolf told me yesterday and congratulated me. I'll start *Kunstoefening* this fall." She chews greedily and speaks with a full mouth, careful not to drip on her dress.

"Great. You'll have to sign up for the general first year courses," he advises with the air of the initiate.

Hanne is all wrapped up in her future.

"I know. I'll make metalsmithing my major. I like what Eddie is doing."

"Twice a week, Tuesdays and Thursdays, with Mr. Zwollo. Room ten."

"I can't wait," Hanne says.

They pedal on, silent, meditative in the hot, heavy, humid North Sea air of the Low Countries. The sky is hung with pearly wads, cloud mountain ranges in shades of white-gray-blue-black. Occasionally they obscure the sun that sends golden flashes through their furrowed channels. Hanne wipes her brows.

"If we keep on eating, we'll have no berries left by the time we get home." Werner stuffs another handful of strawberries into his mouth. He checks his watch.

"There's plenty of time until eight. We could use some rest. Stretch our legs."

"Good idea. My butt hurts," Hanne says.

"How about that grove over there?" Werner suggests.

They pull over, lean their bikes against a tree and sit down in the grass, their baskets between them.

The peace and quiet of a sleepy summer afternoon descends upon them. Relaxed, Hanne pulls up her knees. Ants crawl in long trails along the earth. Big black horseflies flap wings, a loud buzz in flight. Bees and early yellowjackets hum serious business in their hunt for nectar, honey, blood. Transparent dragonflies meditate on tree stumps, green airborne scintillation. Through half-closed eyelids Hanne watches the sculpted swirl of clouds above her. The atmosphere is full of dreams. She senses the nearness of the male next to her. Somewhere below her midriff a fountain of warmth starts its flow. Upward bound. She fights getting limp in her legs. Something in the back of her mind tells her to be on guard.

"Cotton layers, glued upside down," she says, trying to sound casual, out into the blue air to divert her attention. "Look, that one bows like a dancing bear. And over there a huge bird stretches for flight. They keep on the move. Forever changing. Like a slow minuet."

"Looks like mountains to me," Werner says, disinterested, chewing on a grass stem.

She glances at him sideways, surprised.

"See that flamenco dancer over there? Ruffles on her skirt? Reminds me of the dancers at that show in The Hague we went to last year, when Lien Yaldati gave a performance for the refugees," Hanne says.

She stops short, realizes that she is unable to make him see her visions.

She is quiet. His mind is somewhere else. On another wavelength. Suddenly, not knowing where the thought comes from, she blurts, "I miss my parents. Never would have thought that I'd miss my mother this much," she adds faintly. Stops abruptly. It's like admitting to a deep secret wound, to something impossible, something not to be expressed.

They lie quietly in the lush grass. Dream into the clouds. Hanne thinks of home. How angry Mutti was with her last time she came inside fifteen minutes late after shmoozing with Emil Wollheim in the entrance that ended with the longest kiss ever. Those fifteen minutes late. Mutti's slap on her cheek still smarts.

"You're late." Mutti's five fingers burned red stripes into her cheek. Not that Mutti's slaps had ever prevented her from kissing, or from being late. The worst part of those homecomings was that Mutti still insisted on getting her Good Night Kiss. After the slap. Mutti with her soft, wet lips. Yucky, warm, with a wet imprint. Double yuck. Hanne hated to kiss her. She shudders, remembering.

Why on earth does she miss her mother? Contrary feelings tear her apart. Still, she has to admit that she misses Mutti. Perhaps because she hates being a refugee. Hates being a poor refugee. Hates the way deHartogh and her socialite friends look down on her.

"I didn't live with my mother," Werner interrupts her memories. Says it with that strange sarcastic, metallic undertone of his. Like admitting to a secret he does not want to share.

Hanne looks at him, startled, shocked. Don't all children live with their parents?

"You didn't live with your mother? Why not?"

"No. My father died when I was small. She had to work and couldn't take care of me. So she put me in an orphanage. She lived with my aunt. We visited on weekends."

"Then you're used to living like this?"

"What d'you mean *like this*? With other children? We visited regularly. I just lived there."

He obviously resents her remark.

"That's what I mean. An institution. The way we're living here at Jongenshuis. Without parents." Hanne feels embarrassed. Pushed into a corner. She wants to get herself out of the squeeze. Didn't mean to hurt his feelings. "Where's your mother now?"

"She's in London with my aunt. Got their visas shortly after our orphanage left for Rotterdam. All the kids. Peter. Horsey. We left as a group. Dr. Wolf became our director."

"And remained director when you moved here," she concludes.

She looks at Werner, all curiosity now. His brown cowlick hangs like a constant dare across his forehead. Gray-blue eyes between long, curly lashes stare straight and full into her face. She has never known anyone from an orphanage. Orphans are poor. That fact somehow diminishes him. Or does it? She feels sorry for him in a confused, mixed-up sort of way.

His assault is sudden. Overwhelming. She feels his lips on hers, warm, wet, demanding. A few growing hair stubs tickle her upper lip. Like Vati's mustache. There is that warm flow through her body again. Unleashing a storm. She feels faint. Limp. Wants to give in. Kiss. Hug him tight.

"We need to go home," she says faintly and pushes him away. She does not know why she does what she is doing, or where her impulse comes from. No limpness there now!

He looks at her. There's malice in his face. She can feel hate.

"You look horny," he says. His voice grates. She looks back at him, hard. There's that sarcastic undertone that drives her crazy. His eyes stare, half-closed gray-blue slits, full of hatred. His body warm. Full of desire.

She stares back through squeezed eyelids. He is cruel. Good-looking cruel. A flash of truth, sensed somewhere in her groin region. Her body stiffens. She stews inside. Gulps hard. Swallows her stinging reply. Straightens up. No need to show him her hurt. She can't see herself, or what she looks like. But she can see him. His eyes are every bit as horny. The fellow's a cad. Is it resentment? Something like fear snakes up in her.

"We better not be late," she says. "There's quite a distance to pedal yet. And it's getting dark."

She stuffs a handful of strawberries into her mouth to divert attention. Feeling like criminals, they get on their bikes. Sweaty. Mouth and fingers strawberry-red. They pedal silently into the waning, warm Sunday peace on the road. Her basket is empty by the time they get home.

*

Hanne loves the easygoing, individual self-service of Sunday supper. It means fixing your own plate. Tonight it's coleslaw, cucumber, tomatoes, lettuce, radishes, potato salad, and macaroni pudding. The tables stand in their usual diagonal formation. No kitchen duty people on call.

Shaken by the day's events, Hanne fills her plate and sits down in a corner by herself. Away from Werner. Deep down she is angry. She can't explain why. Werner is a riddle she needs to mull over.

The others mill around too. Darn Peter. There he goes tinkering on the piano again. She can't stand the noise right now. That piano is a magnet to many. But no one else is as bad as Peter. Won't anyone teach him to play properly?

It's hard to brood with that much noise around. "Can't you stop? Your tinkering is crude. Downright disgusting," she shouts.

"Yeah. Someone ought to smash your fingers. So we can get some peace in here," Hans Kohn gets into the act. Annoyed, he too. Hans is the house scholar. Thick, brown glasses and all.

"Let me try," Hans Andress wants to push Peter aside.

"Oh, no."

It's hopeless. Neither pleading nor threats help.

"Heini, can't you play something? Ask Dolfi to get his violin. Please..." Hanne suggests above the din. Heini, the real piano player, is the only one who can get Peter away from the piano without a fight.

She tries to put her best pleading into her request. If it has to be noisy, let's get some decent noise.

The crowd chimes in.

"Yes, why don't you give a performance? It's Sunday," the crowd pleads.

They don't have to ask long before Dolfi goes for his violin. "Klärchen, you want to sing? How about *Ständchen?*" Dolfi coaches her.

"All right. You start. I'll sing later."

The Bettelheim brothers often play by popular demand. Easygoing Viennese romantic fare. Dolfi is quite an accomplished artist on his violin. Heini no less a piano player. So the kids think, most of them untrained in anything musical. The boys' repertoire is not large. Monti's *Czardas.* *Menuet* by Boccarini. Some short Beethoven pieces. No matter how often they play them, the youngsters love to hear them. Romantics at heart. Always ask for more.

Like Klärchen, the two Bettelheim brothers have come only recently to Jongenshuis. The three musicians have become a trio. They have added Schubert's *Ständchen* and *Ave Maria* by Gounod to their repertoire.

Unlike the others who came on Kindertransports to Holland, the two boys escaped from Vienna *with* their parents. Lucky ducks. Klärchen is here with her father. They are from Cologne where her mother had died recently. But all three parents now come to visit their children every chance they get on their days off in their camp. Actually, Klärchen's father, a small, skinny man with a woolly white mustache, is almost ever-present. The two are especially close. The Bettelheim mother is quite good-looking. Blond, lighter than Dolfi. The girls tussle about whether her golden blond hair is natural. Or dyed. There are blond Jews all right. But that golden a blond? They think that it must get some artificial help every once in a while to keep its golden luster.

Hanne is jealous. So is everyone else. Imagine being able to see your parents! Talk to them. You just don't talk about missing your parents. What's the use?

While Dolfi is off getting his violin, Hanne suppresses a drawn-out yawn. It's been a tiring day. The strawberries are gone. She wipes the remembered kiss from her mouth.

Mutti's warning the night before they took the train trip to

Krefeld rings in her mind. That was the first time Mutti ever talked about boys. The only time. It wasn't really a talk either. She sensed Mutti's discomfort when she said, rather stiffly, "Hanne, you must be careful…" That was all. Hanne could see her reluctance, watched her squeeze the words out into the open. They never discussed what she should be *careful* about. But Hanne knew instinctively what she meant. She let it go at that.

Unlike a few years earlier, after Gisela Gerler had described for her what married people do. How they do it. That was on their stroll through City Park. It had sounded strange, so unlikely. She still can't picture it. Can't believe that her parents do anything like *that*. Coming home, she had gotten up her nerve to ask Mutti "Where do babies grow?"

"In their mommy's tummy. It takes nine months to grow in there." Mutti's answer to her question was straightforward.

Hanne had mulled over the practical sides of the information. She had seen a few of her parents' women friends grow big before going to the hospital and coming home with a baby. When she discussed her information with her best friend Edith, they had decided to check the encyclopedia. Edith knew that there were pictures of a growing fetus at various stages in a woman's body in the book. All right there to see. The fetus growing bigger every month. That much she had known. But what about the rest?

"How does it get in there?"

She remembers the long, strained silence after her question. Mutti stiffening up. Her voice wretched, miserable. Her face drawn. All reluctance to talk.

"Yeah, it has to get in there first, before it can grow," Hanne repeated. Insistent. Nasty. She had remembered Gisela's description that didn't make much sense. Not in a practical way. She had embarrassed Mutti. Intentionally. Insisted on her explanation.

"Hanne, you'll learn once you grow up."

That was all she had gotten from Mutti. She never even got around to ask how the baby got out. There was nothing more the day she left in Krefeld, except that warning to be careful.

Hanne snaps out of her reverie when Dolfi comes back with his instrument.

"Peter, stop goofing around. Let the Bettelheims play." The demands are communal. Voiced out loud in the room. Peter moves on. The Bettelheims take their places.

The kids congregate around the piano by the sliding glass door. Dolfi tunes his fiddle for a while. Then he nods at Heini. Ready. The crowd is quiet. Grateful, rapt listeners to Boccarini's *Menuet*. Hanne taps her foot in rhythm under the table. She nods at Helga who slides in and sits down next to her.

"Beautiful, isn't it?"

Hanne nods assent. She hears the music, but her mind is back home. Vati used to sing in the bathroom mirror, shaving. Or in the bath. She can hear his voice boom from the bathroom through the house. Rigoletto's major theme was one of his favorites. – *Oh wie so trügerisch sind Weiberhe-erzen/Mögen sie lachen, mögen sie scherzen.* Then there was his other favorite, from Undine, *Vater, Mutter, Schwestern, Brüder hab ich auf der Welt nicht mehr/kehrt' ich einst zur Heimat wieder fänd' ich alles öd' und leer.*

How that verse reflects her present predicament. Undine leaving her family. Although not willingly, she has done the same. Hanne's leaving was necessity. She feels homesick. Hearing the music compounds her longing. Is Vati still singing in his new bathroom in Sweden?

Vati teasing her. Especially for her habit to ask questions. Endless questions. Ever since she was small. "Too many questions," he would tell her, laughing, teasing.

"Are you playing peek-a-boo with Hanne?"

She must have been two. Certainly not older. The time when she watched him prepare for morning prayer during the week. She watched him unwind his phylacteries, place the *Rosh* on his forehead and wind the *Yad* around arm and finger. Count the number of times. Kiss his large blue-striped woolen tallith, turn it and wrap himself, totally absorbed in his communion with his God inside the huge prayer shawl.

"Are you playing peek-a-boo with Hanne?"

She remembers asking this question. His happy smile every time he had reminded her of it. Teasing her for years afterward for her question. As recently as the morning she had left. Her childish question had turned into a sort of private joke between them.

She misses him. His mustache. Prickly kisses. Strong, male kisses so unlike Mutti's.

She sees him still, the tallest Cohen of three on the *Bima* in the synagogue, preparing for the blessing of the priests over the community. The Levites coming up to the *Bima* to wash their hands. Then, shrouded in their prayer shawls, blessing the people, Vati the loudest voice, "*Bar'chu et Adonai ham'vorach.*"

The congregation was supposed to turn away, just listen. But she would peek anyway. Wasn't she the daughter of the priest? His eldest?

"*Barchu... Blessed... the Lord Our God... Bar'chu... Bar'chu... Blessed... May God bless you and keep you.*"

"They're wonderful," Helga says next to her, all appreciation for the performance of the duo up front. Hanne returns from her inner universe. Agrees. It's the *Czardas* by Monti now. Has she missed something? The violin sings, sighs, implores, cries and laughs at the same time. Hanne loves the violin. More than the piano. If she ever has a chance to learn an instrument it'll be the violin. It has soul.

The program follows its usual routine. Kläre gets ready to sing.

"Bet Gounod's *Ave Maria* is next," Hanne whispers.

Eddie and Werner slide in on the bench next to them. Hanne looks up, her mind singing along with the music. It's obvious that Kläre and Dolfi have become a pair. They sure match. Compatible interests. Hanne remembers Werner's warm body. No, she's not going to fight with him. They'll be friends going to school together. Nothing more. She's going to be polite. She's not going to get emotionally involved with a cad.

Music nights never end voluntarily. Van Gelder usually ends

84

them by speaking up in no uncertain terms. By force, that is. As she does tonight.

"Nine thirty. Time to break it up." Van Gelder stands in the door clapping her hands, a reminder of higher authority still functioning. "All right. Wrap it up. It's getting late."

"Ohh, can't you give us an extension?"

"Hey. We thought you'd forget us."

"Well, no such luck. Come on."

Playfully van Gelder switches the light off and on again to make her point.

"All right, already."

Up front Dolfi beds his fiddle gently in red velvet lining and snaps the lid of his black case shut. Heini closes the piano lid, slowly, gently, but with finality over Peter's fingers, who is right there, eager to fool around again. Van Gelder moves forward to thwart his intentions with her solid, starched presence.

"Peter, it's bedtime."

"Ohh. Just a sec."

"No sec, sorry."

They slide off the benches. Reluctantly. Move slowly out of the room. The bedrooms are upstairs.

Most of the children sleep in the large rooms in the back on the second floor, large rooms with fireplaces and parquet floors opposite the administration bedroom/offices. The boys can easily keep track of what is going on between Sussmann and Wolf. Or think they can.

For lack of room, recently six girls, Hanne and Ruth among them, had to move up to the third floor attic where a bedroom had been carved out in the back past the washrooms. The bare wooden floorboards in the attic creak their own singsong, each board grating its own particular tune.

Hanne and Ruth meet on the second floor at the bottom of the narrower flight of stairs up to the third floor. Music-saturated still. They climb silently behind Ditta and Kläre, two of their roommates. The two Häusler sisters, Edith and Friedel, are already in the room, wrapped in hushed whispers, undressing. They too come from Duisburg, the same town as she and Ruth. Hanne remembers Friedel from grade school back home. Her older sister Edith is almost twenty and the oldest girl in the house. The two stick together like glue, an exclusive twosome separate from the rest. Somewhere inside her Hanne feels a twinge of inexplicable regret. Envy? She does *not* want to be that close with Ruth. Ruth is different. The brat would ruin her life. Try to dominate her all she could. No. She can't let that happen. Out of the question.

"You got here early," Hanne says and flops down on her bed. The others do the same. The room explodes in creaking noises from six metal frame beds. Six shifting straw mattresses emit their own squishes under their human load. The straw smell permeating the bedrooms is overwhelming and constant. The girls have become so used to it that they hardly notice.

The room is stuffy. The required blackout blind is pulled down over the small window in the slanted attic roof.

"Got a letter from Maxerl," Ditta beams. Outgoing, happy-go-lucky Ditta, bliss written all over her body. Totally unconcerned whether she's in tune or not – and she never is – she hums her never-ending repertoire of Viennese waltzes. She arches and curves her tubby body in perfect rhythm to her off-key incantations.

"Why don't you stop your nonsense so we can have some peace in here," Kläre mutters under her breath.

Ditta has no such things in mind. She climbs onto her bed with a self-deprecating chuckle. Ignoring her roommates and the heat, she rummages in her precious box where she keeps Max's letters along with scissors, red construction paper, glue and other paraphernalia. Preoccupied with her Maxerl, a twenty-five year old man she used to date in Vienna, she is deaf to what the others say. Smiling to herself, she surrounds herself with her latest heartthrob creations.

Max is the reason that Ditta is here. He got out of Vienna and came to a refugee camp near Rotterdam. When given the choice of Kindertransport destination, she chose Holland rather than England.

"He says he's coming to visit me next time he has a chance," she says with a dreamy-eyed smile into space, holding the letter in front of her.

"Yeahh. Sure," the five others mutter. They think that Ditta is gullible.

"He will too," Ditta declares edgily.

"Hhhohhummm." They have heard about these visits before. But no Max has yet showed. Of course, no one has the heart to seriously wisen her up. She'd only get angry. And sad. The affair is exciting nevertheless. Just think, fifteen-year old Ditta with an old man of twenty-five!

"Want to hear what he writes?"

"Don't read it word for word. Letters are private," Kläre cautions. "We'd like to sleep."

Hanne turns to look at Ditta, lying on her stomach, her face at the foot end of her bed. Her eyes dark coals glowing with happiness.

"Does he still love you?" she teases.

"Course he loves me. He wants to come and visit next chance he gets," Ditta repeats from her bed. Ditta wrapped in stubborn dreams, cloaked against all the teasing.

"Can he get out of his camp to visit?"

"Of course he can. That's what he writes. It's because of him that I'm here. We had a choice, you know."

"Aren't you sorry now that you came *here*? We're in occupied country. The Germans won't get to England."

"No. I'm not sorry. The English get their rockets."

"Over there Jews aren't in danger."

"It's too late to think about that now." Ditta dissolves in smiles. Her own secretive happiness.

"It's past ten. Van Gelder should be here any minute to turn off the light." This from Edith Häusler. All superior sanity. Easy to tell that she's the oldest.

"It's stuffy in here. We ought to get under the covers so we can open the window."

"Yes, hurry up," Friedel chimes in.

Blackout blinds are an obligatory nuisance since the war. The Germans don't want anyone to beam light signals to the RAF, the British Royal Air Force. Lights show the enemy overhead the location of cities. The Germans on the ground truly know how to enforce their rules. There are endless rumors that the Germans have picked up people merely for forgetting to draw their blackout blinds. Accused them of spying.

"Okay, so I won't read the letter. I'll just write him a note," Ditta says, scribbling away on one of her red hearts. "He misses me. He'll come. You'll see," Ditta declares from her bed. Cocksure. Keeps on scribbling.

Hanne thinks Max is a fraud of the first order. Probably has another girl friend in that camp of his. But that's hardly something she'll tell Miss Gullible, who won't believe it anyway. Ditta fifteen, Max twenty-five. They went together in Vienna. That was long ago. Now she's locked up in a children's home in Arnhem, he in an adult camp near Rotterdam. Fat chance he'll bother with her now. Why does he even bother to write her?

From her bed Hanne watches Ditta scribble, surrounded by her cutout hearts. Red hearts in all sizes. Ditta, exhibit A when it comes to fattening refugee food. With snapshots to prove it. Twenty pounds is a lot. Unlikely a fellow would stay in love with the fat lump anyway, even without that distance between them. But why destroy her dream? There she sits, clutching his letter. Happy, humming her Viennese waltzes, way out of tune. No, her Maxerl dream is alive and well – in her mind. A lost case.

"A poem for Maxerl. I'm almost finished." Undaunted, Ditta pens on her red heart cut-out.

"You're last. It's your turn to switch the light off and open the window. It's stuffy. Hurry up," Kläre urges from her corner.

"Aw, shucks. Just a minute."

There is a tense silence in the room. Finally the scribbling stops. Paper, scissors, crayons and pen drop noisily to the floor next to Ditta's bed.

"Okay. Tomorrow I'll put Maxerl's letter up on the wall over my bed," Ditta sighs.

"There's no wall left, with all those hearts and other stuff." Hanne, on edge like the others, expresses the common irritation.

But Ditta shrugs, used to taunts. Smiles her inward all-knowing smile. Heaves herself out of her creaking bed.

Everyone else is in bed, edgy, waiting. Finally. Ditta bends to gather her things. Plops them noisily into her box. Shoves everything under her bed.

"Ditta, open the blind. We're dying for some fresh air! We want to breathe."

"I heard. I'm *going*."

A rotund pillar, Ditta pads to the electric switch by the door. Hanne has a fleeting glimpse of fat ankles. Round billboard ankles on pudgy feet. Solid sturdy masts at the bottom of her pajamas. Through half-closed lids Hanne follows her move to the light switch. Funny, even her ankles have gained weight. The light goes off. In the dark Hanne follows Ditta's voluminous shadow rolling and curving through the room to the old tune of *Geschichten aus dem Wienerwald/So ewig jung und ewig alt/*. Hanne hums along with her. Watches the shadow stop before the window. The black blind scrambles upward with a noisy flap.

"Ta-daaah." The windowpane creaks as Ditta rolls it out and sets it on the hook. "Satisfied?" Ditta challenges. "You have your air."

"Great."

"There's a moon out, in case you want to know," Ditta announces airily. Humming, gyrating in rhythm. Happy as a lark.

"Thanks."

Hanne takes a deep breath. Watches the pillar pad back to the tune of *Stories of the Vienna Woods*. Off-key. Flop into her bed whose metal parts creak, full of suffering heartache.

Her voluminous bulge disappears under her blanket. Good-natured, gullible Ditta. She never gets really angry, at least not for long. No one takes her seriously about Max. Why doesn't the fellow ever live up to his promise to visit? The girls don't know him. But they know there's something fishy about this whole business with him. Poor Ditta.

*

In the dark the Häusler sisters tussle in their own corner. Their outline emerges slowly as her pupils widen in the darkness. These two are almost as bad as the Flesch girls back in Ten Vijver. Friedel was one of her classmates in grade school. How long ago is that? In a former life. The era of Before. Better not think. Even then Edith acted like a mother, making sure that little sis wore her coat, cap, gloves, galoshes in winter. Rotund Mrs. Häusler was one of those worried, protective mothers. Hanne had often felt envious. So unlike her own. Think if Mutti were like that. Worried about her. Just a little bit. Hanne feels a twinge of envy, still.

She couldn't possibly be like Edith. Not with Ruth. The kid would ruin her life. Take over. Kill her. No. Never. It's enough she manipulated everyone else at home. With her looks. Well, Hanne is still the smarter of the two. She got good grades without really trying. Ruth had to sit and study her head off. Still. Conscientious. She has to be best. Be first. Always on top. Can't stand anyone to be better. Hanne turns in her bed, searches for a comfortable position on that flattened straw mattress now disintegrating into its parts. No, she couldn't possibly let that kid take over.

*

"I started a letter home. We ought to get it off this week. The mail takes forever to get there," Ruth announces in the dark. Hanne hears reproach in her voice. She, the older one, should really take care of the mail. But she finds it an effort to sit down and write when there's not much to say. What can she tell her parents? What do they know about her life? They never knew back home.

Even less so here. Her friends used to talk with their parents. She never could. Just couldn't. She kept her own counsel. They never understood. Got angry, no matter what she did.

"We haven't heard from them for a long time," Hanne says with a bad conscience.

"Three weeks."

Leave it to the brat to count the days.

"I wonder what Sweden is like," Ruth whispers. "Do you think that people wear native costume?"

"I doubt it. Before we came here, I thought all the Dutch wear native costumes. Only a few do, in backwoods villages. On holidays. It's probably the same over there."

"That's what I thought. I don't see any in the snapshots we get."

"Let's just hope the Swedes stay out of the war," Hanne says. "It's good to know Mutti and Vati are in neutral territory."

"I made a list of what I want them to send us."

So like Ruth. The practical one. No one would ever accuse Ruth of being a dreamer, the way they do Hanne.

"I'll write tomorrow," Hanne promises.

Hanne tries to picture life in Sweden. No war. No Germans. Must be heaven. Right up there under the North Pole with long summer nights and northern lights, Eskimos and reindeers, glaciers and eternal snow. She remembers Mr. Frank's map in Geography where Scandinavia looked like a tiger lying in wait, ready to jump, it's furrowed brown back of Norwegian coastline, cut by fjords and rivers. The greenish underbelly the Swedish lands bounded by the Baltic Sea. Its folded hind legs Lapland, all the way up into the Arctic Circle. Land of the Midnight Sun. Knut Hamsun. He describes the northern provinces where Sweden and Norway meet. She loves Selma Lagerlöf's Nils Holgersson ride on the snowgoose across the immense, dark Kolmården forest, where elk, moose and other wild creatures roam, to the land of the icy Snow Queen. Bears too? Probably.

"Can you imagine Mutti in Sweden?"

"Why not?" Ruth is baffled.

"Oh, well. I just thought it strange. Never mind," Hanne says. How can she explain to Miss Practical that the country doesn't match chain-smoking Mutti whose greatest interests in life are to play bridge, dress in the latest fashion, gab with her lady friends in the ritziest coffee shop downtown and discuss recipes every afternoon? Whose aspiration was to be bridge champion. All things that Hanne has decided she will never, never, ever do.

"Göteborg looks like an ordinary city. And Mutti is her old well-dressed self in the pictures we've gotten," Ruth emphasizes. Black shadow talking in the dark.

"You're right. It's only the Lapps way up north who need to wear seal or reindeer skins for protection against the cold," Hanne says.

"You're dreaming again," Ruth says. There is that contempt in her voice. Dreaming is not a highly valued preoccupation in the life of a Jewish refugee. How often has she had to hear that phrase back home!

"I'll have to stop fantasizing. If I can," Hanne mumbles to herself. No one needs to hear her. Least of all Ruth.

She thinks of Werner and his kiss earlier in the day. Though she's two years younger, Ruth knows a lot more about IT. Ever since the time that this fellow kidnapped her on the way to Fräulein Stolpa, their seamstress. They called Mutti and Vati late that night from the police station. Kid cried all through the night in her bed after they brought her home. Hanne never dared to ask for details of what happened. What did that fellow do to her? She still can't picture it. All she knows is what she picked up from what Mutti told others. The police found Ruth on Hüttenfelder Strasse, where they used to go to the cheaper movie house on Sunday afternoons. Alone, crying on the street. The man had threatened Ruth with a gun in the stairwell of Stolpa's house. Told her to come along. So she went with him. Afterward he let her go. Hanne wonders what happened in between.

"Thank God, nothing really happened. The doctor examined

her. They picked him up for *Rassenschande*," Mutti used to end her tale.

Rassenschande, the word the Nazis coined to describe sexual relations between Jews and Gentiles. A crime under the Nazi regime. Usually against wealthy Jews and girlfriends, married or not.

Hanne is dying to know what happened to Ruth. Still, she can't bring herself to ask her. Talk about things like sex has always been taboo in her house. What had happened to her sister that night she spent with a nasty man with a gun? Nothing good, that's for sure. She can still hear her crying all night. Perhaps she should've talked to her then.

"You know why I came to Jongenshuis?" Ruth sits up, black shadow on her bed, talking to Hanne.

"Not really. Other than that the deWinters didn't want to take care of that refugee kid any longer." Like all the other nice Jewish families.

"Imagine! I took a cookie. Mrs. deWinter always counted the cookies on her teacart. I took one! One morning."

"For crying out loud, you stole a cookie?!! What kind of theft is that?"

"I was hungry."

"Don't let it bother you. I never told you why the deHartoghs returned me. They accused me of stealing a bar of soap, which I didn't do. The bar I had was a present from fatso Goldberg in The Hague. Accusing us of stealing must be a convenient ploy in the community to get rid of unwanted refugee kids."

"She dismissed her maid when I came. I was the maid," Ruth continues. "Talk about being a cleaning freak – the woman pulled the picture nails out of the wall to dust them, then stuck them back in."

"No kidding. What a nut! Well, I had gotten the maid treatment back in The Hague. Staying with our cousins back then, you didn't get wise to it until coming here," Hanne says.

"Living with them wasn't such a picnic either. Adolf was

a nervous freak, always shouted for no reason at all, even with Berthe. Though she's nice. She has no easy life with him. I pity her. And little Miryam, she's so cute. "Hmmm. You know, Berthe said something that made me think."

"What did she say?"

"She'd never send little Miryam away by herself the way Mutti sent us off to strangers. Her family would stay together, no matter what. Wherever they'd go."

Hanne reflects in silence. She would like to be with Mutti and Vati in Sweden. Right now. Mutti is selfish. There's something to what Berthe said.

*

"Klärchen? Are you asleep?" That is Friedel's low voice, pleading.

"No, not yet."

All of a sudden everyone is wide awake. They know what is coming. All agree.

"You want to sing for us?"

"Aren't you asleep yet?" Kläre asks into the room.

"Not really. Sing for us? Please?"

The fresh air coming through the window seems to have invigorated them.

"Yes, pretty please? It's a unanimous request."

Silent expectation settles in the small room. The moon shines outside, dips the outlines inside the room in silver gloss.

"All right."

Kläre clears her throat, sits up, and leans against the head of her bed. The moon's silvery sheen colors her outline against the bed's frame. She clears her voice.

"*Schlafe, schlafe, holder süsser Knabe,*" her voice fills the tiny room.

Happily, gratefully, the other five listen to her repertoire. Lullabies, the *Shepherd Song*, other songs. They could listen for hours.

Van Gelder opens the door, checking on her charges. Her

bedroom is on the other side of the attic. She listens for a while, then softly closes the door again with a quiet "Good night, girls."

The floorboards outside creak as she traverses the attic to her room. They can hear her door open and shut. Kläre sings on for a while. Then she is quiet.

"I'm sleepy."

"Me too."

"Thanks, Klärchen. You know we love to hear you sing."

"You ought to become an opera singer."

"You have a gorgeous voice."

"Good night."

"Good night." Each one rolls into her comfort space.

I'll have to write my letter tomorrow, Hanne thinks. Can a Jew become an opera singer these days? Or will Kläre have to wait until the end of the war? That pesky war.

If it ever ends.

Silence descends on the little attic room and spreads through the house. The building grows quiet. Another day at Amsterdamsche Weg 1.

Chapter 5

I think I'm finally getting the hang of it," Hanne mumbles, halfway satisfied. Sighs. She steps back to get a better look at her drawing.

The three artists in residence. That's their common nickname these days. They work together in the backyard. Hanne prepares for the fall term. Eddie gets up to survey what she has accomplished, ready to critique.

"Not bad. You're improving," he says and measures the distances on the paper with his pencil against the original next door.

"It isn't easy," Hanne says, flushed after trying all afternoon.

"It's your own fault. Why start with the most difficult thing?" Werner pipes in.

"Why do you always have to gripe at me? I think it's smart to tackle difficult things first, then take it easy with the rest." Hanne shrugs. Werner is getting increasingly under her skin. "That's the way I work," Hanne persists, sulking.

"It's time that school starts," Eddie chimes in.

It's hot, one of those steamy late August afternoons of the Dutch lowlands. Mountains of clouds hang heavy in the air. The glittery sun drugs the landscape to sleep. They sit in the shade under the huge oak tree. Still, they have to keep wiping the sweat out of their eyes.

"My paper sticks. It's glued to my hands, arms, everything. I'm getting us something to drink," Hanne says. "I need some water, but it's hard to pry myself loose from the bench."

Hanne stretches gingerly. After sitting for hours bent over her work, it feels good to grow vertical. She sets herself in motion. The two boys keep on working silently over their designs.

She walks through the sliding door, past the silent black piano, through the dining hall. Wooden wainscoting covers half the walls. The oak parquet floor gleams. She passes the ornate fireplaces, evidence of past glory. Fancy. For the local doctor. Before becoming home for a bunch of poor refugees on the public dole. Peter, Herbert and Dicky play at keeping the parquet floors shining by sliding across the length of the room on rags dipped in paste wax. Betting on who can slide the farthest. Marcuse's method! Miss Sussmann hates it. Dr. Wolf too. Though they haven't outlawed it. Lately Wolf has turned neutral in the matter, probably under van Gelder's influence. She chuckles about the whole thing, secretly of course. The noisy game repeats every four weeks or so. No one can argue with the result: shiny parquet floors. End of discussion.

The kitchen across the hall is a veritable steam bath in this heat. The pots steam. Freda stirs. Hanne walks to the faucet, fills a glass. Gulps the water greedily. Then she fills a pitcher and takes three glasses to take out to the boys. Back in the hall she sees Dicky come in through the large wooden entrance door. He slams it shut with a bang.

"Hi Dick," she calls. Dicky is the Jongenshuis baker, an apprentice at the local bakery down the road. Out of the house before dawn, he is the first to leave and the first to return home in the afternoon. Hanne follows his stride down the black and white marble squares of the hallway. Square, solid figure in striped flour-dusted baker's pants. Something seems out of order here.

She has a strange premonition. She tries to shake it off. Must be the heat. Storm in the air.

"Hi. Did you see our new neighbors?" Dicky stares at her. His face is distorted. His sturdy figure one electrified upset.

"Nope. I've been working in the back all day. What's there to see?"

Black thoughts ramble through her head. Fear is never far from their thoughts.

"Moving in. Well, go look for yourself," he says, at a loss for words.

She leaves her pitcher and the glasses on the side and runs up front to the living room. Its windows face the street. Dicky is right behind her.

"See them?"

"Hmmm." She sees them. No explanation necessary. Black uniforms. An old familiar sight. She has seen them for as long as she can remember. Feared them as far back as her memory can reach.

What now? The ss moving in on the other side of their street? Neighbors? Dread invades her bones. Settles in her organs. Especially her stomach.

"When did they come here?" she mumbles, feeling helpless.

"The building was empty when I left this morning. They're setting up the guard house too."

"Only a blind person can't see them now. We'll hear them too, for sure. Shouts. Boots crashing on asphalt."

The trees in the triangle across the street shield the house somewhat from view. That's why they didn't hear anything during the day. Now no one can help seeing the guards, hearing their goose-step up and down the street past the guardhouse in front of the circular driveway.

"On our street!"

Others come home from school and flock by the window.

"D'you think they're here to stay?"

"This looks pretty permanent, wouldn't you say?"

"To have the guardians of Aryan supremacy right across the street… Trouble!"

"For sure. Does Dr. Wolf know?"

"I told him. He's been watching them move in from his window upstairs all day long," Atze says. He and Ruth have just returned from middle school.

"Wolf says, that as long as we keep a low profile and behave, they won't bother us," says Ruth.

A general sneer.

"Want to bet?"

"He has to say that."

They know better. They have lived with the black menace for years. Aryan elite. Blond, non-entity faces under black helmets. Steely blue-eyed stares full of hatred, malice, death. Booted terror in high decibels. Malicious guffaws. Boycotts. Concentration camps. Parades with flags. Beatings.

"What else could he say?"

They shrug off the inevitable.

"Can't see why blond hair or blue eyes would make them smarter. Or better," Ditta says.

"It's their idiotic idea. Nordic race. Ha!" Shrugs.

"Most Germans are neither blond, nor blue-eyed. Including the Führer."

"They divide humans into five different races. Top race is the Nordic. The rest are inferior by degrees. Lowest on the scale is the Mediterranean. That's us."

"Yea, my social science teacher in Berlin once called me to the front to demonstrate my 'typically Aryan cranium,'" Ruth Pestachowsky scoffs. "I was too scared to tell him I'm Jewish."

"Interesting. So you have an Aryan noodle. I'm impressed," Hanne sneers.

"It's an old anti-semitic idea Hitler picked up."

Sarcasm helps to digest bad news. Hanne looks at Ruth Pestachowsky. "With your square forehead, prominent jaw, strong, straight nose and long dark-blond ponytail you could easily pass for a German."

"Believe me, it wasn't funny at the time. I didn't want to risk my good grade on the last day of school before summer vacation. That's why I let it ride. I was lucky. I had a different science teacher in the fall. Then I had to leave the school anyway."

"Don't you ever wonder what this fellow would have done if he had found out that this perfect cranium sits on a Jewish neck?" Hanne muses.

"I hate to imagine."

*

Hanne remembers. Sure, it had all started with the Nazi takeover in 1933. That's when Hitler was voted in as Kanzler and he and his cohorts gained access to rule Germany. They made no bones about their hate of Jews. The Führer pronounced it and the German people screamed agreement. Applauded. The official stance of the government changed on that day, and with it their politics. Their laws. His book *Mein Kampf* became the gospel for the people. His propaganda machine did the rest. Hindenburg, the president, was too old to object.

*

But anti-Semitism is much older and far more universal. Hitler and his henchmen only expressed it openly, acted on what had been going on for ages. Centuries. Millennia. Two thousand years plus on record. After the Jews refused to recognize Jesus as Christ and Messiah. Jews still wait for Isaiah's prophecy to be fulfilled. Hatred and rejection of the minority in foreign territory took hold wherever Christianity spread, tacit and open, at intervals, expressed with ghettos, burnings, expulsions, during crusades, inquisitions, pogroms, holocausts. A people vilified in folklore as the Wandering Jew. Jews who eat matza made with Christian children's blood. Anti-Semitism now made into official law. Mechanized. Methodical. Eradication by scientific means.

*

Hanne remembers the incident from a few years ago, back home. Not long after *The Takeover*. She may have been nine. Or ten years old. Shortly before Passover. As usual, Pinchas Horowitz, their Passover grocer, a bearded Chasid, had brought matza and the special holiday stuff to their house in the morning. Afterward Mutti went out shopping and she and Ruth were alone in the house. Suddenly she heard heavy footsteps. Boots clomping up the marble steps from the vestibule outside. Stop by their door. Dark shadows in the milky glass. The bell rang. Shrill, urgent, impatient. Nearly jumped out of its socket.

Hanne watched the shadows. Shivering. Goosebumps crawled up her arms, legs, spine. What was she to do? Mutti's rules were clear. Never to open the door for strangers. Under no circumstances. She stood motionless by the door. Ruth behind her. She couldn't breathe. She waited, hoping against hope for the shadows to disappear. Dissolve. But they remained, moving back and forth, relentlessly. Threatening. Her hands were icy. Again the bell shrilled through the house. Demanding. Once. Twice. Three times. A nightmare come alive. Her throat went dry.

"Open up. Or we'll break down the door!" The voice came through the door, loud and clear.

Hanne was petrified. A sudden crash. Boots crashing against the door.

The house shuddered in its foundation.

"*Aufmachen!* Open up, right away, you in there."

The voice got meaner, louder. There was no escape.

Another kick against the door.

"My mother is out. I'm not allowed to open for strangers," Hanne stammered through the glass. She need not have bothered.

"I'll show your mother."

Another kick rumbles against the door. It jumps on its hinges, frame broken. The lock hung by a splint in the center. Three SA-men steps through the opening into the foyer. Broken glass all over. Everywhere. Mean, brown-booted danger enters Hanne's well-organized life. If only the ground would open up. Protect her and Ruth. Hide them. But nothing like that happens. The brown-booted danger remains. There is no rescue.

Outwardly calm, she shivers inside. Faces the unholy trinity in uniform. Ruth behind her.

"Yes?"

"You had a visitor here this morning, a man with a beard. What was his business?"

Hanne marvels how he knows that. The grapevine is quick. Neighbors? There's an SA-home around the corner. Do they watch what is going on in her home?

"That's our holiday grocer."

"He came with a big package."

"He brought our Passover groceries."

"Didn't he bring any pink leaflets? Printed matter?"

"No." Hanne shakes her head. Absurd idea.

"What *did* he bring?"

"Matza and wine. Some other groceries. Food for the whole week. That's a big package."

"You sure there weren't any leaflets in there? Pink papers?"

"Quite sure."

This inquisition is ridiculous. Pink leaflets? Her Dad? Her intuition tells her that he means politics. Communists? An unknown term in this house. Dad never engages in politics. He hates to get involved. He had even canceled the local *Rhein and Ruhrzeitung* because they ran an anti-Semitic editorial.

"Does your father ever get printed papers?"

"No."

Hanne swallows hard to keep her composure. Shakes her

head vehemently in negation. How often would she have to answer this question?

The spokesman turns to the others. "Search the house. You go this way. I'll take the opposite side." They walk off. He turns to the girls. "Show me those packages," he commanded.

Hanne leads him to the living room where the matza, the wine and the other Passover things are stacked, away from everyday food. Unleavened must never come in contact with leavened. The SA-man tears the packages open, sniffs them. Even the oil was under suspicion. Disappointed at not finding anything objectionable, he questions again.

"Is this all he brought?"

"Yes."

"Does you father have many friends like that?"

"Like what?" Hanne has no intention of making things easy for him.

"Dressed funny. With a beard."

"No. He's the only one. He needs the money and so Dad orders from him."

"Does he come often?"

"Once a year. Before Passover. With the holiday food."

Hanne has no desire to defend Pinchas' eighteenth century Chasidic garb. She thinks it's old-fashioned. Stupid. Out of style in modern society. Strange. But is his brown uniform less strange? For that matter, are any of the other Nazi uniforms?

"He never brings any printed matter here? Leaflets? Magazines?"

"No."

"Do others?"

"No."

"Or do they come through the mail?"

"What?"

"Printed matter?"

"No."

Hanne is getting tired and impatient. He keeps repeating himself. She isn't sure whether he is doing that on purpose to confuse her. The fellow tries to set Dad up as a spy. Or Communist. She has to play dumb. And keep her calm despite the chill creeping up her spine. Was it anger? Fear? Printed matter indeed! Her Dad!

The other two come stomping back.

"Nothing." They shake their heads.

The leader turned to the girls again.

"Does your father get any papers through the mail? Foreign newspapers, perhaps? Or magazines? Or anything like that?"

"Never."

Hanne keeps up her guard. There was a catch somewhere. Foreign mail is censored.

"Have you ever seen printed matter in this house? Red leaflets, for example?"

"No. Never."

These leaflets became monotonous. Pink? Red? Hanne looks at her sister. Recognizes the same fear in those big hazel eyes. Hazel with tiny blue specks at the outer edges.

The leader turned to his two companions. They shake their heads. Shrug their shoulders. Disappointed. "Let's go." Then, turning to the girls, he says with emphasis, "We'll be back!"

They stomp out of the house. Slam the door shut behind them with a vengeance. The upper panel's remaining glass shards clink angrily for a while, then stop. The door hangs in there by a thread. The frame ripped, it remains hanging on its hinges.

Frustrated, furious, Hanne tries to push the door completely shut after they are gone. The fight was uneven. A child is powerless against gun-wielding authority. Jewish children are doubly powerless.

After she came home, Mutti called the carpenter. And the locksmith. It took two days before they finally came and fixed the damage as well as they could. Afterward the frame had a huge dent and the door creaked. Mutti complained about the outrageous charges. But when all was said and done, the lock was a sham.

Anyone could invade the privacy of their home. A simple kick at the door was all it took.

* * *

"There's no security in this world," she mutters now.

The world has become unsafe with the spread of the Nazi nightmare. An Octopus. She, her family, all Jews are free game for cruel uniformed men, intoxicated with power.

Hanne shivers despite the heat. She watches tubby Ditta waddle down the hall.

"Wolf is dead wrong," Hanne pronounces to the crowd around them. "The ss will never leave us alone. Never in a million years. Ruthless supermen. All-powerful. Schopenhauer ideas. Nietzsche creatures beyond good and evil."

"Let's go watch them from the front window," Ditta suggests.

"Not me. You can. Haven't you seen enough of them?" Hanne says. She thinks it's a stupid idea.

"Get to know your enemy," Dicky says.

"He's right," Ditta agrees in her singsong Viennese lilt.

"As if we didn't know them already," Hanne mumbles.

But she goes along with the others to see the two black stooges parade on the other side of their street in their quiet middle class neighborhood. Devil incarnate. Their white armbands with the bright-red Indian fertility sign degraded to a crooked cross, the Nazi swastika makes her squirm.

"In Austria they made us scrape the sidewalks to remove their graffiti. I scraped next to a lady with long polished fingernails in a mink coat," Ditta recalls.

"That's the difference between us. Austria and Germany. I can't remember a time without them in Germany," Werner says. He and Eddie have joined the group.

"My parents talked constantly about *before*. I got tired of listening to everything that *used to be before*. It doesn't help to think of the past. We have to tackle the *now*," Hanne says.

For a while they watch the helmeted black uniforms goose-step up and down the street.

"It's no use," Hanne says. "Lets go back to the dining room." She watches Ditta's solid, sturdy ankles in motion.

Hanne is tired. Tired of looking at ss. Tired of their predicament. She feels like a fish caught in a net, gasping, maneuvering to keep alive. Trying to think of gimmicks to keep going.

"Tada!" Out in the hall Peter and Hans parade in goose step like their new neighbors.

"Funny-y-y-yyy!!!" No one is in the mood to laugh.

"They haven't conquered the whole world yet. There's still Britain. And the United States," Werner insists.

"Come on. They're all over Europe. In North Africa. Italy and Japan are their friends. The Axis. We were born on the wrong side of the globe. No one cares what happens to us."

"It may seem that way. The United States won't let them. They won't let England down, for their own good. They know the fix we're in."

Hanne sighs, wanting to be convinced. Time would tell. There's precious little they can do now from inside the octopus. Jonah must have felt that way in his fish. Trapped.

"I wish they'd hurry up. What's taking them so long?"

"Lovely new neighbors," Ruth comes down the hall.

Hanne looks at her younger sister. *How pale she is*, shoots through her mind.

"Yep," she shrugs. "It's best to calm down. Don't let it get to you." Hanne tries to be nonchalant. After a while she adds, "I'll finish the letter tonight. We'll mail it tomorrow."

*

Aunt Scherer, Mutti's aunt in the United States, and her family had sent an affidavit and her parents had applied for visas to emigrate there. That had been years ago. Before Kristallnacht and before things got really nasty. But the Americans had stalled. The German quota was filled, they said. Small wonder, with so many

Jews that wanted to get out. Then they had finally gotten their registration number, long after their application and waited for their turn. Still waiting with nowhere else to go after Kristallnacht, the girls went on Kindertransport to Holland. Then Sweden had allowed their parents to wait there for the visa, like Uncle Henry before them. Mutti and Vati were lucky. Got out in August 1939, two weeks before the war with Poland would have stopped their emigration. With England at war and the mines in the North Sea, they are stuck in Sweden. They wouldn't want to move on without their girls anyway.

"We're hopelessly mired in occupied Holland," Hanne says,.

When they went on Kindertransport no one had imagined that the Nazis would overrun the Low Countries and then France, opening another triple front in the west of Europe.

"Will we have to wait until after the war?"

"How long does a war last? This one is going on forever."

Questions. Questions.

No answers.

"Let me address the envelope. I have the stamps," Hanne says. She takes Ruth's pages and her own, folds the handwritten letters slowly into the envelope with the foreign address. Licks it shut. Licks the stamps and glues them on. "There."

Their parents will hold the same papers in a few days. Days? Weeks? Months? Who knows.

Hanne looks at her younger sibling. People are right. She is pretty with her dark curly hair, those large hazel eyes.

"I'm jealous of her," her mind throbs with sudden, uncanny honesty. "I've wanted to kick her off Mutti's lap for as long as I can remember." Ever since that little shrimp came into the house and took Hanne's place on Mutti's lap. Her place no longer. Then this little impostor had turned into a manipulative, cunning, selfish little monster who knows how to hold center stage. Her looks help. She's the cute favorite all around. The world is unfair.

Hanne sighs quietly. Shrugs.

"On top of all that, she hates me too. Who can live with this selfish monster?"

Hanne bristles defense. She knows that jealousy lies behind her demands: *poone haben*. She wanted *poone*, wanted to nurse from Mutti's breast. Vati teases her about that still. No, they had never understood. They thought it was cute. But never knew what she meant.

But why does this brat hate her so much?

She doesn't know. Never asked. Riddle unsolved.

"You're the older one. You are smarter. You give in." That had been Mutti's and Vati's constant refrain.

She will always be the older sister. All her life. Dammit. Damn her.

*

Dolfi Bettelheim tunes his violin. Hanne watches absentmindedly. Lost in thoughts. Dissonances all around. The room is noisy. The general discussion centers on the new neighbors. Heini runs his fingers across the piano keys. Hanne looks for Peter. Did he really give up his tinkering without a fight? Must have missed that one today while she was absorbed in thoughts of home. Music. They must have changed their minds. Music should help us to take our minds off the new neighbors. Someone calls for Kläre to sing. Dolfi and Heini are playing already. *Czardas* by Monti. Dolfi's fiddle trills. The music permeates her body. Like waves. Her foot moves in rhythm. She's a musical automaton set in motion.

"It's stuffy in here. I need some fresh air," she mumbles. She gets up, irritated, feeling an inner need to move.

The piano shakes the rhythm. She sleepwalks across the shiny parquet floor. Pushes her way through the half-open sliding glass door. Out into the backyard. She can feel the music throbbing through the walls.

Dusk. The twilight wraps the dark green trees and shrubs in an eerie purplish veil. Nettles weave through the tall, uncut, wild grass. Cling to her shoes. Black clouds hang low over the landscape beyond the trees. Uncanny sunrays from a sun hiding behind the cloud cover flip between pregnant dark gray powder bellies. Turn their edges a pinkish-rose. Slivers of dark blue sky in between. Searchlights scan the heavens at regular intervals. Reminders of warring humans on earth. War for power. The atmosphere is dense. Charged with electricity. Storms brew. Fill the earth.

Listless, heavy, on edge, Hanne saunters down the narrow path to where the wire fence marks the end of their grounds. A steep incline behind it leads down to the railroad station of Arnhem. Hanne bends over the bushes and looks at the diverging railroad tracks below in the settling darkness. No illumination tonight or any other night these days. The Germans want the general blackout to prevent enemy bombers from detecting strategic points. People must make certain that their curtains are drawn before they turn their lights on at night. The war breeds fast learners, especially those who suddenly find themselves in enemy territory.

Hanne follows an express train flitting through the station without stopping. Secretive, like a snake on erratic errands. It is too dark to see whether it is a passenger train. Where did it come from? Where is it headed? Why the hurry? Unsettling questions. Like, where is she headed? What lies in her future? She knows where she comes from: an ordinary middle class family, Jewish, modern Orthodox, with an ingrained belief in God – a God of justice and mercy. Yes, there's the rub. Vati is the believer. Mutti the mutineer, chafing under ancient, stale restrictions. Thinks nothing of switching on electric lights on the Sabbath. Hanne has caught her smoking in the bathroom too. Even without seeing it, any idiot can smell her smoke. Whom is she trying to fool? But then, Hanne can understand her rebellion. Dad doesn't notice. Doesn't want to. He is gentleness itself with his family, though ever so strict with himself. Steeped in tradition, he believes that women and children don't have to be as strict as men about the laws. Hanne wonders about his God, Mutti's God, her own. Better not think.

"I'm like Mutti, in a way. But I love Dad. I love his stories."

She tries to picture her own future. Art school is ahead. And then? The Nazis are blocking her way. Insurmountable? That's the question. What are those uniformed fanatics planning to do? Control her life? Throttle her? Her ambitions? Why her? Why us? She gasps for breath. The air feels sticky. What have we done to deserve this? Where is God? Justice? Mercy?

A lightning flash zigzags between gray-black rain clouds bulging in the distant sky. Wart lumps in the heavens. She counts, waiting for the thunder to roll. "One, two, three, four, five, six..." The storm is still a long way off. No rain. No relief.

Total darkness descends. She meditates into the starless, pregnant, impenetrable sky.

"Hanne! Hanne!" she hears van Gelder call. Bedtime. She ought to go back inside. She hesitates. Tries to breathe. She hates the thought of the stuffy bedroom under the attic in this humid heat.

"Hanne! Hanne-e-! Time to go upstairs!" van Gelder's call is more urgent the second time around.

"I'm coming!" she calls. Reluctance mounts thick inside her. Rules. Rules and regulations. Every move she makes goes according to what others decide. A wonder they let her breathe on her own.

"What's the matter?" van Gelder stands in the door, lets her through with a well-meant slap on her rump.

"Oh, nothing, really. The heat is choking me."

"Well then, why not answer the first time?"

"It's sticky. Everything sticks on my skin, like glue," Hanne evades an answer. Lifts the front of her blouse and waves it back and forth to make her point. Fans herself. She feels air rush through the opening.

Indoors, things are still lively. It's funny that bedtime is the time when everyone finds a million urgent things still to do before calling it a day. Seems to go with restrictions. The Bettelheims play the last notes of a Beethoven sonata. She watches Dolfi Bettelheim put his fiddle softly into its red velvet groove inside the black case. Heini waits a minute with closed eyes. Then he lowers the piano lid. Ever so gently. Peter is right there to open it up again. Ever the con-artist.

"Wait, I want to play," he tells Heini.

Heini shrugs. It's not his business. Peter tinkers on, certain of his magic ability to wheedle his way to a few more minutes of tinkering. Restrictions? Don't apply to him. Must have learned wheedling through life in the orphanage.

Van Gelder steps up beside him. Folds the cover down over his fingers.

"Peter, it's enough."

"Aw, shucks." He pulls his hands out, but remains on the stool.

"It's late. The lights are going to be turned off in a few minutes."

"Aw shucks." Peter saunters off.

Van Gelder moves over to the door behind him, shooing her charges before her.

"Upstairs with you. It's nine o'clock. Tomorrow is another day."

"Nine is way too early to get up," they complain, to no avail.

They have an hour. The lights are turned off at ten. No excuses. The boys say that Wolf wants an early curfew because he's in a hurry to visit Sussmann.

Hanne walks the wide staircase to the second floor. The boys live in the large master bedrooms in the back. Wolf and Sussmann can keep a close eye on them from the front. And vice versa. Freda lives downstairs, a room near the kitchen. Van Gelder sleeps in the attic front. Her room faces the street. The girls' bedroom is on the other side. The back of the building.

"Hi." Werner greets Hanne at the landing. "You can copy my Havinga anatomy notes. That way you can catch up with his class. I have them here." He holds his papers out to her.

"Thanks. It's awfully thoughtful of you," she says, grateful for the help. She takes the bundle but she is in no mood to talk. She is too tired.

"What's eating you tonight? Something wrong?" He searches her face.

"I'm in a foul mood," she confesses. "Let's blame it on our new neighbors. And the weather. We'll talk tomorrow."

"Cheer up. The world hasn't come to an end yet. I don't need the notes until school starts," he calls after her.

"Good. That'll give me plenty of time," she mutters and walks on.

She climbs the second, narrow flight to the attic, deaf to the world outside herself.

*

The wooden door creaks on its hinges, unwilling to let her in. If the attic is hot, the enclosed space they call their bedroom is a thousand times worse. It's like a steambath. The air hangs still and stifling between the slanted rafters over the six cots. Hanne gasps for air. The obligatory black blind prevents her from opening the window. She sits down on the edge of her bed. The wooden beams loom large and pressing. The atmosphere feels out of joint tonight. Electrically charged. Threatening. She feels uneasy.

As from afar she hears the other girls trundle in – Ruth, Ditta, Kläre, the Häusler sisters Edith and Friedel. She hears them argue. Their loud voices hurt her head. Hanne feels an uncanny dread. A nasty spirit that hovers over the building. Evil spreads like an ugly, greedy octopus.

"Let's hope they leave us alone."

"Wolf is dead wrong. To think they won't bother us if we keep a low profile."

"They never did. So why would they now?"

"Wishful thinking. Those sentries parading up and down the street. Keeping watch."

Hanne has a mental glimpse of shiny boots, white armbands

with red crooked crosses on black uniforms. Non-entity faces, steely blue vacuous stares under square helmets. Indoctrinated hatred blind to any reason. Blond superior *Aryans*. Race experts on Nordic blonds. Elite SS, a select band of vile loudmouths. A vicious scramble in her head.

"Can't see why hair or eye color would make them better, or smarter! If you look at them, most Germans are neither blond, nor blue-eyed. And that includes The Führer!!!"

The girls are right. She's heard these arguments a million times. Used them herself. A voluminous lump settles in Hanne's chest. The lonely, dreary lightbulb overhead stings in her brain. She hears the girls' chatter from afar, like an echo coming from another planet. She tries to take a deep breath. There is no air to breathe. The lump spreads through her stomach region, clear through to her back, settles in her spinal column somewhere between her shoulder blades. It prevents her from breathing. The walls threaten. Grow huge. Close in on her.

She flops down on top of her blanket. Tries to keep still to find relief from the pressure. In the next bed Ruth stretches out between her sheets. Her mop of hair a curly, espresso colored spot above the pillow. Hanne feels a sudden urge to talk to her.

"Ruth?"

"Hummm?"

"You asleep yet?"

"Almost. I'm sleepy. What's the matter?" Ruth mumbles. Turns toward the wall, away from her.

"Ohh. Nothing."

What's the use? The brat wouldn't care anyway. Her stupid premonitions. She needs to get a handle on herself. Go to sleep, Hanne. Like the others. Mutti always told her not to take things too seriously. Dad echoed the same line.

"I shouldn't make a mountain out of a molehill," she tells herself. It would help if the window were open. We'd get some fresh air in. Ditta's still scribbling on some heart, or whatever. Perhaps a letter to Max. Or a corny poem. The born dawdler.

"I got some snapshots today. And I have a new poem. Want to hear it?" she says into the room.

A negative mumble from the other beds. "Finish up. We want to breathe some fresh air."

"Just one more minute." Then, with a sigh, "All right, pests from Dullsville."

Ditta lumbers out of her bed. Paper, scissors, coloring pens drop noisily on the wooden floor. Feet underneath barrelshaped pajamas pad to the window. The sudden noisy thud of the blackout curtain. The window crank squeaks and grates.

"Goodnight." Ditta pads back and plops onto her mattress. The whole room shakes.

Electrically charged air hangs outside the window. Still. Unmoving. A storm is brewing.

"Klärchen, you want to sing tonight?" Ditta's muffled voice Ditta cuts through the heavy stillness.

"Gee, not tonight. I really don't feel like it."

"Aw, why not?"

"I'm not in the mood. Really. Perhaps tomorrow."

"Well. Goodnight then. Sleep tight."

Ditta's bed squeaks its particular bleep as she settles into it. Each one of the six beds has its own particular groan.

As through a haze Hanne hears the soft breathing. Snores. The occasional moves of the others in the still room. She looks at the window, a light square cut into the midnight dark of the sky. The clammy air hangs motionless within it.

Has there ever been a normal life? Hanne can't remember a time without Nazis. Normal Life. The Before. Before they took over the streets with their hateful parades and marching songs. Hitler's voice blaring through public microphones in public places. Shrill. Overbearing. The Voice of Hate. The Voice of Malevolence.

*

Though long ago, the elections in 1933 are a vivid memory. When Hitler and his cohorts fought for power with riots in the streets, nasty, hateful graffiti on walls and fences, fat round billboards in public places with nasty ads all over the city. She had no idea what was at stake. She remembers one afternoon especially when Alwine, the maid, had taken the girls on their regular afternoon walk to the park. Ruth played in the sandbox while Hanne sat next to Alwine on the bench, reading the names off the wooden fences. Thällmann, Hitler, other names she can't exactly remember. Proudly showing off her reading. Ever since she was in first grade, she read everything in sight. Alwine explained that these were the leaders of parties running for government in the upcoming elections.

"Which one is better?"

"They're both no good. They promise you heaven on earth until they're elected. But Hitler is worse for you."

"Why?"

"He hates Jews."

"Oh." Hitler? Hanne had never heard of him. She hoped he wouldn't win.

That afternoon flares up in her mind. Hitler did win. Alwine had to leave them shortly after the Nazi take-over. Jews were not allowed to employ German maids. She hears their boots echo through the streets. Brown SA, black SS, Gestapo green. Loud. Stomping. Sees them parade their flag with the ominous crooked cross. Hears martial songs in lockstep with *Judenblut* to squirt from their knives. Remembers helmeted goons with guns posted in front of Jewish stores, swastikas and signs painted on the store windows. *Kauft nicht bei Juden!* They had prevented anyone from shopping there. Kept files of people who dared enter. Signs went up in public places and parks, Für *Juden Verboten.*

The Führer's voice suddenly everywhere. Piped through schools and market places to preach his religion of hate. Breeding contempt for anyone not belonging to the *superior Aryan race. Razzias* is suddenly a new household word, a search for Jews, or *other public enemies,* to be shipped off to concentration camps. *Der Stürmer,* Julius Streicher's new tabloid, sporting his expert opinions on Jewish character. Jewish habits. Jewish religion. Talmud. The paper is displayed in special windows around town where crowds of men gather to read about the lecherous, deceitful, greedy Jews. Hanne stops a few times too, wonders at the hateful attitude of the editorials, the vile jokes, the cartoons of fat Jews with oversized noses, the size of sea lion trunks, and their even fatter wives hung with diamonds. Is she really like that? Or the Jews she knows? Mrs. Kempgen, the custodian's wife upstairs, comforts Mutti, explains, "*Wir meinen ja nicht Sie, Frau Kalter. Nur die Juden im allgemeinen.*"

Miss Gaspari, the big-bosomed old maid who rooms with them, agrees. "*Ja. Wirklich. Wir haben ja nichts gegen Sie.*"

Not they? Nothing against them? Jews in general? Who are these general Jews? Different? In what way?

*

She walks home after school, her regular route from Am Buchen-baum Street through the city down Königstrasse. Behind her she hears a parade marching up the street. SA. The brass band booms. They sing "*...und wenn das Judenblut vom Messer spritzt, ja dann geht's nochmal so gut.*" Jewish blood squirt from the knife? An incentive?

Frightened, she turns. She sees them tramp up the street in step with the song. The standard-bearer leads with the hateful flag. Traffic stops. People line up on the sidewalk. Their backs straight, they raise their right arms in the hateful salute when the flag passes by. She looks for an escape. The Kö's sidewalk is wide enough. She steps into the portal of the department store behind her, pretends to be interested in the window display. The parade comes up. She shrinks back further into the entrance.

Suddenly a Hitler youth stands in front of her, pulls her out on the street, throws his arm straight into the air in the ominous salute, his metal heels clicking together, "Heil Hitler!"

Hanne shrinks under his grip.

"Salute the flag!!! It's the law," he shouts. He slaps her across the face. "Dirty Jew."

His five fingers burn in her cheek.

"I... I didn't see," she stammers, stops short, at a loss for something to say.

She looks into his hate-filled face. He is not much older than she. A punk. Her fists ball in a heartfelt urge to hit back.

The nerve! She wants to scream her violent anger into his visage. But she knows better. It's dangerous. Suicidal. Useless. All she can do is shake in helpless rage.

"That's to teach you. For next time," he screams. She watches him lift his right arm again in another stiff salute, click his heels, snap, "Heil Hitler."

He turns and follows his parade, a watchdog for public behavior. A powerbroker anxious to show his might. Her eyes follow his steps. Her right hand holds her burning cheek. A few onlookers turn away in silence. They saw what happened. Why don't they say anything? She is terror-struck. Her cheek is on fire. This pipsqueak. This...this...she grapples for words but there are no words to express what she feels. Shame, humiliation, powerlessness battle inside her. All she can do is to run home... home.

"Mom, Muttii... Muttiiiiiii... Muttiiiiiiiiiiiiiii...

She hears herself scream. The scream has a life of its own. An endless scream out of her guts... she wants to run, run away from danger, from hate. Run for her life. Escape. Away from that infernal, callous hatred she sees in their blue steel-eyes. Run home to safety. But there's nothing. Only despair. She is stuck. In mid-air. Her heart races, pounds, a machine run wild. Smoke snakes upward. Fills the heavens.

The sky is aflame. This heat is too much. Her feet are mired to the ground. She struggles to breathe.

There is no air. That lump in her chest chokes her. Run. Run. Quick.

"Muttiiiiiiiiiiiiiiiiiiiiiiiiiiiiiiiii."

Where on earth is she? Help me, please! Something inside her wants to be safe!! Help!!!! Please!!!!

"Muttiiiiiiiiiiiiiiiiiiiiiiiiiiiiiiiiiiiiiiiiii."

∗   ∗   ∗

"Hanne... Hanne... Child... What's the matter? Hanne? For goodness sakes, what's gotten into you? Stop screaming. Please. Stop it!!!"

Ruth's voice comes from somewhere in outer space. Or is that van Gelder standing over her? The blackout curtain growls, rolling down. The light comes on. Hurts her eyes. She can feel the girls crowding around her bed.

"Shush, Hanne. Hanneke. Child."

She feels a cool hand on her forehead. Soothing. Reassuring.

"Hanne? Child? Calm down..."

Van Gelder's voice.

Outside thunder rumbles, roars to full force. Lightning zigzags through the window, flashes of infernal intensity bounce off the slanted rafters. Sudden heavy raindrops hit the roof in singular drone, tap, tap, tap, collect into streams, float in quirky rivulets across the window pane, spatter droplets in geometric patterns.

"Hanne? What's wrong?"

Her body is wet, clammy. She shivers. A wind-driven leaf. Her pajamas stick to her like an unwanted second skin. She tries to stop shaking. A heap of stones presses on her stomach. Clear through to her back. Has she been screaming? She aches in every muscle, every tendon, every ligament. That cool hand. She grabs van Gelder's other hand. Grips it. Feels van Gelder's clasp around hers.

The rain smashes against the roof overhead. Batters the building in ferocious torrents. Overhead the light bulb dances a wild jig. Goes dark. Flares up again.

"Hanneke?" van Gelder's reassuring voice is right above her.

Hanneke! It's ages since someone called her by her diminutive. Had anyone, ever? She can't remember. Dad? Everything is a blur. Visions float behind her eyeballs.

"Hanneke, child."

That cool hand on her forehead. Hanne tries to open her eyes. Her lids are stuck. Glued shut. The sweaty mildew smell in the wooden beams nauseates her no end. She gags.

The lightbulb overhead stings in her brain. Her bones ache. She is exhausted. Spent. She stretches, supine, her stomach a churning quagmire.

"Nurse?"

"Yes?" The white starch apron solidifies next to her, spreads a hint of chlorine. The solid white globe expands on the edge of her bed. Reassuring. Protective.

"I don't know what came over me. It's terribly hot in here. Everything closed in on me. Sort of choked me. I was afraid. Angry."

She lies back. Limp. Exhausted. The rain pelts the window. Translucent waterfalls canter, criss-cross the pane.

"Yes?"

That soft hand strokes across her forehead. Hanne lies still. She does not move, afraid it may stop.

"There's still a ton of cement, like sitting on top of me. Clear through to my back, between my shoulder blades. I can't breathe."

Hanne tries to inhale from the core. The lump sits, stolid, stuck behind her ribs. Eyes closed, she tries to sit up. The pressure persists. Is she going to be stuck with this load of stones inside her forever? She falls back, giving in to exhaustion.

"You're all flushed."

It's wonderful to hear van Gelder talk, feel her hand stroke her forehead, sense her care.

"It's stuffy in here."

"We had to pull the blackout curtain down to switch the light on."

"It was stuffy even with the window open."

"Would you like to move over to my room? It's a lot cooler in there. There's a breeze blowing from the other direction." Hanne has a vision of space. Quiet. Away from here.

"I'd love to." She needs to get out of this stuffy, overcrowded room.

"Can you manage?"

"Sure."

She gets up. Walks small steps. Van Gelder behind her, across the attic. The raindrops smash heavy against the roof overhead, steady, forceful, insistent. Lightning. Thunder. Waterfalls. Plop. Plop. Plop.

Nurse van Gelder's room is not much larger than their bedroom. But for one person only, it is far less crowded. Much airier. The open window helps. The storm blows a spray of rain in onto the windowsill. Van Gelder runs to put the window on the hook to keep the rain out. Quiet. Hanne heaves a sigh of relief.

"We won't turn the lights on so we can keep the window open," van Gelder says.

She helps Hanne to bed down on the sofa in the dark.

"Try to relax now. I'll have to take care of the others. I'll be back in no time."

"I'll be all right," Hanne assures her. She feels ashamed. What kind of nonsense is she pulling? A sane girl, screaming like that.

Nurse van Gelder's footsteps echo on the wooden planks. Her voice reports from the room across the attic, "Hanne is going to be fine. She'll stay with me for the night. Let's roll her bed out onto the attic. To the far corner there."

The floor rumbles, heaves, shakes, creaks. They push her iron bed across to more privacy.

"Now get down under your covers, gang, so I can turn the light off. Sleep tight."

Hanne stretches her bones out, relaxes on the sofa.

Through the thin walls she hears the light switch click, then the familiar rattle and thud of the blackout curtain. The window creaks as it is cranked open.

A meek flash of light again, then another rumble in the sky, much fainter now, like a distant afterthought. Streams of rain hit the roof in a steady flow.

Peace. Quiet. Hanne lies back, eyes closed to give herself to the dark hush around her. The storm has passed. Outside, the rain brushes with soft lambskin gloves against the window frame. A cool breeze surges through the room, erases the stuffy smell, brings relief. Hanne inhales deeply. She wonders what is wrong with her. What made her act up? She feels like an utter dolt. Crazy? For crying out loud. Not that! No. For goodness sakes, not that! She can't let that happen to her. She needs her brains, now more than ever. They're all she has.

Hanne watches the clouds through the window. Far above they dissolve into fluffy wads with silver rims. Moonbeams flit through lacy edges. The beams sparkle rainbow color rings in the droplets hanging on the window glass. They settle in the wet bark of the tree branches behind it. One slender beam crawls through the pane, rests on the window sill, then fans out in tiny nets of light that criss-cross the white plywood partition between room and attic. Private space separation. Better keep a cool head. She needs to go on. No one is going to think for her. No one will figure for her how to live. She must do it herself. No more crazy stunts. Moonbeams glitter through the room, lighten the private space. Van Gelder returns.

"You all right, Hanne?" she asks in the darkness.

"Huhummm."

Hanne watches her undress in the moonbeam space. Her full figure bare in a white slip. She has never seen, never even imagined van Gelder without her heavily starched uniform, the white apron always sticking out in all directions like a safety zone. Her ashblond hair, braided, halfway hidden under her nurse's cap, now hangs loose down to her shoulders in soft waves sprinkled with moon. Taut, translucent white skin. People are different when they undress. They look more human, approachable, almost defenseless. Do they change in private life? Cloak their internal humanness with a tough professional mask? To live up to expectations? Demands on appearances?

"Nurse van Gelder?"

"Yes, dear? How do you feel?"

"Fine. There's just that clamp on my stomach."

"We'll have Dr. Wolf look at you tomorrow morning. Rest now."

"I'm sorry I created all that commotion. I couldn't help it."

"I know."

"I just couldn't help screaming. The room was hot, burning, like an oven. And crowded. Everything closed in on me, like a threat. Danger."

"There's a breeze now. Can you feel it? Feels good, doesn't it?"

"Sure does. Air. Peace. Just that pressure over my stomach bothers me."

"Try to relax, child."

"What d'you think is wrong with me?"

"Nothing."

The word hangs in the air. Reassurance.

There's that cool hand again on her forehead. The closeness of another body. Hanne inhales down into the depth of her lungs. A veritable blowout. The clamp is palpable. A nasty incubus roots in her chest. Invades her privacy. Extra weight to carry in the foxtrot of life.

"Thanks for letting me sleep here."

"Don't mention it." The hand stops. Leaves.

The full moon shivers in the window, a hazy corona surrounds the gleaming globe in the velvet sky. Hanne freezes. She cannot remember who, or when someone told her that a halo around the moon bodes evil. An old wives' tale. Nothing to fret about. She is not superstitious. No. Not she. That's for babies. There must be a logical, scientific explanation for the halo around that lunatic satellite. But! Just suppose there is some truth to that old belief? There's proof, ample proof that the moon influences life on earth.

All the sea creatures. Life on the shore. The changing outline of the land. Down to her very menstruation. Conception. She shivers under her sheet. Better not think. Bad things can happen without evil omens. She can name a few. No need to add to the list.

Van Gelder comes over in her nightgown, voluminous, soft shadow, sits on the side of the sofa. She takes Hanne's hand and strokes it gently.

"Now, Hanne. I had the girls move your bed out to the far corner of the attic. If you like, you can sleep here. But if you prefer your own bed you can sleep out there."

"I'd better go sleep in my own bed, Nurse."

"All right. Can you manage without the light?"

"Sure thing."

It feels good to sense her concern. But, heck no! She's no baby! Van Gelder walks with her to her bed, tucks her in.

"Nurse, what do you think is wrong with my stomach?"

Hanne worries about that stupid lump that has invaded her against her will.

"It could be a number of things. Probably nerves. We'll have to wait for Dr. Wolf to examine you. He'll tell us."

"Then, can you tell me what happened to me?"

"I think you need some rest. Don't get up with the others in the morning. Sleep in. Take it easy for a day or two." She bends over and plants a kiss on Hanne's forehead. "Good night, Hanneke. Sleep tight."

"Good night, Nurse. And... and... thanks a lot."

Hanne hears van Gelder tap back into her room. A bright round shadow in the dark. Barefoot dabs on wooden flooring growing faint. Disappear. She listens to van Gelder's bed creak. Snores from the other side of the attic. The girls have left their door open for her. Just in case. Then everything is quiet. It's really so much cooler out here. She savors the space, the absence of others crowding her. She crouches over the last remnants of straw mattress under her. Prone.

Sleep late? Great. There'll be too much noise not to wake up with the others. But it's wonderful not having to get up with them. At least for once. Forget about chores, cleaning bathrooms, kitchen duties. Be special. If only that examination with Dr. Wolf wouldn't loom so large. She hates having to deal with people who don't like her. She'll shrink under his sarcasm about her screaming. It's useless to confront hateful people. They don't change. They just tear you apart where you are most vulnerable. Odd, how they sense your weakest spot. And play on your weakness like a cat with a mouse in its claws. Relish it. Savor it. Malice is the word.

Chapter 6

Hanne loves school and everything connected with it. Suddenly her life has meaning. She is going to be an artist, and a good one. She knows it in her bones. Her artistic pursuit is a source of happiness she has never known. Now that she is finally enrolled, she goes about her education with all the innate intensity she can muster. More than ever, she, Werner and Eddie do everything together, walk to school, help each other with homework, gripe about teachers. Almost inseparable, they are the recognized artists of Jongenshuis. The *Trio*.

*   *   *

Less structured than dinner and without moving the tables, breakfast is a noisy affair for the sixty youngsters. Most of the older boys have jobs and have to leave very early. The younger set can take their time. Public school starts at 8:00 in the morning, art school not until 8:30 AM.

Hanne checks her watch. She has to hurry if she does not want to be late. She finishes her slice of dark bread with jam, gulps down the brew people call coffee these days.

"It's pure chicory and roasted wheat, or whatever they burn for coffee these days," she declares.

She doesn't care. Her books, pads, box with brushes and charcoal, the box of watercolors beside her, she brims with excitement. Gulps the coffee.

"Hurry up. We'll be late."

Werner and Eddie stand in the door, ready to leave.

"All right, already! I'm coming. Don't rush me. Haven't been late yet, have I?" She grabs her stuff and runs after them down the hallway. "Now, you wouldn't leave without me, would you?"

"Lord only knows why you always have to dawdle! *Always!*" Werner complains.

Angry with them, and even more with herself, Hanne swallows a quick reply. Can she help it that she doesn't wake up fully in the morning? It takes her a while before her brain gets going. Never before ten or so. Lord only knows how hard she tries to change. Anyway, so far they have always made it on time. So what's he babbling about? She keeps her mouth carefully shut.

She is at a definite disadvantage. The boys are at least a head taller than she is and have legs to match. It takes them half the time to cover the same distance she does. No wonder they're always ahead of her. She grunts. Her great dream has always been to be one of those long-legged fashion plates she so admires in women's and movie magazines. To be a skimpy five-three is one of Hanne's major frustrations, secondary only to her weight problem. Only her height she cannot change. Ever.

She puffs behind the boys. Now, Eddie isn't so bad. It's just his habit of picking on those three shiny strings of hair sprouting out of that huge mole on his right cheek that bothers her.

Just watching Werner's back, she knows the way he is squeezing his lips into two tight, narrow strips of disgust. Temperamental, as usual. She can't take his temper tantrums. They make her cry in secret.

She is losing ground.

"You could slow down," she mumbles behind them, insulted,

out of breath. "Remember, it takes me a lot more energy just to keep up with you."

"If we'd started out on time, we wouldn't have to run like this."

There is no compassion in Werner's voice.

"Oh, never mind."

Hanne knows that she should have kept her mouth shut. No use arguing with him. It isn't that late. At least the weather is great. Hanne loves these early fall days. An occasional nip in the morning might remind of the approaching winter. But the sun is still warm around noon. Winter is far away, yet.

This morning the sky is a cloudless blue, unusual for the Low Countries, famous for their warty low-hanging cloudcovers á la Paulus Potter, the famous painter. The sun sparkles in the meticulously scrubbed windowpanes of the red brick homes lining the streets. Behind the gated front yards they stand, colorful, silent guardians of their owner's' privacy.

"It would be wonderful to belong behind one of these tightly drawn white curtains," she wishes into the air. An impossible dream.

The tardy bell rings its unconcerned buzz just as they enter the school grounds.

"See, we made it," she hisses at the boys.

She races behind the two up the flight of steps into the building in a last ditch effort. The front doors close behind her as she runs down the corridor to the last door on the left, where Frans Zwollo teaches the ancient arts of silver and coppersmithing two days a week, Tuesdays and Thursdays.

Out of breath, she slinks into the room. Pleased with herself. Made it. The pungent smell of vitriol engulfs her. She loves the smell. Identification of her craft.

"Hi," she greets the other students.

Most of them are still standing about, gabbing, in no hurry to start. As usual. The school has the reputation for providing an alternative to society girls, too dumb to make it in academics.

They are the majority here. Of course, there are the others, the serious artists who make their art an inspired profession. They are the busybodies already working at their benches. That's where she belongs.

She runs for her work coat in the little side room where the students keep their projects and other paraphernalia locked up overnight. Tying her belt, she inspects the little round copper pin she left on the shelf the night before – her first try at chasing and embossing metal with steel punches on jeweler's pitch. The red copper with the embossed design smiles back at her, inflames her with pride. The other students loved it. Even monosyllabic Zwollo contributed a few of his rare, telegram-style grunts in praise. Reasons to be proud.

"It's finished. All I need do is to solder the findings on the back," she says. Then pickle, stain and polish it. Sounds easy enough.

She takes the pin into the classroom. Findings are commercially available. But Zwollo firmly believes in teaching his students to make their findings by hand. She is eager to learn how and needs his directions. Pin in hand, she walks over to her teacher who is standing in the corner beside the enameling kiln.

"Mijnheer Zwollo?" she addresses the back of his stolid, bony frame in the dirty-yellow, stained work coat.

She waits with awe, her hand holding the pin stretched out toward the back of her teacher. He stares in the opposite direction with unseeing eyes behind gold-rimmed specs. Meditates against the wall, as usual. Hanne shrugs. A strange person, a theosophist. She keeps staring at his back, a haggard Buddha spaced out on his personal Cloud Nine. He reminds her of Hindu carvings, dancing gods with multiple legs and arms reaching for Nirvana, fakirs trying their endurance to physical pain on nailbeds, beggar priests in wide yellow robes preaching universal peace, soul transmigration – strange concepts and foreign to Hanne's western world that glorifies raw power, wars, tyrants, supermen. His facial features indicate some Indian ancestor, Hanne speculates. The other students make fun of him and his strange habits. Hanne feels an odd sympathy for the lonely man before her. He is an outstanding craftsman, famous in his field all over Europe, if not the world. Even his enemies admit that. He and his father before him have published several books on the art of metalsmithing.

She waits some more. Then decides to call him back to present reality. He is her teacher.

"Mijnheer Zwollo, what do I have to do next?" she asks his back with its mustard-colored work coat, its stains and acid holes the trademark of his ancient profession. She waits patiently for him to tear himself off his lofty cloud and return to his prosaic existence. Standing behind him, she can feel him collect his soul. Then he turns and gives Hanne a vague nod.

"Oh, yes. Juffrouw Kalter."

He takes the copper piece from her outstretched hand, inspects it with care from both sides. Hanne waits patiently for his verdict. But he is in no hurry. Slowly his gaze rises toward her and his watery blue eyes scrutinize her through his gold-rimmed glasses.

"Hm... hm... hmmmmm... Nice work. Very nice work indeed, Miss Kalter. Very nice indeed for a beginner," he grunts, slowly, meditating into her face. As usual, he chops his sentences into a series of interconnected fragments. She waits eagerly, happy with his sparse praise.

"Let's see. You need to make the findings. Then solder them on. After that you pull some silver wire to the correct thickness for the pin and set it in the finding."

He pauses again. Sticks his head into the air for yet another meditation. She waits for instructions on how to carry all this out. A beginner, she does not know how, or where to begin.

She watches his face light up. Inspiration in action. His mustard frame turns abruptly. Stalks down the aisle of workbenches. Dumbfounded, she follows like a well-trained gosling to the last workbench in the front row under the window, where a senior in dark gray work coat wields his hammer with deafening noise. He is fluting a copper vase over a stake. The fellow stops his hammer in midair as they approach.

She had noticed him the first day of school. How could she miss a visage like his? A mousy-blond mop of hair atop an upside-down-turned pear of a head with a huge crooked nose á la Cyrano de Bergerac sticking out into the weather. The mouth underneath is far too wide to fit the narrow underchin that literally merges into the neck, a huge Adam's apple bobbing in the center. Pale blue eyes and pale pink skin. He looks almost like an albino. His narrow, sloping shoulders do nothing to improve his anemic appearance. His pointy Adam's apple dances in the long skinny neck like a yo-yo. She tries to hide a faint smile when she watches him talk. Right out funny. So far they have not talked. But she has stopped by his bench occasionally and watched him bang away at his vase with a mixture of professional admiration and envy.

"Gorrissen, I'd like you to help Miss Kalter to finish her pin. Show her to make findings. Let me see them before she solders them on."

"With pleasure, mijnheer."

Gorrissen's voice has a high pitch. He looks at his teacher. It's almost as if he avoids looking at her.

"All right. You take care of that." Finished with one errand, Zwollo turns his attention to the line of students waiting behind him. They need his help now.

Gorrissen looks at her with a shy smile. She faces him head-on.

"Hi. My name is Hanne, Hanne Kalter."

"My name is Bert. Nice to meet you."

They eye each other, strangers thrown together by fate.

"I saw you run down the hallway with two other fellows first day of school," he starts.

"Yeah? My fault. Werner and Eddie are mad at me for making them late in the mornings."

"I know them from Art History. You from Jongenshuis too?"

"Yes."

He has pegged her. *Refugee.* Natives tend to label you. Outsider. Stranger. Not regular stock, or something like that. Why can't she be normal? Like all the others?

"The two boys lived in Rotterdam before. I used to live in The Hague. In the woods between the city and Scheveningen. Then the moffen ordered foreigners to leave the coast. Our home was dissolved and I came here with my sister."

He smiles at her using the Dutch derogatory term for German invaders.

"Posh section you lived in. My relatives lived there. They escaped to England with the Queen."

"You should've seen the estate – like something out of the movies. The only problem was too many noisy kids around."

Both chuckle. A comfortable chuckle. At ease now.

"Your Dutch is pretty good. Where did you learn it?"

She thinks for a while, trying to remember. Julie was part of it, but only in the beginning.

"I really don't know. Must've picked it up here and there. After all, I've been in this country for two years now. Everyone speaks Dutch."

"Where are you from? In Germany, I mean?"

"Duisburg. Industrial city. Not far from here. Just down the Rhine."

"So you and your sister are here. Where are your parents?"

"She's two years younger and goes to MULO, middle school. My parents are in Sweden. Got there two weeks before Germany invaded Poland. Just in the nick of time before war broke out with England and the Germans spiked the North Sea with mines. And U-boats. The original idea was that we all go to the United States. Now they're stuck in Sweden. And we here."

Lord knows why she stands here answering all his questions. She is not usually this patient with people who give her the third degree about her past.

"Well, your parents are okay then. Can't they take you over?"

"Dunno. Guess the Germans won't let us go," Hanne surmises. She has asked herself the same question a million times. Mutti and Vati are living with Uncle Adolf and Aunt Regi, she thinks. In their house. In transit, her parents have no place of their own. And it costs money to take them out. All they could take out of Germany at the time was ten marks each and the clothes on their backs. They may not even realize how desperately she wants to get out of this communal uniformity of refugee existence. On top of all the political problems with the Nazis. She sighs. She does not like to discuss her problems with strangers. They can't help her. No use complaining.

She holds her pin out to Bert. He takes it. Examines it carefully.

"Hey. This is pretty good. You chase and emboss like an old pro."

"D'you really think so?" Hanne beams with pride. She points to the vase. "I wish I could do things like that."

"Give yourself some time. You've just started. I've four years of training behind me. And this is my master project for graduation next year."

She sighs manages an impatient smile. "I need to catch up. I've lost more time than is good for me already."

He looks at her pin in his hand.

"The findings. Zwollo wants us to make them from scratch. Because handmade things deserve handmade findings. Mass-produced looks cheap, he maintains. I agree. Anyway. Don't worry. It's easier than you think. You have a soldering pipe?"

"No." Hanne is crestfallen. Where would she get a soldering pipe? She has no money. And even if she had, soldering pipes are hard to come by because copper is scarce.

Bert shows her his own.

"I made mine myself."

Hanne looks at him, all admiration.

"Tell you what. I have enough copper pipe left to make one for you," he offers.

Hanne melts in silent gratitude. Speechless.

"Meanwhile, you can use mine. Just get yourself an extra mouthpiece. I may even have one for you." He rummages in his toolbox.

"Thanks," Hanne mumbles, embarrassed, ashamed at having poked fun at his looks. All right, so he looks odd. He's nice. And helpful. Hanne appreciates these traits more than she cares to admit.

She has a new friend.

Under Bert's guidance, Hanne cuts and bends the two small copper pieces into the required shapes. Drills holes in one to anchor the pin, curves the other into a hook to hold it. Then he shows her to clean all pieces in vitriol so that the silver solder flows readily under the flame of the torch. Together they solder both pieces to the back of the pin, one on each side. That done, she pulls silver wire for the pin through the slotted plate to the required thickness. Sets the entire pin on an anvil, a peg between its finding, and hammers it shut.

"There."

Bert is delighted.

"It's ready to be polished."

The bell rings for lunch. The class empties. The two hardly notice.

"You can pickle it in a sulphur bath to give it a brown or green patina. Then you bring out the highlights."

Zwollo comes over to the two eager beavers. Without a word he takes Hanne's polished pin. Turns it back and forth, front and back, endlessly, between his fingers. The two wait for his verdict, timid nobodies before an admired god.

"So, so, so. Pretty good," he mumbles. Cleaves the syllables into fragments as usual.

"She's doing extremely well, isn't she?" Bert shoots in. He beams with pride, more than even Hanne herself. Well, almost.

"Sure has talent," Zwollo chops under his breath. He puts the pin down on the workbench. Goes for his overcoat.

Hanne is flushed. At a loss for words. Success complete. She shrugs.

"I'm going to design something more difficult tomorrow in design class. Perhaps a small bowl."

A million ideas dance in her head. Far away in a mental distance she sees the door falling shut behind Zwollo's back. Alone in the room, the two face each other. Silently. The vitriol smell tickles in her nose. The air around them tightens. She has the distinct feeling that Bert wants to say something. She waits, wondering. But he remains silent.

"Well, thanks for your help, Bert," she says finally and turns to go. He mutters something as she leaves the room. She wonders what. Closes the door behind her. She wants her lunch.

* * *

Two days later Werner and Eddie wait for her in the hall outside her classroom.

"Who is that fellow?" Werner examines her on the way home.

"You're quite absorbed in each other," Eddie pursues.

"What's the matter with you two? Giving me the third degree?"

What kind of liberties do these two think they can take? The nerve! Who do they think they are!

"Just thought to find out who he is…" Werner explains.

And then? Hanne thinks. "He helps me in class, if you must know. He's nice," she says out loud. Nicer than you! Anyway, what business of yours is it anyway! she thinks. But she feels too good to start a discussion with *him*. Better let it go.

"I'm starved. Hope we have something decent for dinner tonight," Eddie gets between the two of them.

"Stamppot here, stamppot there, stamppot everywhere," Hanne recites, glad to change the subject. She tries to keep in step with the two.

"Nothing new in the food business, eh?" Eddie picks at the three hairs of his mole. Does he never pull them out?

They sense it as soon as they get inside the front door. A few people stand in the hallway. Tension bounces off the walls. Loud talk. Something is out of whack at Jongenshuis.

"What's wrong?" All three want to know all at once.

"Two ss arrived a moment ago. They're in Dr. Wolf's office."

"What do they want?"

"Your guess is as good as mine."

General shrugs. Heartfelt helplessness against the odds.

"They're across the street; it was stupid to think they'd leave us alone," Gerd says.

"Sooner or later they were bound to make their presence known," Horsey mumbles.

Hanne wonders what on earth they want. A door slams shut upstairs. Male voices, loud, hard, clipped Teutonic gutturals. Heavy footsteps trample the stairs. Hobnailed threats stomp downward, echo hollow on wooden planks. Dr. Wolf appears with his blackshirted company. Masculinity on exhibit. Infinite Superiority. Two bloodred crooked crosses on white armbands. Boots shine.

"These gentlemen need five boys to clean their stables," Dr. Wolf says.

The two ss stand behind him. Heavy. Threatening. Aloof. Looking around.

Icy silence. The boys stand about, try to shrink into nothingness. What price invisibility? If only the floor would open underneath them.

"We'll assign them, then," Wolf announces matter-of-factly.

"You, you, you, you and you." One Mephisto points in five directions. Ernie Schlächter, Hans Andress, Werner Strauss, Gerd Perl, Gerd Hamm step out of the group, the biggest and strongest of the bunch. The others try hard not to show their deeply felt relief. Freddie Boas's face is an unmistakable gloat.

"You're number six." One blackshirt lunges out and slaps Freddie across the mouth. Sound and sensibility echo a losing gulp in the black and white marble-tiled hall. His ss companion lines the six up in single file.

"Get going! March!" he bellows. Short shrift. Shoves. The six march out of the building, the two Blackshirts at their rear. The heavy front door slams shut behind them. They can hear the footsteps stomp up the street.

"Stupid Freddie. His nose bled," Sigge says reflectively.

"Yeah. Ought to know that you can't win. Not with them."

"Did he want to show that he wasn't afraid?"

"I'm glad they didn't pick me."

"Me too. Next time we may not be so lucky," Eddie says to Werner who stands next to him, staring at the closed door.

"The rest of you just aren't husky enough," Hanne shrugs with a teasing undertone. It won't do any good to feel sorry for them.

"They're to help with the cleaning of their stables and the horses. Just for today," Dr. Wolf says. He turns to return to his office.

"Should have kept a straight face as long as they were here. No use fooling around with them," Hanne hears him mumble as he walks upstairs.

"Let's hope the ss has nothing worse in mind," Hanne mutters.

*

Ruth comes running, waving a letter.

"From home," she shouts.

"Finally. Good news?"

"The usual. They've sent us a package. Clothes. I've grown out of my stuff."

"Hope customs won't hold it too long."

Hanne takes the letter. She looks at the envelope, cluttered with foreign stamps plus several stamps from the customs police granting the letter approval to enter the country.

"I'll read it before I do my homework."

Werner and Eddie sit next to her, absorbed in their homework while she reads.

"We're always plugging away. Why not go swimming next Sunday? Take advantage of the last warm days," Werner suggests.

"Great idea," Hanne says. She loves to swim. But not with Werner alone. Better get a group together.

"We can try to get some *punten* and have a picnic by the Rhine," she suggests.

"Good. We'll have to see whether they have any this Friday, then everyone goes to buy some. Ask Dicky whether they are baking any this week."

Hanne looks forward to next Sunday. The others are right. Fretting won't help. Life goes on. They have to go on living, even with the menace across the street. More than that – because of them. She whistles and continues her homework. Yes, in spite of them all.

Punten are a war invention. Brown, sweet, triangular wedges of cake. That's where their name comes from. Points = *punten*. Bakeries sell them at the bargain price of five cents apiece. Punten are lifesavers, almost as important as clothes, shoes, and ordinary food. Like everything else in this war, baked goods are strictly rationed – so many coupons per item per person. Every living individual has a right to just so much of a commodity. Bureaucracy thrives. Non-persons love to lord it over others. It makes them feel distinguished. Power intoxicates.

But you can buy punten without coupons. On Fridays mostly, as long as they last. The youngsters at Jongenshuis are crazy for them. At last, something that's not rationed, and that they can afford, to boot. Heavy, filling punten. Baked brown, sweet, chewy mush to fill their ever-hungry stomachs.

The problem is the limited availability. First come, first served. Like hawks, they watch the bakery windows every Friday for the appearance of this welcome addition to their monotonous diet.

Starved for sweets and a great many other things, they gorge themselves on extra food whenever it's available. Grateful for any amount, they buy as many as they can get from the baker. They carry the bags home, ostensibly to share with buddies. However, more often than not, the punten disappear on the way, one after another. The lot may be gone long before the happy buyer gets home.

Like all fun things in life, punten exact a price. Sticky, sweet, they are heavy fare and lie like a dead weight in the digestive tract long past the time they should have been absorbed into the system. No one knows their ingredients. No one dares, no one cares to ask. The standing joke has it that the baker scrapes his tables, shelves, benches, sink, including floors, for the weekend cleaning, then bakes the scrapings with a lot of molasses into rounds that he cuts into triangles. For extra profit. When questioned about their contents, Dicky Strauss smirks and keeps mum. He never refutes the tales. Stomachaches after punten splurges? Mere inconvenience. Taken in stride like so much else.

"Tummy ache? Bicarbonate of soda helps."

It's exciting to buy something on your own. Revel in your independence. Even with mere punten. They do wonders for your self-esteem. They do wonders for your soul. That's in addition to filling your stomach.

*

Sunday arrives a dull gray. Hanne scans the heavens for some break in the billowing cumulus clouds that obscure the sun. But the sky cooperates for a change. By midmorning, the kapok mass has divided into flocks. Patches of blue appear and spread. Hesitant at first, the sun breaks through, boldens, takes over. By noon only some flirty cirrus stripes remain. The rest of the sky is glitter blue, the sun a golden globe in the center. Time to roll the swimsuit into the towel. Hanne has even managed to save five punten for the day. She packs them with pride, careful not to crush them. Willpower is not her strength. Or is it?

She runs to find Werner. "Werner? Werner?"

She finds him, alone, sitting before the fireplace in the living room. His torso bent over, his head rests between his hands. A figure of utter dejection. A wave of pity for him surges into existence.

"What on earth is the matter with you?"

"Oh, nothing."

His voice quivers in the empty space under the lofty ceiling. He sounds piqued.

"Well, something is wrong if you're sitting here pouting like a diva."

"Leave me alone. It's nothing."

She is at a loss. Feels like leaving. She inhales for one last try. "I'm ready to go swimming."

Her words hang in the room and beg for an answer. She waits out of a sense of duty, but considers ways to go swimming anyway.

His upper body jerks upright.

"All right. I had a fight with Wolf. I HAVE BEEN GROUND-ED." Every letter an emphasis. His words echo hollow in the room. His gray blue eyes stare at her with accusatory hate.

She stares at his flushed face. His metallic falsetto tells her that she better not delve further into his fight with Wolf, at least not now. Keep out of it.

She is furious. He and his stupid temper. Just like him to pick a fight with Wolf. Wolf of all people! Today of all days! Louse up a gorgeous Sunday afternoon. Their precious free time. She has been looking forward to this swim all week. To lying in the sun by the Rhine River, listening to the barges hoot as they float past, dreaming of connections between people in many regions. Just dreaming.

The lunch gong sounds. Werner remains glued to his chair, all immobile hurt.

"Aren't you going to eat lunch?"

"Nope."

"Why not?"

"Damn it! Why don't you leave me alone? Just go and have your precious lunch!"

She stares at him. "No reason for me to go hungry!" She slams the door behind her.

Hanne files into the dining room. Her food has no taste. What a mess! The thought of Werner bothers her. The entire afternoon spoiled. Darn. Werner and that little buckly-back dictator at the head of the table who sits there, eating, joking with Peter Marcuse. Doesn't give a hoot!

Horsey and Gerd smile across the table. She gazes at their smirky faces.

"Werner's in trouble."

"I know. What happened?"

"He called Wolf an inconsiderate asshole. That's what happened."

"Idiot. What possessed him?"

"He does stupid things like that – gets angry and just doesn't think."

She still doesn't know what led up to this outburst. But Hanne can sympathize with anger, especially against Wolf. She feels sorry for Werner. Somewhere in her brain a nagging feeling spreads that Werner likes to be the martyr.

"He won't come to eat," she announces.

"Okay. Let's *organize* some sandwiches."

Organize means confiscate (steal is a more accurate term) in refugee lingo. Together the three manage to collect and hide a stack of sandwiches from the table for the self-willed victim. She adds one of her five punten to the collection. Hesitates. Should she sacrifice one more? Slowly she puts a second punt into the bag. Her sacrifice for the day. It makes her feel good.

"I still have three," she comforts herself. Then she walks down the hall with her bag to help the pighead through the day.

He has not moved an inch.

"Here. It's for you. You must be hungry."

"Nope."

"You don't have to be a mule." Hanne wafts the bag under his nose. "I included two punten."

"Don't meddle in my affairs!"

"Being stubborn won't help. It's stupid."

Hanne keeps waving the bag.

"I called him an asshole."

"I know. Why?"

"He ordered me to help precious Miss Sussmann with some paperwork. On Sunday morning, mind you! It would've taken all day, practically. So I told him to shove it. He wasn't going to ruin my Sunday."

"Now you've done it to yourself. You could've helped her 'til lunch. She would've let you off. That might've been their intention anyway."

"He didn't have to make me on our day off! Tomorrow would've been fine."

"Well, you don't know. Now look at the mess you're in. Me too. And going hungry won't help. You're not punishing anyone else but yourself."

She shoves one sandwich under his nose. Werner glances at it for a second. Then he takes it and wolfs it down.

"You want me to get you a glass of milk? Van Gelder's in the kitchen."

She knows that van Gelder will give it to her without asking questions.

He glances sideways. "Naah. Don't bother. But you can give me the rest. The punten too."

She hands him the bag. "Here."

She tries to make up her mind what to do with the afternoon. Hang around with Werner and take the ribbing from the others for sacrificing her free afternoon? No way. She could go alone, perhaps meet the others by the river. With the weather so perfect, as it so rarely is, she hates to miss the odd chance to swim.

She hears the doorbell ring. Footsteps echo on the marble

tiles down the hall. Voices. A high-pitched voice. She recognizes it even before he appears in the living room door.

"Hi Bert? What brings you here?"

She is happy about the interference. It's her way out.

"I came to ask you to go swimming. Eddie and some of your friends are going too, I hear."

"I can't. I'm grounded," Werner announces from the fireplace, as he stuffs his face. His voice quivers like a dying guitar.

"What about you?" Bert looks at her.

She looks at Bert, halfway torn between her love of swimming and solidarity with the hothead. After all, if he lands himself in stupid scrapes, she doesn't have to suffer.

"Just let me get my stuff. It's upstairs." She starts running upstairs. "YOFEL!" she shouts, the Jewish slang for *fantastic she had picked up recently.*

Free! She returns with her swim gear. Why should she keep this mulish fool company anyway? Let him sulk in peace. He has the punten.

*

She follows Bert down the steep incline to the river behind the art museum. Shock of dark blond hair with triangular nape. They find a spot among the brush and tufts of patchy grass in the ochre-gray sand by the shore. Peace. Quiet. Hardly a whiff of wind. They spread their towels and lie silently next to each other on the soft cotton, hands under their heads, bake in the hot sun that streaks their bodies through latticed cloud fleece. The river plods onward nearby, relentlesssly. The waves gurgle against the embankment. The other side of the river rises lazily out of the murky waters in a hazy distance, pastoral lush green flatland where flecked Holsteins peacefully chew their cud, their tails constant metronomes against the buzzing flies.

Hanne's eyes follow a huge black coal barge ponderously plowing downstream. Coke, anthracite, coal in separate heaps glisten black sparks from the planked deck of the hauler. Two children play behind the living quarters of the trawler. Here in the lowlands the Rhine is wide, a lumbering, dependable link between the countries and cities lining its banks before it reaches the North Sea. Connective tissue with the rest of the world in peacetime. Cut off from much for the time being.

Hanne inhales the pungent smells the murky waters lapping the sand exhale, odors intermixed with the strong must wafting up from sunburned earth, dung, leaves, brush. She senses the steady rhythm of native, ancient, unchanging dependability. Something indefinable that she lost. Perhaps never had. Will never have. The irretrievability of the loss pains her. A tangible lack. Hard to explain. It's something the OTHERS have. Own as part of their birthright. She glances at Bert stretched out beside her, eyes closed, his hairless, fair body baking in the sun. Sweat beads shimmer around his navel. He belongs to that other world. Tidy streets, houses with neat front yards, iron fences, gates he can enter. Proprietorial. The steady river, canal waters feeding long-established farms, their people, their herds. Ties to the soil on which they are born an unquestioned given. She is different. A stranger. An outsider. Separateness is the shadow that follows her wherever she goes. Like an unwelcome ghost. She is from another land, another culture. She has a different past that trails her, persistent, an unwanted yoke around her neck. Outside the proprietary mainstream. She hates it. A slim edge in her brain revolts. No. She is stuck.

"Why is everyone after the Jews?" Bert's words hang in the air, take possession of the clear Indian summer atmosphere.

She sits up, stares at him. "It's an old story," she says. "As old as the Bible. We've been stubborn from the beginning and refused to let go of our tradition. Even in exile as a minority."

She watches him digest her explanation. It's as good as any she has heard to her own burning questions. Something that Dad told her when she asked that very question years ago. Teacher Gottfried Israel thought that it was because Jews didn't accept Christianity, which amounted to the same thing. Yeah, why should they? Is that the whole story behind what is happening now?

"That was two thousand years ago," Bert says from his towel.

"Yes. It got worse as time went on. It's easy to pick on a minority," she says.

Her mind leaps on. Especially if the minority has always managed to come back. Alive. Preached moral superiority. Perpetuated itself, so far, she thinks with pride. No need to elaborate. It's confusing enough for Jews. Unnecessary to get him confused too.

Bert eyes her from his towel. Silent meditation from towel. Confusing thoughts. Questions to which there is no simple answer.

Shouts and laughter waft through the blue transparency. They look to the river. Eddie Silber, Gerd and Horsey stand on the other side, preparing to swim back. There they go. Six arms splash water in regular, powerful strokes.

"They like to race across," she says, glad to change the subject.

"It's quite a distance," Bert says, looking across the water.

"Yes. I've never tried." She is afraid to try the distance, but prefers not to admit it.

"Do you feel like going in?"

"Later," she says.

She turns leisurely on her towel and closes her eyes. The sun strokes her back. It's hot, like the beginning of time. The water is a cold proposition after baking in the sunshine. She hugs the earth. *In the beginning God created Heaven and Earth.*

She lets carefree timelessness sweep over her. Take her along. Forget the war. Forget the Germans. Forget Nazis. The pesky ss across the street. Nothing exists except sunbaked sand, rustling grass, trees wafting pungency into transparent blue air. Cirrus-streaked sky, yellow-purple brilliant, life-giving disk moving round the sky. River water splashes soothing rhythms in the background.

*

The three come running up the beach in a noisy cloud of sand. There goes the peace.

"The water's great. Perfect to swim across."

Hanne feels a cold rill trickle down her warm back.

"What on earth!" she gasps, jumping to her feet.

A chorus of four belly laughs. Eddie holds the tin cup, slanted, water still trickling, a dark wet blotch in the sand. Three grins into her face. One from the towel. Water droplets roll down her warm back.

"Damn you idiots! What kind of practical joke it this, anyway? I'm trying to get a tan." She tries to wrench the tin cup out of Eddie's hand.

"My foot! You're just too damn lazy!"

"None of your business," she wheezes, fighting a losing battle. The cup is out of reach.

"Bet you can't swim across." Horsey belts his challenge. She feels eight smug eyes fasten in her skin.

"Big deal!" she says.

"Let's see you do it."

"All right! Don't think that I can't!"

The words stand fleshed out in the blue air. Solid. Stark.

She feels trapped. Stunned at her own daring. Curious faces hit her with disbelief. She looks out over the river. Measures the distance to the other bank. Her spine hardens to rock.

"Probably thought I'd chicken out." She pronounces every syllable, for everyone to hear. Takes her bathing cap and walks toward the river, determined to prove them wrong. Their stares burrow in her back. Boys! She's going to make them eat their words!

The water is a cold shock. Goosebumps spread upward across her body. Never mind. They'll disappear once I get going. She strikes out. Boldly. One, two, exhale, three, four, inhale; one, two, exhale, three, four, inhale.

Her breathing technique has never been that great and she tires easily. My self-esteem. That's what's at stake. I can't let them get the better of me. They'll laugh me to pieces. One, two, exhale, three, four, inhale.

Even Bert is on their side. Creep. She pushes onward. Doggedly. One, two, exhale, three, four, inhale. Determination. That's all it takes. One, two, exhale…

She begins to feel the strain. Looks at the other side. Funny, it has not come any closer. She was halfway across quite a while ago. Tries to figure how long ago. Seems like an eternity. No. Her mind is playing a trick on her. But why isn't she getting closer to shore? It's been the same distance ever since… Definitely ever since, since…hard to say.

She treads. Looks back. She's in the middle of the river all right. Come on, she tells herself. Get on with the rest. Swim. She strikes out. One, two, exhale, three, four, inhale. One, two…Her arms are giving out. She is tired. Swimming across wasn't such a great idea. Once she gets across, she'll have to swim back again, the same distance. Perhaps she ought to turn back.

Admit defeat? She gazes back at the boys watching her from the bank. Funny, they are not where they were just a second ago. Farther upstream. Impossible. She is still in the center of the river. She is tired. She has to swim back. Keep on, Hanne! Swim! Strike out! Keep going!

The truth is a sudden, cruel flash in her brain. She looks for the boys. They are even farther upstream now. Growing smaller with each stroke. They are not moving. She is…downstream. She is caught in the current midstream. She will never reach either side. Oh God, SAVE ME. A loud cry from inside.

"*Help! HELP!*"

She hears herself scream at the top of her lungs. She swims wildly, tries to get out of the current that pushes her on, relentlessly, downstream. Downstream. The North Sea. She is desperate. If she can't get out of midstream she'll be lost. Blow up on a German mine. She panics.

"*HELP! HELP ME!!!!! HELP!!!!!!!!!!!!!*" She can faintly make

out the boys in a huddle. I must calm down. Keep treading. Stay
afloat. Easy. Tread. Keep above the water.

She sees Bert run down the bank to where she is treading,
trying to swim out. There. He jumps in. She is exhausted. Not yet.
Keep it up. Head above water. I have to swim toward him. What
takes him so long? She treads. Floats. Swims.

An eternity passes. She treads. Then floats, turns, face up to
the sky. Then he is beside her.

"Hold on to me. We'll swim back together. Hold on to my
middle. Just hold on tight."

"Thank goodness."

She gasps. Gulps water. Coughs it up. Grabs hold of him.
They line up, she behind him, coughs up the dirty water. They
swim in unison. One, two, exhale, three, four, inhale, one, two.

She's never going to live this down. Never in a million years.

Still, it's better than never facing the boys again. Far better.

*

"Nothing behind a big mouth. Tra la, la, la, la, nothing behind a
big mouth," Horsey sings, off key, a melody she does not recognize.
Probably of his own making.

The three smirk in unison. Audible grins.

She can feel the sneers as she towels herself dry. Pretends
not to hear or see. Where do they come into the act? Hanne hates
them, their irritating superiority. The brown mole with the three
black wire hairs. The grin in the drooping eye. The singing horse
dentures.

"Damn it! Why don't you shut up!" she flares.

"We should've let you float out to sea. A modern mermaid
without tail or brain," Eddie Silber puts in his two cents worth of
gloat.

"WE. Where does this WE come in, I'd like to know?" she
challenges. Bristles in total defeat. Mad at herself for getting herself into this mess.

"*WE* haven't done a thing," she mumbles loud enough for them to hear.

She glances at Bert, a short sideways peep. He fished her out. And he is silent. Just rubs his back dry. Sunburn-red. She is all limp gratitude. Shivers in her wet half-covered nakedness. Yes, he's a great guy. Despite his odd exterior. She's never going to laugh about him again. Not ever.

*

The three boys walk ahead. Hanne and Bert follow. They don't talk much on their way back. Bert stops at the door to say goodbye.

"See you tomorrow in school," he says and walks on.

Hanne looks after him. Blond mop of hair on top of sloping shoulders. Marvels at the indefinable bond that has been established between them this afternoon.

Chapter 7

It was a hot summer, followed by a mild autumn, this year of 1942. Contrary to all predictions for it to end soon, the war rages on. Gets progressively worse. The good news is that the United States has finally entered on the side of the Allies. Actually forced into the alliance with the Japanese attack on Pearl Harbor. Fresh blood against the tired collective European defeat two years earlier. More planes at night. More anti-aircraft flak. Far more activity in the air. Rat ta tat tat tat. Flickers. Quakes. Booms. Especially at night. Lights streak through velvet sky at night, a constant feverish vigil. Blackout below. The war is a global effort played out in the heavens above. It's a relief to know that the Yanks are part of the picture now. Reassuring. So far, their participation has not accomplished what all the occupied people yearn for. The Jews in particular. An end to Nazi atrocities on the continent.

Rumors of battles in North Africa are persistent. Even more, those of Russian plans for a counter-offensive on the Eastern Front and heavy Nazi losses in the Russian snow. Every night someone else comes home with good news from the Eastern Front they learned from people outside their little refugee world, people who listen regularly to the nightly news from the BBC. No doubt, the Germans are losing. Finally. Bert listens avidly to the outlawed foreign broadcasts on his self-built short-wave crystal receiver. To defy the strict German laws is a challenge that needs to be met head-on. Never mind that it may mean concentration camp or even death.

"The Wehrmacht is stuck in the snow outside Leningrad. The Russians are fighting back from behind their walls. On the other side, the German supply route is cut off. Reinforcements are stuck."

"It's just that everyone's forgotten about us," the youngsters complain.

"It takes time. The Yanks will make it here. You'll see. They're winning in North Africa. From there it's just a short hop to Italy. They may invade from the West too, you know."

"Small comfort when you know the Nazis're picking up Jews in Amsterdam. It won't be long before they're here."

Hanne looks at the map. Russia in the East. Leningrad? It's St. Petersburg on the old map. Gateway to the Baltic. Finland is a continuation of the landmass. Sweden is on the other side of the Bosnian Sea, still free. Norway is not. Crazy world.

Of course, the German broadcasts sound a different tune. Marching deep into Russia. Conquering territory without resistance. Germany winning on all fronts. Baku oil fields. It sounds terribly believable, given their circumstances. The makings of the Thousand Year Reich. Bert's English news from the BBC is preferable by far.

"I wonder whether Mutti understands. Food is scarce and getting scarcer. Many things are not available at all."

"Still. There's always the black market, if you've got the money."

"Or make friends with a farmer."

"A pair of leather shoes is beyond my reach."

"If they just wouldn't rant so much against the Jews. That's the worst."

Since last year the Nazis have been applying the Nuremberg

laws also to the territories. They've found The Final Solution. Whatever that is. Hanne doesn't want to know. Like in Germany, Jews in the Lowlands are no longer allowed to sit in public parks, or visit public libraries. Then there's that terrible thing about wearing the yellow star. Fiendish.

"It makes you feel like an outcast," she complains.

"But you are the same person as before," her inner voice tells her.

"Hogwash. You feel like a hunted animal in open season. Stigmatized."

*

The ultimate blow comes in the summer.

Jews are no longer permitted to attend secondary schools.

"What do they mean?" I can't go to Kunstoefening?"

"No. We can't go there this fall."

"That's the second time I've been thrown out of school," wails in her head. Now they're blocking her career as an art student. Goodbye ambition. Goodbye dream. Finished. F.i.n.i.t.o.

*

Summer recess has just started when the decree goes into effect. Crestfallen, Hanne, Eddie and Werner make their way to school to say goodbye.

The place is ghostlike without its usual crowd of students. Their steps sound hollow, ominous in the long halls, closed doors on either side. Beyond the sparsely manned offices, Hanne and Eddie try the door to the art metal shop. It gives way. Great. At least a sign of life. Zwollo stands by the kiln. Bert behind him. Both deeply absorbed in discussing Bert's project. The kiln is lit. Magenta heatwaves radiate from the white-gray source. It makes the room a thousand times hotter than the summer heat outside. Hanne wipes her brow.

"Hello, Mijnheer Zwollo. Bert," she says from the door.

Her heart drips with sorrow. This is the last time.

"Zoohs, zooh. Hello. You two." Zwollo's head revolves. A faint flicker of a smile dissolves behind round gold-rim glasses and gravitates to their teacher's narrow-lipped mouth as he greets his students with his usual staccato.

"Hi." Bert's eyes light up above the dirty-yellow work coat. Their pale-blue gleam reflects, broadens, spreads across his face in tiny horizontal foldlines.

No secrets here. Hanne feels accepted without words. She straightens up, swells despite her morbid errand.

"We want to say goodbye to you and the school."

Her despair returns like an antediluvian flood in which she drowns. She shrugs, helpless. Turns to Bert.

"I didn't expect to find you here."

Zwollo and Bert gaze at the two Jews before them, silent, at a loss for anything to say.

"Yeah. Zoohs. Zooh. Hm. Hm." Zwollo mumbles under his breath. Ill-at-ease, embarassment is written into the multicolored stains and sulphuric acid holes of his dirty-yellow coat.

"These rotten bastard moffen! These Kraut!" Bert explodes in frustrated rage. "One of these days we'll show them."

"I want to see that day soon," Eddie sighs.

Hanne looks about the room. The steel punches in a round beaker on Bert's workbench. His home-made copper soldering pipe, the tiny gas flame lit at the end, hangs in its stand. Steel hammers in all shapes, round, half-round, oblong, square; wooden and rubber mallets; steel stakes, pointed, round, flat; anvils, small, medium, large; all shiny, polished and greased to guard against corrosion. Leather pads and rings for iron pitch bowls of various sizes. Brown, heavy bowls with reddish home-cooked jeweler's pitch on which to chase and emboss silver and copper items. She inhales the vapors floating through the room, a blend of vitriol, gas, asbestos, pitch. Beloved, intimate fumes of the trade. She seethes. There is nothing to say.

Frustration builds as she looks at her place of education. The sense of undeserved exclusion. The sympathy of the two

Dutchmen before her hits her like a bitter slap. Exacerbates her keen awareness of the scope of her loss. She cringes at the power of her enemy. The impossibility of fighting the gods that are out to break her. Fierce, cruel, evil forces with power to suck life out of her. They strangle the entire European continent. Her future amounts to nothing but her continued ability to breathe. To stay alive and see the next day. Live to become a miracle. Hopelessness takes possession of her. Better not think. Get angry? Bert better save his breath. She hates leaving the place. Not yet. Just make it a dream. A momentary nightmare. Please, let me wake up from this and be normal. *NORMAL.*

"What's that you're doing?" she asks.

"Mijnheer Zwollo is helping me with my enamel. We're waiting to take it out of the kiln. After that I want to work on embossing my vase. Better get my master's project finished during summer recess."

Hanne looks at the urn-shaped copper piece on the pitch bowl filled with red jeweler's pitch before him. An old-fashioned design. Nothing innovative, somewhat like Zwollo's. But Bert's work is meticulous, every detail carefully executed.

"Bert, it's beautiful," she breathes, all admiration for his craftsmanship.

"It's going to be a birthday present for my mother in the spring."

"I'm sure she'll love it."

She sees him swell with pride. Sees his buttons burst open – pop, pop, pop – under the swell.

A sigh escapes her. No future plans for her. Eddie inspects the vase from all sides. Eddie the expert. Keeps on turning it in his hands. Nods approval.

Hanne looks at Zwollo. Time to say goodbye. No use staying around and breaking your heart.

"Mijnheer. Mijnheer Zwollo."

She is talking to his back. Square-shouldered, dirty-yellow work coat. She stares at the many stains, the countless holes the acid has burned into it over time. He is facing the wall. His soul a private space on his cloud nine again. Exchange of meaningful glances between his students. Crazy old fellow. She waits. Shuffles her feet, not patiently.

It seems an eternity before his mind swings back to the present. Pale-blue eyes behind gold-ringed glasses gaze at Eddie and her. At a loss for what to say, they wait in the enameling hot silence of the room.

"Hm, hm. Zus. Soo." His staccato stammers hang overhead in the heat. "HHmHmm. Hm. How would you two like to work in my studio? Zus. Ssssoo."

He chops his words as if wanting to get rid of them in a hurry. Coughs slightly, clears his throat. Obviously pleased that he got it out. Then continues, "Working for me will give you a lot of practical experience. Once the war is over you can always come back to school and get your official degree. I'll pay you twenty guilders each per week."

Hanne and Eddie stare at their teacher. Lost for words. Speechless at the sudden prospects that open up for them. There is hope after all. Hanne gazes at the reflection of the room with the window and a bit of bluish sky in the corner of his glasses. Nowhere in her wildest dreams had there been a chance to continue her metal-smithing. She sees Eddie's large brown eyes flicker. He stares in silent emotion. The three hairs on his dark-rimmed brown mole stick wildly in the air. The money isn't overly much. Actually laughably low in comparison to a normal salary. Never mind. Hanne looks forward to being a wage earner. Even a low-wage earner. She can use every cent. Suddenly her future is not dead. There are ways to fight. Fate is a quirk.

"But that's great," Eddie gasps, in a hurry to confirm.

"Of course, I'd love to," Hanne chimes in. "When do we start?"

She reels. Afraid the mustard-yellow coat opposite her might change its mind.

"Well, you could start tomorrow. I have enough private orders to keep you busy. Be there at nine."

Hanne's gut dances jigs. The reversal is so sudden. Her feet itch to get moving. The kiln's timer rings shrill into the charged silence. Zwollo grabs his spatula and walks over to the kiln. Bert walks next to him and lifts the red-hot enamel out of the white-glowing furnace. Hanne watches them. Awestruck. Soon she'll be doing the same.

*

The trip to Zwollo's house in Oosterbeek, a municipality adjacent to Arnhem, is cumbersome. There is no streetcar cooperation between the communities. The Arnhem cars tingle to a stop at the end of Arnhem. There is a long wait at the interchange before the Oosterbeek car arrives to snail back to deliver the passengers to their destinations.

"It's an hour and a half each way," Hanne gripes.

Eddie shrugs.

"Wasted time," Hanne harps on.

"Better than sitting at home."

"True."

They are too happy about their new lease on life to mind for long. Their leisurely morning gets hectic. Despite her tendency to run slow and be late in the morning, Hanne doesn't mind getting up at the crack of dawn. Not at all. Not that it's easier to get out of the warm bed into cold stark reality. But the work makes getting up worthwhile. She is anxious to get to the studio on time.

"But it's a lot of wasted time."

Eddie nods. No use to answer the obvious.

They walk down the quiet residential lane to Zwollo's house. Hanne rings the bell. Zwollo's teenage daughter lets them in and shows them to the studio in the back. Hanne inhales the vitriol pungency. She feels immediately at home among the racks of metal stakes on the side of the workbench, the vast number of homemade steel punches for embossing and chasing metal, blow-torches large and small. Familiar territory.

She hears the family in the dining room. Steps clomp down the narrow staircase. Zwollo appears from his bedroom upstairs, neatly scrubbed, ready to put his two new helpers to work.

"Zus. Szoo. Good morning," he clips.

"Good morning."

She watches Eddie get a soldering job.

"Zus. Szoo." Zwollo pulls several cabochon amethysts out of the top drawer. Graduated in size, he spreads them out on the workbench before Hanne. Purple teardrops. A client wants him to make a necklace. He spreads a coil of heavy square silver wire over the workbench, scribbles some doodles on a stenographer's pad. Points at the indecipherable doodles.

"I've drawn some sketches here to give you an idea of what I want," he says. She looks at the inky lines on yellow lined paper. Chickenscratch.

"Hhum," she mumbles.

Then he gets up and leaves for school. He will be gone for the day.

Hanne stares at the paper. Stares again. And again. Slowly, gradually, her mind fills in what his inky doodles left out. She bends the wire. Cuts. Saws. Shapes. Solders. Links that eventually will become a necklace with amethysts. A large, stylized swanlike silver hanger with a large amethyst in front, lesser links with lesser amethysts graduating toward the back. She is working. The work makes her forget the world around her. Her mind shapes ideas, bends and forces them into focus. She is busy.

Zwollo is delighted with her work when he returns in the evenings. They discuss. Shape some more.

He leaves in the morning. She works in the studio. Creates. Turns his vague notations into stunning jewelry.

Every morning begins a new, exciting adventure. Working in his studio, she realizes that he is no more exacting there than he is at school. She knows by now that she needs to help her boss with all his designs as the work progresses. She needs to learn his craftsmanship. Working for him personally will give her more experience than she would ever get in school. The war is in another life. She pushes the thought of Nazis and obnoxious German decrees far out of her mind. If just those stupid streetcar rides were more convenient…

*

It doesn't take long before the Nuremberg laws go into effect in Arnhem. Hanne and Eddie need no longer complain about tedious, time-consuming rides to and from work. Jews are forbidden to use public parks, libraries, public transportation. Et cetera, et cetera, et cetera. If they want to continue to work for Zwollo they will have to walk the distance.

Of course they will.

It's a long walk between Arnhem and Oosterbeek. They trace their route on a map. Amsterdamsche Weg up, turn left through the woods, across the heath, past the Old Cemetery for World War One veterans, then across the railroad tracks, straight into the Oosterbeek section where Zwollo lives.

They comfort themselves that walking the distance takes no longer than riding the streetcar. The weather is cooperative too at first, Indian summer with the rising sun burning off the early morning mists. Hanne inhales deeply the fragrant, moisture vapors the dark-green foliage emits. Sturdy old oaks, beeches, sycamores nod by the wayside, whispering old forgotten tales as they walk along. She loves these walks. Marvels at the rainbow colored dewdrops that glisten from grassblades and heather like lost pearls from a million torn necklaces.

Fall turns verdure slowly into a symphony of burnished tan, crimson, ochre, carmine, rust, yellows in all variations under the slanting rays of the pale sun. Shrivels it before it falls to the ground for a short, independent rustling rest for a coda of wind-driven, loose-jointed mounds that warm the soil before the mixture gradually composts into moist, moldy food for dank-dark earth.

Then mornings turn cool. White rim-frost paints the heath an even deeper purple. Having lost their leafy robes, the trees stick their denuding limbs into the air. Dark patterns clad in iceblue crystal. The paths freeze. Mists wrap heaven and earth in loose milk white veils.

Winter arrives with rains. Leaves dance furiously their last ballet in the winds that sweep them into way corners to rest. Eddie and she must be careful not to slip on heaps of wet leaves when they walk home in the fading daylight of crimped afternoons. Long shadows spread over the ground, getting longer as time passes. Hanne breathes brittle blue air, exhales whitish vapors.

"I love our walks," she tells Eddie, intoxicated with fall, nature and professional progress. Zwollo is pleased with her work. He considers her talented, creative. Taciturn as always, he is sparse with words. She feels her teacher's approval like something tangible.

"I wish the walks weren't that long. We're ruining our shoes. My feet blister," Eddie complains.

He is right. Hanne has spent a good part of her salary on soles. New shoes are rationed. Expensive and flimsy besides. Made of surrogate material that doesn't hold up. Better repair the old leather gear as long as they hold up.

"My feet are used to walking. The blisters healed long ago." Hanne doesn't want her enthusiasm dampened.

"Keep your fun to yourself. If the moffen find out, they'll take that away too," Eddie grumbles.

"Come on, Eddie. Look at our gorgeous world! It's still here."

"Yeah. What gives them the right to ruin it?"

"Yeah. Who gives them the right!" She stumbles over a brown stump. Almost loses her balance.

"Hey, better look where you're going, dreamhead!"

"I'm trying hard."

Hanne's eyes follow a flock of birds up high, a black, self-contained entity in the heavens moving south. A long tail of stragglers struggle in the wake to keep up the pace behind the leaders.

Everything in nature fits into a pattern of natural laws and habits established in a historical twilight long lost in myth. A huge flood of envy surges up in her.

"To have the freedom to go wherever you want," she frets. Why can't she go wherever she wants, whenever she wants?

She remembers the time she was five years old and caught scarlet fever at the beginning of first grade. Doctor Jülich came, advised Mutti to put Hanne into the hospital so Ruth wouldn't catch it too. Ruth. Always Ruth. How lost she had felt in the separate infectious disease section of the *Diakonen Krankenhaus*. How she had cried whenever Mutti and Vati appeared to visit outside her window, "*Ich will nach Hause, ich will nach Hause!*"

Inconsolable. She had wanted to go home. Inconsolable long after they had left. The nurses tried their level autocratic, carbolic best to comfort the screaming child. Nothing helped. They advised her parents not to visit. Drastic measures that had quieted her down, all right, for the six weeks of her stay in the hospital. Perhaps forever after. Along with *poone haben*.

"Only your mind is free to roam," she decides.

> *Kommt ein Vogel geflogen/setzt sich nieder auf meinem Fuss,*
> *Hat einen Zettel im Schnabel/von der Mutter einen Gruss.*
> *Lieber Vogel fliege weiter/nimm einen Gruss mit und einen Kuss,*
> *Denn ich kann Dich nicht begleiten/weil ich hierbleiben muss.*

She hums the melody to the old lullaby. Almost forgotten, a surprising presence. A bird comes with greetings from home, but she needs to send it back. She is stuck.

Something went wrong here. Right from the start. Adam and Eve. Lilith. Cain and Abel. Jacob and Esau. Leah and Rachel. The powerful, the self-serving, the overbearing twist rules to serve their own ends. Shape them to their convenience. They own the

world. Where does that leave the weak and the meek? The righteous? The underdogs? The dispossessed? Shove them aside. Put
them away. Who wants to listen to the silent screams of Jews?

She smarts at the unfairness of it all. Her fate. How much
easier things would be as one of the others. The loud majority.
The lucky crowd!

*

They reach the woods. A few straggler leaves rustle overhead in
their last dance toward eternal rest. Then they step out into the
long alley lined with huge, stately beeches and sycamores. They
walk silently. Hanne meditates into the patterns the pale sun
throws through the trees on the damp, dark, uneven ground. A
sudden misgiving shivers through her. Makes her look up. A
lonesome dark figure appears at the end of the alley where the
first residential homes begin at the outskirts of Arnhem. It moves.
Comes closer.

"Isn't that Bert?" she says.

"Sure looks like him."

The figure grows, takes shape. It's Bert all right. She wonders
what prompts him to come out all this way to meet them.

"Hi, fellow metalsmiths," he greets them. "What's up?"

Hanne senses tension in his voice underneath his cheerie
words. Or is that just her imagination going wild again?

"Fine," the two say in unison.

"What brings you out here?" Eddie wonders.

Hanne thinks of the other necklace taking shape. The settings
for the cabochon moonstones are finished. She is busy bending,
shaping and filing the links of the chain. Zwollo is visibly pleased.
Without many words other than an occasional, approving, "Zuss.
Sooh. Zuss. Sooh." Every morning he leaves her alone with the
work while he teaches at school. The approval is in his voice. His
trust is in his demeanor. She wants to tell Bert.

"School started this morning and we thought of you two. They want you to know that we miss you in class," Bert speaks into the wintry air before him.

They walk on toward the city.

Funny, busy with her work, school has become an issue of secondary importance. There is a sting of slight running through her. Like having lost something irretrievable. With the exception of Bert, her relationship to the other students was never too close. Now that she is no longer in school, she misses hearing the teenage pleasures, aggravations and sorrows that are exclusively theirs. She feels ostracized, excluded merely because of what she is.

The feeling is not new. It's an old shadow that has followed her since her childhood. Secretly she may have wanted to compensate for that old loss when she enrolled. Recapture her lost childhood. This is the second time she is thrown out of school. Older now, she fathoms the scope of what is denied her. Neither lament nor crying helps. She can comfort herself with the thought that she would never have learned in a classroom what she is learning in Zwollo's studio. Working with him is her lucky stroke of fate. School in session also means that from now on Zwollo is going to disappear two days a week from the studio. More freedom for her. Don't grudge! She pushes her pain deep down inside.

"Well, what's the latest gossip? There's always so much going on in school." She wants to sound lighthearted.

"I told everybody I was going to meet you this afternoon. They send regards. As for latest gossip, Hettie Hovekamp and Piet Havinga got engaged over the summer. Want to get married after graduation in the spring."

"Congrats. Give them our best when you see them," Hanne says.

"No surprise. They've been dating for as long as I can remember," Eddie adds.

"Hettie has talked about nothing else," Bert agrees.

Hanne falls silent. Sighs. How great it must be to make plans for the future. And know that you can make them come true. Will she ever be able to? All she knows is uncertainty at what may happen today or tomorrow. Her sole certainty is the separation between present and future. Living from day to day has become the only way to live. Survive the moment and take life from there. Insecure by experience, she is suspicious of what may happen in the future. She has the nagging feeling that Bert has not come all the way out here just to meet them and gossip. It's so unlike him.

The wood ends. They walk on in silence, each hanging on to his own thoughts. She has a sense of leaving a protective cover behind as they step out on the paved street. It leads to the city. Her sense of dejection deepens as they walk on into the orange-violet-purple fringes of the setting sun. By the time they reach the residential area, evening dusk with its long shadows hugs the red brick homes lining Amsterdamsche Weg. The unreal postcard quality makes her cringe. What lurks behind all this sane, orderly beauty? Or is her feeling of dread an adumbration of wisdom garnered in her past? She scrutinizes Bert. Meets his searching look. Watches him gulp and take a deep breath.

"Rumors have it that the moffen are rounding up Jews in Amsterdam. Not just the men this time, but entire families."

Bert turns his gaze forward. Away from her.

A feeling of *deja vu* creeps up in her. She looks at Eddie. Their eyes meet in a common bond. Like, "Isn't that a repeat of what we already know? Or some such thing that this outsider can't know." They walk on, step by step, right, left, right, left, right, left. Automatons. The steps echo hollow on the hard pavement. An ominous dread flutters in the air like a lost bird.

"They say that these people are no longer going to Vught. They're sent to a place called Westerbork. That's way up in Dren-the… of course, they're just rumors. Nothing confirmed." Bert presses it out, an unwilling messenger. He falls silent again with a wan smile.

She wants it to stop, but her brain propels into overtime. Vught has an ominous reputation for mishandling its prisoners.

Many of them are sent on to work in German plants to help in the war effort. Westerbork, on the other hand, has long been a camp for German refugees up in the sandy wilds of Drenthe. Northern Holland. What do they want all these Jews for now? Families? Children? To work in Germany? It doesn't make sense. Of course, neither do concentration camps for Jews, communist, gypsies, homosexuals and all kinds of other social minorities the Nazis have declared outcasts. Dangerous to the *Reich*.

"Do you think they need these people to work? Families with children?" Hanne vents her thoughts, addresses Bert.

He shrugs. Helpless.

"Just in Amsterdam?" Eddie presses further.

The possibility of rounding up Jews in other cities takes shape in the fall dusk.

"Men in mixed marriages can choose between castration or roundup. A few chose to stay," Bert reports.

"You mean these men had themselves neutered?" Eddie throws out in disbelief.

"That's it."

"I can't believe it. What about their children? Legally they are Jews."

"I don't know the details. I think these families may stay together. You know, these new laws are confusing. One thing today, another tomorrow. It depends a lot on the official in authority. You never know."

Hanne grits her teeth. Her stomach is churning again, as so often these days. The pain under her ribs spreads. She breathes heavily. Nazi catechism. She is a full-blooded Jew. Does she envy the half-breeds, *mishlings*? Yes and no. Despite all her difficulties, she is proud of what she is. She can't imagine being different. She's angry at the boors, hecklers, uneducated ruffians. Brutal animals with unwarranted ideas about other people. What do they know about Judaism. Its great writings. Its ancient culture. Its proud heritage. To act like them would be to lower yourself to their level. She sighs. All right. It would be more practical to be one of them. Even a half-breed. Safer at any rate. Stupid though the others are.

"In that case, Horst Garnmann can wiggle out if they pick us up," Eddie supposes. He says it out loud. The thought that is on all their minds. *Pick us up.* She shivers.

Hanne's stomach cramps. Eddie mustn't paint the devil on the wall. So far it's only in Amsterdam. Far removed from our daily lives. It may never get here. The thought is half prayer, half fervent wish. Eddie mustn't give up hope, for crying out loud. They need hope to survive. Horst's mother is gentile, his father a Jew. His parents placed him on Kindertransport to escape to Holland. He has uncles and cousins in the German army, some are party members, male cousins in the *Hitlerjugend*, girl cousins in *BdM* = short for *Bund deutscher Mädchen*. As a Jew he is hunted down, as a German he may be drafted for the military. A no-win situation. With some luck, he may be able to remain on the sidelines in Holland . Survive. No. Bert's news is horrible. She hates Eddie's logic even more. The issue is survival. Survival by all means. Any means. The overriding question is, *HOW*.

The dusk is dark purple by the time they reach Jongenshuis. The two black sentries on the other side of the street are very much in evidence. Clop, clop, clop, clop. Their boots have a special resonance on the pavement. Mere wishful thinking won't make them disappear. Foolish thought that. The ss remain. A giant steely octopus whose slimy tentacles spread all over Europe. Chokes its lifeblood. But the land and its nations will survive. Only the Jews are in danger of being utterly destroyed. They have no land. The ultimate victims because they have no country. Victims to their stubborn divergence. Martyrs to their cohesion.

They stop in front of the house.

"I'm hungry. Good night," Eddie says and disappears behind the heavy door. Hanne is about to do the same when Bert stops her.

"Hanne, I want to talk to you. That's the main reason I

came out to meet you. I've just been waiting for him to leave us alone."

"Funny, I've had the feeling all along there's something else"

She searches his face, wondering what he has to say. It must be urgent for him to meet her that far out.

The black helmet across the street glares into her field of vision, the face hidden under the steel brim. The polished boots on the other side stomp their monotonous clomp, clomp, clomp.

"Bert, you put yourself in danger out here with me," she says quietly. "Why don't you come inside?"

"All right."

"With luck we'll even find a quiet corner in this beehive where we can talk."

Thoughts race, scramble in her head trying to figure out what he may want to talk about. Futile. No clue. The house is very quiet during the day when only the staff and perhaps some sickies are in. But beware of the late afternoons after school lets out! Then it becomes a pandemonium of activity where boundless teen-age energy bounces off walls and tables seeking affirmation. She checks the front room. It's empty. Hanne motions Bert to come in, then closes the door, careful not to arouse suspicion. Her thoughts dance a jig at her luck. Curious at what he has to say.

"We should be fairly undisturbed here," she says. "Shoot."

She watches him in surprise. His feet go limp in shy embarassment. His head bent over, he pulls a small package wrapped in silky paper out of his pocket. He shivers as he unwraps the tissue paper. She follows his hands turn slowly from pink to reddish. She can literally feel his blood climb slowly up his trunk under his dark overcoat, across his long, thin neck with the funny, slightly bobbing Adam's apple, then spread a glow across his bent face, flush into his eyelids all the way between the shiny blond eyelashes, color his forehead up to the roots of his dark blond shock of hair. There's an element of enormity in the air as he unwraps a small silver ring. His head tilts upright, watery blue eyes burrow into hers. She can feel his fingers shake when she takes it from his outstretched hand.

"Here. For you." His voice quivers. Fills the atmosphere with nervous excitement.

Overwhelmed, Hanne takes the ring. Doesn't know what to say. She looks at the small circle of embossed leaves and flowers, a garland soldered between two delicate parallel silver wires.

"I made it for you," he says. The quiver is still there. His face is a deep purple.

She is all admiration for his work, his craftsmanship. If only she could learn to work this well.

"Oh, Bert. It's gorgeous. What an intricate design. And such delicate, painstaking work!"

She pulls it over her ring finger. Grateful for his attention. Unable to put all her feelings into mere words.

"And it fits!"

"It should." His feet cross, one ankle bent outward, his entire body a vision of delighted embarrassment. "Remember when we played with the ring measures in class? I did it on purpose to get your size." Proud of his trick, the purple-red blush expands around his moving Adam's apple. Its mobile tip is aglow.

"Gee. I remember, now that you mention it. I never suspected."

"I'm happy you like it."

"I do. I really do, Bertie. It's beautiful. Thanks so much."

A long, weighty silence descends in the room. Pause. Hanne does not know what to do next. She can hear the kids gab, laugh, run down the hall outside their door. She looks at him. Is there something else? She sees him swallow, take a deep breath. His Adam's apple bobs a wild cha-cha.

"There's something I want to discuss."

"Yes?" She rolls the ring between her fingers, round and round. Mulls things over in her head. What else can there be?

He swallows, takes a visible mental leap. Charged, the air hangs thick between them.

"No one knows when the moffen are going to decide to pick up Jews here in Arnhem."

There. Of course. The unspeakable truth has come alive. Reality. Foreboding. Threats to her existence. Goosebumps crawl up her arms. Her fingers grow cold, stiffen around the ring. Her mouth is dry, runs out of saliva. Bert's voice sounds from afar.

"What I want to say is that I have a place for you to go underground. Hide. I have access to food coupons for you too, so there's no need to worry on that account."

His words reverberate in her ears. Solidify. Take on form in her consciousness. A place to escape from the Nazis. Many Jews have disappeared from the scene lately. *Gone into hiding* is the term. She knows that he has connections to the underground. She has never asked. One doesn't talk about these things unless they're necessary. The less one knows, the better all around. No chance to spill any secrets that way. Here's her opportunity to escape. She knows that she can trust him. Although… and here's the big if… put her life into someone else's hands? She doesn't know the others who work with him. The idea is too murky. What about informers? There are plenty of them around too. The daily papers are full of reports on *hiders* and *hidees* summarily shot on the spot. Danger lurks either way. She hates to face the imminent truth. Better put it off. Push it out of her mind. Just a while longer. Tomorrow might bring a change for the better. Tomorrow. Who knows?

"What about my sister?" she asks.

"I have room for only one person." He shrugs his shoulders in regret. Regret is in his eyes.

She looks at him. Intently. Silently. Her mind a blank in a raging storm. Can you turn the thought off? Please!!! Ruth is a pest. Has always been. Made her life miserable from way back.

But can she really leave her? They are family. Sisters. She is older than the brat. She can't leave her here. Alone.

A mountain builds up between her and the fellow standing opposite her. No. She fiddles with the ring in her hands. Turns it between her fingers. Aimlessly. Round and round and round and round. Things will be better tomorrow. Next week. Next year. The Americans will come. Now that they have joined in the war. The Germans can't win. Mustn't win. She has this inner compulsion to go on. Survive. It sounds stupid, given the circumstances. She can't explain why, but she can't go off and leave Ruth. There is Mutti looking at her.

Internal sighs funnel through her pores into the open. Ruth, the pest. But no! A thousand times *NO!!!*

"Bert, I can't. I can't just go off and leave her. I appreciate your offer."

Her words reverberate through the air. Hang there. They eye each other. He has small pupils, tiny black dots in pale blue. An expanse of silence builds between them. She fidgets with the ring, feels the rough, cutting edges of the silver flowers that stick out beyond the wires on which they are soldered. She must stay here, in this house, remain with her sister. And the others. Breaking away is like losing her identity. Though that isn't the problem here. How can she ever face Mutti and Vati if she abandons her younger sister? She tries to find a way to make him understand her position. She can't. Language fails her. She doesn't have the words to explain. The silence turns awkward.

It is an eternity before he speaks. Dark sounds in the emotionally charged air.

"Hanneke, I so wish I could help. But I can't find a second place. Lord only knows how hard I tried. I was afraid that you'd refuse."

His words feel good. She looks at him. Sees anger take over, reddish glow slowly creeping up from his chicken neck, across the aquiline nose, sideways over the forehead, covering the entire pale face. Flushed, frustration in his voice, he rants, "Damn! Damn these moffen! To hell with the lot of them! Who asked them to come here, anyway?" His arms flail about in consuming fury, a cock on the attack. "Damn them!"

Hanne is speechless. She has never seen him this angry before. Her heart goes out to him in pity.

CHAPTER 7

"Hush, Bertus. There's nothing we can do."

She knows from experience that they can do nothing from inside German territory. From where they sit, they can only support help coming from outside. There's nothing on the horizon that she can see.

She is afraid that Dr. Wolf or one of the staff members will find them here. Suddenly he stands close to her. She feels his trembling body enfolding her, his arms an awkward grip around her waist. She stands stiff, almost petrified, not knowing what to do. His body heat makes her dizzy in a strange, wonderful way. She melts, limp in his embrace, her body against his. Like from afar, she feels herself throw her arms around his shoulders and return his kiss as if she had never wanted to do anything else in her life.

"Oh, Hanne..."

She feels his voice breathe into her ear. Lost, she lets the wave engulf her. Wishing for nothing but to let it persist, feeling nothing but his presence around her, interlocked, kissing, his warm breath against her mouth, drowning all thought in the embrace, forever, forever, forever.

The dinner gong rends them apart. Its echo reverberates in the walls. They straighten up, too shy to look at each other. Outside, the staircase comes alive, rumbling under the onslaught of a million feet. Youngsters who want to live run to get their food.

"Dinner. I have to go," she says into the cold void where his warm body has been.

Lucky that no one has come in, it flits through her mind. She wonders momentarily what would have happened if someone had.

"Yes. I have to go home too."

She walks with him down the hall to the heavy wooden front door where he turns to face her.

"Take care. I'll see you tomorrow after school."

They shake hands in a formal way. She watches his dark coat disappear through the heavy wooden door. Then she turns abruptly and walks slowly over the black and white marble tiled floor down to the dining room. Oblivious to the commotion around her. Her mind grinds one refrain: "Have I done the right thing in refusing his offer?"

*

After that day, Bert waits for her every afternoon at the same spot at the end of the woods where Eddie and she step out on the alley. Only a glance, perhaps a slight smile, of recognition, then the threesome continue their walk home, a silent togetherness of a meager half hour as the days grow shorter. Hanne looks forward to their walks. Each time she sees him waiting at the end of the alley her heart takes a silent leap. It would be nice to get rid of Eddie and be alone.

Oh well, he really doesn't bother them that much. Sometimes one of them breaks the silence with some story of how he has solved a problem at work. In this respect, Eddie is part of the club anyway. Other times, Bert brings the latest gossip from school, or even the latest news from the BBC he heard on his short-wave receiver behind closed doors the previous night.

*

Lately, the news isn't all bad. First there is the Russian winter. Stalingrad. Nothing official, but rumors persist. The tide has turned there. Then, the Germans are fighting fiercely in North Africa. Rommel lost at El Alamein.

"He took a good licking," Bert assures the two.

"But that's in Africa. Far away from here," Eddie argues.

"Yeah, what good is it to us? It can't help us in our predicament," she wails.

"The Allies – we need them *here*. Before the Nazis destroy all of Europe," Eddie says.

"The Jews above all."

"Hmm. Humm."

"But at least the moffen are losing."

Unanimous agreement.

*

Autumn is turning cold. The frosty winds and snowy rains drive the leftover leaves through the air. Lift them, whirl them in mad St. Vitus dances before they settle in wet, darkbrown, molding heaps on the open earth. Hanne and Eddie have to be careful not to slip as they wade through them on their way to work.

In the mornings, dense fogs hang in whitish layers across the heath and shroud the brush in opaque secrecy. Lacy spiderwebs hung with round, pearly dew droplets shimmer between dark knotty trees and branches that guard the alley like arthritic, gouty old wizards. Silent, foreboding ghosts hold their breath in a grayish-white dampness. On the street, yellow lights flash through rain, drizzle and haze where cars and bikes are shadows that darkly grow, spread and disappear.

These gloomy days alternate with days when the sun takes a late stand and slants her lemon glow into frostbitten mornings. Hanne watches the heath turn purple, then pale blue. Cold and nasty, daylight shrinks to some short grayish noontime hours. Slowly the wind turns icier and fiercer, batters the stark trees, gnarled specters that ache in defiance to an uncaring, twisted universe, their accusing fingers pointing skyward where leaden, defenseless wads scud across the heavens in hopeless despair.

Hanne and Eddie bundle up to withstand the cold and sleet on their way to work. Despite the weather, Bert waits faithfully by their tree every afternoon and keeps them silent company on their way home. Hanne marvels at his stubborn steadfastness.

"Hot and horny," Eddie says. His breath curls white out of his mouth.

"What d'you mean?" Hanne glowers into his face. The three black hairs on his brown mole flutter in the wind disconcertingly.

"Your silent admirer."

"Why don't you shut your stupid mouth."

He shrugs his shoulders under his coat and gulps, obviously swallowing a nasty answer. Like "you're too stupid to see." Or something like that. The usual things boys tell girls.

"It's none of your business," she mumbles under her breath. It's like having the last word without a fight.

Boys. Girls. God.

She has been thinking a lot lately. About faith. God. She used to argue with herself, with Him, with the world. Endless questions. Why? Why? No answers anywhere. She has decided to stop this. At least stop for now. Put the questioning on the backburner. Shelve the matters like something defective. Faith is internal. Brain. Things that can neither be confirmed, nor used. Even less discarded. Is it indoctrination working in her? A nuisance her forebears have saddled her with.

Let others do the thinking. I bow out. For now. Perhaps at some future time. No, definitely. At some far-off, unknowable future time. When I'll be better equipped to answer this kind of questioning. Like, is there a God? If so, what does he want? From me? From the Jews?

*

October arrives dull, dark, dreary. Somber days that envelop life. Enclose, clutch the world. Thick black clouds hang low in the sky. Dismal threats all around pervade, smother their minds. The wet wind frets cold through the countryside, plants frost over the sodden earth.

Eddie is at home with the flu. She is alone, huddled in her winter coat and boots when they meet on her way home at the usual confluence between heath and woods.

"Not that I wish him ill, but it's nice to be alone for a change," he grumbles with secretive bliss.

His eyes are inscrutable black dots in pale blue that make her uneasy. Obscure reasons. They walk close. Take comfort from each other's presence. Insulated sparks flow between them, connect.

He reports the latest news from school, lighthearted gossip from another universe that excludes her these days. She listens, tries to pay attention. She talks shop. Zwollo and her work. She has some questionable news about the master's private life. Not that Zwollo ever says anything outright, but problems between him and his wife permeate the atmosphere in the house. It's palpable every morning when she walks through the hall to the studio in the back. The woman's hateful black looks. Hanne is an expert on hateful looks. Zwollo's embarrassed mumbles after loud fights in the dining room they can't help hearing.

"Zus soo, zus soo." Hanne imitates the master's staccato phrase.

"No. It's not that I'm rooting in his private life. And I'm no tattletale. But it takes all kinds to make a family. Perhaps they enjoy playing cat and mouse. Or got used to it during years of married life. What do you think?"

"I don't know. I'm no expert on married life."

"Theirs seems like living hell. At lunch he complains that there isn't enough for him to eat. She tells him that the children come first. How'd you like to be one of the children and sit at that table eating lunch? Of course he knows that Eddie and I can hear them. Then he comes back to work with his zusssoo's and mumbles something about punishment. Having done something awful in his former life. Can you imagine such crap?"

"It's nonsense, but he believes it. He's a theosophist. They believe in soul transmigration."

"I know."

She mulls it over in silence. Jewish mystics believe in an eternal soul. The soul returns to God. Strange beliefs that too, but she's used to this. Christians have an even better defined system for afterlife.

Ever since the day she refused Bert's offer to go underground, they have not mentioned any Nazis and have carefully avoided war and politics. They chatter on about small insignificances as if nothing else matters. Kiss passionate, wind-frosted kisses in haphazard intervals on the frozen path, continue in the deserted alley under the protection of knobby, gnarled, naked trees. They walk arm in arm down the road. Disconnect, reduce intimacy to holding hands when they reach the open street. His hand feels warm in hers, reassuring between homes with drawn curtains on either side of the road. Despite her longing for sun, warmth and summer, Hanne wishes that nothing changes, ever. She wants time to stand still. Her fingers close in Bert's hand. His hand presses hard around them.

As if on sudden impulse, he turns to her. His eyes lock into hers in a sharp pale-blue gaze with tiny black center dot. Then he looks forward, chin stretched out into the wind.

"They've rounded up Jews in the city during the night," he commits to the frozen afternoon.

Her heart somersaults somewhere inside her body. Her blood curdles. Her stomach shrinks. Ties into knots. Her intestines cramp. That's why he kissed her longer, more urgently than ever out on the heath. A dull ache settles in her spinal column.

"Oh," she says into the wind, mindful of her wish just a minute ago.

It's all she can say. Her throat is dry. The heavy lump in her stomach spreads outward, pushes against her ribs. She has trouble breathing. Her feet are sudden leaden obstacles, moving forward on their own accord without connection to her body.

When will they come for us? Jongenshuis? The thought stands out in heavy, freakish unspoken letters. She has met all this before, way back in her young past. How many times?

Something inside shuts down. An eerie feeling of unreality possesses her. She keeps on walking next to Bert. An impenetrable wall between them has ripped them apart. The regular stomp of the two black sentries across the street echoes hollow in her brain. They stop in front of Jongenshuis.

She stands removed from herself, observes what she is doing from somewhere outside in space. From her distance, she looks at Bert. He gazes back at her. She shrinks under his powder blue gaze with the two tiny black center dots.

Say it isn't so, something inside her screams and tries to scramble out of her. But she is dumb. Her voice is not functioning, locked inside. The silence turns awkward. When will she see him again? She feels like running, running away from it all, yet she is glued to the spot in front of him. The ss are on the opposite side of the street. Her feet are mired in a nightmare.

"Goodbye, Bert." She holds her hand out. Her arm is a piece of lead.

"Goodbye, Hanneke. Take care."

He takes her hand into both his hands for a second. Then he drops it, turns abruptly. She stands still, alone. Watches him walk down the incline of the street until he is out of sight. Then she turns and drags herself into the house. Halfway through the hallway Werner stands at the foot of the staircase.

"Hi. I hear you're getting real chummy with that goy of yours. Be careful that they don't run both of you in for *Rassenschande*. It's a crime these days, you know."

"Concerned?"

They stare at each other. Hate stands in their eyes. Sudden open enemies.

"Spying on me?" she challenges into his silence.

"Ha! Don't make me laugh! As if I had nothing better to do." His voice has this strange, metallic timbre again.

"Then what are you doing out here?"

"Don't act as if I were jealous. Stupid skirt!" Derisive curls pucker his lips. She watches him saunter up the stairs.

"Always your pleasant self," she mutters against his blunt back atop the slightly concave legs. The sound of his steps rebounds on the bare wood.

His comments sting. Of course the danger of meeting Bert has occurred to her long before his reminder. It's always with her. It's not only the Germans. She knows that her parents would never approve of her meeting a goy. If they're old-fashioned, now Hitler proves them right. Or something like that. She shrugs them off. Now is now. She has voiced the Nazi danger to Bert. He refuses to listen.

"We're entitled to talk and meet. They have no right to prevent us."

Of course he is right. They had never discussed the subject again. Besides, how many people wander about the heath anyway? Certainly not many in this weather. Germans least of all. They parade in uniformed clusters on the streets, noisy presences to thrust fear into normal folk who want to go about their normal daily business.

The doorbell pierces through her meditations. Sounds of commotion outside. Loud voices from the street she has heard before. Her memory runs overtime. German voices. Boots. Familiar sounds of terror. Hearing German is not uncommon in their home. They speak German among themselves still. Wolf and Sussmann don't speak anything else. Dutch is reserved for natives, staff members such as van Gelder, people outside the home, school, stores. Learning Dutch came fairly easy for all of the youngsters.

Hanne is closest to the door. She turns to open it.

The three ss-men outside click their heels. Black uniforms over shiny gloss of black boots. Metal spurs glitter. Danger lurks in the atmosphere.

"Heil Hitler!" Their arms shoot forward in their odious salute. Another click of the heels. Metal on metal.

"Good evening," she says. Calm encloses her frame from outside. "Not yet. Dear God. Not yet, please. Please," her inside prays.

"We're looking for Arthur Natt. He lives here."

They brush her aside and stomp inside. She is right behind them.

"I don't think he's home yet," she manages to utter, far too softly.

"Where's your director? We want to talk to him."

"He should be in his office upstairs." She leads them up the staircase.

What do they want from Atze? They don't look like the ones from across the street, although she can't be sure. They have been over to requisition boys a few times before, to clean their stables, or help with the horses, shovel manure. The boys dread this slave labor. So far they've always returned unharmed, physically that is.

Their boots echo. A menace on the wooden stairs. The ss behind her, Hanne knocks at Dr. Wolf's office door.

"Yes."

She opens the door. Sees Dr. Spinoza buttoning his overcoat, on his way to leave.

"Three gentlemen to see you," she announces. Her insides scoff at her use of the word *gentlemen*. She bites her lips. It's suicide to call them openly what she thinks they are.

Dr. Spinoza bids Dr. Wolf goodbye. Then, on his way out, greets and passes the black booted furies with their hateful armbands. She glimpses Dr. Wolf welcoming the three as she closes the door behind them.

Dr. Spinoza is a local physician who has taken on the voluntary job of treating the youngsters, since Dr. Wolf has no official Dutch license to treat them. She walks down the stairs with him. "Anyone seriously ill?" she asks him. She wonders whether Eddie's five-day cold is more than just a mere old cold. Kids can pick up all kinds of infections in school. Or at work. Lately the flu has been making the rounds.

"Huhh hummm." His grunt is non-committal.

A group of scared youngsters stands around the bottom of the stairs.

"They want Atze. Anyone know where he is?" she says.

"He was with us at the *Sportsfondsenbad* for the weekly cleaning this afternoon. We haven't seen him since," someone announces. *Sportsfondsenbad* is the communal bathhouse they visit every Friday afternoon for a thorough body scrub.

Dr. Spinoza calls for attention. "Dr. Wolf wanted to announce it himself. But since he's busy at the moment I'll do it instead. We have five confirmed measles cases in the house. I'll have to report them. There may be more. It's a highly contagious disease. Jongenshuis must be under quarantine. That means no one may leave the building. No outsider may come in."

"For how long?"

"Four weeks after the last case."

Dr. Spinoza finishes buttoning his overcoat. Looks at the youngsters. Pats Herbert, who happens to stand near him, on the shoulder and walks out of the building.

"Great. Jailed. Lord knows for how long!" they wail.

"Stuck," she sighs.

The idea of being locked up is revolting. She can't go to work. She can't see Bert.

She is not going to get the measles because both Ruth and she had them when they were little. Ruth first. Then she. She remembers them both in bed, burning with fever in their darkened bedroom, the window curtains drawn to protect their eyes. Dr. Jülich visiting with his big black bag. Mutti taking their temperature, sticking the fever thermometer into her bottom so that it hurts. Her screams made Mutti angry. As always. The maid coming with lots of liquids.

Voices from upstairs cut into Hanne's ruminations. Boots. Dr. Wolf and his unwelcome trinity stand by the rails. Dr. Wolf bends across.

"Is Arthur home yet?" he calls down.

As if summoned by magic, Atze enters through the back door.

"You're wanted in the office."

Atze walks slowly through the room. His boots track mud through the hall. There's soil on his hands. He glances at his friends as he makes his way up the stairs under the stares of authority from above. The youngsters are silent. Don't know what to make of this. Watch his body move upward, join authorities. Then they watch them all disappear into Dr. Wolf's office. They all look at each other with question marks on their faces. "What's all this about? First measles and quarantine. Now the ss in their house." Silent thoughts written in invisible script. Disasters never cease.

"Actually, if we're under quarantine, they won't pick us up." Who knows, maybe it's a blessing in disguise?

*

It's an eternity before Dr. Wolf's door opens again. The three black uniforms have Atze between them. Dr. Wolf's humpbacked little figure trails behind them, down the staircase, then out into the backyard. The youngsters watch through the glass doors as Atze stops and points to the rhododendron bush. They see one of the Nazis bellow a command. Atze bends down and digs in the soil. Pulls at an object. Shakes it clean. Earth clumps fly. He straightens up with a gun in his hands. Shiny black steel glimmers. They stare through the glass.

"Looks like a revolver to me," Horst says.

"Hm Mm hmmm." Common agreement.

A ridiculous sight. How did Atze come by a revolver? The Germans take the weapon out of Atze's hand, handcuff him, and march him through the gate. Out on the road. Dr. Wolf trips after them. Slowly closes the gate behind them. His large silver mane shakes in disbelief. His ashen face stands before them in the hall.

"What on earth is all this about?" They question in disbelief.

Dr. Wolf stares at them. It takes a long minute before he gets his speech back. "Arthur took a revolver from one of them in the public bathhouse last Friday, then buried it in our backyard. They traced him here."

His head keeps on shaking on his infirm frame.

"He wanted to join the Underground. Probably wanted to take the thing along," Gerd says into the silence.

As if the shocks from outside aren't enough already.

"Foolish to think that he could get away with it. Stealing from them in broad daylight! Putting all of us in danger." Dr. Wolf's head jiggles on in aggravated disapproval.

The dinner gong rings through their consternation, calling them back to mundane reality.

"Food is ready," van Gelder shouts from outside her kitchen door. Freda next to her directs her boys. They push the big kettles to the dining room with the usual noisy rumble.

Shaken, the youngsters file into the dining room. Hanne is not hungry. Foolish Atze. Who gave him that idiotic idea? Fat chance they'll ever see him again!

Hanne has visions of torture. She shakes her head, unwilling to think any further. Does he know any secrets? Like about the Underground? What about his connections? Questions, questions. Endless questions to which she has no answers.

What with the local roundup of Jews, the logical thing is to disappear. Go underground. If you have the right connections, that is. Ernst Schlächter's place remains empty. Dolfi, Heini and Kläre's seats too. Hanne wishes them luck. They'll need it. Has she made the right decision in refusing Bert's offer? She looks at her sister on the other side of the room. Who can tell what's better or worse?

Before grace, Dr. Wolf taps his glass. "We have a few measles cases in the house. We're under quarantine. No one is allowed to enter or leave," he announces. Then he sits down and turns to Peter Marcuse. "A blessing in disguise. A respite. The Germans won't pick us up as long as there are measles in the house," he says out loud for everyone to hear.

As long as there are measles cases in the house. No one knows for how long. But every day counts. Every delay from falling into the German clutches means a faint chance. Suppose the Americans catch up with them?

"May all Germans roast in hell," Horsey hums to the tune of the Hatikvah. Werner chimes in.

"Amen," says Gerd.

Eddie nods, all consent, his mole included.

"The English are going to bomb the Germans to smithereens," Peter predicts.

Dr. Wolf chuckles above his hunchback. "You'd better start grace," he tells Peter.

Peter's words hit home, heartfelt wishes put into words. Bomb them to smithereens! All of them!

"I wonder what's keeping them," Hanne mutters. Americans just don't move fast enough.

*

The weeks go by. Three bedrooms full of measles, mostly light cases. The house stinks of carbolic acid and chlorine. Like a hospital.

Chapter 8

anne! Hanne!" She hears Eddie's voice as he runs upstairs, two steps at a time. All breathless hurry, he bumps into her at the top of the flight.

"What's the rush?"

"I'm looking for you," Eddie puffs, out of breath.

"Yep, and now that you've found me?"

Eddie catches his breath. His dark eyes glint like coals on fire.

"Your lover's outside the window. Wants to talk to you."

"My what?"

Her self-esteem radiates outward. Lover? She feels like Greta Garbo, smiling, in *Anna Karenina*. She's seen the movie and read the book.

"Oh well, you know. Bert's standing outside on the street. Go down and talk to him through the window."

She bounds downstairs.

They have not met since that last walk together, the day the quarantine started. She wonders what has brought him here. It must be important. Locked up, she misses their walks through the woods, across the heath, down *Amsterdamsche Weg* even more.

She must tell him to come to the side window so the ss won't notice him.

Werner steps into her way in the hall. "That boyfriend of yours is cluttering up the street."

"Nut. Get out of my way." She hates the mean vocal metallic vibrations of his voice. Who needs him? She runs to the window.

"Hi, Bert," she shouts into the windy roar outside.

She can see the wind flap his overcoat. Black danger lurks from across the street. He shouldn't stand here, in broad daylight, right under the nose of the Gestapo. She motions him to come around the side where she can open the window a slit. She is careful to close the door to the room behind her – no need to have the entire house listening in.

"Hi. What brings you here?"

They beam up and down at each other.

"Just wanted to see how you're doing," he says.

She watches his fingers play with the center button on his coat. Blond hair fluff on the back of his hand.

"How's school?"

"Fine. Everyone says hello. We talk a lot about you. How are you?"

"I'm all right. We're getting on each other's nerves, shut up inside."

They chuckle into a sudden cold blast.

"We miss you." His words vibrate in the cold.

"How's Zwollo?"

"He sends his best. I told him that I was coming here."

"It's Tuesday. You must've seen him this morning."

"He's busier than ever in his studio. Bella Heckscher is still working there. So is Bernard de Vries. Lately Fietje Dekker and Hetty Hovekamp have joined them."

"That's a lot. How does he have so much work space?"

Bert shrugs. "He made a space in his living room. The studio is too cold. No heat."

Bella is a Jewish student at school who had joined Hanne and Eddie at Zwollo's house months after the Jews were expelled and she and Eddie started in his studio. Back then Hanne never knew that Bella lived in the deVries' household. An adopted niece. Both her parents had died in an accident, but Bella had never talked about it. Her cousin Bernard did. Bernard had come to Zwollo after the first roundup of Jews when he lost his job. Working for Zwollo just might provide some escape route. Who knows?

"So they're still in town," Hanne says.

Once Hanne had felt a twinge of envy for Bella for living in a normal household.

"Far as I know. I talked to Bernard and heard that Bella is getting worse. Bernard still works for Zwollo."

"How's that?"

"Didn't you know that Bella had a nervous breakdown? Before she came to Zwollo. That's why they started her there last year – art as sort of therapy."

"I never knew that!" Perhaps better that she hadn't known. Bella, the beautiful redhead she had envied for her secure home life, perhaps even for her looks. How different reality looks now that Hanne knows her background! If Bella had never talked about it at school, she talked about it even less at work. She really never talked. And when she did, it often didn't make sense. Hanne thought that Bella just lived in her own world, without catching on that she had emotional problems. Now she feels sorry for her. But that won't help Bella. No matter how sorry she feels.

"How're your measles coming?" Bert stands patiently under the window, waiting for her answer.

"Fine. We had a new case this morning. That'll ground us for the next four weeks."

The happiness of seeing each other glows in their eyes. He stops fiddling with the coat button. Sticks his hands in his pockets.

"Can't you come outside?" His eyes plead.

"I'm not allowed to spread measles."

"I realize that. But I've had them and so has everyone I know at school. Can't you get out of the house, like perhaps after supper tonight? It gets dark early."

"What d'you have in mind?" Her brain races.

"Kootje invited the gang to her birthday party tonight. We want you to be there too. Can't you find a way to get out?"

The idea presents a tempting challenge. "But what about the measles? I'm a carrier."

"Aw, come off your conscience horse, will you. We've all had it. I checked."

She feels flattered. They want her there. Want *her*. She weighs the obstacles. To get through the front door is impossible. Too heavy. Creaks. Locked. Too many people around to watch. Besides, the sentry across the street. That leaves the back. The sliding-glass door is a lot easier to manage. With the blackout, no one will notice if she walks out after dinner and leaves it unlocked. The fence? The shrubs on the side between them and the neighbors are a cinch. If necessary they might have to get through the hedge in the back, down the incline to the railroad tracks.

"I'd love to come. What time?"

"Around seven?"

"Good. Wait for me outside the fence in the back."

They smile at each other in secret conspiracy. She watches a group of shiny blackshirted boots trample up the sidewalk on the other side of the street. She cringes. The world's best butchers.

"Wait for me to show, in case I'm late, will you?" she says. Her eyes follow the boisterous parade. "Better get going before we draw suspicion."

"All right. See you."

She closes the window and steps back. He waits until the boots stomp out of sight, gives her a last look, then saunters off, leisurely, through the front gate, in the opposite direction, down the incline. His body shrinks and gradually disappears in the wind.

She'll have to tell one of her roommates what she's up to, just in case. Ruth? No. Hanne shrugs. The kid would squeal.

It's an eternity since she's been outside the house. Cooped up with the same people all that time. She can't wait for evening to come.

*

"Hi! Thought I'd never make it," Hanne whispers through the fence. She jumps across, mindful of the steep incline a few feet away.

Bert pulls her down to safety. "You all right?"

"Sure. Been waiting a long time?"

"Nahhh."

They stand close to each other. The bushes around them provide protection. The settling darkness helps. Hanne takes a deep breath to dissolve her inner tension, built up planning her escape from the house. She feels his warm body against hers. A fleeting kiss. She straightens up.

"I took that stupid star off my coat."

They know that if the Nazis catch them for any reason they'll both be in trouble, big trouble, with or without the yellow star.

"Let's get going. I left my bike in the bushes around the corner. You can hop on the luggage rack. Just hold on to me. Kootje's house isn't far – it's in Beethoven Laan. We'll take back alleys."

They saunter to where the bike stands and step out on the dark street, trying to look casual.

"Let's walk slowly away from here to the alley behind the houses," Bert directs, leading his bike. Mindful of the black menace across the street.

"Now."

She climbs on behind him. Bert has padded the steel rack. She appreciates his thoughtfulness in thankful silence. She feels almost safe when she puts her arms around him to hold on as he pedals away.

"It's just a few blocks away. I know a shortcut."

He pedals into the wintry night with the self-confidence of the young native son.

The night sky is mottled, cloud-covered ebony without stars. The air feels cold against her cheek. The city is draped in the black shroud of mourning – the war permits no light. Their eyes get used to the dark in the familiar surrounding. Intermittent searchlights criss-cross the sky in search of the enemy.

Fest steht und treu die Wacht/die Wacht am Rhein, the melody hums through her brain. She wants to shut it off but can't. *Fest steht und treu die Wacht, die Wacht am Rhein.*

Her memory rounds off the refrain. Bert's shaded light under his handlebars throws ghostlike circles on the narrow path ahead. The English will have to cut through this watch, Rhein River or no Rhein River.

No German patrols in these backyard alleys, she assures herself, half-believing. Even without the star on her clothes, her ID has the big J stamped on it. It's insane of her to tempt fate, a crime to endanger Bert's life. She tightens her grip around him. His body's warmth, his closeness is reassuring. To hell with the moffen! The night stands cold, dark and quiet. The searchlight sweeps in regular intervals across the heavens. If only her brain would shut up and leave her alone.

"Here we are," Bert says.

They stop. Hanne looks around, climbs stiffly off the bike, wondering what the people who live behind the blackout curtains in this upper-middle-class neighborhood are like. It's so long ago that she lived this kind of life. The de Hartoghs don't count. Some powerful force has yanked her out. She lives outside the norm. Sidelined.

"You're sure they want me at this party?"

She dances a quiet jig to get the circulation in arms and legs going again.

"Now, don't be silly. I told you that Kootje told me to bring you along."

Might have been out of pity, her inside yells. She doesn't want any pity. She hates to be pitied. The very idea of being considered less than equal appalls her.

Hanne shrugs. Bert will never understand. Even if she could explain her feelings. Which she can't. He may love her, but in his way he pities her too. She can feel it in the fibers of her body. She sighs. It's not easy to be dumped on the wrong side of the tracks, like excess garbage. Trash determined to live on. That it's through no fault of her own, except for a matter of birth, *that's* what makes it doubly frustrating. Innocent prisoners behind bars must feel this way. Caught in a snare others set for you!

They stand within the narrow door entrance. Laughter rings out from inside. She senses Bert's hesitation to ring the bell. He lifts, then drops his outstretched hand again. Then, like an afterthought, he turns to her and folds her into his arms. Sort of clumsy. So they stand, silently, breathing, feeling, wanting. He draws her closer. His lips find hers. A warm spurt surges down her neck into her spine. Spreads. Embers glow through her body. She puts her arms around him and answers his kiss.

"Hanneke."

They cling to each other for a moment that is like an eternity. Locked in an embrace in willful defiance of the world around them. Trapped in a hostile present without a future. Fully aware of the futility of their desires.

Roaring laughter from the other side of the door yanks them back to reality. Hanne's arms grow limp.

"We've got to get inside. They're waiting for us."

He straightens up. Adjusts his clothes. Rings the bell. It's shrill tinkle ends the boisterous roar. Footsteps. Kootje opens the door.

"Hi there! We were worried…"

"No need to. Everything's fine. Even getting out of the house wasn't too difficult. Let's just hope no one finds the unlocked backdoor and locks it before I get back."

"We'll make it a short evening," Kootje says and takes their coats.

Hanne gazes at Kootje, blond, blue-eyed, dainty, much more graceful than the average sturdy Dutch girl. Hanne sees Kootje as the epitome of secure Dutch womanhood. She envies her that self-assured sense of belonging she herself so sorely lacks, that fate denies her.

"It's good to have you here tonight," Kootje says when they enter the living room.

"Yes, it's nice to be here," Hanne agrees. Doubly appreciated because it's a dangerous enterprise. We've jumped only half the hurdles, her mind intrudes with a warning. Don't cut me in half with your fears, she argues with a silent shrug that no one must notice.

They've all come, Miep, Fietje, Hettie, Joop and Frits too. A noisy welcome greets them.

"Haven't seen you since you became a professional," they joke, showing their genuine pleasure at seeing her again. No one mentions measles, or the fact that it's only because of the quarantine that she is still in town. She wonders whether there'll ever be a time when she'll not have to face persecution and deportation at every turn in her life.

"How's school?"

"Well, Zwollo is his strange old self, hu hu hu," Hettie mocks his staccato speech. They burst into laughter.

"His private life is just as odd, if not more so," Hanne volunteers. "I feel sorry for the guy. His wife hates him. Sounds as if she isn't feeding him enough. He's turned his living room into a workplace this winter. The original studio has no heat. The door is closed between us and the dining room, but we can't help hearing every word they say. Lunchtime especially. Perhaps I shouldn't talk about this, but it's too sad." Hanne mimics his speech: "'Hu hu hu, isn't there any more food? hu hu hu,' and she tells him, 'No, there isn't. The children come first.' They have three. Two enemies living together in the same house. After three offspring, mind you. In the morning he comes downstairs, right into the studio to work, while she's having breakfast with the children. Makes you wonder about marriage. Nice kids, though. Wonder how they feel, I mean about it all."

There is a hush in the living room while everyone digests the information.

"Could be that's why he's so kooky," Kootje says.

"Always off in the clouds, somewhere on Puff Nine," Fietje says.

"He's a theosophist. That's probably why, if you ask me," Hanne argues.

"They don't eat meat. They believe in the transmigration of the soul."

"Fine. But after a noisy fight about food the other day during lunch, he returned to the studio with a 'Hu hu hu, must be punishment for having been bad in a former existence,' and goes right on with work. Knows that Eddie and I must have heard every word. Then he stands in a corner and stares off into space, the way he does in school."

"Wonder what he sees out there," Frits muses, loud in the hush.

"He has a whole library on theosophy. Gave me one of his books for my birthday. *JINAJARADAJASA.* I've been reading in it. Difficult. Don't know what it all means. Far-out ideas I need to take with a grain of salt. I don't want to get mixed up by all this metaphysical stuff," Hanne says.

"Hm. True. Meditating on these things can turn you into a crackpot all right, if you're not careful."

"That's the danger with all those religious cults. Look at the Nazis. It's easy to sweep people off their feet when they swallow stuff wholesale and fail to use their critical faculties," Bert says.

Most agree. Only Kootje contends, "I don't know. I think there's something to it, though. Some people see more than others, feel more than others. They're sort of on a higher, supernatural level. I like to dabble with the supernatural myself. It's exciting. I'm convinced there are people who read the future. It's like religion – you either believe, or you don't."

There's a general silence. They look at each other.

Then Kootje starts again, "Matter of fact, I have a Ouija board. We ought to try it out tonight. I've done it before."

Everyone consents except Hanne. Life is bad enough. Why tamper with the unknown? The future is bleak. What good is it to know things before they happen? She looks at Bert for support. But no, he is as hooked on the idea as the others.

Oh, well. She can't be the only spoilsport. She'll have to play along with the crowd. Kootje is already busy setting up the board in the center of the big dining room table. She watches as Kootje lights a candle.

"Come on, let's each take our seat at the table," Kootje says. All ceremony, she sets the candle on the mantelpiece.

They settle around the huge round table. Excitement fills the air. Hanne stares at the Ouija board in the center.

"Everyone ready?" Kootje switches the electric lights off. Only the candle glows in the dimly lit room. Hanne watches her sit down.

"Like a ghost," Hanne thinks, ill at ease. Hushed anticipation permeates the overstuffed room.

"Place both your hands on the table, fingers touching the board," Kootje directs.

They do as directed. Hanne does too. An inexplicable fear overcomes her. She shudders and waits. The silence in the room is palpable with expectation, overwhelming.

"Someone isn't cooperating. Let your doubts go. Concentrate or it won't work," Kootje commands into the hush.

"It must be me. My cynicism," Hanne thinks. She hates to be the Doubting Thomas here. She wills herself to concentrate. Believe in what we're doing? How can I? Like believing in God? She isn't sure of him either. She is tired of her doubts. A million for settling the case. Where is the certainty?

A sudden tug. The board jerks under her fingers. Catches her soul.

"Enter," Kootje commands. Her voice a deep, hollow sound from the grave. All hands follow the jerky dance of the board under their fingers. It rises aloft. Takes their hands along.

"Are you a spirit, you who has entered?" Kootje's voice sounds eerie, hollow, as if from a cave in the candle-lit hush.

The board sails slowly downward, then up again. All hands with it. No one wants to break the spell. Tension mounts throughout the room.

"That means *yes*," Kootje says.

The board takes a small leap. Settles down again.

"Are you a friend?" Kootje pursues.

The board takes another leap in acknowledgement.

"Friendly spirit, are you alive?"

The board remains still.

"Then are you a departed spirit?"

The board jerks aloft to confirm that he is. Or is it a she? Hanne's mind crackles.

"Do we know you, friendly dead spirit?"

The tug on the board confirms the fact.

"Are you a relative of someone present here?"

The board remains still in denial.

"Then do we know you from school?"

The board comes alive, moves slightly a few times, then lies still.

"All right then, are you from Jongenshuis?"

The board jiggles violently, almost leaps out of control.

Hanne shakes with anticipation.

"Are you Arthur Natt?"

They all feel the board stir under their hands. Hanne waits for more. How did Kootje know that name?

"Will there be peace soon?" Kootje asks the question that is on all their minds.

The board tries to rise. Falls limp. Hanne feels her fingers twitch as if they had a life of their own, far removed from her body. Ghosts.

"Are you happy where you are now?" Kootje resumes her queries.

The board remains still. Lifeless. The connection is broken. If there ever was a connection, Hanne's mind interjects. What if someone, perhaps Kootje herself, had moved the board? How can she be sure?

"It's gone," Kootje says. "Something interfered." The others are disappointed.

"It was great going, as long as it lasted," Frits says.

"How did you know to ask for Atze?" Hanne wants to know.

"I don't know. Inspiration. From out there. Sort of leaped at me," Kootje explains.

Hanne is dumbfounded. She thinks of Atze. Caught weeks ago for stealing a gun from an ss. So full of life. Atze. Arthur Natt. Eddie or Werner must've mentioned him to some from school. Have the Nazis killed him? Or was the séance just a hoax?

Her head spins. Her body shivers in the overheated room. Afraid to believe that this spirit, any spirit, can float through this room to connect with a group of live human beings. She doesn't want to believe that mortals can communicate with the dead. It's just another trick of her overly fertile imagination! she decides, suddenly angry with Bert for having brought her here. Did he know what Kootje had in mind before he asked her to come? Soul transmigration? Hindus? Yes, the rabbis too believe in the soul's eternal life. The *Zohar*? What is the difference, really. Only a matter of belief? Religion?

"Wasn't Atze the fellow the ss picked up for stealing a revolver in *Sportsfondsenbad*?" Kootje questions Hanne.

"Yes."

"His message may have been for you," Kootje says.

"What message?"

Hanne is determined to doubt there ever was a spirit, much less a message, whatever the others think. She is going to stick with reality. Life's reality is confusing enough. Why add to the confusion?

"I don't want to believe that he's dead," Hanne explains, fumbling for an excuse for doubting Kootje's spirits. "It's time to head back," she tells Bert.

"Yes, we need to go," he says.

Thank goodness. Hanne draws a deep breath. Bert's agreement is an escape hatch. Kootje can believe whatever she wants.

*

The cool night air feels refreshing after the emotional drain of spiritual communication with the beyond. What a relief! She feels free. Hanne inhales deeply. She climbs behind Bert on the bike.

"Bert, do you believe in spirits?"

"I don't believe they exist in ways we picture them."

"That's funny for you to say, an agnostic."

"The séance tonight seemed real enough. The board moved, didn't it?"

"I don't really know. That's my dilemma. "

"I didn't see anyone moving it."

"That's what makes me wonder. The power of suggestion? Concentration turned into energy of some sort we don't understand? There were so many hands. Someone might have given it a shove, subconsciously, perhaps."

"I don't know. There are so many things beyond the grasp of our understanding."

"True. But I don't want to believe in this hocus-pocus. You've got to draw the line somewhere." She is still shivering from the experience. It has taken much more out of her than she wants to admit, even to herself.

No, she's not going to subordinate herself to matters beyond human comprehension. Logic must prevail. That's essential for survival.

She has seen the Nazis pick people up. Watched ss kick

CHAPTER 8

men in their groins. Heavy, polished boots practice punting on live offertory. Paddywagons were well known, dreaded transport vehicles back in Germany. Their back doors swallow human flesh, maul bones. Once they close behind people, the people are lost and eventually disappear. Transformation smoke curls.

"I can't imagine that Atze is really dead. As long as a person is alive, there's hope." She's stubborn. She insists. Her mind is unable to accept the idea of death.

A truck loaded with Germans rattles down the road. It's smart of Bert to take the back alleys. No telling what these characters would do if they'd see us, the words form in her brain. She keeps them there. Tightens her grip around Bert. Subconsciously seeking protection.

There's a curfew. Bert picks up speed. They reach Jongenshuis. Bert turns off the shaded flashlight on his bike. They stand in the dark by the fence in back of the building.

"Thank goodness," she exhales.

"I'm glad we went," he says quietly. His voice brims with satisfaction, even pride.

Across the street they hear a horde of black shapes stomp out of the mansion. Jeers, roars, loud laughter rend the still night air. The pavement reverberates, echoes danger under the clomp of metal-tipped boots. Bert pushes his bike into the bushes, careful not to make any noise.

"I'll help you jump across," he whispers.

They stand huddled, close by the fence atop the steep incline to the railroad tracks. Embrace each other as if not wanting to let go. Her heart quakes.

She feels more than hears the rustle in the bushes on the side. Sounds that do not belong to where they come from. Strange sounds.

"*Ist da etwas los?*"

"*Ich dachte dass ich da etwas gehört hatte.*"

Male voices. Gruff. What are they doing here? A flashlight beams in the general direction of where they stand. They shrink further back into the brush. Stand rigid. Hold their breath. The light keeps searching. Misses them by a hair. Flickers off.

"*Nee, war doch nichts.*"

The voice sounds satisfied. The flashlight settles a few bushes away from where they stand. The rustle continues. A girl's muffled cry. On the defensive. A male's heavy breathing, faster and faster, a loud groan. A dull thud. The girl, crying. The light dies.

Petrified, Hanne leans back into the fence. She has seen enough in the dim flash before the light goes off. Not one, but several Germans stand around the white flesh of a stark-naked girl, gagged, squirming in the grass between two Germans who are holding her pinned down. A third kneels over her, his fly open, his dark-purple protuberance between his hands, ready to straddle her. Several others stand behind them, egging him on to get going. Waiting for their turns. Hanne remembers the girl's eyes – white globes. A silent scream for help. Her milky flesh below the black uniform a ghastly chiascuro in the night. The white armbands with the red old Indian fertility sign a diabolical excuse for the crime.

Shocked, Hanne turns away from Bert. Further back into the bushes. More shouted commands desecrate the night. Heavy panting again, accelerating, like a locomotive picking up speed. Groans, a faint whimper, another thud. Sounds repeat, once, twice, three times. Hanne stops counting. Her eyes adjust. She can see the shadows move in and out of the dark recess.

She wants the nightmare to go away. This mix of brutal power and carnal pleasure. Where does one end and the other begin? Is this act of animal gratification the ultimate goal of love? An exercise of power? Hate? She suppresses a rasp in her throat. Repulsion in her stomach area. Bert is close to her. She feels his body. Warm, protective.

The girl is quiet now. A prone sacrifice to German bestiality. Does she realize the futility of her resistance? Or has she passed out? Hanne shudders. There, by the grace of God. Pure luck that she…

Where is love? No, there must be more to it, she decides. Her relationship with Bert, his caring, his consideration, his warmth, the gentleness in his touch. That is different entirely. Self-gratification? Sure. But real love also means the wish to consider, to satisfy the feelings of the other at the same time. Hanne reaches for Bert's hand in the dark. Feels his reassuring pressure. Their world is worlds apart from what is happening just a few steps away.

She hears them argue. Some want another turn. An eternity passes. The two huddle, immobile. Wait by the fence.

At long last the boots clomp off in the other direction. German clomps, wane, dissolve in the distance. The girl is left alone on the ground. Hanne hears her muffled sobs as she frees herself of the gag. Her legs seem bloody, but that may be an optical illusion in the dark. Hanne moves, wants to help her. Bert holds her back.

"Are you nuts? Don't get involved. You don't know who she is."

They watch the shadow of the girl limp away.

"I feel like gagging," Hanne says.

"Don't compare beasts with humans."

The night hangs dark and indifferent about them. The starless sky is full of unanswered questions. There's no one to solve them. She shivers in the cold night air. She hates to leave. This may very well be their last time together. They press close, unwilling to let go, wishing to extend the other's presence into eternity.

"I better get inside," she says at long last.

"I'll wait here. If you're not back in a few minutes I'll assume that you're all right. Take care."

A fleeting kiss. He helps her across the fence. She jumps down, hits ground with a thud.

"You okay?"

"Yes. Be careful," she whispers into the night.

"You too."

Her heart boils over as she makes her way to the building.

"Please, let the door be unlocked the way I left it," she prays, a request to someone who wants to grant her wish. The door gives way, moves aside, slides open to her push. A heartfelt sigh of relief. Thank goodness! She squeezes through the crack. Slides the door shut in the opposite direction from inside. Locks the latch quickly, careful not to make a noise.

I made it! She slides to the floor. Sits there, motionless, leaning against the piano. Lets her built-up tension dissolve in the protective stillness of the large room. She does not know how long she sits there. Her mind is a scramble of thoughts, feelings, wishes. Unfinished arguments. A cry for normalcy. *Help!*

She can't sit here all night. Pulling herself together, she tiptoes upstairs with a fervent prayer that no one hears the creaking boards of the staircase.

"Without me Bert is safe. He knows the city well enough to get home without being seen."

The attic is hushed. Everyone is asleep. She undresses and drops into her bed, though she can't fall asleep. The events of the evening keep rushing through her mind, keeping her awake. She tosses and turns. Watches the horizon turn pale in the little window between the slanted rafters before she finally falls into a fitful, haunted sleep.

Chapter 9

December 1942. Cold, windy, somber, swathed in dull-gray. From inside Jongenshuis they watch the drenching rains solidify to icicles on buildings, shrubs, trees. Harden into sleet on the ground. The last measles case is a week old and improving. They pray for someone to get sick to continue the quarantine. No such luck so far. Those who never had the sickness before have come down with it by now. The rest are immune.

They have been housebound for weeks and are getting on each other's nerves. They follow their routine. Do their daily chores. Then crowd around the little iron stove in the dining hall. It's the only warm spot in the building outside the kitchen, where only kitchen personnel are allowed. The tiny heater does its best to sputter its coke-fed heat within a few feet's radius. The rest of the large room remains cold. Eager beavers secure their places in its vicinity early in the day. The rest sit nearby as close as possible, bundled up to keep warm. Trade places as soon as someone closer to the stove needs to leave.

Cut off from the rest of the world, they have no news except from the official newscast or the administrative personnel. Whatever the source, the news is depressing. Hanne, Werner and Eddie stick together. Paint, draw, design, study anatomy books to keep up with their profession. Comment on one another's efforts. Help each other. Try to raise their spirits.

Der Wind hat mir ein Lied erzählt
von einem Glück unsa. a.a.a. agbar schön
er weiss was meinem Herzen fehlt
für wen es schlägt und glüht.
er weiss für wen,

Hanne sings with feeling Zarah Leander's tune to herself.

er weiss für we. e.e.n.

She holds the note, all soul.

Komm, komm... Ach,

She can't remember the next line, but hums the melody. The disappointment of waiting in vain for the beloved.

Der Wind, der Wind.

She lets her voice trail off the way she has seen Zarah Leander do it in the movie. A German movie way back at home. What was the name of it? She can't remember. She loves Zarah Leander's voice! She has seen every Zarah Leander movie. And that long, thick red mop of hair. So unlike her own baby-fine hair that will never hold a hairpin. Never keep a hairdo in place. Tiniest whiff of wind blows it apart. No, Zarah is not as rail thin as the American movie stars. But her voice! Dark, Full-throated. Mysterious. Full of longing. Hanne is lost in memory. Humming. *Der Wind.i.i.i.n.d.*

It's such a romantic song of love. Real love. Longing. That voice makes the song.

"Zarah Leander? I had her records at home. This one too,"

Ditta hums behind her. Off-key, as usual. Right into her ear. It hurts.

"We ought to ask Herr Felsenthal whether he has this record. We could play it on the gramophone."

Mr. Felsenthal has joined the staff recently. Hired to keep them occupied, especially the boys. To prevent mischief between boys and girls. He came right after the big stink with Horst Hamm and Rosie. When Rosie thought she was pregnant and they put Horst to sleep in the attic as punishment for messing with her. After a few days of anxiety and Rosie crying, she found out that she wasn't pregnant after all. But the incident spooked Dr. Wolf, the staff and the Committee. Horst is still up in the attic. Made himself a nice private corner. Curtained off.

Frau Felsenthal and their two boys visit often. They live nearby.

"I think the melody is from a ballet by Delius *The Girl with the Enamel Eyes*. I'm not sure. We ought to ask her, not him," Ditta suggests.

"The Felsenthal family hasn't been in the house since the measles."

"Zarah Leander is Goebbels's girlfriend."

"Really? He has a wife and five or six children!"

"I think she's married, too."

"But she's Swedish!"

That's a definite plus in Hanne's esteem. The Goebbels connection throws a damper on her admiration. Hair and all. Except that voice. What a waste. That gorgeous voice misplaced on a Nazi floozie.

Der Wind...

Hanne hums the tune. What a shame.

The longing remains.

Longing. Love. Is she in love? With Bert? She is torn. Between romantic longing and reality. She closes her eyes. Her body says one thing. Her mind another. Bert is no Adolf Wohlbrück. Or Robert Taylor. Or Clark Gable. Now there's a man. A man. The way he defeated Captain Bligh! Dream and longing fuse when she closes her eyes.

*   *   *

With a sense of foreboding Hanne sits by the window between the slanted rafters in the attic. In defiance of the house rule not to go upstairs during the day. Rules are not that strictly enforced these days of quarantine and carbolic acid smells.

"Rules are made to be broken. A person needs some time to herself," her brain eggs her on. The old story of *My Room*. She still has that silver coffee spoon with the Bergen aan Zee coat of arms.

Foreboding, bad conscience, memories, reflections on life.

At least some quiet! Away from the din of crowd-filled rooms downstairs. She fills her lungs with fresh air that surges through the open window. She watches as trains change tracks down below, hears their sharp squeaks that drown other noises. The railroad station is always busy. Trains puff in, shriek to a halt. Passengers exit, others enter. The stationmaster lifts his round red sign. The trains roll on. Promise the next destination. People bustle in a steady stream. Laugh. Shout. Hellos and goodbyes. Why can't she be a part of that happy, careless, unconcerned humanity? Why has she to be separated? Set apart? She gazes down at the tracks, iron lines in parallels that meander, connect, branch out, float together. Continue as solitary entities in pairs. Always in pairs. Like human lives. Where do they lead? Who connects? Who disconnects? Who guides their destinies? Is there a guide? A brain behind all this confusion?

She wonders about God. Why doesn't he listen to Jewish prayers? Can't he hear? Understand that we need help? See what the Nazis are up to? It's impossible to fight them alone. Does he care? Whose side is he on, anyway?

Has she provoked this disaster? That nagging feeling of guilt.

Since last Yom Kippur, the Day of Atonement. She remembers home. How proud she was at age twelve when she fasted all day through for the first time. Dad said half the day is enough for her age. But she made it, from sundown to sundown, like an adult. It isn't that difficult if you put your mind to it. Don't think of food. Push the thought into another compartment of your brain and lock it shut for the day. Think of other things. Of course, it's hard when everyone else talks food. How hungry he or she is. She must change the subject. That helps. To the movies, or the weather.

But this past Yom Kippur something went grossly wrong. During morning services everything was fine. She forgot the fast. That splitting headache began during mincha services, the afternoon prayer. Faint at first. Some knock-knocks over both eyes. She tried to imagine something else. Forget the *chazan*. His singing. Only she couldn't. His voice pounded inside her head like a hammer crashing on steel. A million clangs kept resounding in her head. Steel on steel. Clang, boom, clang, boom. Faster, faster, and faster still. A mad rhumba between her eardrums. An evil ring dance in knock-knocks. Madness incarnate between her eyes. Her pupils went blind in fiery flashes. Lightning rods zigzagged under her closed eyelids. Stabs on her brain. She felt nauseous. Gagged. Nothing but bitter bile. Green bile. Acrid yuck-yuck spilled across her tongue, filled her mouth. She spit. Then suddenly van Gelder was beside her. Her voice filtered through excruciating stab wounds into her consciousness. From distant, far off, outer space.

"Hanne, you don't have to continue if you don't feel well."

"I feel lousy."

"I can see that." Van Gelder had held Hanne's head between her fleshy hands. Soft. Warm. Caring.

"I'll get some milk for you. A few crackers."

"No. I've always fasted. Easily. I'm a grown-up," she had babbled. Cut to pieces with unknown desires. She pressed against her temples to stop the madness between them. To give in would be weakness.

"There's no need to torture yourself. Even the Rabbis say so. I'm going to get you something," van Gelder resolved. Disappeared without another word.

Then she was back. Hanne heard the tray set on the table. Her mind wanted to refuse.

"I'm not hungry. Honestly I'm not."

"No. You're beyond that. Your system is. Hungry, I mean."

Van Gelder held the glass and Hanne sipped the milk in small glugs. Slowly.

"I shouldn't…" She said as she nibbled the crackers. Cautiously. The sky was going to crash down on her for sure. She lay back on the cot.

She remembers how the pounding in her head slowly stopped. Her vision gradually cleared. Her headache went. Miracle of miracles. Don't fast and God saves you? She has a bad conscience and doesn't want to be punished.

* * *

She has tried to put the incident out of her mind. She couldn't help getting a headache. The Rabbis teach that you don't have to fast if you're ill. Or pregnant. Dad had said so. Mr. Israel said so in school. Van Gelder was right. But she can't help it. Having eaten on Yom Kippur haunts her. From her window seat she prays, "Good Lord, don't punish me for something I couldn't help! Don't send me off to who knows where! And punish all the Jews with me!!! It's unfair!!!" Her inside cries out. But her screams stay locked inside her.

"Others do worse things without getting punished! Aren't you supposed to be the Lord of mercy? Lord of Justice?"

She sits by the window and wonders about her God. Why doesn't he listen to our prayers for help? Has he closed up shop? It looks as though the Nazis have the answer. Not the Jews. No, everyone but the Jews. God is unfair.

"You have broken trust with the very people who trust you.

No. Make that trusted you. Not just once, but throughout the millennia. What kind of a God are you, anyway?"

* * *

The doorbell shrills, shaking the attic walls. Pulls her back to the present. Must be the mailman. It's that time of day. She hopes for news from her parents. In her last letter she told them about the roundups. *We may have to change address*, she had written. She couldn't be more explicit. Mail sent abroad is censored at the border. People actually sit there reading letters. Then strike over everything that sounds suspect. Don't they know in Sweden what is going on here? What about the rest of the world?

* * *

"Hanne! Hanne!" Van Gelder's voice echoes up to her.

Hanne walks to the landing. Tries to think of a plausible excuse for disregarding the rules. "I'm up here."

"There's a telegram for you."

She bounces down the stairs, three steps at a time. She can't keep up with her feet. Signs the mailman's receipt. Then she holds the yellow paper in her hands. Shivering.

"Thank you," she breathes toward the mailman. He is already halfway outside. The heavy door slams shut behind his blue uniform.

Out of breath, her fingers jittery, she can't tear it open fast enough. The black letters dance before her eyes.

ALL ARRANGED FOR YOUR SWEDISH CITIZENSHIP. MUTTI.

What does this mean? Her heart pounds a jig. Her knees want to buckle. Not now! She takes a deep breath. Tries to compose herself. Ruth appears in the kitchen door. The kid is on kitchen duty this week. Hanne gives her the telegram. Van Gelder, the kitchen staff, the youngsters all gather around.

"What do you make of it?"

The sisters gaze at each other. Hanne shrugs.

"This may help us somehow. Let's see what Dr. Wolf says." Excitement rushes through her bones. They speculate.

Dr. Wolf reads the telegram, slowly, thoughtfully. Scratches his big head of silver hair with his long manicured fingernails. He looks at the girls.

"If you're Swedish citizens you're no longer under German jurisdiction."

His voice trails off. The very thought is too much. He looks at the other grown-ups around and smiles.

"But you need proof. More than this telegram, I suppose. That may take some time. Hold on to the telegram for now."

Chastened, Hanne runs upstairs to put the telegram into her suitcase where all the things not necessary for daily use hibernate. Well, this sheet of paper is a special treasure. Another buried dream?

*   *   *

December 10, 1942. Five AM. The bell rings through the house. Loud. Demanding attention. Impossible to ignore.

"What's the matter?"

Men's voices. Boots clomp the stairs, doors slam. The ss is here to round them up. Despite the quarantine. Only those sick in bed may stay, along with the administration. They have an hour to pack their gear. Include the two woolen blankets from their beds, compliments of their Jewish benefactors who years ago tried to save Jewish children from the Nazis.

They pack in silence. Too sleepy, too intimidated, too shocked to wonder where they are going. They pack. Three ss stand in the hallway downstairs and bellow commands. They have a list. Dr. Wolf stands next to them. Freda the kitchen genius from Frankfurt is dead. Committed suicide during the night. Twenty-five years old. The others have more immediate matters to worry about. Hanne runs down with her telegram. Confers with Wolf who shows it to the black trinity. They look at it. More discussions.

Hand it back to Dr. Wolf. Suggest that Hanne show it to the reg-istration people on arrival at their destination. She and Ruth need to get ready. Come along.

Hanne goes back upstairs. Packs. Her arms are leaden. She is leaden. Unable to move. Her suitcase is full. One by one the youngsters line up on the black and white marble tiles in the hall downstairs. Black uniforms, lists in their hands, shout. Read names. Upstairs on her bed, Hanne's head swims. She cannot get her suitcase shut. Her stomach flutters in an uproar. The old lump spreads its tentacles behind her ribs. Cramps. Stings. Her body refuses to cooperate. Her brain is a hollow void. Empty. She sits down on the bed beside her suitcase. The single lightbulb over-head stings in her eyes. The room grows hazy. The hollow in her head has tightly drawn curtains that shut the light out. Far away she hears voices pierce through her semiconsciousness below the drawn blackout drape.

"*Einz, zwei, drei, vier, fünf, sechs, sieben… vierzehn… Achtun-dzwanzig… zweiunddreissig… Neunundvierzig… sechsundfünfzig. Einer fehlt.*"

A short pause. The count begins again.

"*Einer fehlt.*"

Pause. Mumbles. Shouts.

"Hanne. Hanne is missing."

Hobnailed boots reverberate in her head. Dull, hollow echoes against worn wood. Deliberate. Insistent. Louder with each tread. Clomping upstairs. Getting nearer. Coming close. The black uni-form fills the small door of the bedroom. The red crooked cross on white armband stings her eyes.

"*Sind Sie fertig?*"

Hanne sees the revolver dangling from his belt. Her eyes flash burning heatwaves Her legs are jelly, ready to fold.

"I can't get my suitcase shut," she wheezes toward the door.

He steps inside the room. Bends over her bed.

"I'll close it." He sits on the suitcase. Clicks it shut in no time. "There."

Her mouth is dry. His presence fills the room where empty cots gape. The straw sacks bulge bare in odd-shaped loneliness. He stares down at her.

I can't go on, she thinks darkly. She needs to wangle her way out. Impossible. No matter what. The guns. The power. That's how they control us. Everybody.

"I don't feel well." She tells him the truth.

"Gehen Sie 'runter," he commands.

She glances at his closed face. Mouth a shrunken line. Blue porcelain eyes bulge. Lifeless globes in his face. Circumscribed, dull vision. Like the dead eyes of her Käthe Kruse doll back home years ago, when she broke the doll's porcelain face and the double eyes fell out. Glared up at her, unseeing pale blue orbs on a lead rod. Ruth had covered her eyes and run away, stricken with fear.

Hanne stands up, straightens up on legs that want to wobble. Steadies herself. Pulls her suitcase off the bed. Her legs begin to propel themselves forward. Step by unthinking step. An automaton. Right, left, right, left, right.

The uniform stomps behind her, metal spurs clang a steady clop, clop on wooden stairs. The revolver bangs in ringing dissonance. Dislodged. She wants to run. Escape this madness. But she continues to walk, step by step by step, down the stairs, first the narrow servants' staircase from the attic, then the broad stairs from the first floor master suites down to the dining and living rooms. Turns a sharp left. Treads the familiar black and white marble tiles in the hallway where the others stand lined up by the door. Three to a row. They watch her come, join them. Next to Ruth. She is the last in line.

"Your name is Hanne Kalter?" The blackbooted uniform asks. Checks off his list with a yellow pencil.

"That's it," he reports to the others.

Dr. Wolf and the other staff stand on one side of the line-up.

The other black uniform calls roll again. Checks all names off on his list with finality. Counts. Fifty-seven. Okay. Ready.

"Make sure you show your telegram to the authorities in charge once you reach your destination," Wolf and van Gelder remind her.

Vaguely she wonders, what destination? Where? When? Apparently the telegram is worthless. She must find a way.

The three count again. Fifty-seven.

"*Fertig! Los!*" The leader bellows into the air from up front to no one in particular. Wolf, Sussmann, van Gelder stand aside, tears in their eyes. Secretly delirious to be left where they are.

"*Marsch! Los!*" the leader shouts.

The group jerks slowly forward. Behind two black uniforms. Through the door. Out into the wintry street. It's cold. The third black uniform draws up the rear.

Like stupid sheep led to slaughter. Robots rule the universe. Empty thoughts flash through the empty room that is Hanne's brain. A void. Out of commission. Non-functioning. Dead.

*   *   *

The group inches forward, behind two black uniforms with armbands, four boots attached. Hanne sleepwalks. As in a trance. Aware of the third uniform behind her. His boots clang the dirty snow-covered asphalt.

Like a herd of sheep, flashes again through that empty space in her head.

She is aware of moving shadows outside herself. No, these are real people. They line the street and watch the flock being herded past. In rows of three. Horsey, Gerd and Eddie walk ahead of her. Werner, Ruth and she bring up the rear. The world is a hazed daze. Hanne's legs move forward, step by step by step. Hanne Kalter. Automaton. An empty shell. Devoid of will. Hanne doubleforked. Split in two. Hanne watching from a distance what Hanne's body does. A robot without soul. A puppet on fiendish strings.

Like a zoo, another flash.

A chill wind blows up the incline of the street. They walk

down. The streets are slippery with ice. Yesterday's snow lies in dirty heaps by the wayside. Reality suspended.

They turn the corner under the bridge to Velperplein. Cross the plaza. Reach the school where Arnhem's Jews are being collected. Those who escaped the first roundup. A ten-minute walk under normal circumstances. The door opens. They enter. Pass through the door. Slowly inside. Leave eternity behind.

∗　∗　∗

An unripe ss man orders them to sit down in one corner of the great hall. The group huddles together for companionship, emotional flickers between siblings no one can dispense with. Line up their suitcases next to them on the floor. They sit down. Listless. Stare at the other Jews brought inside. Unwilling companions.

"Hey, you there," one of the ss bellows.

"He wants you," Werner says to Hanne. Hanne looks up.

"Yes, you there." She sees the uniform. White rose-ringed fleshy fingers point at her. Slicked-down ashblond hair.

Hanne gets up, sleepwalks toward the uniform. He leans against the white wall, nonchalant, hands stuck in his pockets. He ogles her. Iceblue rocks behind half-closed pallid eyelids. All superiority.

"You. Get me one of those chairs from over there." His head motions toward a stack of folding chairs at the other end.

Hanne feels an urge to kick this supercilious, bleach-topped specter. Too weary to entertain the thought further she slips the thought into the empty space behind her eyes. It's useless. Bites her lips in frustration.

"*Dally, dally. Wird's bald werden?*" he eggs her on. Watches her squirm.

She gets the folding chair, drags it over and leans it, still folded, next to him against the wall. Careful not to bang it. Turns in a rush to get back to her group.

"Unfold it," he orders into her back.

Hanne blushes with fury. Does stiffly what she is told. Their eyes meet, cherry black and steelblue hate between them. She opens the folded chair. Fury incarnate. Puts it down. Then remains rooted to the spot.

"Bring it over here," he commands from two steps away. His voice an icy hammer.

Her hands unsteady, she inches the chair in his direction. He stretches one leg and pulls the chair the remaining half-inch to where he stands. Sits down. Stares into the Jewish crowd before him. A blank stare that doesn't see her.

Hanne picks her way back to her friends. A few friendly slaps of comfort on her back acknowledge her predicament. Ruth pats her hand. No one speaks. They will have to take these humiliations in stride. Hard as it is. Fear stalks the hall. It's palpable. Solid.

The Jongenshuis group is not the first to arrive in the school on that tenth of December. Other Jews, entire families, are already sitting among their last belongings when they shuffle in. More arrive steadily as the day progresses. On into the night. The entrance doors of the school open and close continuously with new arrivals – old, middle-aged, young. Healthy. Feeble. Sick. It makes no difference. Mothers with tiny babies. Infants cry, children run about, scream. Fathers scold frightened offspring. Mothers shout. Or try to soothe. Hand out the food provisions brought along for that uncertain, indeterminate journey. An icy wind blows in every time the doors open for the new arrivals. Pandemonium reigns. Doomsday for Arnhem Jewry. The ss lord it over all.

"They're rounding up the left-overs," Eddie says. Hanne nods apathetically.

"Except those who're in hiding."

"And the Jewish Council. They're still here."

The noise around her is unbearable. Her limbs are stiff. The floor is hard, cold. Her back aches, her eyes burn. Her body one suppressed scream. She stares at the young mother on the floor breastfeeding her baby.

In a fog, she watches another ss shift arrive in the gray morning hours. Come to relieve the previous crew. A group of Arnhem volunteers dispenses lukewarm brown liquid they call "coffee" out of habit. With a roll. Breakfast for the involuntary charges. Prisoners without a cause. No one feels much like eating.

"But you don't know where your next meal will come from. Or even if it will come."

Horsey lumbers over first for his share. The others follow. Stand in line. A break. Better take what is offered. At least the warm water warms your guts after the cold, sleepless, destructive night.

Hanne thinks of her parents far away in a free country. Her hand reaches into her pocketbook to feel the telegram. Make certain it's still there. She thinks of the mess Ruth and she are in. Ruth dozes next to her. The injustice of it all…

Where is God in all this? Is He in exile too? Or merely on vacation?

Chapter 10

February 1943. Frostbitten winds howl across the northern Dutch province of Drenthe, sweep clouds of black grit aloft in their frigid wake. In the center of this Dutch nowhere lies Camp Westerbork, far away from civilization and at a safe distance from society's economic activities.

Originally the Dutch government had established the camp to house the flood of Jewish refugees surging across the border from Germany. Steeped in humanitarian tradition, the Dutch had accepted the refugees. But times were bad, so they did their best to exclude the German Jews from the Dutch economy. Hence the camp. Here the Jews were fed and allowed to exist in small barracks to wait for visas abroad or for conditions in Germany to improve. Of course, neither Queen Wilhelmina nor her government had anticipated the German invasion and the occupation that followed.

The Nazis found the ready-made camp convenient and designated it a *Sammellager*. Thus Westerbork became a collection depot from which the Germans transported all the Jews from Holland to some destination in the East. No one knew where. For the camp inmates *The East* is a hazy, dreaded concept. Nazi heaven. Or Hell. Try to delay the ride by all means. Any means.

*   *   *

Sand is everywhere. It grits between their teeth, lodges in their throats, itches their eyes, cakes their eyelashes, clumps up in their ears. Sand permeates their hair, their clothes, their shoes, the folds of their skin.

Sandstorms are a permanent feature of Drenthe winter. Sandstorms have been whirling nonstop ever since their arrival after a depressing ride through flat Dutch country. Prisoners, separated from their fellow prisoners because of their continuing quarantine. Insulated in the train compartment, some young ss punks hardly older than they are supervised them, mere boys in uniforms indoctrinated with blind hate, convinced of their superiority. They are Jews, second-class humans, open to any provocation, unable to strike back. It's revolting to be at their mercy.

Mute, they see the country fly past their window, snowgray, flat, a barren, wintry landscape that matches their mood. A slow drizzle against the dusty pane turns to snowflakes. Iridescent teardrops shiver in the wind, melt on the glass panes.

In the late afternoon the train jerks to a halt in snowblown no-man's-land. Their cars unhooked, they watch the rest of the regular train disappear on its scheduled route. Abandoned, they stand for hours under guard on the platform. Finally a locomotive chugs in and pulls their cars the short distance into the camp.

They're caught. Barbed wire surrounds them. Guards in watchtowers watch. ss bellow, organize, disappear. Low, heavy scuds flee across a leaden sky, the howling wind in merciless pursuit. A few bent human shapes, dull-gray, scurry between dull-brown barracks in the distance. Inmates appear, take over from the Nazis. German Jews all, they guide the new arrivals to the administration building, offices run by the Jewish Council. German Jews they too. Gruff, harsh Germanic officialdom even here. Another German Jew comes and separates the Jongenshuis group from the rest of the new arrivals because of the quarantine. They are the last to be processed and catalogued into the camp. German efficiency. Hanne makes certain that Ruth stays by her side. She has to take care of her sister. When their turn comes to register, Hanne shows her parents' yellow telegram. She watches the heated tussle on the other side of the table. Pomposity in action.

"Have you heard from your parents since you got this?"

"It came the day before yesterday. My parents don't know our new address... yet."

"It came in the nick of time. They don't know we're here," Ruth puts in.

"Right."

Another conference on the other side of the rickety table.

"With this we'll keep you here for the time being. Set you aside. Your group will be under quarantine for the next two weeks anyway. Longer if there's another case. Let me make a copy for the *Kommandantur*."

She disappears, then returns with the original.

"We'll keep the copy. You take good care of the original. Don't lose it."

Their formal registration is over. They are the last for the day. The others are gone, dispersed through the camp. Hans Hellmuth leads them to their new living quarters. Barrack 65. Their temporary home, he says. For the quarantine period.

"The registration people all speak German," Hanne says.

"Yes. Including me," says Hellmuth. "All Germans. No Dutch."

He means German Jews. The *real* Germans are in uniform. They live outside the barbed wire fence.

They wonder why German Jews run things here. But they don't question this fact. German Jews ran Jongenshuis. That was logical. They took care of German Jewish children.

Like all the other communal barracks, Number 65 has two wings that spread from either side of the common entrance in the center front. Each sex has its own wing. Men in the left wing, women in the right. Each a large hall with several rows of three-tiered metal bunks. A few tables are set up in the space behind the entrance for eating purposes. At the end of the hall is the washroom consisting of several military cold-water faucets over a large zinc tub running along the wall and three open toilets. In their case, they are to live in the left wing of Barrack 65, set aside these days just for the Jongenshuis children under quarantine. The occupants of the right wing stare at them as Hellmuth walks them through to their new place. For the next two weeks. Perhaps more.

They take possession. Divide the large hall into two sections, girls in front, boys in back. Set a schedule for each group to use the bathroom. It's the easy stuff because there are far more beds than they need.

Hanne and Ruth choose a bunk in the window aisle. Hanne feels claustrophobic in the lower beds and settles on a top bunk. Ruth takes the bottom bunk. They pile their suitcases and other stuff in the middle. At the boys' end of the wing, Hans Markbreiter and Jackie Bergmann argue furiously about something. Hans Hellmuth appears out of nowhere.

"Hi. I'm the barrack elder in sixty-five. Just checking, how you're settling in."

"Oh, fine," the two agree," sudden buddies.

The whole group gathers around Hellmuth with questions.

"Where can we put our stuff?"

Hellmuth produces a corrective smirk.

"You have plenty of space around here. Keep the small things you need every day on top of your bed. The rest goes into your suitcases under your bunks. That's the rule."

They don't know yet that their present accommodations are an unheard-of luxury under normal circumstances in the camp where every inch of living space is at a premium, fought over with all the energy camp inmates can muster. Only much later will they come to appreciate the privilege of having had the entire wing all to themselves. A mere fifty-seven youngsters. But by then they are an integrated part of the camp.

Separated for now, the new camp tenants look at their new

leader in silence. Hellmuth continues his information. "Now. Let me explain the general schedule around here. The siren calls at five o'clock in the morning. At five thirty AM I come with breakfast from the main kitchen. Six AM the siren goes off for roll call in front of your barrack." He stops to lend emphasis to his instructions. "Now, everyone has to be there. In line! On time!" He stops again. His eyes burrow into theirs, one after another. "That's when you get your work assignments for the day. Lunch is at your work site, wherever that is. You work until five PM. Then return to your barrack. At six PM I roll in with your dinner from the main kitchen. That's about it."

"Of course, none of that applies now while you're quarantined. You're not to leave this hall until the quarantine is over. Meanwhile I'll just come with your food."

"How about mail?"

"After chow in the evening."

Hellmuth grins, heaves his body off the empty cot on which he's sitting, relieved to have explained his official functions. Hanne expects him to leave. To her surprise he settles down to smalltalk instead.

"I'm from Berlin. Any Berliners here?"

There is instant camaraderie between Werner Levy, Peter Marcuse, some others and their barrack elder.

"*Icke Ballinner*?" Gerd Perl joins in. They exchange common memories in their lingo that bind in this place of displacement. There are Margot Kneidel and her friend Greta, also Berliners. Then Ditta cuts in with her well-known Viennese tirades, her love for *her Maxerl*, which made her come to Holland instead of going to England.

"And now I'm stuck here. And I haven't seen him even once," she wails, fluttering her dark eyelashes. As if Hellmuth could help.

"Seems that Germans run the place," Hanne cuts in. She means German Jews, not the real kind. She's noticed this before. The idea is to get to the facts.

Her question strikes a raw nerve. Hellmuth squirms, ill at ease. It's obvious he doesn't like to talk about the German Jews' leading position in the camp.

"Well, yes. Look, we've managed this place ever since they established it. The Dutch government felt that we were a threat to their economy, so they put us here into this nowhere to keep us out of their precious Dutch life. A threat to the Dutch economy," Hellmuth scoffs with the general bitter feelings of the refugees.

They sympathize. Hanne thinks of her experiences with the Goldbergs, the deHartoghs, and Ruth's deWinters.

"Who lives in those small cottages at the far side of the camp? I saw them when we came in," Werner wants to know.

"My, you're observant. It was almost dark."

"Just curious."

The youngsters nod. Walking past, they've all noticed them. Buildings much smaller than the large barracks they inhabit.

"Those are the barracks they built for us, the original refugees."

"Who lives there now?"

"We still do. The German refugees live in them. Families. They're the Old-timers. The ones that run the place for the Germans outside."

"And you?"

"Me too."

Hellmuth leaves. They look after him. Someone to envy?

"I'm sure none of us minds, *gel*?" Eddie nods behind Hellmuth's retreat.

Of course no one does. Why should they? German origin will be another feather in their own caps. They can use all the feathers that flutter their way.

The youngsters settle into camp routine without being part of it. Hellmuth comes at regular intervals with food. Morning, noon, evening. No mail just yet. No measles either. They are still a unit for another two weeks.

Then they break up. No longer a group, they dissolve. Become regular citizens of the camp. The boys stay to integrate into the male left wing. The girls take their suitcases and move over to the women's side. Disperse throughout the right wing of Barrack 65 wherever they can find an empty place. Hanne finds an empty top bunk by the window again. Ruth claims the center bunk underneath her. The bottom happens to be vacant for their suitcases. Odd stuff like towel, soap, toothbrush, eating utensils, remains on their bed. Bottom bunks are usually reserved for the older generation. The worst part of this move is the far greater lack of private space. And their integration into the workforce. Hellmuth is still the barrack elder.

*   *   *

It doesn't take them long to feel the deep rift between German and Dutch Jews within the camp.

"It's basically the envy of the haves toward the have-nots," Hanne informs Ruth.

"Sure. The former have-nots have turned things upside down. They're on top now."

"Changed pedigree. That's the reason for the gloat."

Westerbork, they learn, with its German-speaking population was the ideal site when the Nazi authorities went looking for a place for the *Sammellager* they wanted to establish: a camp away from civilization where the Nazis could collect all the Jews, and others. Could cart people away without much fanfare. All they had added were the large communal barracks where they now house the transitory occupants for further transportation to an unknown destination. Then surround the place with a barbed wire fence and manned watchtowers at strategically located intervals to keep them securely locked up. And run a rail connection right into the center of the camp. Outside the fence is *The Kommandantur*, their own administrative building from where the Kommandant and the other Nazis reign supreme.

The ss run the camp with thorough German efficiency from outside the fence and the help of the German Jews inside. The latter are the *long-term-residents*. Speaking the same language helps. Set aside from transport on order of the Kommandant, the long-termers deliver. *Divide and rule.* The ss demand delivery of a set amount of live cargo each week. Needless to say, the system is open to graft and preferential treatment of all kinds imaginable. And the most intense hatred between German and Dutch Jews.

"There isn't much love lost between victims and victims. Bloodbrothers," Hanne says.

"We German Jews have been victims since 1933. Some came from the *St. Louis*. No one cared. No one helped us. Now it's the Dutch's turn."

"They weren't occupied until 1940."

"The Dutch call the Germans arrogant, impervious, ungrateful."

"Well. Listen to them. The way they carry on. Bark their commands. They sound like the real Teutons. Disgusting."

"Yeah. Real *Wichtigtuers*."

"Pompous asses."

"Listen, it's unfair to blame their misery on the Dutch," Hanne says.

"Well, what can you do?" Hellmuth shrugs and beats a quick retreat.

Hanne finds the German Jews' argument vindictive. Actually downright criminal.

"The group doesn't need to go quite that far. We're still Jews."

"The Dutch pitied us, Gentiles and Jews alike. They provided an asylum. Only that wasn't exactly what we needed. We needed rehabilitation. Needed to regain our self-esteem after years of persecution. We needed our humanness. A sense of hope for the better. And that never came. The Dutch said they couldn't afford us. And with the occupation the tide turned."

"You ought to appreciate belonging to the privileged class here. Use your common sense."

It's a powerful argument. Hanne must agree. It means survival. For the moment at least. Still…

"It's a disgrace, Jews hating each other under these circumstances. We're all in the same boat."

"Yes. Only where your life is concerned you try to keep your neck attached to your shoulders as long as possible. At any cost."

Those were Hellmuth's words the first day they moved in. They still ring in her ears. Those two weeks in quarantine gave the Jewish Council in the administration building enough time to get the Jongenshuis youngsters a stamp of deferral on their ID's.

"You're not going to be on the list next Tuesday. That's the day the weekly train comes and leaves."

Hanne stares at the floor. Yes. Life is a game. A cruel game of playing for time. Survival. No holds barred.

The Nazis hogged them all, those ideals. They spout them – faith, honor, love, – in stiff parades up and down their own country. And now in the occupied lands as well…

Love of what? Love for what? Honor? For whom? For what? Parades of robots with flags.

It's a net. We're caught in it.

Chapter 11

Suppertime. Hanne and Werner stand in line, patient, tired. They hold their mugs and plates ready. Hanne looks at their tin utensils.

"Mine is dirty. Can't get it properly clean."

"Who cares?" Werner gives it a sideways glance.

Hellmuth's voice booms above the general din from behind his cauldrons up front. He ladles the contents in small measured portions, spices them with jokes and native Berliner's so-called wit. The foodline's forward movement is slow.

It is cold inside the barrack, despite the many people. The wind sweeps straight through the cracks in the thin walls. Hanne hops from one foot to the other to keep her circulation going. She grits sand between her teeth. Sand is everywhere, on faces, under eyelids, under fingernails, under her tongue, in her nose, the creases in her skin. She wipes her inflamed eyes and realizes the futility of her effort. Her fingertips are covered with grit.

"Tons of sand. Our lungs must be sandbags," she says and tries to spit grit out of her teeth. The grit sounds hollow in her brain. It's supposed to be a joke, but it doesn't come off. Nothing really does. They are exhausted, physically and mentally. Nothing matters. She remembers the gray inmates she saw that first night, the grayness of the camp overall. A future glimpse when they arrived of her own grayness as part of the whole.

"Camp life gets to you after a while," Werner says.

Hanne agrees in silence. The odds are stacked against them and they know it. Three months of communal living under these conditions have drained them of the last vestiges of energy.

"I'm a rag, too tired to work, too tired to fight, too tired to even think. A human zombie. A ghost with flesh on her bones. I wouldn't have the strength it would take to escape," she nags her frigid innards.

If she had ever entertained the thought of escape, she has stopped thinking of it. It's a futile effort. Barbed wire surrounds them. Watchtowers with ss guards, vigilant eyes with machine guns and dogs, are forever on the lookout. They are far away from human habitation. Even if she scales the fence and gets out, she can't get far. Clothing, manners, her accented speech pattern would give her away. Sure, some tried and even made it. But these are special cases with outside connections. Native Dutch speakers. Like the two who were sent to take laundry to Hooghalen and never returned. Or the woman commissioned to buy books in Amsterdam… a fool if she had come back to this. Then there were the fellows who suddenly disappeared and afterward were found hiding in another barrack, still waiting for a chance to get out. No, you need pull to get outside. She has none.

Caught in the vortex of an immense, vicious cyclone.

Welcome to the crazed logic, the inverted rectitude, the connived, diabolical justifications of an immense killing machine for which no one takes responsibility. Marketing human flesh.

*   *   *

"It's tough to get out. Even tougher to be outside," Werner muses next to her. It's as if he reads her thoughts.

"You're right. They sell you out for money."

"Uh huh. The dregs of society. Barrack 66, the penal barrack right next to ours, is full of their victims. People with the penal S-stamp on their ID don't remain for longer than the next train departure. Independent, revolutionary characters take their chances and go into hiding. I've heard there are squealers right inside the camp."

"I can't believe that Jews squeal on Jews."

"It's hard to believe, but true. You've got to be careful."

"I still would like to know where all these trains are going???"

Hanne is quiet. She can't tell Werner that she feels special. Set aside. As long as she is set aside from transport. It's foolish to jeopardize her chance of getting her Swedish passport from the authorities. If she ever gets it, and it's a big IF, no one would be able to find her in hiding. She'll have to trust fate. Her fate. It's hard to trust if you don't believe in fate. Perhaps it is a cop-out. An official excuse for not daring.

"I'm hollow. Exhausted. Barely manage to coast along. Can't even care one way or the other. I need something to eat."

"Wonder what's on the menu tonight?" Werner wants to keep the conversation going.

"They say it's green," Dicky joins them from behind, plate and mug in hand. "Spinach, I suppose."

"They got us used to stamppot back at Jongenshuis," Hanne says.

"This is worse," Werner says.

"Far worse. At least then we had van Gelder's desserts."

"Especially her rice pudding." Gerd, Ditta, Erika and Pferdchen join the line behind them.

They look at each other. Heave a meaningful sigh of longing. Even though they are falling apart as a group within the camp, they still feel the old solidarity, or kinship, a community of quasi-siblings away from their home in Arnhem.

"The food globs here are far stickier," Dicky sighs, his eyes thick, shiny with longing.

"Homesick?"

"Don't lose our place," Werner pulls Hanne into line.

They inch forward. Hanne pulls herself back to present reality with an icy stare at some pushy outsiders trying to cut into their line.

"Is it true that they put carbonate of soda into the food?" Hanne wants to know.

"I've heard those rumors. Do they really lace our food with the stuff?" Werner wonders.

"It's true. To keep your sexual urges down. I've seen the sacks," Dicky says.

He should know. As a trained baker, they've put him to work in the central kitchen. He's become hot stuff. They feel lucky. Whenever possible he *organizes* potatoes, carrots and other loose edibles for himself and friends. *Organisieren.* Like *yofel, organize* is a word that imperceptibly crawled into Hanne's refugee vocabulary back at Jongenshuis. Means filching. It came with the boys. Excusable filching. Permissible. Out of necessity. A matter of pride. A feat. Accomplishment. Organize to keep on living.

"Any extra provisions today?" Werner's eyes gleam at the thought. In cahoots with underground camp currents.

"A couple of potatoes."

Hanne can see them bulge Dicky's pockets.

"We'll roast them on the stove later."

"If you can get to it," Hanne cautions.

Hanne doesn't think the soda helps much. Stamping out sexuality in cramped quarters like these is a joke. Even if they separate the men and have them sleep on the other side of the barracks. The air is thick with desire. She feels the glances of the old geezers whenever she walks through the men's wings. Despite the solo sleeping arrangements, an alarming number of women are pregnant. She doesn't need to be convinced that rumors about rakish camp leaders and long-term residents are true. They have private nooks, separate rooms, and the power to grant favors, exemptions, food…

They reach the end of the line.

"Hi, gorgeous," Hellmuth smiles at Hanne and takes her plate. She watches him dive into his cauldron. Wield his ladle like a power tool. His muscles bulge under the shirt. Polyphemus? No. More like Max Baer. Jack Dempsey. She likes him. Good-natured underneath all those muscles. Something more than regular food must sustain him. Ah well, long-termer. Married.

"Here."

His upper body comes up, red-flushed skin. His hand returns her plate. She sniffs at the green glob with an air of appreciation.

"Meat in it today! What's the occasion?"

Hellmuth wipes sweat beads off his forehead. The cold doesn't affect him much.

"Hot stuff," he smiles. Pushes his kerchief into his pocket. A red tail hangs down.

"The occasion? Extra treat for good behavior? Plain chance? Probably some leftovers. Who knows what moves them."

"Next?" He is ready for Werner behind her.

"Any mail for me today?" she insists.

"Let me finish here first. People are hungry. I'll get the mail later," Hellmuth shouts out of the depth of his kettle.

Hanne and Werner take their food over to the tables and benches set up between bunks behind the entrance. They save seats for the others, Gerd, Horsey and Dicky, to join them.

"Heard anything from your parents yet?" Werner asks, chewing away.

Back in the shadows of her brain she hears Mutti's, "Don't talk with your mouth full."

Hanne stifles a caustic, silent chuckle. How far away these concerns are now. Table manners. Who cares about talking while chewing? You're lucky to have a full mouth. She swallows her own mouthful before she answers.

"No. It's months since the telegram. Their letter must have gone to Arnhem first."

"Or it's stuck at the censors for someone to read and cross out half the text," Ruth says, joining them.

"We're doubly checked here. Our mail goes to the ss first, then to the post office inside."

"Leave room for Eddie," Ruth says and slides into the bench from behind.

Eddie is her latest flame. Violet-eyed Eddie Silver, another good-natured Viennese. What a change after Atze! Hanne marvels at her sister. She shrugs with an inaudible sigh. Their hopes are on pretty shaky grounds. It's hard to figure what's behind the telegram. The ss in Arnhem did not take it seriously. It's just a ray of hope they've established here in the camp. Like a straw to pull you out of the water when you're drowning. Better than nothing. Needed to cope with all this squalor. The others don't even have that.

"Shame on you," her brain scolds. Look at Werner. His mother sits in London. He can't correspond with her at all. Last he heard from her was through the Red Cross – a mere card. And that was months ago. More months, years before his mother gets his answer.

"It's just so nerve-racking. This uncertainty," she wails back to her brain.

"How was your day?" she asks Werner, turning their conversation in a different direction.

"Not too bad. A large contingent of geezers came in this morning. An old folks home from Apeldoorn. Including the nurses. Didn't want to leave their charges."

"You wonder about that kind of heroism. Whether it's worth it. We got the women in our section. Not really sick. Just old. Helpless. Not used to taking care of themselves. They depend on the nurses. I know one of them. Ruth Pestachowsky. Good old Pesta. Met her this morning. We used to be together in The Hague. She went into nursing. Just like her to volunteer for this. The oldies need her, she says. One woman is blind."

"Public Enemy First Class," Dicky scoffs.

"Needs to be imprisoned. Eliminated. Fodder for next week's train," Werner says.

"It's the loopy limit. They'll never survive another train ride, wherever they're going. Not these trains," Hanne says.

"We're getting callous. Like the rest, I suppose. Talking about shipments, trainloads – as if people were merchandise and the whole thing didn't concern us."

"What else can you do? You see the same thing repeat, week after week after week. Secretly you're happy not to be one of them. You need to develop some kind of distance. Or you'd go nuts."

"Didn't take us long to fall in line."

"Everyone schemes to stay. By hook or crook."

They have learned about the subterranean traffic of privilege permeating the camp. To know *the right person* becomes a matter of deferment. A matter of life and death. Choice foods, cigarettes, sexual favors can be traded for extensions to stay. Get on a *list*. There are quite a few. Some go out of style, others come in. Foreign countries, Cuba, Costa Rica, Nansen, Mixed Marriage. Certain young girls find it easy to stay. Correction: *Easier* to stay. Life is a commodity.

Sarcasm is another way of coping.

Hanne's eyes sweep across their accommodations. Five rows of three-tiered metal bunks, each bunk piled high with the entire earthly possessions of its current occupant. The total remainder of a former normal life lived somewhere in human society shrunk to between a metal frame built to contain a sleep-hungry body at night. The washroom at the far end: twelve faucets over a common zinc tub hugging two walls. Three open toilets on the other side. Has anyone ever heard of privacy?

The noise level is even worse. Nights are especially bad. Children yanked into this life are out of order. The crying never stops. Neither does the traffic of people running to the bathroom at night. They cough, wheeze, vomit, cry, sigh, talk, whisper, snore, scream. Nightmares galore. And the smell! In addition to the sandy grit. Dank straw mattresses, urine, sweat, food, filth blend in a wild concoction. It permeates their clothes, sticks in their noses, ears, armpits. The first days after arrival were especially bad.

CHAPTER 11

Hanne sniffs. Globby food. She ought to have gotten used to it by now. The little iron stove in the center aisle is much like the heater at Jongenshuis. Same type, making the same heroic efforts to spread warmth from its round, red-flamed belly. The heat doesn't go far. People crowd around its vicinity to catch some of what it manages to radiate within its narrow circumference. Older people who do not have to work during the day fight over the seats on benches nearby. Stamina, larger muscles, vilest mouths, chutzpa usually win. Less assertive characters give up. The same people hang on – until the next transport takes them out of competition. Room for the next contenders.

The spirit of enterprise is alive even in a concentration camp. Especially in a concentration camp. She watches an elderly couple toast bread slices on the stovetop. Another uses the stovepipe to toast their bread. Probably saved from some meal. Or a package from outside. The woman monitors the slow browning process. The man stays on the bench to guard *their* seats. The smell of toast wafts through the barrack and mingles with other odors, old and new, clings to walls and cots. And whatever is on and underneath them.

Others sit and wait, protect their turn in line to roast or toast on the little stove. Eagle-eyed, they watch the progress of things cooking or toasting: sliced potatoes, whole potatoes, cans of soup. Anything to expand or vary the camp food dished out to the inmates. The toasty smell tickles up her nose. Once she contemplated toasting her bread. She gave up. A waste to devote endless hours to getting near the iron red belly. She has no time, much less patience, and no nerve to fight with these hawks. Best forgo the luxury of toasted bread. Though it sure smells inviting. No, she has no energy left at night after tending to her sickies all day.

The lump in her stomach is a constant these days. As soon as she gets tired or upset it spreads like wildfire through her chest. Being tired is another regular state. Hanne thinks of Dr. Wolf when she visited in his office after her strange screaming session back at the home. His stupid prescription, one teaspoon of bicarbonate of soda in a glass of water sipped in small clunks twice daily while walking back and forth with the glass for fifteen minutes never worked. She can still taste the salt on her tongue. Did he ever know what was wrong with her? She has her doubts. She did not want to contradict him, just wanted to get better. Still does. Desperately.

Then the attack came and went. It's a companion now. Settled inside for good.

How lucky and happy she felt when he told her about her acceptance to *Kunstoefening*.

Hanne has seen old women come and go in their bottom bunk. Ruth in the bunk underneath her is the only unbroken regular in her life now. Her Jongenshuis buddies a close second. More companionable. It's a callous and selfish world.

"Hi, can you shove over to make room for us?"

Hans Markbreiter and Horst Hamm are behind them with their full plates.

"Sure. Squish in."

Hanne gazes at her old siblings in fate. Camp life has put its mark on all of them soon enough. The typical colorless, grubby, gray camp look. Down to their behavior.

"How're things in the kitchen?" they ask Dicky.

Permanent kitchen duty is the most envied job in camp. A close second to administrative work. The hospital a far third. Administrative jobs are unobtainable. They're the prerogative of the original camp inmates, their families and close friends. They're beyond the aspirations of mere camp mortals.

"All's well on the kitchen front. I've organized some spuds and carrots."

"Yofel."

It's a good thing that Dicky shares so faithfully with us.

"Downright wonderful," Dicky shakes his head in self-mockery.

"I've just heard that the Russians launched a counterattack in the East. Cut off the German supplies behind the lines. The moffen are trapped and getting creamed outside of Stalingrad. In the snows of the Russian winter. And in North Africa the Allies finally got their act together against Rommel," Horst Hamm spreads the latest political news.

"Yofel."

"Fantastic."

"Time they get here."

They sigh. Hope. Flotsam in a sea of wishes. Mauve-crested thoughts suppressed. Hanne wonders how Hans and Horst know. Where do they get all this latest news? They're always in on it. No one asks for the source.

"Hard to believe. It had to start sometime." Werner mops his plate with great satisfaction. They feel connected with the outside world. North Africa. Russia. The Yanks are moving.

"Yep. We're ready for an invasion. It's the only hope for an end to the war," Horsey says.

"It's the only way out of here beside that train. Hope they get here before it's too late."

"Wonder what's keeping them?"

They don't understand what's keeping the Allies from coming to free the European continent. Don't they understand that every day counts? Every minute even? Or don't they care?

Hanne wonders. She is trapped with the others. Her Swedish passport? An impossible dream at the other end of a rainbow-tinted straw. No one knows exactly what happens to the people at the end of these regular Tuesday train rides! Still!! Perhaps better not dwell on the subject. Better not know. There are rumors. The cleaning crew mumbles of slips of paper. Notes found in cracks of the returning wagons on Monday nights. Poland? That's on the other side of the world. Hanne shrugs. Scare tactics? Tales of rumormongers? People with too fertile an imagination? The Nazis need people for work. Here and everywhere. Why would they send them to Poland, of all places?

"Who knows? The war might be over before long."

Wishful thinking? Hanne is looking for comfort. The others

nod. Anything to soothe their jolted souls. A reed. A straw will do. It's out of their hands.

Most of their group now work in the hospital. The assignment puts them at a relatively safe distance from the weekly trainlists. Somewhere in between the original inmates and the Dutch *hoi polloi*. Kid cousins…

* * *

That first night after they integrated is forever etched in her memory. The unexpected pitfalls of camp life. Camp life, an existence with creaky cracks. A live cage with shrieky joints. Each crying for special lubrication.

The care she had taken to select a decent bunk. Another disaster. She waits for the bulb in the wooden beam overhead to switch off. In vain. It remains lit all through the night. Burns holes through her eyelids. Burrows into her brain. An evil eye from which there's no escape. She tosses and turns. It's difficult to sleep on your stomach through the night. The light scorches the back of her head. Her nape. Enters her brain the wrong way. Her back hurts.

"What's the matter with you, dancing solo up there?" Ruth complains from below.

"The light bothers me."

"Let people sleep down here. The whole three tier-contraption wiggles under your weight."

The old woman in the bottom bunk that night did not complain. She was in the john. Gagging.

Hanne complains to Hellmuth the next day.

"Can't you do something about that light? It's on all night!"

"Can't help it. Folks need to find their way to the bathroom in the dark. Sorry."

He's no help.

The joys of communal living at night! It's not just that infernal light. It's the constant shuffle for which the light stays on. Feet on wooden planks. Tap. Trudge. Trample. Run. Shuffle. Loose boards shriek creaking complaints. Moans of grown-ups caught and regimented like animals. The cacophony of imprisoned humanity a thousand times multiplied at night. She cannot remember a decent night's sleep since she integrated into the regular women's section. Suffering absorbed without getting used to it. Is there a breaking point? Where? When? How much is too much?

* * *

The following day is worse. Hellmuth wakes them with his supercilious Berliner accent. It's five in the morning. Dark. Cold. The wind blows through cracks in the walls. Hanne crawls deeper under her blankets. Two woolens, pink with two green stripes on one side. Compliments Jongenshuis. Jewish community. She tries to make up for lost sleep. While everyone else scrambles for a faucet in the washroom.

"Hanne, get up. Roll call's in twenty minutes."

Conscientious little sister from below. Vertical in pajamas. "And you want to eat breakfast before that."

Miss Conscientious runs to the washroom with towel and soap.

"Yep. I'd better."

Hanne opens her eyes into the light overhead. Rolls out. It's icy. Trots off to the washroom with soap and towel. In this filth you can't skip that part of habit. She waits for someone to leave to get to one of the ice-cold water faucets. She feels the dirt layering on her skin. The washroom empties slowly. She climbs up into the tub and lets the icy water from the faucet run over her legs. Sponges it over her entire body. It wakes her up. Somehow helps her face the day. Towels dry while running back. Ruth returns with two slices of bread and ersatz java from Hellmuth up front dishing out breakfast. Hanne gobbles, chews, dresses all at the same time. Still chewing, she files out of the barrack for roll call. Last in line behind Ruth. She stands upright for her call. She needs to learn to get out of the sack first thing. And fast.

It's dark. Five-thirty AM. Two ss watch as Hellmuth calls

the names from his list. Each name is accounted for with a *Here.* Hellmuth checks off. Leaves. The ss take over. Divide them into two groups. Older women do general clean-up jobs. Older men clean latrines. The smallfry stay for kindergarten, or something they call "school." All inside the camp. The rest march out of the camp. Through the barbed wire fence. The ss with rifles march front, sides, back. Out onto the heath. The cold wind blows harder. More sand. Mean streaks of sand. The sun rises. Cold yellow ball of fuzz in pale blue over dark purple heather. Woody, gnarled shrubs.

There are heaps of jute sacks. The ss pass one out to everyone. They have to pull the heather out of the ground. Fill the sack. Exchange the full sack for an empty sack. The ss want to see them all filled. Let's see who is fastest. Who pulls the most.

Hanne's hands are white icicles. Raynaud's syndrome. Inherited from Mutti. Her fingers are a deadly white. Numb. She can't feel them. Unfit to pull shrubs out of frozen ground. She can't enter the competition. Lacks desire too. To be a slave for the Nazis is one thing, a willing slave quite another. She blows into her lifeless fingers and sets about her task. Nature is unwilling to cooperate. The bushes stay firmly rooted in the ground. They belong there. Her fingers remain white. Bloodless. Waxen. Numb.

"Hellmuth is late with his mail today," Werner complains into her memories.

"Do you remember the first day after quarantine?" Hanne spins on her train of thought.

"Sure do."

She remembers it well. How could she forget?

The stubborn scrub that wouldn't submit. She pulled hard. Put all the energy she could muster into the task. But no matter how hard she tried, the heather stuck its ground. The earth was frozen. The brush in it unyielding. It remained rooted in the earth. Where it belonged.

"What do they do with all this heather?"

"Make brooms," Werner explains. The others listen.

"Nearly killed my back. It's as stubborn as hell."

"It's busywork. Can't have the Jews sit around all day doing nothing but shoot the breeze," Hans says.

She thinks of the icy breeze out on the heath. Her sack never filled up.

"They never got rich on my work."

"Keeps you out of mischief, doesn't it? Lets you earn your keep. *Arbeit macht frei!*"

"Slave labor? After looting us to the poorhouse? Ha!"

"We work. Either out on the heath, or inside the camp – KP duty, clean latrines, mop barracks, nurse sickies." The list goes on and on.

"All work that needs to be done to keep this dump going. Can't just let things run wild."

"It's just that the cushy jobs are for *insiders. The Long-termers.* The original inmates. Because they were here first."

"They run this place."

"And their protégés."

"Me, I cleaned latrines that first day. All my enemies should land in that stink," Werner announces, not wanting to be left out.

"We're lucky. They rescued us soon enough. German refugee kids, needed for regular work."

"Not the top jobs."

"Still, just below."

"Don't knock it. Keeps us off the weekly *lists.*"

"What d'you take me for? I thank our good fortune. Every day that I'm here."

A collective silent stare into some pregnant void follows the mere mention of *the* List. They don't usually discuss these internal intrigues. The List. The ghost that stubbornly permeates the very camp air they breathe. It dominates every thought, every breath, every sigh. It's ingrained in the woof and mesh of Westerbork, with its companion – the iron reptile that wheezes into the camp every Monday night on its weekly mission, only to wail on its way out the next morning with its high-pitched shriek. Filled to bursting. The function of the place.

* * *

That first day out in the freezing cold sticks in Hanne's memory. Haunts, confounds her. That day out on the heath. Outside the confines of the smelly camp. The group marched out. Past the gate into free nature with its merciless storms. The hoary frost lay stiff on the heath in the wild winter universe. The sundisk rose in pale pee. Sunrays glittered on purple, sparse, frostclad landscape. The distant fire globe on the eastern horizon curved in slow motion to its slanted zenith. No screams. No putrid smells. No busybody humanity. No frets on one's nerves. Just clean, crisp, translucent air. Pungent earth and heather. She was sick of camp. Of sadistic Nazis with guns. She breathed. Alone with the outside. Her back hurt. No one was around. She was tired. Apathetic. Hollow. Weary of life.

She remembers sitting down, uncurling into vertical position. Normal. Human. Upright. Her spinal column grateful. Leaning against a clump of purple brush. Relieved. She remembers inhaling the aroma of surrounding heather. A sun ray stroking gently over her face. Cirrus fluff fingering cerulean sky. Soft. Wispy. Sparrows quarreling noisily in some bare trees. Lively specks, black freckles in blue between white fluff. Wings rushing. Spreading across the turquoise expanse. She remembers looking after them. Envious. To be able to rise and sail into freedom just like that. Free to move! Free to do! Free to speak! Wherever. Whenever. She is dead tired. Through and through, body and mind.

She loses her sense of time. Just sits. Outside her misery. Watches the sun roll westward in the cutting winter air. Cold creeps out of the ground. Up her legs. Spreads through her rump. Stiffens her spine. She doesn't care. Too weary to move on. The sparsely filled sack slumps listlessly beside her on the frozen ground.

Suddenly two black boots stand before her. Yellow light

reflects in their polished shine. She looks up. Bland blond face under party cap stares down at her. Young. Nose red-tipped.

"*Was machen Sie denn da?*"

She gazes back. Embarrassed. Trapped. Comes up slowly. Stiffly gazes at eyelevel. Wow. He addresses her with the formal *Sie*. Double Wow. Wow. Wow. He can see what she's doing, can't he?

"*Mein Rücken tut weh,*" she says. Touches the small of her back for emphasis. Her throat is a dry husk. She puts her hands out, bloodless, waxen-purple fingertips, torn. Black, blood-caked ridges in colorless parchment. She blows into her stiff hands. Circulation nil.

"*Sie sind hier um Heide zu rupfen,*" he reminds her. She looks at five rose-bedded nails beyond the glove that clamp around his rifle butt. The sun is a gleaming dot in the metal shaft. Why should he care whether her back hurts? Let him break his, for all she cares. They all should break their backs. But all he does is move his rifle over the heath. Away from her. Bland blond. Young. He reminds her of Fritz Hohenstein, their neighbor's son back home. Ilse's older brother. He had carried her on his shoulders when she was little. A dream she carries around? A lost truth?

Bland blond and his rifle stand, a black shadow, wait until she gets her stiff joints going again. Bend, pull, bend, pull, bend, pull. She stuffs brush clumps into the greedy slack of her sack, bends, pulls again. He watches her for a while. Then leaves her alone. Most of the afternoon is gone anyway. By the time they call the group to march back her sack is almost full. Others have six or seven to their name. Experience makes the man, Mutti used to say. They march into the sunset. Frozen brown heath in purple glow. A unit of prisoners. Jews. Slaves. Barracks rise dark behind the fence. They marched in unison through the gate back into the camp. She remembers that day vividly, grateful for not having to pull heather any more.

"Nursing is far better than pulling heather. At least the hospital is heated, Hanne says. She looks at her fingers. Dirty pale pink. She can't get them properly clean.

"Beats latrine duty any day," Werner agrees.

"Hell, yes."

Long-term residents. Indeed. They can shuffle the lists. Priorities. Pull. Pull above all. Plus the accidental luck of birthplace. Where you were born. Thanks our lucky stars. With Ruth she enjoys the extra status that had blown their way with Mutti's yellow telegram.

Double luck. Luck? Hanne wonders about Bland Blond who let her march back with the rest. Didn't peep another word! She wonders why.

She shivers with the sudden chill of utter, scary aloneness. Alone in an overwhelming mass of humanity. Everybody for himself.

* * *

Latest reality check. Fear. Terror rules her world. Conquers resistance. That's how it works here. Everyone for himself. No more moral imperatives. No more hypocritical defenses. Only a lot of sane hypocrites. Scramble for chances. Makes people putty. Pliable. Because there are those with rifles. Guns. And dogs. Grovel on. Anything to live another day.

Arbeit macht frei!

* * *

Up front Hellmuth clanks metal lids back on huge cauldrons. Hollow sounds kill your eardrums.

"Done." He wipes his forehead. The KP, short for "kitchen personnel," come from the central kitchen and roll the kettles away. The witches' dance of the hour. Metallic rumbles out the door in the center of the barrack where women's and men's sections meet. They watch Hellmuth return with his mailbag. Anxious expectancy permeates the barrack. Like a cloud, hope-filled, hope-torn. Unspoken wishes. Let me have some mail. Connection to the world. Real life. Mail is the link.

Where is *Real life*? Inside or out?

Hellmuth dips into his bag. Heaps of letters and parcels rise to the surface. He pulls them out, one by one. Spreads them before him on the table. He begins to call their owners. Slowly. Connections. Deflect brown and white rays from the lonely bulb overhead.

"Hanne Kalter."

Did she hear that right? Her off-center mind shrinks back to active mode. Sudden alert.

"Go on," Ruth orders, "that's you!"

Hanne pushes her way through the throng around the mailman. Privacy, where are you? She expects mail from Sweden. He hands her a package. Brown wrapping paper. Tied with string like curdled paper rope. The cheap war kind that falls apart. The package is heavy. She carries it back to her friends. Nonplussed.

"From Sweden?" Ruth asks.

"No. Dutch stamps."

They crane their necks. Stare at the name of the sender. Hanne recognizes the slanted, even handwriting.

"It's from Bert," she says.

"For heaven's sake. Open it!"

Curious stares at the things emerging from old newspaper wrappings. Excitement. Hanne places each item on the table before her. Two jars of strawberry preserves. One jar of peanut butter, the smooth kind. Two cans of sardines in oil. A can of sausages.

A windfall. The newspaper wads pile up around the jars. Eddie straightens the crumpled sheets.

"Interesting reading from the *Arnhem Courant*."

No one listens. Their eyes are glued to the package contents.

"Food!" Ruth shouts. "Oh boy!"

Hungry eyes. Envy.

"Remember your friends," Horsey reminds her.

"This is rationed stuff."

"We're still customers for spuds and carrots, Dicky," Hanne reminds him.

"Sure thing."

"I wonder how he got it," Ruth mumbles.

"Me too."

Hanne is overwhelmed. No one in his right mind gives up his regular rations these days. Just can't afford to. Bert doesn't have enough money to buy things on the black market. Anyway, his mother would never approve. *Black Market. It's not aboveboard. You don't support clandestine money-gougers.* She can just hear her. So where *does* all this loot come from? She rescues his letter from underneath the heap of old newspaper wrappings. It doesn't say much. Kunstoefening friends miss her. Eddie. But he himself misses her most of all. A wish for "happy eating."

"Regards to all," she tells Eddie and Werner.

No use worrying about where it comes from. It's a welcome addition to their brown ersatz-coffee, stale bread slices that turn moldy if you keep them too long, the monotony of colored potato glue, the carbonate of soda taste each day in another color shade. She puts the treasures on her bed, one by one. Her heist. She looks forward to eating it. With Ruth. Plans to pass some out in small portions to her buddies.

She slides onto the bench by the table between the bunks inherited from former inmates who had *organized* it to have something to sit on besides a bed on the third tier. Then left it behind because you can't take benches or tables along on a goods train. A cattle car. With a one-suitcase allowance. Her mind composes a letter to Bert.

Dear Bert, you're the best reliable, unselfish friend I have ever met. Wherever you got the food you sent me, with this package you have given me something far more valuable than the food. You have restored my faith in humankind. Reassured me that not all is lost with our human race.

Hanne bites her lips. Perhaps she should qualify that last phrase. To read that not all is lost with *some* part of humanity. The ss fellow that afternoon on the heath flashes through the back of her mind. She shrugs. Unsure whether she'll ever mail this letter.

⁎   ⁎   ⁎

The Train. The train is a freight train consisting of about forty to forty-five cattle cars. She isn't sure of the number. Perhaps she should count them. But the number may vary anyway, depending on the number of people going. It comes silently during Monday nights on the single track right into the center of the camp. A paved square at the end of a well-trampled dirt path that the inmates, with coping sarcasm, call *Boulevard de Misère*. It leaves with a marrow-piercing toot on Tuesdays before noon. Regularly. Every week.

The Train dominates life at Westerbork. A carnivorous beast. A segmented, dirty, tilebrown, blood-thirsty monster. Its malevolent fumes cast their special shadow across the camp. The life of the inmates whirls around this train in a mad dervish dance. It is the dead center in the vortex of camp existence. The division. With status, you're outside the loop. Without status, you're on The *List* for the Train. Whether patrician or *hoi polloi*. Tensions rise and fall with the snake's malevolent weekly rhythm. Life pushed between the coming and going of The Train.

Hanne has never seen it rolling in. But it stands there in the center of the camp, cordoned off within the paved section that serves as the platform for departure on Tuesday mornings. Boulevard de Misère. With the arrival of The Snake tension rises to unbearable heights, palpable throughout the camp like a clammy cloud. It reaches its crazed crescendo when Hellmuth enters the barrack with his infamous *List* late Monday nights after curfew. Tension permeates the barrack, an inferno of oxygen thickly laced with carbon dioxide that prevents you from breathing in the ensuing silence. The inmates sit on their beds in the growing dusk. Or lie on their beds. He reads his list. Names. More names. Doomsday. Tomorrow morning's travelers.

On Monday nights the inmates are divided into two distinct classes. No longer human. Those Leaving. Those Remaining. The Haves. The Have-nots. The Rich. The Poor. Wealth no longer counted in money. It's not the accumulation of things that divides the two groups. It's whether your name is on The List. Or off. The Doomed and The Living. The Doomed cry, scream, fall numb, remain stoic or silent, go into convulsions, have anxiety attacks, all according to temperament. Upbringing has a lot to do with their reactions. Then there are the others. The Patricians. The Upper Class in the camp. Embarrassed to show their relief. Hate and despair mingle, intertwine. Dumbed-down compassion. Dumbfounded guilt. Spared for another week. An infernal, unbounded chasm exists between the two groups: camp life versus the Unknown Beyond That Train.

Life outside, the Real Life Outside from where they all come, was never as divisive as these infamous Monday Nights with their List that governs life inside the barbed wire fence. Hellmuth folds the sheets of paper after reading the names. The paper crackles into his pocket. He leaves. Then a long night looms inside the barracks. Wails. Prayers. Cries. Packing. Shouts. Retching. Children run. Constant shuffles to the bathroom. Urgent. The traffic never stops.

Dumb silence on the other side. Thank God my name wasn't on it!

No one sleeps.

Waiting for tomorrow.

Until around noon the following day, Tuesday. When the "cargo" has been loaded, pushed, squeezed into the segmented monster, then safely bolted behind its iron fangs. The rusty limbs screech into line behind the locomotive.

The snake comes alive with the deafening toot that pierces all guts. Like a victory hail to hell.

The ss with their rifles step on the boards along the outsides of the train cars. Like leeches. They grip the iron bars, hang on to roll to their quarters outside the fence. There they'll jump off. Duty done. While the train picks up speed. Moves toward its unknown destination. With its unwilling cargo.

Those on the platform hear muffled cries, watch fingers and hands appear between the slats of the air openings in the wagons. They watch the snake slither away, sinister, sated, the sacrificial lambs in its innards rolling to their destiny. A destiny no one wants to contemplate.

Then with a silent heartfelt sigh of unutterable, guilt-ridden relief a deathly calm settles over the remaining Patricians. Another week of respite!

* * *

It's a godsend to be out of the loop.

* * *

The weekly Westerbork-rhythm repeats with new arrivals later that night or Wednesday morning. Crowded conditions repeat. Gradually. The bunks fill up, toilets clog, overflow, foodlines lengthen. Tensions rise around the sputtering stove. Come to their weekly climax on Monday nights with the reading of The List. Week after week. Until the shrill whistle of the train announces the finale and the train's slow, heavy crawl out of sight dissolves another climax of accumulated tension. Those left in the camp too exhausted to feel anything but relief, for a few hours anyway.

It's good to be exempt.

Only the cleaning crew knows when exactly the train rolls in. It's their job to clean it. Rumors float about small paper scraps found in cracks and crevices. Scribbles mention places deep inside Poland. At the other end of Europe? They have a hard time reading the unfamiliar names. It seems implausible. Why would the Nazis go to the trouble of moving the Jews from here to there? All that distance? It doesn't add up. Many things don't add up. Take the hospital. Its very existence. Why cure people before sending them on their way? If not for some needed work? What kind of work?

* * *

As nurses, Hanne and Ruth are exempted from the curfew. They wear white armbands on their right sleeves to show their status. All the nurses do, male and female. During the week they work the dayshift from six AM to three PM. Except Tuesday mornings when they have to report to work at five AM. Early. To get the hospital's List-patients dressed and ready for transport. After the train leaves, usually shortly before noon, they have free time. By that time they are exhausted. Drained. Incapable of lifting another hand, another leg. Or of thinking a human thought.

*   *   *

It's time to sleep. Noon. Tuesday is the only time during the week she can sleep without the lit bulb burning overhead. The barrack is relatively quiet. Most people are out at work. Except a few old-sters who sit and gab far off around the stove. Cook some soup. Or toast bread. Hanne drops onto her bunk. She hears Ruth climb into her space underneath. Routine. The tension is gone. It's quiet. Her ears close with the hum in the halfdark of the barrack. She drifts off into a fitful sleep.

*   *   *

Hanne wakes into the dusk of the barrack. Peers into the lonely, unlit bulb overhead. She feels Ruth's eyes peep across the side of her bunk.

"Hanne? You awake?"

"Hm hmmm."

"Did you hear the rumor?"

"Which one? There are so many, with all these Jews." Jews are famous for spreading rumors. In the camp they have no other mental exercise.

"I mean the ones that these trains go to Poland."

"I've heard them."

"What I mean is, like – why are we sending sick people on these trains? I mean, really, we send them from the hospital right to the train. Sick, feeble. To ride in cattle cars to some far-off destination – Poland, no less. It makes no sense."

"No, Ruth, it doesn't make sense to me either. But nothing does anymore. Like why are we here? All of us? To nurse them back to health and *then* send them off. In cattle cars?"

"Right."

No, it doesn't make sense. If someone is on The List, no matter how sick or feeble, they – the nurses – have to get them dressed and packed. Then call the od Jewish Police. They come with their stretchers, put the patients on – prone, sick, blind, or whatever – and carry them to the train. Hanne doesn't want to complete the thought.

"Ruthie, I can't answer that. Better not think about it at all. We're here to survive."

"Hmmm. Right." Ruth's dark curls descend from the side of her bunk. "I'll go and visit the boys."

Hanne sees her disappear down the long hallway of the women's quarters. The boys live on the other side with the men.

*   *   *

Hanne settles back. Thinks of this morning. Tuesday morning. On their way to work. Meet the black iron snake, silent, ominous, famished for live cargo in the pale dawn. Cordoned off in the center of the camp. Squatting in its usual place. Boulevard de Misère. A fitting name. Hanne wonders who named it. Someone who knew French. Probably no longer in the camp. Hanne and Ruth walking around the yellow string. The hospital barracks are right behind.

*   *   *

Take last night. Monday night. Hellmuth walks in at 11:00 PM. With his *List*. Reads the names that make up next morning's cargo. Hanne lies on her bed. Like everyone else on her own turf. Helpless. In agony. She closes herself off. Wants to avoid getting emotionally involved in what's going on around her. Better get some rest. It's late. She has to be on duty very early in the morning. That bulb overhead singes her brain. Prevents her from getting her sleep. Hellmuth pronounces every name. Slowly.

Hysterical screams intersperse his reading and pierce Hanne's self-willed isolation. A young mother with her three-week old baby. She has come right from the maternity ward in Amsterdam. The husband is somewhere in hiding. She needed to go to the hospital. Thought it was safe for her to go there to give birth. Then join her husband again. Hanne listens to the steady rain smatter against the barrack roof. A hollow beat against wooden planks. She watches drops seep through the ceiling. Pearls congregate. Alive, heavy, a funnel of silver glister down ceiling and wall to ease its overload. Collect in a rainbow rivulet. An act of independent defiance. The repair crew has fixed the roof leaks countless times, they say. The water pearls persist. A stubborn breed.

The tension in the barrack rises to unbearable heights. Chokes her. She doesn't want to hear. The wind howls outside. Adds yet another dimension to the pandemonium inside. A channel of teardrops flits down the wall. Collects in an expanding puddle on the floor under the window. Hellmuth's voice stops. All the names have been called. He is done. Through closed eyelids she sees him fold the paper. It crackles into the sudden silence laden with disaster. Disappears in his pocket. He leaves. Heavy tread on loose wooden planks.

The light overhead! An evil eye that stings. Red glare through closed eyelids. She turns in an attempt to escape. Rests her stomach across the straw mattress. Diminished, shredded, cut, life resumes around her.

Terror sneers from every airpocket inside the barrack. Terror stalks the night with invisible fangs that rip every soul to shreds. Terror gloats from the drumbeaten ceiling. Terror bloodies the toilet seats in the washrooms. Terror clasps each breath they breathe with clamps unseen. Terror sticks to her fingers, her breasts, her legs. Terror suffocates.

There is no defense.

Shuffles to and from the bathroom disturb her precarious slumber measured in spooned fits. Voices whisper, trying to calm panic. Coughs rise in all decibels. Children's cries for parents are shushed. She pictures the quagmires outside she will have to slide through in the morning. Her shoesoles are worn. Holes that leak. She will have to sidestep the puddles.

The deHartoghs are in the camp. They arrived on Thursday. She met them on her way back from work. All three – Mister, Mistress Teacozy with her muscular shinbones. Flipje as skinny as ever. They're next door in Barrack 64. She went over to see them. Teacozy's still her limited, self-centered old self.

"I've come prepared for the *trip*," she tells her former house-guest, proud as a peacock over her wise foresight. "I got all three of us new winter coats, fur-lined. See?" She holds them out to Hanne to finger the plush, soft lining.

As if they were headed for a ritzy winter vacation in the Alps. Hanne thinks of the train.

"And new boots. Mine are almost up to my knees. They should keep us warm," she breathes. Holds the three pairs up for Hanne to admire.

Her boots especially catch Hanne's attention. Bally. Green envy invades her heart.

"They're nice," Hanne says. Teacozy pulls her treasures away to put them with the rest of her belongings. Ah, yes.

"Black Market. Cost a pretty penny," she beams with pride.

Hanne takes it in. Wonders what good their social small-town pedigree and their money, inherited or otherwise, will do once Teacozy gets stuffed into the train. Hanne's toes itch inside her shoes. Scrape against the soles, conscious of their holey reality. A wave of envy crawls into her bowels and climbs up her spine into her brain.

I wonder whether these three are on tonight's List? She'll find out in the morning. On the platform.

The wind blusters through the cracks. Rocks the flyspecked

evil eye overhead to its rhythm with a smug, self-righteous sneer. Hanne remembers the hurt when Mrs. deHartogh after a two-week stay had accused her of stealing a bar of soap. Had she really believed that? Or had it just been a calculated scheme to get rid of a refugee kid without losing face in her decent community?

That suspicion has been with Hanne ever since she met the woman on the street a few weeks after Hanne's send-off to Jongenshuis. Hanne had again assured the woman that she never took any soap from anybody.

"I know. Miep confessed to taking that bar," Teacozy admitted, somewhat sheepishly, into Hanne's repeated tirades of innocence. Hanne had stopped short. Speechless. The woman never bothered to apologize for what she had done. It was as if the feelings of refugee kids don't count. If they hadn't met by chance on that street, and if Hanne had not brought up the subject again, she'd never have known. The very idea of Teacozy going through her stuff while she sent Hanne out shopping was revolting enough. Behind her back! No. The woman had treated her like a common criminal!

"Useless thoughts," Hanne reminds herself.

"Their accusation was devastating," her gut fights back. How could they? Indignation takes over. Lord knows what kind of tales these ladies spread about *poor refugee children* from behind their translucent china cups and quilted teacozies in their stuffy rooms. Who of them had believed her, Hanne? Protesting her innocence had probably made it worse.

On balance, she's not going to cry if the deHartoghs are on that train tomorrow. The thought clogs her brain. Serves them right? She has second thoughts.

"Don't let me wish such things," Hanne prays to no one in particular. It can't be God. She's lost faith in Him long ago.

She pulls the cover over her head. Tuesday morning. There's a rough day ahead of her. Delivery Day. She has to get up at four to start at five. The only nurses in the barrack, Ruth and she have the washroom to themselves at that hour. It's great to get washed and dressed properly without being rushed. In all this filth it's important to keep clean. It's not easy. If only that darned light overhead would go away. It fries her brain. Right through her eyelids. She is desperate for sleep.

Exempt from curfew, Hanne and Ruth leave Barrack 65 early to go to work. Their white nurse's armband over their left sleeve shines in the dark morning chill. The rain has stopped. A merciful frost has iced over the top layers of mud. The solid, slippery clumps make walking hazardous. They slither forward. But at least their feet remain dry. Hanne is more conscious than ever of the holes in her soles. An icy wind howls along the pathways between barracks. Cuts into their cheeks. Hanne looks forward to the heated hospital on the other side of Boulevard de Misère.

As usual on Tuesday morning, the loading zone is cordoned off. The sisters walk around the yellow bands of the enclosure. Inside, the Train lulls in predawn repose in its appointed place. A nubile monster. Black, brazen, arrogant. Ready for the assault. A vile reptile lying in wait to devour its human sacrifices. Treachery incarnate.

They tread forward, carefully measure their steps so as not to slip. To keep their balance. They watch the horizon turn bloody red behind the black monster. Their steps quicken in a slow jog to the hospital.

*   *   *

In the ward the night nurse routinely receives The *List* during her shift the night before. It is her duty to wake the people concerned before she leaves in the morning. Then she passes The *List* on to the incoming day staff. They have to get the deportees ready. Hanne receives her copy. Scans it while she thaws out her frozen fingers by the stove. More people than usual. Mostly from the old age home in Apeldoorn. It means a lot of fast work, to get all these oldsters dressed and packed for transport by seven A M. What makes things worse is that many of them don't quite understand what is happening to them. Some have begun to get dressed. It's obvious they're used to getting help. Realizes that a few are senile. Hanne tries to be calm. She helps with potties. Washes those who need her help. Ties shoelaces, buttons dresses, folds blankets, rolls them into bundles, closes overstuffed suitcases.

In between all this she attends the three patients not on the list, registers their temperature, counts pulses, brings them their filled washbasins and towels. Two are older women in their forties, one a severe influenza case, the other a heart patient. The third is her secret favorite: Paula, a girl her age, recovering from tuberculosis. She had already been in the ward when Hanne started her nursing career in December. They have become friends, sort of. The doctor prescribes nourishing food and lots of rest for Paula. Despite the care she gets, her temperature remains stubbornly elevated. All three may leave their beds so the nurses can straighten them properly. According to the doctor they are not ready for transport. Hanne suspects some higher protection that keeps all three off The *List*.

"Hi, Paula. How're you today?" Hanne puts the thermometer into Paula's mouth. The question is rhetorical because Paula is unable to answer right now.

"We're fine. All three of us. How's the weather?" is the answer from the next bed.

"Not too bad. Cold. But the rain stopped, so people won't get soaked." Hanne stops herself in time from ending with *before being loaded on the train*. She takes Paula's hand, takes her pulse, records the result on the chart, then checks Paula's thermometer, shakes her head as she records the inevitable elevated count in the designated square.

She repeats the procedure with the other two.

"You can get washed whenever you feel like it. You don't have to rush. I'll have to get the transport people ready before I can straighten your sheets."

Gerda puffs in, a few minutes late. She is the nurse on duty with Hanne. Leaving the remaining patients in her care, Hanne proceeds to help the oldsters who wait for her directions. They are helpless. So used to being told what to do it's frightening. Does that come with age?

"I'm not going to be that helpless." Hanne is full of sympathy for their dependence on others. "Better not get old altogether, but if I do, I'm never going to lose my independence," Hanne decides then and there.

"They ask you whether to wipe their bottoms," Gerda snickers in disbelief.

"Can you believe it? I just wonder what the Nazis will do with them on the other end of the train trip. These people can't work!"

"I often wonder about that. We wait for patients to get well before sending them off. But these?"

"I wonder about the entire hospital set-up. We nurse them back to health because only healthy people can work. But they send children, the feeble, the blind, oldsters."

"Makes you wonder, doesn't it?"

Hanne doesn't want to complete the thought. Is the whole thing just a sham? Dr. Spanier is the director in charge of the medical unit. An Old-Timer, he is friendly, if not downright chummy, with Gemmeker, the Kommandant. The hospital provides jobs and exemptions for a lot of people in the camp. Questions, questions. And no good answers.

She shrugs. As long as it keeps her and Ruth off The *List* she has nothing against that state of affairs.

Breakfast rolls in from the kitchen. They set it up. Hanne runs back and forth with the breakfast trays, the hot brown brew they call coffee, and slices of bread. She finds lost shawls, misplaced gloves, ties belts, buttons dresses and coats. Old people are slow. And gabby. She listens to their aches and pains, illnesses, tales of children, grandchildren. They rummage through purses, show her the latest snapshots of loved ones, eager to hear her comments. She helps to put the pictures back into folders, careful not to ruin them. She works mechanically. Tries not to get emotionally involved. Not to think. Every Tuesday morning the same nagging questions. The same upsetting thoughts. What is she doing here? Conspiring against her own people? Getting them ready for transport? They would have to go, regardless... Better not think! Turn it off! Off! Please!

At seven sharp two Green Police enter. Gemmeker's men. Rifles over their shoulders. Flaunt their might. They're here to supervise. Several OD men, the despised Jewish police, arrive with them. Their duty is to carry invalids to the train, on stretchers if necessary. Hanne scans her list. Checks against theirs. She hands her list to the Germans. They call the names, arranged in alphabetical order. Then line the people up in rows. Hanne runs to get her coat. She has to help the group to the train. The Germans count again.

"*Stimmt.*"

Everyone on the list is accounted for.

"*Marsch! Los!*"

The group shuffles to their destination. The stretchers go first. Then the others. Across soggy, melting muck. Through puddles of every consistency. Sobs and cries drown in the general commotion. Hanne steadies individuals wherever she can until they get to the platform. Here her job ends. The Greens and the OD take full charge. They do the loading. Hanne watches the spectacle unfold before her eyes. Her senses shut off from reality out of sheer necessity.

The doors of the wagons are wide open, black gaping holes to be stuffed. The loading is in full swing. One wagon filled, move on to the next in line. The old, the cripples, the blind first. The OD load. Shove the cargo up into the wagon. Greens help from inside the opening. Humans and luggage. Cram both onto the bare floor. Like canned sardines. The Jewish OD scum shout and kick and push. Like their German masters. No wailing, no crying tolerated. Kommandant Gemmeker in impeccable uniform supervises the loading from the platform, his shepherd dog by his side. Dr. Spanier, in business suit, stands next to him. Schlesinger, Head of Camp Registration (commonly called Sir *Machtsichwichtig*), VIP, hot shot, wears riding breeches and matching boots. They fawn on either side of the Kommandant. Hospital doctors stand by in the background to assist "in case of emergency."

Hanne's nurse's badge protects her. She walks slowly along the platform looking for familiar faces among the people waiting for loading. They stand in groups with their barrack elder, ready with his list, on the platform among their suitcases, knapsacks, cartons, bags. There are the deHartoghs. Hanne walks over to say goodbye.

"One suitcase only."

Mrs. deHartogh is flustered. They are three, Mister, Mistress, Flipje. Three suitcases. She decides to redistribute her material wealth in them in case the family gets separated during the trip. Flipje gets his own suitcase. Smart thinking. Hanne looks at the display on the platform with a new wave of wonder. Another pair of boots. In addition to the pair she is wearing. She sure has come prepared. Disinterested in her provisions, Flip and his father watch for their turn on the train.

Hanne watches Mrs. deHartogh, fascinated. Her mind hops in fantasies. The long, red fingernails stuff one suitcase to the brim. Suddenly the woman takes off for the other suitcase farther off. The extra pair of boots stand on the ground, alone. Hanne's brain runs wild. What if she forgets them? Or she's called to the train before she has a chance to cram them on top of the bulging contents here or there? Their barrack number is called from the wagon. The eldest walks over to the train and hands over his list. The group starts to move behind him. Mr. deHartogh calls Flipje and returns to his wife. Starts to close the overstuffed suitcases. Hanne watches, apprehensively, with her eye on the solid pair of boots on the side. She ought to tell him.

From the train opening the Green Police shout their name, "De Hartogh!"

"My boots," Teacozy shouts frantically. Hanne heaves a sigh. No. These are not her boots. She runs over to help. Gets the boots. Handsewn Bally boots. Hands them to their rightful owner. The fingers with their red nails grab them, heap them on top of her neatly folded clothes in the open suitcase. Mister deHartogh tries to close the lid over them.

"Help me," he puffs from below.

Mrs. deHartogh sits down on top of the suitcase next to him. Hanne too. They push and press. Finally, the bulging suitcase snaps shut on the new handsewn leather boots inside. He lugs the cases to the wagon. A last, indifferent goodbye. Then the three are inside. The last to be crammed into the black hole. Hanne sees a lot of people sitting on top of their luggage spread on the floor inside. Space at a premium. Sardines in a can. The Greens shout, push, shove. Stuff people and luggage. Squeeze the overflow inside between the closing doors. Shut the door over the bulge.

"That's a full one all right!" They wipe their brows. Proud of their efficiency.

The next cattle car. They stomp over. The next group. Herded. Stuffed in like animals. Human voices emerge from behind the tile-brown slats, muffled, subdued, indistinguishable. Hanne wonders about their living space. Water? Toilets? Food? Two pairs of beautiful, handmade boots. She looks down at her own worn footgear. Shrugs.

"These are mine," she says with emphasis to no one in particular.

Hanne walks around the triad Gemmeker-Schlesinger-Spanier. An unholy trinity. Preoccupied in pleasant conversation. Gemmeker laughs out loud. What kind of jokes are they telling each other while all this goes on? In his riding outfit, Schlesinger looks worse than the Nazi. More dangerous too. Definitely the most despised, hated, envied, flattered person in camp. Manager over life and death. Gemmeker states the required number. Schlesinger provides the people. Exact amount. Culled from the masses. People grovel to save their hides. A Green Police stomps up, confers with the three. A nod.

The policeman shouts, "No more luggage. Just one small bag for each!"

"One small item per person only from now on."

"What about the rest of the bags?"

"Leave the rest on the platform."

With less baggage you can stuff in more people. Simple logic. There aren't enough wagons for both.

The deHartoghs are lucky. She didn't have to leave her boots on the platform.

The next group is called for loading. They are rushed to the train. A few kicks, shouts and knocks with the rifle settle any protest over suitcases left behind. Without the luggage, the loading goes much faster. Smoother. More *material* goes into the space. Hanne stands glued to her spot. Watches the final car being loaded. The door rolled shut. Their job done, the OD step aside. The Green Police walk along the platform, pull the slanted iron bolts over each closed door. One by one. The finale. Securely locked to prevent escapes. Ready and sealed. Those inside have some straw, a bucket of water, an empty pail to relieve themselves. They have become a universe unto themselves.

Muffled screams, wails from inside the train rent the cold air. The leader of the Green Police signals Gemmeker. Job done. Ready to roll.

Hanne is dead tired.

The Kommandant interrupts his animated conversation with Dr. Spanier and Schlesinger. Looks up and down the train. God incarnate. Walks a few paces down the platform. The dog follows. At the end of the train the Master of the Universe lifts his hand. His sign to the engineer up front that this "shipment" is ready. The train whistles its piercing wail that cuts the marrow of every camp inmate. The blast calling the crime…

It takes a few minutes. Then the gorged reptile twitches into action. Straightens up. It creaks in every hinge with its heavy load. Every joint. Over three thousand this week.

"Three thousand individuals. Each one a separate world," Hanne mumbles.

Humans once upon a time. Cargo now. A "Shipment."

Rifles over their shoulders, the Green Police jump on the steps outside the sealed train. Slowly, very slowly the reptile inches to the camp boundary. It stops by the gate for the official exchange. Gemmeker's adjutant hands the list of names to the German military. Each Jew must be accounted for. From here on the German military is responsible for the cargo. The transfer is businesslike. Orderly. The familiar Heil Hitlers. Arms raised in salute. Clicking of heels. Then the military step into the empty passenger car provided for their use. They accompany the cargo all the way to its destination. Somewhere.

With a shudder the reptile straightens to its full length. Slithers out of the camp to fulfill its mission. The Greens ride along, hanging on its sides. They'll jump off at their Headquarters just outside the fence.

Hanne stands, transfixed. She sees the Greens jump off one by one outside the gate. Rifles included. The reptile moves on. Picks up speed. Then disappears around the bend with a creaking wail. She shudders on the platform. Her feet are cold and wet. Her shoes caked with mud.

Tuesday morning. Eleven A M. The usual time.

Hanne draws a deep breath. A sigh really. She is dead tired.

*   *   *

The Camp. It looks a uniform, strange entity to any outsider at first sight. It seems a melting pot. That's the impression she had when she first came. That first glance from outside when she looked at the drab uniformity of the barracks. Every moving creature looked drab. Bent. Scurvy. Scuttled. Like rats. One big lump of degraded humanity behind a fence.

But it isn't like that at all. Most of the prisoners hardly know one another. They come from different communities. Different homes. Different backgrounds.

Now they have to live together in close quarters. Thrown together by higher authority. They arrive in a lump, but each one an individual. They make certain to keep their individuality. They leave in a clump, each one a person. Each one concentrates on his own fate, not on his fellow human. They may live side by side, in too close proximity that makes for discomfort, engenders hate. They grate on each other. Each a person still.

There is a well-defined social structure within the camp. A self-contained hierarchy that lives by its own rules that over time have become tradition. Status is all-important, a status that takes its power from the German authority outside the fenced-in confines and passed on to those individuals it favors. They in turn pass their reflected glory down the line to their eclectic favorites.

The camp is a breathing universe running by its own rules. Developed over the years of its existence. A feudal society greased by flattery. Cunning. Its power is godlike since it rules over the life and death of each individual. It guides the lives of the hodgepodge millions of displaced, solitary strangers collected within its crowded confines. Each one a life. Each one in a scramble to keep his own life intact. Natural selection? Circumstance? Fate?

Life is precious. It comes in an allotment of one. There is no more than one. One life. Make the best of it. It's up to you!

*   *   *

Hanne is exhausted. All she can think of is rest. Lie down. Sleep. Done for the morning at the hospital. Gerda will take care of the three remaining patients until later that afternoon. She turns to leave. The cleaning crew is busy removing the enclosure. For another week. The left-over luggage, suitcases, bundles, packages, what have you, so prominently lonely on the platform just a minute ago, is gone. She wonders where all the flotsam went in such a hurry. Someone will make money on the contents. Barter is big around here. They might be worth lives, futures, aspirations. An eerie silence settles over the camp once the train has left. It's audible, tactile. She feels and tastes it with all her senses. In all her nerve tips. Like a subterranean sigh of relief. Spared. Everyone tries to forget The Train. It won't come for another week. Another week of grace. Back to normal! For a whole week! Did she say *normal*? She walks past the cleaning crew. Heads back to Barrack 65. The bunk on the third rung that is her present *home*. She's had so many lately.

The weather is clearing. A feeble ray of sun fights through dark, low-bulging kapok crags. Glimmers around its edges. Timid. Like an intruder. A pale gold stripe hits the ground in front of her. Frozen crystals glisten in their melt. She steps around the squish of defrosting puddles. Mindful of her holey footgear. She'll have to do something about that. Find something to cut insoles. Hellmuth might have some thick cardboard.

She steps out. Returned to life once more. It occurs to her that she has plenty of time to walk past Barrack 66, the penal barrack.

Barrack 66 is for *criminals*. *Criminals* like those picked up for not wearing the Jewish star. Or for hiding from the Nazis. Informers get paid for squealing on Jews. The pay must be terrific. There are enough informers around judging from the heavy stream of *criminals* going through Barrack 66. They get an S (for *Strafe*) on their ID's or passports. And all the S'ers are the first on the weekly List. Barrack 66 has its special guards. Round the clock. No outsiders allowed in. But prisoners are permitted to come to the window and talk to visitors.

Ernst Schlächter may have come in with a group of S-pickups. Gerd thought he had seen him come in. He wasn't sure.

"It's quite possible. Ernie went underground shortly before we were rounded up," Hanne argues.

Gerd could be wrong. But if he came in last night he'd be too late for this morning's List. She is going to look for him.

Hanne stalks through the expanding mud mounds. Careful not to sink too deeply into the sloshy muck outside one of the windows of 66. She knocks at the glass pane. Puts her nose against it. No one inside? Of course, they went on transport in the morning. She knocks again to make certain. A fellow with a bushel of flaming red hair and a mustache to match appears behind the glass. A stranger.

"Hanne?" he lights up.

She has to look twice to recognize their old pal.

"Ernie. How did you get here?"

Stupid question. At least he's still here. They gaze at each other through the window. He's put on some weight.

"Guess your Titian hair didn't fool the ss," she tries to joke.

"Nah. The milkman in Apeldoorn ratted, I think." He shrugs. His eyes broadcast fear.

"How are they treating you in here?" she wonders. She has never had the occasion to look for one of these *S*-people before.

"Okay, I guess. Considering the circumstances." His broody eyes stare out at her. The red glory around his head provides an eerie halo.

The circumstances. How give comfort to someone when there's no comfort to give? What can she do? Essentially she's in as much danger as he is. Only hers is delayed, by official consent.

"Gerd said you're here. He saw you come in."

"He was here this morning."

"Did you tell the receptionist that you're one of us? We're on deferral."

"I told the woman. I didn't know about any deferral. Gerd said something about talking to one of the bigwigs here, Schlesinger or something, on my behalf."

"If anyone can get something done, it's Gerd. You know him. He can put on the *schmoozer*. At least he has the gall. He knows some *machers* here. Lord knows how he rigs it."

She keeps talking hope. It's difficult to get rid of an *S*. A literal impossibility, unless you have extreme pull. She doesn't think that Gerd is in that league. She sighs. At least he'll try. She knows that much. There are miracles. Who knows? There's still another week.

" I got a package. I'll bring you some jam and peanut butter," Hanne offers.

"Awfully nice of you."

"Camp food is lousy. It's free. Compliments of the government. I'll see you later."

She turns to go. Her feet are wet and cold. She needs to find some heavy cardboard. Packages are a good source.

"Say hello to the others," he calls after her through the window. She turns and waves.

"Will do. I'll drop by later with the stuff."

*   *   *

The women's wing of Barrack 65 is almost empty when she arrives. The grown-ups are at work. The small children in school. Only a few oldsters, too old to work, sit around the stove. Gabbing family matters. Children. Grandchildren. Many bunks are bare. Mourning for their former tenants. They could tell stories galore after watching people come and go these past years. For a while the inmates will have plenty of storage space for their stuff. Until the next transports roll in. And the fight for living space resumes.

Hanne is surprised that Ruth isn't in. She has seen her on the platform. Probably visiting the boys in the men's wing, she figures. Hanne climbs up to her top bunk. The kid ought to get some sleep.

She folds her arms under her head. Tries to relax. No evil eye to spite her sleep, thank you. At least during the day the light is off.

Life in camp is confusing. It continues. Even social life – despite mess, dirt, filth, transports. Some famous entertainers from Amsterdam have formed a group. Including a few celebrities from Berlin who had escaped to Amsterdam and worked there entertaining the refugees. Last Saturday they staged *Cabaret Night* in Barrack 62. The place was crammed. Lots of good jokes. Intelligent jokes. Jokes with grip. Hanne likes smart jokes. Hates slapstick. A baritone, a German tenor, and a mezzosoprano sang Italian arias. There was a chorus. Harmonica players accompanied for lack of a piano. Hanne hums quietly and tries to remember the words –

We're tired of the war
Back to Mokem we wanna go.

Everyone chimed in. Grateful for the entertainment. Grateful for the relief it provided. *Mokem* is the nickname for Amsterdam. A Yiddish word, meaning *place*. It proves the long relationship between the Dutch and its Jews. Unlike in Germany. Inside the camp there are the usual fights between old and young. Traditional and modern. Hanne understands the mixed feelings. Entertainment and music while others go on transport. The younger set argues that people need diversion to go on. Crying isn't going to help. That's why she went. The transports are going. Whether she laughs at the jokes or not. The performers work hard to make the performance a success. They're great.

Gemmeker was there too. With his goons. Rumors have it that he wants to support a symphony orchestra. Hanne loves the idea. She loves music. Beethoven above all. Mozart a close second. Besides, performing keeps the performers off transport. Gemmeker, the patron saint of the performing arts. Ha, ha!

We're tired of the war
We're tired of the war.
I wanna go home.

She hums. Changes the last line of the lyrics to fit her case. Where is her home?

The aroma of toast is all pervasive around her. There must be bread slices on the stove. It smells great. Some old ladies having tea. Her stomach starts growling. It's a while until dinner yet. Ruth is still out, somewhere. Her arms are crampy. She turns on her side. Relishes her solo peace in the halfdark. The panes are dusty. The unlit bulb overhead covered with flyspecks. A black net on dusty white.

Apropos Gemmeker. The Kommandant is a calculating case.

The way he runs the camp aggravates the friction between the Dutch and those *arrogant Prussians*. Jews that is. Different backgrounds. Upbringing. Training. Outlook. Two different types of Jews thrown together under conditions too crowded for comfort. Where everyone tries to save his own skin. Sure, the Supermaster over Life and List prefers the *Yeckes*. They speak the same language. Yeckes are efficient, as streamlined and organized as their language. With an established, well-run administration long before July 1942 when the Germans decided to turn the refugee camp into a *Polizeiliches Durchgangslager,* a police transit camp, for all the country's Jews. Crafty, Gemmeker plays buddy to his *Yeckes*. A thousand Jews on the next train? Fine. He leaves the selection to his Jewish buddies. Master and slaves in cahoots. You want to stage your Cabaret? Symphony concerts? By all means. I love them. They break our dull routine out here in Nomansland. I bring my girlfriend and my honchos too. Mingle with my slaves in the front seats. The *Kommandant* likes to see happy faces. His obedient vassals may get swelled heads. They may shout and bark, just like their masters. He doesn't care. Divide and rule. Let the Jews fight it out. He's the winner. Nothing new under the sun. Funny, this god from Valhalla is good-looking. Some girls have taken a shine to him.

Der Wind hat mir ein Lied erzählt
Von einem Glück unsagbar schö... ö... n
Er weiss was meinem Herzen fehlt
Für wen es schlägt und glüht
Er weiss für wen...

She whistles the melody softly under her breath. What makes her whistle Zarah Leander's song all of a sudden? It's still her favorite. She loves Zarah's dark, full-throated voice. Whatever her private life. Singing of the wind. Telling of unspeakable longing, happiness. She thinks of Bert. Is she in love with him? She isn't sure. Nothing is sure.

Komm, ach komm... m... m... m...

she whistles on, softly, holds with a flourish, longing through her flesh, her bones, her entire being.

Ach... ch... ch...
Der Wind... der Wind... der Wind...

She longs to get out of this dump.

*   *   *

"The boys want us to come over on Friday night. Sort of an Oneg Shabbat get-together," Ruth says over the edge of her bunk.

"Hi. I didn't hear you come in."

"You were asleep. In the middle of the day," Ruth says with emphasis.

"I must've dozed off. In the middle of thinking."

"Thinking. A waste of time," Ruth declares. Convincing.

"Can't help it. You and your practical advice. What's this Oneg Shabbat for?"

"Dunno. Just to get together, I suppose."

"I don't want to get drawn into any Orthodox fight again," Hanne says.

That was last Friday night. They landed right in the middle of it in the men's wing. As if the rift between German and Dutch weren't enough for one camp, there's the deep chasm between the religious groups. Even before they get here. Inside, the fights get magnified. Old rabbis with yarmulkes and long beards from Eastern Europe team up with old devout halachic Dutch Jews against socialists, agnostics, all kinds of factions and shadings of the clean-shaven assimilated crowd. Mostly youngsters. A generation gap. Strict adherence is inconvenient, obsolete, out of touch with the real world they live in. The Middle Ages are long past. The seventeenth century in the Polish shtetls too. Not to mention the Jewish baptized *goyim*. Catholics, protestants, even *nuns* and *monks* in their habits, with tremendous crosses and rosaries dangling all over. It's a first for Hanne. She's never met *them* before.

The friction between pious and assimilated is familiar. Old hat. A continuation of her discussions with Vati. But she has no sympathy for converts. None whatsoever. No sir!

"They're traitors."

There's no other term for these turncoats. Their arguments are bogus. Look at this mess. What do they think? That baptism changes their Jewishness? Makes them Aryans? Ask Hitler about that!

"How can they claim that our Messiah has come?"

"Look around you!"

The Sabbath and holidays provoke clashes. Right here, in their own barrack last Friday. Julius Streicher would've had a ball hearing us argue. Good for a juicy headline in his *Der Stürmer*.

Friday. Sundown after work. They were with the boys in the next wing. The Orthodox wives were on the other side and kindled the Sabbath lights. With shawls and benedictions. Arms outstretched above the lights. Pray with closed eyes. "Bless the Sabbath bride."

They remind Hanne of home. The lights on the table glow. They watch the services, the women behind the men. The chazan chants the familiar *Kabbalat Shabbat*. Hanne and some of the boys hum along. An atmosphere of serenity in the midst of squalor. Remind of Friday evenings at home. Vati coming home from services. The Sabbath dinner. Singing *zemiroth* between courses. Fish, chicken soup with noodles.

Friday night services are short. Afterward everyone in the barrack pursues his own interests. The Orthodox sit in their corner with their Rabbi, debating Talmud, Torah, the sages. Heated, intense arguments, arms swinging, hands flapping, as if their lives depend on who is right or wrong on some fine point in the Scriptures. Endless debates since ancient times.

"What on earth are they fighting about?" Hanne mumbles. As if there's not enough fighting going on already.

They are still a group. Jongenshuis from Arnhem. A clique that draws together. They relax with talk. The latest camp news. Personal news. Discuss earthshaking politics from Hellmuth on up to the world at large.

"Someone escaped from Barrack 66," Horsey reports.

"Really? Wow." They're speechless. "Despite all the supervision?"

"Must've had help from outside. Higher up."

It's hard to believe. They shake their heads, dumbfounded, envious. Envious most of all. To think... no, it's hard to think that one through.

Gerd and Hans light a cigarette to share between them. Weedsticks are a special treat because they make them feel grown up. And they're hard to come by. Hardcore addicts trade them for food. Or other valuables. A pack might get someone off the deportation list. There's even a busy trade in butts. Hans got his in a package from a friend.

Suddenly one of those holy bearded men stands at their table.

"Smoking on Shabbat! You should be ashamed. A Jew!" he shouts into their faces.

They look up. Suddenly aware that the whole Orthodoxy is up in arms.

"Children without reverence. No tradition. No respect for our laws!" Their eyes fume hate.

"You mock the Torah!" a pinched face shouts.

Gray earlocks shake. His moonface wife puts a fleshy hand on his shoulder to calm him down.

The Jewish Orthodoxy refute them. Their youth. Their ideas. The aroma of tobacco hits their nostrils. Hans keeps the burning weedstick between his fingers. Hesitant. It's not the first time the old fellows object to things they do. Like treife food sent them in packages. Now this! They sit, resentful. They don't want to offend the old generation with their ancient laws. It's just that times have changed.

Werner can't keep his mouth shut.

"Look. It's none of your business. We're old enough to think for ourselves."

Werner stands there. Bluegray eyes, swollen veins in his forehead, his cowlick quivering.

They sit behind him. Tacit defiance. These old *knackers* sure have a nerve! Who gives them the right to tell us what to do? We don't tell *them* how to behave! Or what to believe!

The opposition is alive and well. Old versus young.

"Old codgers!" Gerd sneers under his breath.

"Think they own the world!" Hans mumbles.

"You *are* Jews! The Torah belongs to all of us. Thanks to her we survived. It is forbidden to light fire on Shabbat!" Earlocks shakes his finger at them. Beard and stomach shake in unison with his voice. Moses on his mountain smashing the tablets in self-righteous fury.

They are the rocks. The tablets are broken.

"You and your old-fashioned laws. This is the twentieth century!" Werner shouts.

"Better stop this," Hanne mumbles, disgusted with the entire scene.

But Werner needs to get it out of his system, all of it.

"Leave us alone. We don't interfere in your affairs. Besides," Werner takes a deep breath for the finale. "Besides, smoking has nothing to do with work. And even less with religion."

"You tell him," Dicky snuffles under his nose. He takes the cigarette from Hans and puffs on it. Exhales blue rings that rise defiantly through the barrack air. Defiance in action. War between the generations.

The chazan jumps to his feet. Delegate for the beards behind him.

"You pipsqueaks. You young nothings! We're old enough to be your fathers. Your grandfathers!" Fists pound the table.

"No respect for your elders! You trample on our traditions!

Defy our Torah! Disregard our Rabbis! *Phooey*!!!" He spits on the floor before him to show his disgust.

"It's you who've brought this disaster on us! Hitler is what you deserve!"

"Yes. Hitler shows you all right!"

The barrack is aghast. All the way up the walls.

"What gives those fanatics the right?" Hanne explodes in her head.

The Sabbath candles flicker. Frantic agitation hangs heavy over the sudden embarrassed quiet.

"They're nuts," Hans decides. He stands up to walk away.

"Who gives you the right to be the judge? You're not God!" Werner screams.

He stops for breath. He is going to tell them! Who is he to consider them idiots. Nincompoops.

"You blame us. US. Why don't you blame yourself? Where has all this Orthodoxy gotten you? Your traditions? Grow *peyes* in this day and age? And kashruth? It means clean. So you decide that mixing meat and milk is *unclean*? A cow mixes both. And what about body cleanliness? Throwing a few scoops of water over your hands before meals doesn't mean cleanliness! Where's the law for stinking bodies!" The youngsters breathe silent agreement. They know the oldsters find them rude. Upstarts that challenge ancient laws. Three thousand years of tradition.

"No respect. No respect at all!"

They sense it more than hear it from the other side. It's not the first time. Hanne is weary of hearing the same argument over and over again. A house divided against itself. She can see Julius Streicher's caricatures in his *Stürmer*. The Nazi gloats.

"Werner. That's enough. You're getting too personal. Vindictive. You're going too far."

The Rabbi on the other side gets into the act. "Calm down, all of you." He looks at both sides. Turns to the youngsters.

"Listen. Your insolence has nothing to do with religion. Your behavior degrades all of us, including you! All right. Don't keep the laws. Don't keep kosher. But have the decency to respect those who do. They *are* your traditions or you wouldn't be here. After all, we live in Jewish surroundings. Don't offend others with your smoking on Shabbat. And you know that you do."

The Rabbi's quiet authority spreads sense between the warring parties. The Sabbath candles flicker quietly.

Only hothead Werner needs to have the last word.

"I have nothing against traditions. And nothing against prayers. But I resent people interfering with what I'm doing. My smoking is my business. Mine alone. If it's a sin, fine. It's no one else's sin but my own."

"You've made your point, Werner."

The group wants to end the fight. They've discussed this a million times. They grew up with these controversies between diverse nationalities, different mores, changing generations. They agree with Werner. The laws are ancient. Behind their times. They need to be revised. For Torah and Talmud to be a living law it's important to reinterpret the laws time and again the way the ancients did. Throughout the centuries. The *Shulchan Aruch* is not the final decree. Even if some Ashkenazi sects in eastern Europe want to have it so.

* * *

It's an old issue for Hanne. She knows both sides well. Dad and his old-fashioned laws. Mutti smokes on the Sabbath. Secretly, in the bathroom. At least she thinks it's secret. The tobacco stink smells throughout the house. Vati keeps the Sabbath. He waits until after havdalah. First thing then, and only then, he lights his cigarette. But he keeps quiet about Mutti. It's her business. And since her own run-in with the Agudah boys in The Hague Hanne's reservations about this entire Orthodoxy bit have risen skyhigh.

"To blame us and smoking for Hitler is downright crazy! Simply nuts!"

* * *

Hanne wonders whether it's only that fight with the Agudah boys in The Hague that began her doubts. They're deep inside her brain. They linger. Smolder. Fester. What do these Orthodox do with their prayers? Jews have prayed for two thousand years. And look where it has gotten us!!! Is there anyone listening up there? Not that I can discern! On leave of absence perhaps? Finish the thought

"Is there anyone out there? Anyone? Hello? *Sh'ma koli*?"

*   *   *

The issue is moot the minute the door opens and three ss-men trample into the barrack. Suddenly the walls fill with silent dread. The air is loaded with fear. No ss has ever entered a barrack. This is new. Blackbooted, they post themselves inside the entrance door.

"No one leaves," their leader barks. His voice is hollow against the Shabbat lights. The cigarettes are forgotten. Smoking on Shabbat is no longer an issue – the Nazis are. And their laws.

"We're worse than these predators," Hanne mumbles. The accusation is fresh in her mind.

"Your ID's. Remain next to your beds," the leader orders.

He stands at the front of the barrack. The others branch out. Trample on wood floors. One checks the bathroom.

"No one here," he reports to the front.

The prisoners oblige. Like sheep. They shuffle about to find their ID's in no time. Stand by their beds. Hanne and the other girls stand next to the boys. The Orthodox women stand with their husbands. Their bunks are in the other wing. Their ID's too.

The ss stomp down the aisles from bunk to bunk to check ID's. They run their rifles across empty bunks along the way. The wooden floors groan under their boots.

"They must be looking for the escapees from 66," Werner whispers out of the corner of his mouth.

"For sure."

One of the ss stares them down with icy eyes. Hanne stares

back in a stubborn attempt to resurrect self-esteem. He resumes his checking. She breathes momentary relief. Across the aisle the angry old fellow rummages through his papers. Nervous. Can't find his ID? His fingers shake. His face, so rabid a minute ago, is ashen. What an infantile idea to say that God sent Hitler to punish all Jews. Sure, the Nazis are a scourge. But to explain them in this manner is worse than infantile. Even if you believe that God takes a personal interest in what's going on down here. And that's something hard to figure. Considering that good people are sent off. Meanies stay. Explain that! She wracks her brain to remember who said that God created the world, then left the management to chance. Some philosopher whose name she can't remember. Life a chance occurrence? Is there a God? If there is, how can He let this happen? Nazis. Concentration camps.

She sighs. Tired of thinking. She has no answer. There is no answer.

"Your ID?" The SS stands before her. A black menace.

"It's in my handbag. In the other wing."

He sends her and the other women and girls back to their wing.

"We'll be over there."

It takes the SS over an hour to search the barrack. By that time it's nine PM, the hour of universal curfew.

Another German stomps in. Announces the end of the search. Visitors have five minutes to return to their respective barracks.

The missing man from 66 remains at large. The punishment goes to the inmates of 66. They have to line up in front of their barrack every morning for two-hour push-ups. In the icecaked mud. Until next Tuesday. To punish them with the next transport is grotesque. With their S on their ID they go anyway. Another one of the many idiosyncrasies of camp life.

The Jongenshuis group admires the escapee. Admiration tinged with envy. Lucky fellow! How on earth did he pull it off?

*　*　*

Hanne's arms are numb. She pulls them out from under her head. Stiff. She changes position with a groan. Shakes her numb joints. They hurt. She rubs her fingers to get her blood circulating again. A fly buzzes around the dirty lightbulb overhead. Tiny flyspecks, round black dots on glass. Creature totally out of season. What's it doing in here? She never notices the specks when the light is on at night.

Some smallfry chase each other the length of the aisles. She smiles at their innocent laughter. The kitchen duty people return from the central kitchen. One woman unloads a few potatoes from under her clothes like well-guarded treasures. Puts them on the stove to roast next to some carrots already roasting on space carved out by somebody else. Kitchen people are better off than others for obvious reasons. Of course, nothing is as safe as the job of the camp princes, the administration people who are in constant contact with the Germans. They're never going on transport.

There's a noisy fight around the stove. Priorities. Potatoes versus carrots.

"Don't push my stuff to the side. I was here first!"

"Others have the same right. We don't have time to sit around the stove all day. We work!" Hanne closes her eyes. No chance for a nap in this racket. She'll have to get up and go to work soon anyway. Out of the corner of her eyes she sees Hans and Esther Markbreiter come in. Newlyweds. Got married two days ago. Both came to Holland with a children's transport. He from Vienna, she from Berlin. They met at Jongenshuis. Last week they announced their plan to marry. No use to talk them out of that foolishness. They had *made up their minds. Considered the consequences.*

"Who knows where we'll be tomorrow!"

They're right. Why not get out of life whatever you can? Tomorrow may be too late. The Rabbi in the other wing officiated. The group witnessed. Husband and wife at eighteen. Good luck. Now they can have intercourse without indecency charges from the older generation. The Orthodox are satisfied. The two make good use of their liberty. Hans visits his wife every chance they get. Oblivious to the noise all around they disappear under the pink wool blanket with the green stripes on Esther's top bunk. High enough to be out of the general viewing range. From her bunk Hanne sees the green stripes come alive with irregular propulsions that gradually shift to a regular, steadily mounting rhythm. Hanne waits for heavy breathing and muffled groans. In vain. The playful youngsters and the fighting oven toasters drown them out. Embarrassed, Hanne turns to give those two more privacy. But the vibrations of metal persist in her spine. How come they have time to get in early in the afternoon? Are they playing hooky from work? What if Esther gets pregnant? To have a baby in this dump? Hanne feels sorry for the baby. Some honeymoon! Hanne tries to picture her own. Pushes it years away. Will she ever have one? With whom? Bert?

Tomorrow is a blank.

Hanne has never connected Bert with marriage. The idea intrigues her. Does she love him? Sort of, in a friendly way. He's hardly a fellow to sweep her off her feet. Life does that. More than she would like. Bert is goodhearted, considerate. A nice guy. Yes, nice is the word. Ugly? To look at perhaps. But kindness and caring make up for physical shortcomings. Or do they? She isn't sure. Her brain tells her that Werner can't hold a candle to him by a long shot. With all his good looks. She thinks of his cowlick over his forehead. Sort of cute.

She pictures Bert at home. A bed with sheets. Clean, white sheets. Slightly starched the way Dutch housewives hang them out on the line. She longs to lie between clean linens. In an orderly room. An internal longing to be with Bert now creeps inside her. Feel his warm hands, the warmth of his body against hers. Will she ever see him again? Not unless she gets out of this hellhole. But love Bert? She isn't sure. Rather doubts it.

Hanne sighs. The bunk contraption shakes in its joints. Aren't these two finished yet? With all this noisy humanity around they ought to hurry up. She wonders what other couples do in this place. With the exception of the Markbreiters, she has never seen anyone else copulate. The boys tend to crack jokes about couples. Not impossible in a camp where husbands and wives are separated. Perhaps she isn't smart enough to see such things. Beds aren't a necessary requirement either. The boys rumor about couples taking walks behind barracks in the darkness. Must be a cold affair in this freezing weather. Of course, most people don't stay in camp long enough. Have too many other things on their mind to think of sex. Like staying off the train.

The bed convulsions stop with an abrupt thud. The pink blanket is still. Flat. At peace. Two heads stick out on one side. Curly blond short hair next to long flowing strands.

The original *Long-termers* are a different camp breed. They inhabit the small family barracks at the side of the camp with lots of privacy. They're the envy of the common inmates who live in the mass barracks. The *commoners* have to find their own solutions. More recent additions to the *Old-timers* like barrack elders à la Hellmuth cordon their sleeping quarters off from the great halls with curtains behind the entrances. They have their wives in their cubicles, much to the envy of the others in the communal halls. If it's forbidden, no one complains. Who'd dare? And to whom? God is on the side of the powerful.

*　*　*

"Hi, there. Wake up!"

Hanne hears her sister's voice. Feels her tap on her feet. She opens her eyes.

"I must've dozed off again. What's up?" Hanne sits up. Yawns.

The fly is busy buzzing around the bulb overhead. Now it dives down, circles around her head with a buzz. Hanne waves it off.

"How can you sleep in this noise?" Ruth's face is flushed with excitement.

"I could sleep forever."

A glance across the bunks outlines two motionless bodies under pink wool.

She is never alert after waking up, and doubly groggy after dozing in the afternoon.

"What is it? Something up?" Hanne asks the dark curled head below her.

"Hellmuth has been looking for you."

"What's he want?" Hanne shakes her brain to wake herself up.

"He has a letter for you, real official looking affair with stamps and stuff. He thought you may want it right away and brought it over from the post office. Special Delivery. He's in the men's wing."

Hanne is on sudden high alert. She shoots out of her saggy hole. Hans Hellmuth in person! Indeed!

"Come on," she tells Ruth and slides down the metal contraption. Runs to the other wing. Ruth close behind her.

"It's special delivery," Ruth repeats behind her back.

Hanne sees Hellmuth talking to the Rabbi. The letter shines like a polished treasure in his hand.

"A letter for me?" she interrupts the two men.

"Straight from the capital of the Thousand Year Reich."

Hellmuth has her sign a paper and hands her the thick white envelope.

Hanne tingles. Hesitates. Surveys the three gold crowns over the sender's name and address.

"*Kungliga Svenska Beskickningen,*" she reads slowly, overwhelmed by the officialdom. The feel of the expensive watermarked paper. So different from the dull, brownish paper they get in their war-torn part of the world. She doesn't know the language, but she knows that it's from the Swedish Legation in Berlin, addressed to her: Hanne Kalter, Camp Westerbork, Drente, Holland. A million stamps besides.

"Yikes! This is the letter we've been waiting for." She stares at the envelope.

"Get a hold of yourself, idiot. Open it."

She is too excited to object to Ruth's choice of title.

She tears into the envelope, slowly, gingerly, mindful to preserve the sender's address. Ruth stands next to her, impatient. The paper crackles in her hand.

"Come on. It's not gold. Don't you want to know what is says?"

"Hold your horses, will you? It's addressed to me!" She pulls the letter out. The letterhead bears the same logo. Underneath it's addressed to her, Hanne Kalter. She shakes from the bottom of her feet upward. Out into her fingertips. Overcome with importance.

She pulls herself together. Her eyes fly across the white heavy paper. In a somewhat stilted German the Swedish Legation in Berlin has the pleasure to inform her that the Swedish Parliament, at the recommendation of *His Majesty King Gustaf v of Sweden, on January 8, 1943 has voted to confer Swedish citizenship on the children Hanne Kalter and Ruth Kalter.*

She reads out loud. Ruth reads along with her over her left shoulder. Then her knees buckle.

"This is too much," she says and holds on to the table for support. The letter clutched tightly in her hand she reads on that at the request of her uncle, Mr. Adolf Bindefeld of Gothenburg, Hanne and Ruth Kalter are to come to join their parents in Sweden as soon as this can be arranged. Accordingly, the Swedish Legation in Berlin, entrusted with the execution of this request, has applied to the German authorities to grant the children Kalter permission to leave German territory. To speed up matters the Legation has issued Swedish passports for Hanne and Ruth Kalter and sent these, including photos, to the German authorities for due process. At the request of Mr. Adolf Bindefeld, the Legation has asked for immediate release of the children Kalter from Camp Westerbork to wait for this permission, i.e. *Sichtvermerk* from the German authorities, in Amsterdam.

"My gosh. I can't believe this!" Hanne says. She looks at Ruth bending over as she reads along. She can feel her breath.

"Go on!" Ruth's impatience is volatile. "Go on!" she urges.

The letter goes on to give them directions. After receiving their passports with the proper exit visa from Gestapo in Amsterdam they are to travel by train to Berlin where the Swedish Legation will arrange further passage to Gothenburg and the children's return to their parents. Signed by the Swedish attaché, Sven Lind.

"I can't believe this."

"Don't be silly," Ruth says. "Here it is. Established."

Hanne hangs on to the letter, fingers the paper like precious property. Vellum. Solid, sturdy, genuine. The real article. Swedish citizens. Ruth takes the letter.

"Passports. Imagine."

Hanne pinches Ruth's arm, then her own. Makes doubly certain that this is not a dream.

The girls sit down on the edge of the bottom bunk that held a nice young woman from Amsterdam this very morning. She is now on a cattle train, destination unknown. The bed is empty, waiting for its next victim. Life is unpredictable.

"They make it sound so simple. Just get their okay and leave. They don't know Germans. I won't believe it until I've walked past that barbed wire and see the watchtowers from the other side," Hanne cautions.

Hellmuth ambles by, curiosity personified.

"I have to go and talk to Administration," Hanne puts herself in order.

"What's up?"

"We're Swedish citizens. Going to Sweden," Ruth declares, all factual personality.

"Think of me when you're there, will you?" Hellmuth says, wistful with a good measure of visible envy.

"We're not there yet," Hanne cautions. Nothing in life is certain. She has never been able to make plans, and this is no time to start. Tomorrow is always a dream away. Better not tempt fate with detailed plans. A letter from the Swedes may spell things out.

They don't know fate the way she does. Fate – a mercurial item on the road to the future. Temperamental. Devious.

"First thing, I have to show this letter to Dr. Neuberger in the Applications Office and then to the Jewish Advisory Council. Just to make sure they keep us off the train," Hanne says.

"And make certain that we get released," Ruth says.

"We'll go this afternoon right after work." Hanne takes the reins.

"Okay. I'll meet you outside your ward."

Hanne looks at her watch. "Time to get back to work. I saw Ernie Schlächter this morning in No 66. I promised him some of our peanut butter and jam. We'll have enough to eat once we get out. I'll drop it off on my way to work."

"I'll come with you," Ruth declares.

Hanne has yet another visit ahead of her. Bella Heckscher has come in. Bella, her one-time Jewish classmate at *Kunstoefening*. Thrown out like Hanne, she too had worked for Zwollo for a short while. Then she stopped coming. There were rumors of a nervous breakdown. Hanne never knew the details. Zwollo mumbled something about her aunt calling. All Hanne knows is that Bella lost her parents in an accident and lived with her aunt's family. Artwork was meant as therapy for Bella. Now she's in the Westerbork mental ward, Barrack 85. Hanne feels sorry for her.

"The world we live in isn't made for sensitive people," she reflects. Perhaps Eddie and Werner want to visit Bella with her.

"Come on, we'll be late for work," Ruth reminds her, the peanut butter and jam for Ernie in her hands.

Chapter 12

Rat-tat-tat-tat, rat-tat-tat-tat drums the train. Sings freedom, free, freee, freeee, freeeee. It takes an hour by train from Amsterdam to Arnhem. The humdrum rhythm vibrates through her body. Soporific. Alone in the compartment she closes her eyes. Hangs on to her thoughts. Tries to visualize Bert's face at her unexpected return. Freedom regained. This is her second day. Liberty diffuses her bones, her flesh, every fiber of her ganglia, every tip of her nerves. Her innards burst. Joy. Relief. At long last.

It's two days ago that she left from outside the gate. Wednesday, May 5, 1943. Odd, it's so far removed now. Like a surreal nightmare you know is only that, a nightmare. No more. Westerbork is its name. How can she ever forget?

* * *

The hot bath she and Ruth took when they finally arrived at Abram's boarding house on Jekerstraat 21 in Amsterdam South. That hot bath they had been dreaming about for six months. She let Ruth go first. Why not? While she opened the suitcase and removed all the remaining stars from her clothing. The thread in the lightly fastened six-pointed yellow squares pulled out easily, one by one.

"There. I'm not going to wear these anymore. We don't need to! We're Swedish citizens. You do the same," Hanne yells into the steamy bathroom where Ruth runs the hot water.

"Do you think we should?" Careful Ruth voices her doubts.

"Why not? The Abrams may like to get these stars so they won't need to shift theirs around from one dress to another."

"I'm going to keep my nurse's armband," Ruth shouts out of the steam.

"Not me. I'm done with camp life," Hanne says. "I'm getting rid of mine. The sooner the better."

She inhales deeply. That bath! With lots of soap. Fatso Goldberg's bar. Teacozy's medium for infamy. Lather all over. Thick like cream. Scrub off all that filth. That's when she decided to see Bert. Tell him in person that she's out. Thank him for his concern. The lifeline he provided that kept her from total despair. Will he be surprised when he sees her! She can feel his surprise already. Feel it literally in her bones.

May 5 is the date to remember. A Wednesday, the middle of the week. The day she was born again. Given a second chance on life. Dead for so long, emotions paralyzed still, she is unable to fathom the entire scope of her experience. Register the great joy she should feel. Should feel. She has learned to watch herself from a distance. To record her innermost thoughts, smells, sights, sounds, feelings as if she were watching a stranger. Outside the things that are happening. But something inside her brain has started sprouting since yesterday. Volatile, diffident, transparent. Yet there it is. Her brain knows there is a tomorrow. Hope. A future on the horizon.

"Start working again," she pleads. "Brain. Come alive! Please! I need you to work with precision. Don't let me down."

She can't count the many times after the Swedish letter arrived Ruth and she appeared in the Application Office to inquire about news from the Gestapo. Bombarded the *macht-sich-wichtig* crowd behind their squeaky tables with questions. The Swedish Legation. They can't do much. It's up to the Germans, the Gestapo, to be precise.

Once she goes without Ruth.

"Any news today?"

The fellow at the reception desk grins at her with a lewd smirk. Instead of his usual trek behind the curtain into some mysterious inner sanctum where he usually gets his information from some lofty god, he tells her, "Sorry, nothing yet. They're working on it. It takes time."

"Can't you check?"

He gives her another rutty smirk. "Why not?"

He gets up and motions her to follow him behind that curtain. Curious, she follows him. She stands in a small room with another door, more mysterious than ever. The smirk expands. His gaze fastens on hers while he tries to grab her breast. She steps backward. Stares back. No!

"Wait here," he says and drops his arm. Then turns and disappears behind the door. Shuts it with a loud bang.

She waits, in no mood to get involved. Why should she? Who does he think he is! He can't help her other than look for directions from Gestapo. So what's he so high and mighty about?

She waits for an eternity. Dr. Neuberger, his boss, is famous for chasing skirts. Infamous is a better term. Is this fellow trying to emulate his boss? She doesn't need his or his master's special attention. No googoo eyes for her. She plays dumb when he finally returns.

"No. Sorry. Nothing yet."

She doesn't care for the strange glint in his eye and leaves with a sigh of relief, as if restored after a double threat.

"Our case is under the jurisdiction of higher authorities," she tells Ruth afterward. She still feels funny for waiting in that room. Like a piece of cheap merchandise. Special order refused to be claimed.

*   *   *

They wait for nearly five months. It's the afternoon of May 4ᵗʰ. Tuesday. *The Train* left in the morning. Punctually at 11:00 AM with its marrow-piercing shriek. A cool, breezy spring day in the northern Dutch province of Drenthe. The camp is quiet, recuperating from the last terror-filled twenty-four hours. The barracks are relaxing, emptied of many of its recent inmates. The Train is only a distant nightmare, an eternity away pushed far down into the subconscious. Another week. The wind streaks its usual blasts around the shacks of the camp. Sends streamers of sand flying through the cracks, as usual. The stove sputters, as usual. Does its usual best to spread warmth. A woman dissolves a bouillon cube in a tin cup of water on top of the stove. Soup à la Westerbork. The faint aroma of chicken imitation permeates the usual Westerbork stench. Relaxing on her bunk after the morning's gruesome duty, Hanne tries to thaw her frozen fingers under her coat.

The door of Barrack 65 is suddenly torn open. Everyone looks at the noise. A special messenger appears in the door, a dark outline in the light behind him. The air of the cool spring day outside surrounds him like an invisible halo.

"Close the door. It's cold in here," the bouillon cube woman shouts, tin cup in her hand, stirring the brew.

The boy steps inside the women's section. The white note in his hand shines prominent in the half dark of the barrack.

"I'm looking for Hanne Kalter."

"Hanne Kalter," the bouillon woman shouts down the barrack interior.

"That's me," Hanne calls from her bunk. She slides the metal rail down to the floor.

"I've been here twice already," the boy says and hands her the memo.

"I've just come back from work."

Hanne takes the memo. Her eyes fly across the paper. It's from the *Kommandantur* outside the fence. Hanne and Ruth Kalter are to appear at Camp Headquarters.

"Thanks," she calls after the boy. He is already halfway out the door.

It's like lightning has struck her. Action. She runs to find Ruth with Eddie Silber in the men's wing.

"We're going to see the inside of the *Kommandantur*. Come on."

They both run to Hellmuth in his cubicle. He takes the memo.

"All right. You're free to go. I'll take care of the rest."

*   *   *

Hanne's senses absorb the Dutch flower fields speeding past outside the train window. Rows and rows of colors – tulips, daffodils, hyacinths, crocuses glitter in the blazing morning sunlight. Reds. Yellows. Whites. Pinks in all shades. Patches of crocus in green calyx fingers. Purples.

The strong light hurts her eyes. She has to get used to it again after the dusk of camp life. Daffodils swagger in the breeze. Yellow sun fire in zephyr sky dotted with white fluff. Spring. After an eternity of gray monotony. Of despair. Springtime. Life's profusion before her in all its blinding brilliance. That's what struck her as soon as they passed the camp gate sitting on the open truck that took them both to the train station in Hooghalen. Houses, stone buildings, people, trees. The sun. Flowerpots. Containers with colors. Millions of colors. The world a blinding brilliance. It overwhelms her. No more hopeless drabness. No more camp. She can't believe her freedom.

She would like to be a child again. Has she ever been a child? She can't remember. She must have come a grown-up from the very start. Life goes on, regardless. Flowers in the field. Year after year. Will she ever be able to catch up? How do you make up for lost time? Six months. She hasn't seen her parents for five years. The world is full of colors.

*   *   *

The barracks of the *Kommandantur* stand solid outside the barbed wire fence. It's not easy to miss. Hanne and Ruth show the memo as their pass, then walk through the gate with a sense of self-righteous trepidation. It's a mental leap from here to there. Inside versus outside. They cross the neat gravel path between a well-kept lawn. Flowerbeds. Geraniums. Fuchsias. Flowers in containers. The absence of noise is palpable. She climbs the few steps to the main building. Ruth close behind her. Knocks at the door. Enters. It's like entering another universe. The subdued quiet inside the offices is tonic to her harried, frazzled nerves. Her eardrums relax. Her body tenses up. Germans behind the counter – two males in uniform, two females in ordinary dresses. Flowery sheers. A radio plays Haydn in the background. She feels out of place. The radio switches to a voice. Victories on all fronts. Well, take that with a grain of salt. What about the tremendous German defeat in Russia outside Stalingrad? Even with all the noise in the barracks they can hear the hum of the RAF on their nightly way south. Bombing missions deep into German lands. The anti-aircraft flak with its tarat tat tat tat, tarat tat tat tat a constant staccato echo nearby. The camp inmates are excited. They talk about nothing else.

"For all we know, the war may be over soon."

"Let them talk victories."

They know better than the radio broadcasts. Meanwhile she wants to get out of here. She turns to the fellow on the other side of the counter.

"Good morning."

"*Heil Hitler,*" his right arm shoots automatically into the air. A rocket released for action.

Hanne is not about to appreciate his salute. Narrow-minded megalomaniac!

"*Ich habe die Mitteilung hier vorzusprechen.*" She passes the memo across the counter.

"*Ja. Wir haben Sie erwartet.*" He takes the note.

Hanne is impressed despite herself. He has addressed her with the formal *Sie*. It's for the second time since she has been in camp. It must be the effect of Swedish citizenship. Her ego takes a leap. Up and out of bounds. He scans the note she has given him. Rummages through stacks of paper in front of him. Gets up and rummages through more dossiers in the back. Finally finds what he wants.

"*Hier,*" he says, pulls the Kalter dossier out and returns with it to his window seat. Clears his throat. Opens the folder. Pulls a letter. She watches him as he reads. His lips go up and down. Open and close. It is quiet in the room except for the radio and the tap tap of the girl on her typewriter. A whiff of eau de cologne. *4711.* The radio changes to Beethoven. *Appassionata.* She hums along. Her favorite composer. The fellow lifts his eyes. Fastens them, blue-gray porcelain marbles, on hers across the counter top.

"Your parents live in Gothenburg, Sweden?"

"Yes."

She squirms despite herself. It's like the last Inquisition. She feels Ruth close beside her.

"Here's a letter from the Swedish Legation in Berlin," he says.

"Yes." Hanne has learned the prudence of saying as little as possible when dealing with authority. He meditates on her *Yes.* The music plays on. The famous theme. Tralalala. Slow adagio. It reverberates in her head. Her foot taps in rhythm automatically. He lowers his gaze ever so slowly and meditates into the letter. His hair oil reeks stuffy.

"Your parents want you to join them there."

"Yes."

She has a short glimpse of the letter in his hands. The Swedish crowns. He reads some more. Drags the questions out for reasons of his own. She fidgets.

"The ss Headquarters in Amsterdam has authorized us to release you and let you wait for your *Sichtvermerk* in Amsterdam. You leave tomorrow morning. The truck will drive you to Hooghalen where you'll take the train. Here are your tickets, from the Jewish Council."

He passes the envelope with the tickets across the counter.

"And this is the address of the boarding house where the

Jewish Council has made reservation for you until you leave for Sweden."

Hanne takes the slip and adds it to the envelope with the tickets.

He pushes two short printed forms across the counter. "This is your release from Westerbork. Sign here."

Hanne looks at them. Two pieces of cheap grayish paper. Passes for the Jewesses Hanne and Ruth Kalter permitting them to leave camp Westerbork. Reason: *On Order of Sturmbannführer Zöpf. For departure to Sweden.* Signed for *The* Camp *Kommandant* by *Hassel.*

Official and stamped. May 5, 1943.

He holds his paper forward for her to sign her name. Ruth signs hers on the next. Hanne examines the envelope and the papers. Clumsy. Nervous. Then she puts everything slowly, very slowly into her handbag. Her fingers shake. Her body is a leaf in the wind.

"Thank you," she says across the counter.

"Be at the gate at seven thirty in the morning," he says. "The truck leaves at eight."

Hanne senses a faint hint of a smile around the corner of his mouth. She isn't sure. Could be her vivid imagination. And anyway, what does it matter? She cannot believe her luck that she's done with this. Not yet. She needs to get away from here. Every fiber in her being longs to get out. Out!

Free. Free to walk out of this camp. Free to leave this inferno. Tomorrow morning at eight o'clock. It's unbelievable. How easy it all is. Just sign a piece of paper. A paper with an official stamp. What's the fellow's name? She can't remember. Ah well, who cares.

"*Viel Glück*," he calls behind them.

They are already on their way out.

"*Danke*," Hanne mumbles toward the door.

"Goodbye," Hanne and Ruth whisper in unison. They walk

out. On clouds. His answer is immaterial. She pulls the door shut from outside. Done with it.

She remembers the two of them walk back along the tidy gravel path through the gate into the camp to spend the last night with their siblings. There's no need for words. They would hardly do justice to their feelings anyway. Not now. Not ever.

The train whistle blasts into Hanne's reflections. The train's motions reverberate through her body. Lattice puffs billow across the dusty windowpane, expand, disintegrate in their backward flow. The flower fields outside have made way for neatly divided flats of greens, turquoise, yellows, ochre in all shadings. The Dutch spring whirrs past in geometric patterns outside her window. Cattle grazing, mooing lazily in between lone farmhouses and barns. All exude peaceful, earthy contentment. Unconcerned with the tidal wave of hate and destruction surging through their land. Hanne wonders about the battlefronts. The soldiers fighting there. Where are they raging now beyond Stalingrad? Bert must know more about that. Last they were in North Africa. Winning at El Alamein.

Hanne settles back in her corner. Appreciates the peace and quiet. The last night at camp. Is it really just two days in the past? It seems two eons ago. No, two million planets ago. As many lifetimes. She knows what her siblings are doing at this moment. What is their future like? Ditta, Horsey, Werner, Eddie, Gerd, Hans, the two newlyweds, all the others. Fifty-seven of them. Even Hans and Esther stayed out of bed for as long as it took to say goodbye. They gather around the table beside Hanne's bunk, quietly, reluctant to talk about the good and bad, the beautiful and the ugly they shared these past years. Hanne writes down Horst Garnmann's address. *Mischling,* half-breed, he did not have to go with them to Westerbork. He lives in Amsterdam. She intends to contact him when she gets there. Parting is hard. Like leaving a piece of yourself behind. She opens the last of her jars and cans. They feast on peanut butter, jams, sardines and herring with bread slices Gerd and Dicky snitched, no *organized,* from the central kitchen. *Organized* that's the word there. Werner inherits her leftovers. She senses envy. A sting of guilt invades the back of her mind. She can't blame anyone for being envious. Werner gives her his suitcase with his best suit and other things for safekeeping.

"Here's my mother's address in London. Send it to her when you can."

"Sure," she promises.

There is a huge chasm yawning between them all of a sudden. No one talks about it. But it's there. An abyss they cannot cross. Their future is uncertain. She pushes the thought out of her mind. The way she has done with her own all along. Does so still. She promises to write. Send packages now that she'll be outside. They embrace. Kiss. Say goodnight. Go back to their bunks.

In the dawn Werner and Eddie carry their suitcases to the gate. See them off. The truck's motor rumbles, hums, waits. The two girls show their passes. Pass through the gate. Leave the others behind. Kurt Ehrlich walks with them through the gate. Free with an unexpected Nansen Pass. Like the girls, he heads for Amsterdam. For a short stopover. He wants to go to Spain or Portugal. Then on to Palestine. There are plenty of boats from there across the Mediterranean. He wants to help build a Jewish state. They turn and wave a last goodbye in the direction of the gate with the watchtower. Two forlorn fellows in its center. The barbed wire fence moves backward. Kurt and the two girls sit in the back of the open truck with the humming motor hobbling over the bumpy road. Away from the fence. Into the blinding sunshine of the Dutch countryside in May. She can still see the two boys stand by the gatehouse, two creatures doomed to go as far as fate will permit them. Their outlines shrink into the faint mist of the early morning. Tiny dots inside the gate. Part of her is still there, with her siblings in the squalor of Westerbork, the camp on the moor of the northeastern Dutch countryside, built for German Jewish refugees, then conveniently transformed to a *Durchgang-slager*, a transit camp for all of Holland's Jews on their way east.

One thousand every week. How many Jews are in Holland? A lot. Camp Westerbork. Part of her will remain there. Forever.

*   *   *

Noise from the corridor returns her to the present. People come and go. Outside her window the rural landscape has transformed to clusters of neat brick homes. Red brick with shiny rain-washed roofs. Windowpanes sparkle in the sunlight. Fenced-in front yards, neat squares sporting spring flowers – begonias, lilacs, crocuses, hyacinths, tulips. Tiny marguerites in lush green grass. They are nearing Utrecht, the railroad junction. The house clusters grow denser, less spacious, turn into blocks of apartment houses. The weave of railroad tracks gets complex, separates, divides, widens. The train screeches, jostles between the multi-branched criss-cross of tracks. The train whistle sends shivers of memory down her spine. Trucks, cars, cyclists stand behind booms at intersections. Waiting for the train to pass. Then they puff into the station within a cloud of acrid steam. Screech to a halt.

The acrid cloud makes her cough. Makes her stand back from the window. She does not have to change trains.

"Just a little while longer."

She looks down the platform. German soldiers are everywhere. She sees her fellow humans laugh, shout, wave, cry, embrace. Life lived. Then the doors bang shut. The stationmaster walks up to the locomotive, blows his whistle, lifts his sign. They roll on. She breathes the cool May air and lets the wind fly in her hair.

*   *   *

Life is a kaleidoscope. Haphazard days. Unscripted. They fall into hardly premeditated place. She had no time to write. To think that it is only day before yesterday that the barbed wire fence with the watchtowers closed behind her. She hopes that Kurtchen Ehrlich will make it out of German territory with his *Nansen* passport. After all, it was good enough to get him out of Westerbork. He helped them with their luggage to the tram station in Amsterdam. Then they said goodbye.

"Good luck in Palestine."

"Good luck to you in Sweden."

He waves after them in the streetcar. They will never see each other again. Life is nothing but a lot of goodbyes. Ever since *Kristallnacht*. Then she and Ruth are alone in the streetcar, the luggage beside them. On their own for the first time in five years. Destination Amsterdam Zuid. Abram's boarding house on Jekerstraat 21 is a good distance from the streetcar stop. They lug their suitcases through the quiet residential streets of Amsterdam South. She was smart to have taken her yellow star off before leaving the camp. Told Ruth to do the same. That way they can use public transportation.

"No more. No longer that kind of degradation," she tells the shaking compartment walls of the train. It's over and done with. Finito!!! She is a Swedish citizen. A Swedish subject. Even without the passport.

"No more of that," she repeats. Tells Ruth again when they unpack.

No. She has never denied her Judaism. She is not about to do it now. But the yellow star has to go. She couldn't get rid of hers fast enough.

"To wear that Star of David as an adornment is one thing. The Nazis turned it into a hateful, infernal mark of shame. Ordering us to wear it degrades us. They want to make Jews an inferior people, as if we are a danger to Aryan superiority."

"What superiority? They have made us easy scapegoats for mob violence."

At least the brat and she agree on something.

*   *   *

Jekerstraat 21. Amsterdam Zuid.

Hanne pulls the slip with instructions from her pocket. They check. *Pension Abram.*

"Finally."

It's past eight PM but they don't need to worry. They have official permission to be outside after curfew. Their arms hurt from lugging the heavy suitcases. Sweaty, smelly, tired, they look at each other. Smile. Ruth rings the bell. Secret furtive expectations. Their first home on the way home. Freedom, of sorts.

The door opens with a grinding squeak in its hinges. Mr. Abram stands in the center. Diminutive, wiry, lost in a huge apron. Friendly concave nose on top. The typical wooden wardrobe stands behind him overloaded with heavy coats.

"Good evening. We are the Kalter girls."

"Welcome to our boardinghouse. Come in." His thick, guttural German accent is a familiar sound.

They push their suitcases across the threshold. "Whew," a sigh of relief escapes both. They have arrived.

"Lore, here are the girls," he calls into the kitchen at the end of the hallway.

Mrs. Abram stands in a flow of steam rising from the dinner cooking on the stove. Small. Plump. Pudgy. Wider than tall. Her round peachy soft dumpling of a head peers out from atop her huge apron, a roomy gray affair with yellow dots that enfolds her like an oversized envelope. Her hairbun sticks against her neck with half-loose hairpins. She rubs her hands dry against her apron hips and stretches both detergent-red hands forward for the familiar German handshake. Stubby fingers lie warm, soft, sweaty in Hanne's grip.

"You're right on time. Dinner is almost ready. You must be tired," she breathes.

They shake hands to the soothing tick-tock of the kitchen clock on the wall. Hanne feels welcome. Relieved to have arrived. All excitement for the new life she is beginning.

"I'll call Klas to help you upstairs with your luggage," Mr. Abram calls from the hall.

"Klas is our boy," Mrs. Abrams explains. We put you on the second floor. You don't mind to climb stairs, do you? The other boarders are a lot older and hate to use the stairs, the friendly dumpling excuses their decision.

"Not at all." Hanne is magnanimity in person.

"The dinner gong sounds in a few minutes. Just wash your hands and come back down. There'll be plenty of time to unpack after dinner," Dumpling instructs from atop her apron.

Both Abrams return to stirring their steaming pots with their long-handled ladles.

The girls do as they are told. They are hungry and tired. They nod to the other guests as Mr. Abrams introduces them when they come down to dinner. They take their seats and decide to make this dinner a short affair. Halfway through they excuse themselves. The bathtub calls. That can't wait.

*　*　*

Eyes closed, Hanne still feels that first hot bath. Luxury heaven. Standing by the tub she watches the hot water ripple down in streams. Steam hugs her pores. Water rises in the tub. Up. Up. Almost to the edge. She steps over the bathtub rim, slowly, one foot first, then the other. Warm water floats up her legs. She slides her rump down the slick slanted back into bliss. Heaps of suds embrace her body. Soapbubbles full of inexplicable latent dreams. Soap. Goldberg's bar. Never mind the scarcity. She unwraps the creamy cake, first the outer wrap with the flamenco dancer. Then the gold foil. Voilà. Forget deHartogh. Get rid of accumulated filth. That peculiar stench of sweat, haysacks, urine, overfilled latrines, mixed with stinky potato glue and soda salts in metal cauldrons. Perfumed soap. To scrub away filth of condemned humanity that clings to her like an unwanted hell's halo. She wants herself percolated. An aura of discard emanates from her clothes. Hanne inhales deeply. The odor wafts strong in her nostrils. Sickens her nasal passages. Still there, two days later, despite all her scrubbing. Especially when she opens her trunk to get some underwear or clothes. She doesn't want to think back. Where are her siblings? The train rattles on toward Arnhem. Bert.

She turns her head and fills her lungs with the fresh air that floats through the open window. She'll have to get rid of her clothes as soon as possible as soon as they get to Sweden. Get rid of their memories. Lose herself in another being once she gets to her new home far away. It sounds so easy. Turn a new leaf. A new Hanne. Reborn.

They complete the adventure of rebirth in the morning. The Abrams are grateful for the yellow stars. It makes changing clothes easier. The girls feel outside the loop. Singularly superior. What if the Germans change their mind? Impossible.

"We can do our shopping between three and five only. And we can't take the streetcar. Would you mind shopping for us?" Mr. Abram wonders.

"Why not? It'll be fun to fool the Nazis."

Hanne's guts smile at the prospect.

Outside the landscape hastens past, turns familiar. Birds sidle in flocks on electric lines. The tracks, shiny parallels, divide into multiple strands. Beech, oak and sycamore groves sport their tiny fresh green plumage in the suburbs. The train slows down. Rolls across the bridge into Arnhem. Utrecht Plein below, the plaza that divides Arnhem into residential areas with Park Sonsbeek on one side. Downtown business district and the Rhine River on the other. The dirty red brick wall of Amsterdamsche Weg. The steep incline stretches upward in the morning light. How many times has she wandered that street on the other side of that brick wall? The train shrieks in its joints. She looks up at Jongenshuis shining white in the sunshine at the top of the hill. The jerk of the sudden stop jostles her forward. She holds tight. Keep your balance, Hanne.

Arnhem in big letters on the station walls.

She walks along the platform and looks up at the white building hugging the top. A familiar, double-faced castle, like the witch's apple in *Sleeping Beauty*.

Life in reverse. The many times she has looked down from there onto this platform. Wondered about the people coming and going. She looks up now. Another perspective. The familiar white building turned stranger. She knows its exterior. Even better its insides. Its black and white marble tiles. The wide wooden stairs. The brown wainscoting. The Nazi line-up. Who lives in it now? For a fleeting moment she feels like going up to find out. Perhaps later. First to Bert. Her anchor. Surprise!

*   *   *

She took the early train to give her as much time with Bert as possible. It's mid-morning when she enters the hat store on Hommelstraat. The familiar address from countless food packages. She has never met Bert's family. All she knows is that his father runs the store with Bert's younger brother Max. The family lives upstairs.

"Good morning."

She swings through the glass door. White steam floats in the back. The smell of steamed woolen felt. She turns to the old gentleman behind the glass counter.

"Hello. I'm Hanne. Is Bert home?"

She watches the old gent's puzzled face expand into a wide, warm smile. His hand reaches across the glass countertop.

"Why, of course. We've heard so much about you. I'm Bert's father."

They shake hands like old friends. Hanne notes a family resemblance. Gorrissen senior is better looking by far.

"Aren't you in Westerbork?"

"I was. They released us, my sister and me, day before yesterday. May 5th. We're in Amsterdam waiting for our *Sichtvermerk* from the Gestapo. To go to Sweden."

"Well, isn't that something!" He mumbles under his breath; it sounds like *damn them, moffen, murderers*. Or something like that. His chin set out like a rock, his head shakes in fierce enmity. It's clear where he stands.

"Hi, Max. Isn't Bert in school this morning?"

Max's head appears in a cloud of vapor that sizzles out of a kettle in the little backroom behind him. He keeps on brushing furiously the brim of a felt hat between his fingers.

"He is. He's working on his vase," Max shouts above the sizzle back into the store.

"Hi." Max emerges out of the steam. Puts his regenerated hat carefully on the counter. Then grabs Hanne's hand and shakes it wildly.

A swishy sizzle escapes the kettle in the back room. Dies down.

"Hi, Max." Hanne remembers faintly Bert's younger brother. He's taller than Bert, skinny, his neck even longer than his older brother's. Same pointy Adam's apple bobs up and down. Like a Jack-in-the-box. Gold-rimmed glasses blink across his nose.

"Bert went to school to work on that vase of his. I'm sure you'll find him there."

"Thanks," she says, halfway out the door. "See you later."

Kunstoefening is on the other side of *Stationsplein* in the center of town, only a short walk from the store. It feels good to walk the familiar streets, though the war shows its ugly face on the people. They have a drawn, hungry look. Shabbier clothes. Almost threadbare. Ravaged shop windows groan the rape of the land. In contrast, the German military in all its various colors trample their dominion. World control. The black and brown Nazis, ss and sa. Boisterous, guttural voices rattle their dare to the world. Polished boots drone pavement and cobblestones into submission. They own the world. Despite the latest news from the bbc. Don't they know the disastrous winter campaigns outside Stalingrad? Didn't they hear the disintegration of the Russian front and the African Corps? Rommel? The Dutch listen to the clandestine broadcasts in hidden nooks. Hitler threatens a secret weapon. What if that comes true? She shudders in the spring air. The very idea of Nazis winning the war is unthinkable. No. That mustn't be. Ever!

She crosses the plaza. Stands outside the school grounds from which she was expelled almost two years ago. She is back. Still a Jew. Without the star. Classes are in session. Zwollo won't be in.

It's Friday. Metalsmithing meets Tuesdays and Thursdays. She pictures him in his studio in Oosterbeek. Wonders who's working for him now. It would be nice to see him again.

She runs up the stone stairs. Her steps echo in the long corridor, empty between classes. Voices behind closed doors. Muffled sounds from classes she has taken. Anatomy. Figure drawing. Through a glass side panel she glimpses a naked model on the platform in Figure Drawing. Stained glass shop next door. Fritz Jantzen, with colored glass pieces, bent over a table. Then she stands before *her* door. Metal and silversmithing. She hesitates. Regular hammer blows on the inside vibrate the door. Her arm feels limp.

She collects her courage. Opens the door with a start. Steps inside. The door falls shut behind her. A private enclosure. Sulphuric acid smell. Metal. Welcome! Bert stands at his workbench by the window. His hammer blows drop in regular rhythm on his copper vase sitting on a metal stake in the vise. Absorbed in shaping his work. His back is turned to the door. He can't hear her. The metal clangs under his hammer. Boing! Boing! Boing! The noise drones in her ears. She remains standing by the door. Watches him. His bold strokes on the round shape. Good old Bert. Good to be back. To be alive.

"Hi, Bert."

He does not hear her. She walks through the room, slowly. Stands beside him on the other side of his stake.

"Hi, Bertus."

He looks up, absentmindedly. From another world.

She watches disbelief dawn in his pupils. Recognition. He drops his hammer on the bench. The vase hangs loose on the stake. He knocks his stool over in his attempt to reach her.

"Hanne!" He stops short before her. They stand eye to eye. A shiver reels up her throat. She swallows hard. The sudden quiet hangs in the room like a furtive halo.

"Hanne!"

"Hi." She stands there, smiling at him.

"I can't believe this! What are you doing here?"

"I'm out," she says. Limp.

"When did you get out?" It's almost a whisper. The stool remains lying on the floor.

"Day before yesterday. Wednesday May fifth." Her voice is unsteady. She clears her throat.

"To wait in Amsterdam for the permit to leave the country."

The silence between them is heavy. Pregnant with confounding sentiments.

"Can't believe it's really you."

He breaks the emotional barrier. She smiles with a sigh. She can't believe it's happening to her either.

"Alive and well," she says.

"You look fine."

Her chuckles break the tension. They sit down. Hanne inspects his fluted copper vase, now almost finished. She strokes the design. Inhales the acrid odor of sulphuric acid that belongs here. Their workroom. She remembers when he hammered this vase into shape.

"You're almost done. Was it hard to chisel the design?"

"I filled it with jeweler's pitch and worked it from outside. The problem was to get the right punches to work from inside out. Making them took almost half of last year. Now I'm just correcting some flaws in the shape that crept in with the design."

"It must have been difficult to get all the pitch out after you were done."

"I heated it and let it flow out, then burned off the rest."

"Smelly job. But, Bert, it's gorgeous." She weighs the vase between her hands.

"When do you think you'll get that permit?" He returns to the overriding question.

"*Sichtvermerk*? The ways of the gods are inscrutable. You know that." She shrugs.

"Yeah. Right."

"A few weeks at least."

"And you came here the very next day," he murmurs. His voice trails off.

"I couldn't thank you over the telephone." Does she mean to tell him that she wanted to see him? She isn't sure herself.

"You don't look emaciated."

"Your stuff helped." She chuckles, then goes on to the question uppermost in her mind. "Where did you get all that stuff you sent? Surely not from your mother! And Black Market stuff is beyond your means! That leaves robbing the coupon office."

"Didn't do anything of the kind." Bert's broad smile is an all-knowing smirk indicating that he must have played a good joke on someone else.

"Our rations? Mother's supply? So far, we get by. But our rations are not enough to feed others. The moffen take from the farmers whatever they find and ship it to the front, or home. The Food Stamp Office? Too dangerous, though I wouldn't have any qualms robbing it empty. They rob far more from us than stamps!" His smile broadens.

"Then what did you *do*?" Her curiosity reaches a high pitch.

He hesitates for a moment. Smirks.

"Aw. I guess I can tell you that much. I dispense coupons for people who're in hiding. They don't get any through regular channels. They have no ID's, so they don't exist, see? Hanne, I honestly don't know where they come from, or where they're going. I'm just a middleman. The less I know, the safer for all concerned. So don't worry about it. You needed it as much as those in hiding." His entire person exudes pride in his wisdom.

"How exactly did you do that?"

"Oh, every once in a while I just kept a coupon or two..." Bert's arm makes a wide sweep through the room. Utter satisfaction on his face over his splendid scheme. Hanne sighs intense relief.

"I appreciate your help. But I'm just as glad that now you don't have to steal anymore."

"Steal? Pinch, perhaps. It's a relief to have you out. And not just for the coupons we save."

We called it *organisieren*, Hanne thinks.

The clock ticks loudly from the wall into the settling silence. They look at each other, happiness in their silent gaze. Her stomach growls into the silence. His eyes follow hers to the wall clock.

"Goodness. Past twelve. Let's go home and introduce you to my folks. It's time for lunch."

He collects his tools and puts them in the small side room, like old times. Here nothing has changed. She helps him. No change? Except that now she's no longer here. And will soon leave for good. To go home. Her home.

"When does your train leave?"

"We've plenty of time. The last train gets me home just before curfew tonight. I'm looking forward to meeting your mother."

Their laughter on the way to Hommelstraat communicates their happiness. Only they two exist. Nothing else. An entire afternoon is theirs alone.

* * *

Lunch is over. Mr. Gorrissen and Max have returned to their work in the store. Ma Gorrissen cleans her kitchen. Hanne and Bert sit at the bottom of the stairs behind the store to decide what to do with their afternoon.

"Something special. To celebrate your release," Bert insists.

"Just being here is special." Her voice trails off. Her brain is wild with desires for things she has not been able to do for years.

"How about the movies? I haven't seen one since I left Germany. That Jeanette MacDonald-Nelson Eddie movie they showed us in The Hague was for the entire refugee group and doesn't count."

Flaunting her new independence, she is full of wild expectations. But Bert hesitates.

"You know, the theaters play only German movies." He cautions.

"There isn't much else to do for us in Arnhem on a weekday afternoon." Her voice is full of longing. Why would he object?

CHAPTER 12

It slowly sinks in. Of course, there's the tacit boycott against German movies. No decent self-respecting Dutchman goes to see one. And as a Jew she is doubly obliged not to go. Also, she is forbidden by law to enter a movie theater. That irks.

"Are there many Jews left in Arnhem?"

Bert looks at her. Where is the connection between Jews in Arnhem and German movies?

"A few. Those working for the Jewish Council. Their offices are in the Jongenshuis. I think Dr. Wolf is one of them now."

Hanne hates the thought of strangers living in *her* house.

"No one else knows that I'm Jewish. Boycott or not, I need to dare the system." Strange reasoning.

"What the hell," Bert declares to the dark walls by the staircase. "Let's find out what's playing."

They scan the ads in the newspaper.

"*The Golden City* with Kristina Söderbaum."

"Sounds good. She's Swedish," Hanne declares. Extra loud. Making the actress's nationality a welcome excuse for her guilty conscience.

"Let's go."

They buy the tickets. Walk past the booth into the dark inside. Feeling like conspirators adds a criminal charm to this venture.

"For the first time in my life knowing German is good for something," Hanne mumbles. They sit down in the dark. Double dare.

They hold hands, their bodies warm with spring sun. Intimacy. The romantic love story unfolding on the screen mirrors their own secret longings. Two young lovers, star-crossed victims of small-town gossip. The girl a logical suicide. Turn-of-the century Prague with its elaborate medieval, Gothic and Baroque buildings and monuments as background underscores inflexible, inherited mores and prejudices. Religion turned secular. Smetana's haunting *Moldau* tunes. Veit Harlan directs. Isn't he Kristina Söderbaum's husband?

Transfixed, hungry for art, they absorb the story, the acting, the music, the beauty on the screen. The lovers' defiance of unchallenged rules adds another dimension to Hanne's spirit of rebellion. No, she is *not* a candidate for suicide. The girl should've been careful. She feels Bert's slight pressure around her fingers. A stream of hot desire runs amok down her spine into her abdomen. Their eyes lock by the flickering light from the screen. They look aside, too shy to admit feelings they hardly know they feel. Nothing but the moment exists.

The somber ending. Lights tear into their private cocoon. Her mind is still in the story. Haunted. She hums the *Leitmotif* of Smetana's masterpiece. Saunters behind Bert with the throng. Out into the blinding sun. Its glare rebounds from the warm asphalt. Slowly, very slowly her eyesight adjusts. Bert stops in the middle of the square. Blinks into the church tower to check the time.

"All right. So it was a moffen movie. It was great, in every respect."

"I think so too." The two rebels agree. Both defying an invisible enemy.

"It's barely three o'clock, much too early to go home. We could go for a walk," he says.

They have flaunted wartime society's unwritten rules. Plenty of time to face the consequences.

"Fine. I haven't been in Sonsbeek for a million years. It looks inviting this time of year."

"Why don't we stroll through the park out to where we used to meet. Sort of relive old times," he suggests.

"Great idea."

Sonsbeek Park is almost empty but for a few maids on the benches with their charges, rocking baby carriages, watching their charges play, run after each other, fight. They gossip about madams or boyfriends. Some toddlers chase wild fowl on the grass by the lake where sunrays teeter-totter in golden glitter on ruffled wavelets. Hanne inhales deeply, grateful for life coursing through her veins again. She has been absent for so long. Absent in mind and body. Will she ever break through that crust memories have molded around her being? Or will she remain a stranger looking in from some distant outside for the rest of her life? She would like to throw her arms up into the air. Try to embrace the world. Reach out in an effort to make herself a part of it again. She churns on a sigh in her throat.

"Did I tell you that I met Bella Heckscher in camp?"

"You mentioned it in your letter, but didn't go into details. How is she? They say she flipped altogether."

"Yes."

"She enrolled in *Kunstoefening* about a year before you came. Sort of a shy girl."

"I know. She had lost both her parents in a car accident and lived with her aunt and her family. Art school was supposed to help her over the shock. Therapy. I didn't find out until much later.

"Then she disappeared from the scene."

"I envied her when I first came to school and met her. I thought she was one of the happy ones who live ordinary lives with families in brick homes. How was I to know her background? Then she came to Zwollo's studio to work. Perhaps the wrong word – she dabbled. Her family paid. It was hard to get close to her. But then, Zwollo never talked about her. Probably didn't know all of it anyway. With all my own problems she hardly fit in anyway.

At work Bella seemed fine at first. Then I noticed her saying odd things. Out of context. Remarks that didn't make sense. Zwollo mumbled something like *sad case*. But he was full of balderdash himself with his problem wife. And his theosophy. Two nuts at work. I was too preoccupied to get the real picture. Then she stopped coming altogether. I never gave it a second thought, until Louis came to Zwollo *to learn the trade*. Turned out Louis was Bella's cousin. Nice fellow. So I asked how she was doing. "She doesn't live with us anymore," he said.

"He was embarrassed and I dumbfounded. I felt stupid for asking the question. Hiding? Disappeared? Gone. That wasn't unusual. You don't ask. So, I didn't ask any more questions. I never caught on that she went to a mental institution. Not until Westerbork when Eddie told me he's seen Bella come in with the group from Apeldoorn. I went to visit her in the mental ward one afternoon after work."

Hanne meditates along the pebbled path of Sonsbeek before her. A habitat of memories. Her gaze follows a mother mallard proudly leading her offspring through the grass to the lake. She plops in, six fluff balls drop single file behind her, paddle through the mirror surface, leaving a triangular wake of tiny ripples behind them. Waves that furrow wider and wider across the lake. Mom quacks noisily to announce their presence. Hanne sighs.

"Okay, the visit. She was in her nightgown. A silky, flimsy, flowing affair – in a concentration camp, mind you. Her golden-red hair a wild curly halo around the pale freckled porcelain-skin face. She stopped when she saw me come in, reflected, then recognized me. Real lively. 'Hanne,' she greeted me. I asked her how she was. She was waiting for her parents. They'd come soon. Soon. Soon. She said more things I couldn't understand, as if she'd blocked out the present. I don't know enough of her past to know whether she was living in some fantasy world of her own making. But so it seemed. Bert, she was off on another planet in her own world."

Hanne feels Bert's gaze.

"She did a dervish dance on top of her bed, the red locks flying along with her lacy gown. Otherworldly gorgeous. Like a van Eyck angel. Westerbork didn't mean a thing to her. Or its purpose... Bert, she was so beautiful..."

"The entire group went the following Tuesday. Mental cases have no option for delay."

Bert is a quiet listener. She looks at the fresh green grass under their feet. The sunlight glistens in transparent, rainbow-colored water pearls. Above them a pair of finches twitters spring tunes. Busy building their nest somewhere in the tree. The earth smells black dirt. Soft spring. New life throbbing everywhere. Look ahead, she reminds herself. Don't let old baggage overwhelm you!

They wander through the woods. Safe under ponderous old beeches, ancient sycamores, huge wide oaks. Young green sprouts peep from gnarled limbs. New leaves in fresh green. Winged tree crowns intertwine and spread their protective dome over creation below.

"I was afraid of losing you," Bert muses next to her.

"I can't believe I'm back," she says.

"I stood at the corner across the street and watched all of you pass by last December. You walked right past me with Ruth and Eddie. There was nothing I could do. Not a thing. I felt so helpless. Despaired of ever seeing you again. Though you were never out of my mind. You know that, don't you?" His voice is hardly audible. He searches her face.

"I didn't see anyone that day. My mind was somewhere else. I don't remember much. A wall of people lining Amsterdamsche Weg, gawking. I felt like an ape in a zoo. Caged. Frustrated. Automated. Limp." She looks at Bert. A hint of a smile.

"It's good it turned out the way it did."

They reach the familiar heath. A mélange of purple and green catching its breath in the afternoon breeze under white-speckled turquoise sky. Hanne makes a wide sweep with her hand.

"This the moffen can't destroy."

"Let's sit down."

The air, the freedom. It's just too much all at once.

They settle in the grass under a huge sycamore and lean against the trunk. Hanne looks up at the canopy above her. A shelter of golden-flecked small leaves that rustle a lullaby. A martin warbles its love song from the branches. His mate trills her response. A waterfall tinkles nearby. Hanne closes her eyes. In tune. Bucolic symphony. Longing ache fills her.

"Hanne."

She feels his arm around her. Pulling her closer to him. She opens her eyes for a second. Confirms that this is not a dream. Closes them again. Gives in to the warm wave that courses down her spine and takes possession of her body. The pressure of his arm increases. His body feels warm against hers. The throbs increase, become unbearable. They kiss. Warmth spreads. There is nothing else but their bodies.

"Hanne," he whispers again, "I've wanted you ever since that first day in school when I saw you running down the hall."

"Because I was late." She shakes her head slightly, unwilling to talk. Why spoil beautiful moments with words? She abandons herself to spring's earth and sky. His arms slide around her. Search. Get bolder. Undress her. Himself. She wants him. Wants him with all the heat at the core of her being. She edges close. Helps him until their bodies fuse. Feels, then answers his rhythmic thrusts until their ecstasy bursts through her inner self in red-hot flashes.

Spent, they kiss tenderly. Disengage. For a long time they rest side by side, shoulders touching. The martin keeps singing his trills in a branch above. The tree spreads its crown like a cupola full of blessings over them.

* * *

They arrive home in time for supper. Ma Gorrissen has done her best to make it a festive occasion in Hanne's honor. Her best linen. Her silverware. The three wait for Mr. Gorrissen and Max, who are still in the store with a late customer.

"Did you have a good time?" Ma makes absentminded motherly conversation.

"Yes," Hanne says with a sideway glance at Bert.

Downstairs the store door closes. Gets locked shut. The two merchants trot up the stairs. Take their places at the dinner table.

"Let's have a shot of Jenever. It's not every day that people get released from camp."

"To your future!" They clink glasses.

She feels Bert squirm on his seat next to her.

Ma fills Pa's plate. Passes it on. Gets the next plate. Starts heaping it.

"I hope you like my cooking," she says and holds it out to Hanne. "What have you been doing all afternoon?

Hanne hesitates, grateful for the serving process that provides a moment of delay. She takes the plate from across the table. Sniffs audibly the tantalizing aroma of beef stew. Murmurs appreciation in an effort to please the cook. Ingratiate herself? She isn't sure.

Bert sits up straight on his chair. Decisive.

"We went to see a movie." He tries to sound casual. But this is a definite declaration.

"*The Golden City*. With Kristina Söderbaum in the title role," Hanne seconds his effort at honesty in the surrounding stillness.

"What?"

Mutilation of happy feelings. A hole in the airy balloon of family solidarity. Ma's face turns crimson. The plate she has been heaping for Bert drops on the white tablecloth to steam on its own. Her eyes flash. Anger. Fury. Pa and Max stare at a vacant spot on the starched tablecloth before them.

"No decent Dutchman goes to see a German movie!" It's her declaration of patriotism. Her solidarity with the House of Oranje. Her absent Queen.

The small family at the table is silent under her onslaught.

"What on earth got into you, Bert? You know better than that! You too, Hanne. Really! You of all people."

Treason ensnares the two.

Ma's face is full of disdain. Her eyes wander from one to the other around the table in indignant self-righteousness. Hanne steels herself against contrition. Then, resolutely, Ma picks up Bert's plate, spoons food for her son to a pointed heap and passes it on without another word. Bert takes the plate.

"There *are* only German movies. And there's nothing else to do. We haven't seen a movie since the occupation. Hanne much longer than that."

Bert takes up the heated defense. His anger is bloody red up in his throat, including the Adam's apple.

"You know there's a boycott against everything made in

moffenland. That includes movies. How else are we going to defeat them?" Ma is in her usual combat mood against the strangers that occupy her country.

"Ma. It's inane to link the allies' victory to two measly movie tickets."

Bert has inherited his mother's straightforward temper. And her stubbornness.

"Just imagine where we'd be if everyone said that!"

Silence again. Forks and knives clatter rebellion against the porcelain plates. Hanne looks at her food. Did she detect a bemused smile in the corners of Pa's mouth between bites? Or is her imagination playing tricks? She looks again, but there is nothing.

A good movie. A memorable afternoon. Ma's objections put a damper on her happiness. No, she decides. Not even Ma's righteous objections will ruin the memory of this day. She begins to eat. Tries to catch up with the others who are already halfway through. She has always been a slow eater. The food is delicious. Better than she's tasted in years. The silverware shines. Why on earth does she always have to deny herself even the simplest pleasures? Why does she always wind up on the wrong end of fate? She is sick and tired of sacrifices.

"Well, was it at least a good movie? As long as you broke the rules, was it worth it?" Pa Gorrissen speaks, appeasement into awkward silence.

Hanne takes a deep breath. "Yes sir. It's set in Prague. What a beautiful city! The photography is out of this world. Smetana's music is even better."

She defends the movie, but stops short of recommending it. Not here.

"I'm going to visit that city someday," Bert declares.

Ma accepts the defense. Reluctantly. Against her better judgment. Lets it go at that without questioning their motives. Thank goodness. They eat in peace right through the cherry cake dessert. A special treat for the visitor.

Pa Gorrissen checks his oldfashioned goldwatch hanging on a shining goldchain across his chest.

"I hate to break up this party, but if Hanne wants to catch the train to make it to Amsterdam before curfew you better hurry."

"I'm sorry to have to leave right after supper," Hanne sighs regret at her necessary rudeness.

"Do come and visit us again," Ma shoots Bert a long look full of meaning.

"I'll take you to the train," Bert says.

They walk arm in arm the short distance to the railroad station.

"Ma has a temper. But she doesn't mean half of what she says when she's angry."

Hanne stops in the middle of the street. Faces him.

"Bert, she's dead right. Only thing, I just didn't want to hear the truth."

She waves her hand in a helpless gesture. Walks on, a slight chuckle in her throat. "Like mother like son. I solemnly swear never to see another German-made movie again," she declares. "American and Swedish will do."

They smile at each other with an undercurrent of sadness in their smiles. Why do things always have an edge?

"I wish you didn't have to leave. There ought to be a way to keep you here. Anyway, I'll come and visit you in Amsterdam before you leave."

They stop and kiss on the street. Never mind the people. Take comfort in the thought that this parting is not final. Yet.

They walk through the railroad station. Stand on the platform, wishing the train would never come.

But it chugs in. World on the move. Inevitable, relentless time. A fleeting kiss. Hanne climbs aboard the black iron tube without looking back. Finds herself a seat by the window. Bert follows her outside.

"Take care of yourself," he screams through the heavy glass.

She nods. Waves. Doors slam shut. The trainmaster walks

up the platform. Lifts his sign. The shrill locomotive whistle rents the air.

"Bye, Bert." She throws a kiss in his direction.

"Goodbye, Hanneke."

He walks alongside the slowly rolling train. It picks up speed. She watches the distance grow between them. He gets smaller and smaller under the light at the end of the platform until he is a dot. Then she can no longer see him.

Chapter 13

Mountains of slate clouds droop low over the city of Amsterdam. Sagging bulges, ready to discharge their wet substance any minute. Bolts flash red zigzags between them. Thunder follows with slow growls. Down below the air feels sticky. A typical hot summer day in the Dutch lowlands.

The open window on the third floor of *Pension Abram* brings more humidity. More discomfort than relief. Ruth sits by the window, resentful, complaining.

"I hate to darn stockings. Holes on holes. Hardly any stocking left."

"Do what I do – go without. Bare legs is the latest summer fashion."

Hanne tries to collect her thoughts for a letter to Bert. She has a bad conscience. He has written her twice already since his last visit in Amsterdam. It's hard to know where to start. So much is happening. Especially with the Jews. It's even harder to talk about these things. Impossible to write about. She chews on the end of her pen. Meditates over that empty white sheet before her.

"I don't know what's worse, letter writing or darning."

It is after lunch. The house is quiet. They've been shopping for their landlords in the morning. A daily task since their arrival. Without the Jewish star it's no problem for them to get around. Ride the streetcars. Shop all day instead of just between 3–5 PM. Hanne likes to shop. Find bargains. The task gives her a sense of importance. She and Ruth spend their pocket money on food packages to Westerbork.

Her hands are clammy. They stick to the paper in front of her. She wipes them to get them dry. It is no use.

"It's so much easier to talk," she mutters.

Bert has visited twice since her release. Both times they went to the *Rijksmuseum*. There is so much to see, even a third time wouldn't be enough to see it all, despite the fact that most of the truly great masterpieces are hidden in a safe place somewhere else.

"Are they hiding the great artworks from the Germans or from bombings?" Hanne wondered out loud.

"Both, I'm sure. We'll just have to come back after it's all over," Bert said with utter conviction as if she weren't about to leave the country.

"I'm hungry," she said.

"There's a pancake place somewhere nearby," he said.

They went. She watched him eat his favorite food. Thick pancakes with heaping mounds of preserves. So thick that he couldn't roll the pancake around them. Instead, he cut the huge platter carefully into pointed triangles, then heaped yet another spoonful of the red strawberry preserve on top of his triangle, speared the wiggling double mound of jelled sweets and balanced the whole carefully into his gaping mouth. Clenching his teeth around it.

"Wow," she said, full of admiration.

His blue eyes radiated happiness. With her presence? The sweet pancakes? The successful balancing act? Or all of these?

The waitress came and reminded them that the shop closed at five thirty.

"I know. I'll have to catch the train to Arnhem too." He managed to polish off the three huge pancakes before closing time. And still made the train.

"What am I going to write?" Hanne demands from her paper. Keeps chewing her sticky pen.

This wait is getting on her nerves. She needs to get on with her life after five lost years of refugee existence. A major part of her education lost. She told Bert last time how anxious she was.

"I understand. But *you* must understand how much I hate the thought of your going away," he said when he kissed her on the platform.

"If only the *Sichtvermerk* would come. I wonder what our new life will be like. Life without war is hard to imagine. I dread the thought of another language again," Hanne meditates against Ruth's back by the window.

"It's almost June. You'd think that four weeks is plenty of time for the Nazis to investigate the criminal record of two girls," Ruth says.

"A silly stamp. Meanwhile we shop for the Abramses."

"They're grateful for the help and we get to know the city."

"Hardly a reason to stay in Amsterdam."

"No. It's a shame we can't enjoy the city now that we're here. It's a Dutch shell with German troops and Nazis. Take the Rijksmuseum. Most of the real valuables, the Vermeers, the Rembrandts, the Halses are in bomb shelters for safekeeping. If the Germans haven't carted them off. Whatever is hanging there is interesting, but hardly the real stuff."

"It's wise to protect the famous art underground. I'm sure the Dutch took them away before the Nazis could get at them. You never know when or where bombs hit. The RAF is pretty busy lately. They keep the German flak on their toes at night."

"True. You can't take a step outside without falling over soldiers these days. Have you noticed how many of them are wounded lately?"

"Sure. Hobbling on casts. In wheelchairs. Recuperating. On leave from the front. Must be from Russia."

"And the RAF is busy. I hear them hum every night. Don't you?"

"Whenever I'm awake. It's not too often."

Hanne prays for their success.

"Bomb them to smithereens. Give it all you got! God, you need to take sides. Pay them back in kind. That's the only way we get peace with the Germans. War is a crime. But for the victim not to defend himself is a double crime."

"Hanne! Hanne, come look."

Ruth is looking down the street. Her voice sounds urgent. Her finger points to the street below.

Hanne runs to the window. Only too happy to have a reason to drop her writing. Ruth is bent over the sill. Stares down into the street.

"See down there?"

Hanne looks. A girl walks on the sidewalk on the opposite side. Behind her a small woman with gray hair looks familiar.

"Doesn't it look like Sussmann?"

"You're right."

Ruth is gone. The door slams shut behind her. She hears her sister run down the stairs. There is Ruth on the street. Running. Hanne watches her catch up with the woman farther down the block by the corner. They talk for a while. Ruth points. The woman's gaze follows. Is that a nod the woman sends up her way? Hanne isn't sure. Then the woman trips around the corner. Ruth shrugs. Turns back toward the boarding house. Hanne is at a loss. It sure looked like Sussmann. The way she pattered about.

"I would've sworn it was Sussmann from up here," she says as Ruth enters the room.

"It was," Ruth says and drops into her chair.

Hanne gives her a searching look.

"It was. She's *hiding* somewhere in this neighborhood. She thought no one knows her. Until I turn up. I'm not supposed to have seen her."

"Oh my gosh."

"She didn't want to stop to talk. At first she even tried to deny who she is. Dr. Wolf is still working for the Jewish Council in Arnhem. She knew that we're on our way to Sweden. Didn't want to tell me who told her. She wishes us good luck. Sends her regards." Ruth trips over her words, catching her breath.

"The Jewish Council has moved into our Jongenshuis. Bert told me."

"I promised her not to tell anyone I'd seen her. Except you, of course."

"No one we know would be interested anyway."

Never mind the letter. Hanne flops on her bed. Perspiration droplets roll down her neck. Her forehead is wet down to her eyelids. Her hands are clammy.

"Good Lord. Is that how it is to be in hiding. Such an ordinary everyday word lately. *In hiding.* Stashed away. Incognito. Live in fear of being recognized. Of course, as a Jew you lived in fear anyway in Nazi territory. But this involves hiding your identity. Your entire existence. *You don't exist.*" She sounds the syllables. It could easily have been her fate. To think how close she was. What if? How would she then have known about her Swedish citizenship? Lucky ducks, Ruth and she? Better believe that! Though it's hard to think that way. There's so much wrong in her life. What is normal? *N.O.R.M.A.L.* A human term that doesn't exist for most of humanity right now. Least of all her.

*   *   *

The June days are hot. They live in expectation. Waiting for the Gestapo to call them. In the meantime they go shopping for food packages for the Abramses. Discover the city and its museums. They visit The Hague. Without its government the city has become a stranger. Even the beloved *Mauritshuis* is unrecognizable, stripped of its many Rembrandts. Only the canals are the same as ever, smelly and murky.

"Hanne? Look over there."

Ruth sits by the window again. It's a gray day with summer storms in the sky. The air is sticky. She sits on her bed in her underwear.

"What now? Again someone who doesn't want to be recognized?"

Ruth has keen eyesight. She sees a lot. Much more than Hanne does with her nearsighted vision. Hanne follows the direction where Ruth finger is pointing. Scans the other side of the street.

"See that fellow across the street? He's been up and down the block a couple of times."

"You mean that bum over there?"

Ruth looks cross. "Doesn't he remind you of someone? Look again."

Hanne strains her eyes. Squints into the damp grayness of the street.

"Hmm. He looks wet. Dirty. Reminds me of Werner, the way he stands cocked and stares."

Hanne has flashes of Jongenshuis. Westerbork. Werner staring after them on the pick-up truck.

"It can't be," she mumbles. "It can't possibly be. We left him in the camp just a few weeks ago. Behind barbed wire. Watchtowers with ss all around."

"His bowlegged walk. That forward slump."

"Yes. Even the cowlick." Hanne agrees. She reaches for her skirt and top. Her brain races with possibilities. "I'll go. It can't hurt to check. You stay here. Keep watching."

She slides into her sandals. Straightens her skirt while she races down the stairs. Excitement tingles. What if it *is* Werner? She stops at the foot of the stairs. Thank goodness the kitchen door is closed! The Abramses are nosy. She takes a deep breath then walks out into the hothouse drizzle outside. Crosses the street. Tries to disappear among the few people walking past under their umbrellas. She catches up with the fellow just before the corner. Quickens her steps. Brushes slightly against him as if by accident as she passes him. A few more steps. Then she turns and looks into his face.

"Indeed."

"Hanne," he mumbles without breaking his stride. She walks alongside him at a slight distance. A million questions in her mind.

"What on earth are you doing here?"

"Shhh. Keep walking while we talk."

They turn the corner.

"I need somewhere to stay. Is your place safe?"

She is glad for the cooperative weather. Rain. An electrical storm is brewing.

"Tell you what. I'll turn here. It's No 21. I'll leave the door slightly ajar. You follow and pull it shut. We're on the top floor."

She walks ahead of him. Around the block so as not to arouse suspicion. He follows a short distance behind her.

Luckily the kitchen door is still closed. She hurries past. Prays that it may stay shut for a few more minutes. It's best to leave Mr. and Mrs. Nosy out of this altogether. For all that, she can always claim that he is a relative visiting her. It's true, to a point. She is dying to know how he managed to escape. She waits at the foot of the stairs. When he comes in she motions him to follow. He looks like a dripping wildcat.

"It's good to be inside," Werner whispers behind her.

They enter the room. A lightning bolt flashes outside. The deep growl of thunder follows shortly thereafter.

"Thank goodness. You've made it in here just in time."

"Undetected. So far."

Werner slumps into the chair. The girls bring towels. Suggest a bath.

"I'd rather have something to eat first. I haven't eaten for three days."

"Sure. I'll run downstairs and grab something in the kitchen."

Hanne looks after her little sister. Helpfulness personified. She has never seen her help like that. Her footsteps patter downstairs.

"We're alone up here. The room next door is empty. That

leaves us the third floor pretty much to ourselves. Including the bathroom. You should be pretty safe up here. Until we find a solution for you."

Werner grumbles something under his beard. He looks haggard. Exhausted. Hanne watches him stretch out on her bed. A shaggy dog with his wild stubble.

"I'm tired," he says.

"We'll get you back into shape. First thing we need is a razor. I'll call Bert from the booth downstairs. He'll find a solution." Werner needs to disappear, go into hiding. Hanne is convinced that Bert can help.

"I first thought of making it to Arnhem, but it's too small a place. Too many people know me. I would've waited outside all night, if necessary."

"Impossible with the curfew at eight. The only people on the streets at night are Germans. Nazis, with their paddy wagons. And the Jews they walk off. Someone would've spotted you standing there."

"I was careful not to stand still. I walked around the block. Figured that one of you'd come out eventually."

"Ruth is a street watcher for want of anything more productive to do. Last week she spotted Sussmann. She's living under an assumed name somewhere in the neighborhood. Now you. Thing is, Jewish homes aren't the safest places these days." Hanne shakes her head. "Still, the boarding house has been left alone so far."

Ruth appears in the door with a glass of milk and a heap of sandwiches.

"I was lucky. They were busy in the kitchen so I took all I could find in the pantry. Even milk set aside for babies. Hope no one misses it."

They watch Werner attack the food. He is ravenous.

"I never thought you'd have the guts to get out," Hanne mumbles.

They wait for him to finish. Hanne needs to call Bert. Ernie Schlächter comes to her mind. She shudders.

"The Nazis are unlikely to show up in this place unless they come searching for something else. Or to pick up the Abramses," Ruth muses.

"There." With a deep sigh and a suppressed burp, Werner leans back. Wipes his mouth with the back of his hand. A picture of satisfaction. "Thanks. That was good."

A pregnant silence descends in the third-floor bedroom of *Pension Abram*. The girls itch with curiosity.

"How on earth did you manage to get out?"

"I walked out." Werner grins. A joke.

"Just like that? Walked out of Camp Westerbork?" The very idea seems preposterous.

"Yep. Just like that!" Werner repeats. His smile is a cocky smirk. "I took a lucky chance. There've been some other escapes lately. But that's beside the point. Anyway, getting out wasn't the trick. Staying out was."

"Do me a favor, start from the beginning." Hanne wants to know the trick.

"Okay. We had an old man with Parkinson's on our ward. Mixed marriage. So he got permission to return to his Christian wife in Amsterdam. Gemmeker must've been in a good mood. A few got out that way. Anyhow, I had to take the fellow to the truck that was to drive him to Assen. Same truck that took you two and Kurt.

"Our bums are still sore." The two nod.

"Yeah. It's a bumpy ride. Anyway, watching you disappear that morning got me into thinking. Just didn't know how to do it. Until I got the slip to take the fellow to the truck *outside* the gate." Werner pauses for effect. The silence underlines the enormity of his dare.

"So I place him on the truck and sit behind him. To help. And so we speed off to Assen. I help the fellow get on the train. In case of another check I would've played dumb. He really did need my help. And then I disappeared in the john and flushed my star down the toilet. I got off on the other side of the train and walked into the city. The way I looked, I figured I'd better get a move on. I stayed off the main road. Slept in smelly barns. Lived on raw potatoes, other stuff I dug up in the fields. Berries. Ruined my stomach and got diarrhea. One farmer caught me sleeping in his barn. When he heard who I was he brought me food. Stashed me under his produce on his truck in the morning to the farmer's market in Meppel. I took the train from there and came here. I had your address. It took some time to find you. But it's easier to walk in the city. Except for food." His speech slurs. He catches his breath.

"I oughta take a bath," he mumbles, then turns toward the wall. Fast asleep.

"He did the right thing not to take the train right away. No telling what they would've done if they'd caught him, the way he looks."

Hanne surveys her comrade with an amused gaze. His rumpled clothes. His beard. "I wonder the price his barrack had to pay for his escape." Hanne looks again. That twitch around his mouth is new.

"We can't stand on convention. He'll have to stay here until Bert finds a solution. And clothes for him. Meanwhile he can wear my robe until we clean his stuff. I'll sleep in the tub with our woolen blankets tonight. And he can have my extra towel."

Ruth clears his glass and plate away.

"I'll run downstairs and call Bert," Hanne says, all efficiency.

* * *

Bert arrives with the first train by the crack of dawn. They hold a war council of four on two beds.

Bert is all business. "You need to get to a safer place as soon as possible. The moffen can show up at any time to haul the Abramses off. And you endanger the girls."

"Besides, we may get our permit any time," Hanne agrees.

Werner looks rested, stuffed with food snitched from the breakfast table.

"Right. I brought some food coupons to help you for now. The big question is, where to? Either you go into hiding or you try to get out. Do you have some connection in Switzerland or Spain? The Swiss are difficult. Spain less so. Whatever we decide, you need an ID without the *J*. That, and this razor to clean you up for society. You don't want to stick out in a crowd."

"You really thought of everything." Hanne is all admiration.

"If you want to, I could get you a place in Arnhem. But people may recognize you there."

The room is full of unexpressed ifs, buts, unfinished wishes, repressed desires. Hanne's eyes follow a string of sunshine stripes break through the thick cloud cover outside. It dances across Werner's cowlick on to the bed and up the wallpaper behind him where it perches like a golden marker. Ruth fiddles with the button on her blouse, her forehead in thinking folds. Bert's Adam's apple bobs up and down. His pale-blue eyes absent in deep thought.

"Bert, I'm not good at sitting locked up in an attic day and night. Unable to talk or move. Always on edge. I hate to endanger other people. If you can get me Aryan papers I could disappear in the shuffle of a big city inside the Reich. I'd prefer to get to a neutral place, like Spain or Portugal. Or to my mother in London." Werner's eyes have a longing glint.

"Hmm. There's a fellow in Amsterdam who handles ID's. He may know more than I do in the backwoods of Arnhem. Calling is dangerous, but let me go and talk to him while you clean yourself up. You don't happen to have a snapshot of yourself on you?"

"No. That's the last thing I thought of taking along."

"Of course. Well, don't worry. We can take one. Get rid of the stubble first."

Werner strokes his face. Upward. The wild growth rasps under his fingers.

"Won't take long. I'll be ready when you get back."

"Good. I hope to have a place for you then."

"The sooner the better."

The council is over. Bert walks to the door and turns back to Hanne. "Want to keep me company to the streetcar?"

"Sure!" They close the door behind them. Stop at the top of the stairs for a long, heartfelt kiss. Then they walk in silence out on the street to the next stop a block away. They kiss fleetingly and touch hands before Bert steps up for the ride to his friend. Somewhere in Amsterdam.

She sends a fervent bid skyward. Perhaps she should make a deal with the deity in charge. You never know.

"Good Lord. Make this a success."

Then, as if compelled, adding in her mind, "If you do, I'll believe in you." It can't hurt to invoke all the heavenly powers there may be and ask for success. The thought occurs deep in her throat somewhere. "Whoever you are." She does not want to promise anything further. Let him show his power first!

She saunters back. Takes her time. Yesterday's rain clouds are breaking up into gray blotches against blue background. A watery sun strokes the rooftops, reflects in the shiny windows, lightens the red brick of the residential homes.

"Meanwhile, all we can do is wait."

* * *

Bert returns by mid-afternoon.

"Regards from Gerrit. He's figured a way out. He sends this."

Bert unwraps a package with food for Werner – rolls, cold-cuts, sweets, muffins. Werner's eyes caress the choice morsels.

"You can't be that hungry. We raided the table for leftovers last night and this morning." Hanne is miffed. What they *organized* in their napkins should have lasted him for days.

"He's like a bottomless pit," Ruth says.

Among the many things the war has taught them is that food is precious. No one lets food go to waste. Leftovers are for another meal. To throw food away is a cardinal sin.

"Choice tidbits. It's a crime to let them get stale. Can I help it that my stomach developed a hole? I'll snack while you tell us your plans," Werner says. He sounds pleased with himself.

"You begin to look downright normal with that wool off your face," Bert says.

"Thought you'd never notice. Smooth as an ape's ass," Werner strokes his chin with an aura of extreme satisfaction. "So what about this Gerrit?"

"Sit down. Eat your food."

"Shoot."

Werner unwraps the paper and spreads the items before him. Then breaks the bread apart and shoves the cold-cuts in between. It's a huge sandwich. His mouth an enormous cavity, he bites into it with obvious relish.

"Gerrit knows a Dutchman who's been called to the *Arbeitsdienst* in Germany. Called forced labor. He doesn't want to go. The fellow is about your age, perhaps a year or so older. You could go in his name with this summons and his ID. All Gerrit will have to do is work in your photograph. You'll just have to learn the guy's data, like birthday, birthplace, etc. as your own. He's married. So don't get yourself married while you live under his name." Bert snickers at his own joke.

Werner has his mouth full. He chews. His jaws are going like a machine.

"Must be my lucky break. Go right into the lion's den. Remember old man Topol? He went to Germany from Alsace. His papers were fine. Only then he took a shower with his buddies. Stupid. The Nazis brought him back. Paraded him through the city with a big sign: *Ich bin ein Judenschwein*. Spit on him. Hit him, the works. Topol had a nervous breakdown and wound up in Dachau."

Werner swallows with gusto. Then takes another huge bite.

"You're smarter than to shower with them! We still think that Germany is the safest place to hide. Unless you can get out of German territory altogether. To southern France. From there to Spain. That'll be up to you."

"What about the snapshot he needs?"

"He'll take it when you get there."

Werner picks the crumbs from his lap. Shoves them into his mouth, slowly, carefully, to get every last morsel of his provisions. His eyes shine. "I used Hanne's talcum powder. It smells good. I feel like a human being again," he announces with pride. "Just smell me."

His eyes wander from one to the other for approval.

"And how long does it take to get the papers?"

"If we take the snapshot tonight you'll have your ID tomorrow."

"So when are we going to see this Gerrit? I can't wait."

"Hanne can take you to him now. You stay with Gerrit for the time being. Until you decide where to go. He'll give you directions." Bert pauses and looks at Hanne. "It's best if someone follows and keeps an eye on him. Just in case. Remember – don't walk together. Pretend you don't even know each other."

Hanne looks at the others. "Now?"

"Be sure to get there before curfew. It'll be late. You can stay at Gerrit's overnight and come back in the morning."

"No problem," Hanne nods. Her papers are in order.

"Fine. I need to make the train home today, so I'll leave first. Werner can leave after that and Hanne follows. Not too close, just in case. Call me in the morning."

Hanne looks at Bert. "So where's this Gerrit's place?"

"Patience. It's a windmill. Outside the city limits." He looks at Hanne and Werner charitably as he pulls a paper out of his pocket. "It's an old, abandoned windmill, just about a twenty-minute walk from the end stop of the streetcar. It's been out of use for years and therefore ideal for what we are doing. Here's a rough diagram to get there. Study it. We'll destroy it right here."

The three sit down at the table and study the map.

"Here's where you get off. Walk to the end of the paved street. Bear left at the fork where the two country roads diverge. Continue past the wooded area and turn right. That path leads to a clearing with three birches. Turn left. There's a farmhouse at the end. If something should go wrongs. for any reason, knock at the farmhouse and talk to the farmer. If everything is okay, pass the farmhouse. Go to the windmill in the field behind the property. One long, three short, two long knocks. Gerrit will let you in. Make certain you're in before curfew at eight."

Hanne knocks on the dresser behind her. "One long, three short, two long, tra la la," she taps.

"Right," Bert says. They smile.

"You smell great," she tells Werner and holds her nose.

"As long as there aren't any funny surprises, it's a cinch." Werner is full of confidence.

"What if? Better to be prepared," Hanne says.

"Here's the telephone number. Memorize it," Bert says.

"I know your number."

"Werner ought to know it too. And Ruth. You call me if anything goes wrong. Forget the rest of the instructions. You know nothing."

Ruth nods.

"Left at the fork, turn right, then left," Werner repeats.

"All right. Destroy the notes. And good luck." Bert turns to Werner. They shake hands. Like the buddies they never were before. And never wanted to be. They're fighting a common deadly enemy now.

"Ruth, don't forget to call..."

Bert leaves the rest of the thought unfinished somewhere in space. He walks to the door. "Take my raincoat, Werner. You'll be less conspicuous dressed like a normal person. Rain is not unusual in this part of the world," Bert says, door handle in one hand, holding out his raincoat in the other.

"Thanks a lot for all your help."

Bert nods. He is past the threshold. Pulls the door shut behind him. Hanne waits for the slam of the entrance door downstairs.

"Thanks, girls. Good luck in Sweden," Werner mumbles

something about a raincoat and unnecessary bother. His shaky voice belies his nonchalance.

"Good luck to you," Ruth says. She walks out and looks down the stairs. "The coast is clear," she reports.

Werner steps outside, past Ruth, raises his hand in farewell, walks down the stairs. Hanne follows behind.

The streetcar screeches from one stop to the next in the pale Amsterdam afternoon. Passengers come and go. Downtown the stops are short and frequent. Their distance increases as they near the outskirts of the city. The number of passengers decreases in proportion. Hanne sits by the window. She watches the orange-frayed sun disk paint yellowish-violet streaks in the west and dive into the horizon behind purplish farm buildings. She checks the time. Seven. They are close to the last stop. Make the rest in an hour.

*   *   *

Out of the corner of her eyes Hanne checks Werner sitting in the back of the car. He finishes the rolls Bert has brought him. Now that his beard is off he looks even skinnier. Downright haggard. No wonder his stomach is a bottomless pit. She sighs. Let him remain free! So far everything has gone according to plan. Cleaned up and shaven he no longer looks like a fugitive.

The conductor calls the last stop. The two remaining people in the car walk past her to the platform. Werner saunters up the aisle behind them. Puts his newly acquired raincoat next to her seat. She stands up and buttons her sweater.

"I'll walk ahead. You keep your distance as long as we're on the paved street. I'll wait at the fork for you to catch up with me," he mumbles without looking at her.

He looks downright cocky. Only once before has she seen him like this. That Friday night when they had that terrible fight with the Orthodox geezers in the men's wing of Barrack 65. She nods, rehearsing Bert's and Ruth's telephone numbers in her mind. She wonders about Gerrit's clandestine operation in the empty windmill. How safe is he? Are they? The streetcar jostles to a halt.

"Last stop," the conductor calls at no one in particular. There is no one left in the car. The driver emerges from his cubicle and lights a cigarette up front. Werner steps off to begin his journey outside. She follows.

"Not too close. Keep your distance."

Hanne's head whirls with thoughts. Strange ruminations. Here I'm walking behind Werner. Bowlegged as ever. Remember the Sunday bike ride for strawberries? Miss Horny indeed. She wonders whether he got close to another horny idiot in the camp. With the lack of privacy there probably not, although she wouldn't put it past him. Hanne, stop this. Stick to your job. You're to deliver him to Gerrit. In one piece. Yourself too if you want to see your old folks again. Know what's good for you. Sure. The task you're on isn't the healthiest job you've ever done. Could be worse, though. The sky has cleared. Dusk is setting. The veined globe of the pale full moon hangs in the sky. A few buildings and a row of trees strike stark silhouettes by the rural wayside. Werner keeps a brisk pace ahead of her. They need to disappear before dark. There's a good distance between them. She better quicken her pace.

Ahead of her the two men disappear into the last house on the street. She hears them talking a blue streak on the other side of the fence. Except for Werner the landscape lies deserted. A dog howls somewhere far off. A lonely tomcat jumps the fence with a screechy meow. She sees him run off across the field. She gets jittery. No, don't give in to that! She takes a deep breath. That always helps.

"No need to get frightened." She straightens her back.

Sudden loud men's voices at the end of the road pierce the early evening air. Her heart leaps. Three Germans stand with Werner. Screaming. Suppose he needs her help. She quickens her step. Catches up. They are screaming in German. Want to know the time of day. Werner is shaking his head.

"*Niet verstaan.*"

Werner turns to Hanne coming up the road.

"Excuse me, do you have the correct time?"

He addresses her in polite Dutch. As if talking to a stranger. She is relieved.

"Yes, Sir." She looks at her watch.

"A quarter past seven," she says. Then turns to the Germans.

"*Viertel nach sieben*," she repeats, quite the sudden translator into their language. Why not make it easy and get rid of them. The soldiers are politeness itself. Click their heels.

"*Danke schön*"

Like drilled automatons, they raise their arms.

"Heil Hitler." Metallic clicks of heels. Boots turn and stomp off in the opposite direction.

"Shove off," she mumbles. The paved road reverberates under their hobnailed boots.

Werner whistles relief through his teeth. "Thank goodness."

Hanne echoes with a heartfelt sigh.

They walk to the end of the street and turn into the deserted country road. The fields on either side do not afford much protection except for a few trees farther down the road. They walk briskly. Once aroused, Hanne cannot shake the feeling of impending danger. This stupid incident with those soldiers works on her still. Or is it the danger of her mission? Another dog howls into the evening stillness. Howls from various places answer. A secret code?

Suddenly there is a sputter of motorbikes nearby.

"Let's hurry," she says. Alarm creeps up her spine. "I'd like to avoid meeting more Germans."

She hardly finishes the thought when two soldiers on a motorbike come up behind them. Hanne shivers an instant prayer for nothing more than another hour of this day. The two stop alongside the two youngsters. An aura of alcohol spreads with them.

"*Was machen Sie denn hier?*"

Hanne and Werner pretend not to understand. The questioner leaves the balance of the bike to his comrade, steps off the bike and posts himself in front of the two. The smell of alcohol is all pervasive.

"*Wohin geh'n Sie denn?*"

He shouts at the top of his lungs trying to make himself better understood. The two shrug their shoulders. The fellow before them weaves unsteadily on his legs. The alcohol stench is nauseating. Suddenly the bike makes a loud *Boingggg!!!* The other fellow topples off the motorbike. The machine crashes to the ground with an earsplitting crash of metal.

"*Verdammt noch mal!*" The two Nazis weave themselves with difficulty into a vertical position.

"*Wohin?*" the first yells again. His body shakes toward them.

"My cousin!" Hanne shouts back, less loud, in Dutch. She tries to play for time.

"*Wo ist Ihr Cousin?*" the first German wants to know. His eyes are as unsteady as his body. He looks like he wants to throw up.

"*Ja, wo ist er?*" number two echoes him.

Hanne turns her head away from the stench. Frustration creeps up her spine. They are so close. Do these drunks have to spoil it?

"Over there!" she points in a noncommittal westward direction away from their real destination. In a way it's good they are drunk. May the devil take them! They'll have to figure a way to get out of this. German Number Two turns to lift up his fallen bike. He curses as he labors. Halfway up, it topples again in metallic convulsions. The noise is deafening.

"*Verfluchtes Ding!*"

"*Zum Teufel damit,*" growls Number One.

"*Ja. Hilf mir dann doch!*" Number Two yells at Number One.

Hanne glances at Werner. He has been quietly standing aside thus far. Almost invisibly he motions her while he stares at the sky. Then Hanne hears it too. It's unmistakable. The faint rumble of approaching airplanes.

"*Nun zeigen Sie mir Ihren Ausweis,*" Number One demands

again with a one-track mind, too drunk to hear his companion, completely deaf to the faint sound in the sky.

Show him their IDs? That order spells trouble. She has her ID. And her letter from the Swedish Legation in Berlin. The problem is Werner. They have to get away from these pests. They're drunk anyway and don't know what they're doing. Hanne gives the soldier a blank look. Lets him know that she does not understand his demand.

"*Verfluchtes Gesox! Ihren Ausweis! ID! Dally, dally,*" he yells, drunk, angry, impatient.

She watches him fumble with his gun. She rummages in her purse and prays. Wants to gain time. There must be a way out of this! The rumble overhead comes closer. Still faint, but close enough for the air-raid alarm to be sounded soon. Number Two is still busy raising his fallen bike, unsuccessfully. Does she see right? Werner helps him? She sees the bike reel, pulling the Nazi down and sideswiping the other as it thuds to the ground again, both soldiers in tow. Has Werner done that on purpose?

Overhead the rumble of airplanes grows louder. Air raid sirens start screaming. The anti-airflak adds their smatter to the roar. Mayhem. Utter confusion. She sees Werner drive his pocket knife into the front tire. The air begins to escape slowly with a sizzling whooosh.

"Come on. Let's go," Werner pants, pulling Hanne back out on the path.

"Let's get out of here. We need shelter!" They run for their lives without a look back while all hell breaks loose.

An air raid! The Tommies have finally come! And just in time!

*   *   *

They have run quite a distance by the time the sirens stop. The anti-aircraft sputter their rat-tat-tat-tat. Out of breath, Hanne looks at the faint, tiny metal birds overhead glitter black in the early evening light. Fireballs burst between them. Like firecrackers. A hit. A fiery red explosion rocks the northern sky. Flames spatter. Lick the expanse. Parachutes spread out in the silver sky. Or is that just her imagination. They are gone when she looks again.

"Come on! We don't have time to lose," Werner grates. He runs. She runs behind him.

"We've got to be inside after curfew!"

"We can't be too far away from Gerrit," she says. Her feet are automatons in motion. She can't feel them. They rotate on their own somewhere underneath her. She thinks that she hears shots behind them.

"Without their bike those lushes will be stuck for a while," Werner puffs.

"We better disappear in time."

They reach the windmill at last. It looks deserted. The millstones lie outside on the ground. Unused. A picture of long-time abandonment. They knock their code – one long, three short, two long. They wait. Overhead the rumble of planes slowly fades into the southeastern night. Hanne makes a silent wish for a lot of bombs over Nazi Germany and the planes' safe return. Including a farmer, or any good Dutchman, for the parachuters. She looks at the weather-beaten mill, that sturdy, winged guardian of the Dutch lowlands that provides its people with constant power. After her recent experience, the light of the rising pale moon makes the scene doubly frightening. She shivers. What if nobody answers at the mill?

A young fellow saunters leisurely around from the back and looks at them closely. "Hi. You Werner? I'm Gerrit."

"Werner Levy. Hanne Kalter. Bert sent us."

"I've been waiting for you. How'd you get through the raid?"

He leads the two around to the back. Makes certain no one is about nearby.

The sirens blare the end of the raid. It does not mean much out here anyway. The planes are meant for Germany. A loud explosion shatters the distance.

"Sounds like a hit. I wonder where," Gerrit says. His eyes sweep the neighborhood. The sky.

"Let's go inside," he directs.

Hanne wonders how long the raid has lasted. How long ago was it they left the two lushes in the woods? Minutes? Hours? Years? What if they found the puncture already? Are they coming to look for them? She takes a deep, audible breath to steady her fears. Best to get out of this area as soon as possible.

Werner loses no time telling Gerrit what has happened. Hanne is surprised to find several other young people sitting around on sacks and crates. Gerrit introduces the two newcomers by their first names.

"They're waiting for instructions," Gerrit says. "Where did you leave the two moffen? We're pretty well camouflaged. But I don't like them in our neighborhood."

"Better help them out of here," the others agree.

"Curfew. Not until tomorrow morning."

"They're smashed anyhow. We left them about halfway down the main path. They won't move far on their motorbike. It's got a bad tire."

Gerrit surveys his crewmembers.

"All right; Karel and Flip, you pass them, quite casually. The woods are personal property so don't go in for a lot of nonsense. Help them get out of this area. All the rest, get a move on to find the crew of the downed plane before the moffen find them. You have your instructions."

One by one the group disappears into the night. Gerrit turns to his two new guests and smiles. "This old mill hasn't been used for decades. With the millstones outside it looks even more deserted. And it is. Except on occasions." Gerrit smiles at the word. *Occasions* has a special meaning for him. No need to ask. It's none of her business. He must've said this to reassure her and Werner.

"Now. I understand that you need an ID We better take your picture."

Hanne looks around. The mill is bare, except for some crates and heaps of empty flour sacks.

"Where's your equipment?"

Gerrit smiles, as he had at the word *occasions.* "We don't keep it up here, in case the *kraut* come and nose around. The equipment and other essentials are in our hideaway. Below."

Gerrit lifts the pocket lamp from the rafters. He walks to the back of the mill and pushes a heap of bales aside. A man-sized wooden square appears in the cut stone slab. Werner helps him lift it out. A ladder folds out from its underside.

"A trapdoor to the dugout," Gerrit explains.

The three climb down into the cellar filled with newspapers, magazines, books, folders and leaflets in all shapes and colors. A large map of Holland and Belgium hangs on the wall. At the other end stands the photo equipment, including the development area with darkroom light, tubs, even a water faucet from outside. Several scouts' sleeping bags lie rumpled in the corner.

"It's pretty complete for clandestine work." Gerrit states the fact with pride. Shows them the air ducts, the water pipes, the electric wire.

"Now let's take your picture."

He positions Werner before a dark background, then snaps several times. The flashes are blinding in the murky dark. Hanne shuts her eyes momentarily. It smells musty down here.

"I'll work on this tomorrow morning. Now I need to go upstairs to keep watch. You bed down here for the night. The farmer up the road will pick you up in the morning, Hanne. He drives his vegetable truck to the open market in Amsterdam. That will keep you out of sight. Werner stays here until we figure out what to do with him. See where he can go. Good night, now."

Hanne watches Gerrit climb up again. Notes the bulge of his revolver under his arm with comforting satisfaction. In all this hazard it fills her with a sense of security. Not that Werner, or she, are out of danger.

But things are looking up. June 1943. The RAF is finally getting busy. The Yanks are coming with fresh ammunition and more people. They'll head for Germany and the Thousand Year Reich. If the Nazis don't want to yield any other way, then they'll have to destroy the dear Vaterland. She smiles, satisfied. Werner has arrived at his first destination in one piece. Tomorrow he'll be relatively safe with a good clandestine ID.

"Let's hope that help doesn't come too late for the many victims," she says into the half dark where Werner pulls the sleeping bags into place. His flashlight throws long grotesque black shadows, moving silhouettes, across the floor, beams and walls. They spread sacks on the floor.

"Horny?" flashes through her mind.

They crawl into their spaces.

"Better here than Westerbork. There's hope here," Werner says and flips the light off. It's ghostly. Dark. Hanne makes herself comfortable on the hard floor. Curls into fetal position. The musty odor has something fertile, fecund about it.

"Sure. Let's call it a day, Werner. I'll see you in the morning before I leave." Tired to the bone, Hanne is half asleep already. A satisfied exhaustion.

"I want to thank you for your help," Werner says into the dark.

"Hmmm."

"I mean, it's pretty decent of you and Bert." His words echo faintly in the early June darkness.

She is fast asleep. With her usual regular slight snore.

* * *

Bert appears suddenly the following weekend. "It's a surprise visit," he says.

"I like surprise visits. What's up?"

"I'll have to show you this city properly before you leave," he declares. His tone has that familiar fatherly tinge.

"I've been shopping enough. Seen the *grachten*. The Queen's Castle. It's in the Center," she says.

"Seeing the old city and its canals is as important as the castle, the Rijksmuseum and the other museums. Right after Mauritshuis, the Peace Palace and the Binnenhof in The Hague. There's nothing original in these buildings at the moment anyway. The art is gone. So is the government." A knowing smile plays on his lips.

"Fine. I like boat rides," she says.

They take one of the many excursion rides through the darkly glittering canals that meander through the city. The dark water is brackish, unhurried, ponderous, slightly nauseating under the curved bridges. Wood and stone that link proper burgherdom. Countless bridges whose names she will never remember. They glide smoothly within the cobblestoned narrow streets lined with endless rows of quaint sixteenth-century patrician homes, their individual gables the mark and signature of their original owners.

Hanne counts the three major canals that ring the original city with her fingers: "Keizersgracht, Prinsengracht, Heerengracht, all in proper feudal rank," she lectures Bert, who smiles indulgently.

They glide out into the choppy harbor. Testimony to a wealthier past. Center of world trade since the late Middle Ages, rich, sedate and self-satisfied. Straightlaced, stodgy, ingenious, but now separated from its colonies. New home to unwanted half-breeds like Nurse Zindel. All trying to survive the onslaught of utter brutality. Cope with treachery, deceit.

"I'm looking forward to Gothenburg. It's designed and built by Dutch engineers following the Dutch pattern as a gateway to the West."

She wants to break a lance for her new country against his overweening local patriotism.

"I'm hungry. Let's eat," Bert says as the boat docks again.

They step out on the clean scrubbed cobblestones.

"Pancakes again?"

"Goes without saying. The only decent food available these days."

They're as hungry as wolves. The red-cheeked waitress brings a huge round platter heaped with yellow brown-black cakes and sets it in the center of the wobbly little table by the window with the lace curtains. Hanne looks out into the dark-flowing water of the canal. The sun jitterbugs in the slow-moving undulations that roll forward. Sunjangles. Dancing gold chain links. One-way, out into the North Sea. The Gulf Stream surely picks up a few and leads them across the Skagerrak to Gothenburg. Hanne takes a pancake.

"Smells good." She inhales the steam.

The Gulf Stream... she isn't certain of its route. Around England? It's in the neighborhood and floats up the west coast of Sweden. Waterborne greetings to her new home.

She doesn't much care for the thick Dutch pancakes and jam. Mutti used to make thin Crêpe Suzettes filled with sweetened crème cheese. She picks a few cherries out of the sugary concoction and spreads them across her floppy flub. Mutti's were thin. Crisp. Hanne rolls hers up omelet fashion the way she remembers from home. Mutti took pride in making hers paper-thin. These pancakes are solid and sturdy, like the Dutch people. She watches Bert. His mode of operation intrigues her still.

He dips his spoon into the red jam mass, lifts it, an overflowing heap, and flops it down in the center of his pancake. Once. Twice. Three times. He reaches for a fourth spoonful that nearly empties the glass container. Pushes the heap slowly from the center in a circular direction across the pancake, which disappears under the inch-thick load. A slight overlap of pancake hangs over one side. Carefully he lops off the overhang, then wiggles the rim precariously on top of the inch-thick jam. His eyes glimmer.

"That's how I like it," he smiles from ear to ear. His teeth shine white. He starts cutting into the jam. Yellow double strips of pancake between red jam. He lifts a cut piece carefully onto his fork, balances it upward, shoves it into his mouth. Chews with delight. One bite after another disappears."

"I know." Hanne watches him eat his favorite food. Strange habits. Fun to watch.

"Any news from Werner?" She wants to lead her thoughts away from watching Bert eat. It's not nice to look at other people's plates. That's Mutti way back in her memory. Besides, she is eager to find out what happened since she left the windmill the other day.

"You'll be happy to learn that he's sitting safely in England," Bert manages between chews.

"Don't tease me about such matters," she says angrily.

"It's true." He beams blissfully back into her face, ignoring her anger.

"How on earth?"

"It's one of the rare happy endings. Gerrit's men picked up three Tommies that night from a burning plane. Hid them in the mill for a day or two. To keep Werner company," he joked.

"How'd they get them home?"

"An English rescue mission picked them up a few days afterward. They took Werner along. Neat, don't you think? Fellow has more luck than brains."

"How'd they manage to get them out?"

"You're asking too much. You know too much already. But honestly, I don't know the details. Even if I did I wouldn't tell. All I know is that Gerrit has radio contact with England. I know too that occasionally they pick up their men and take them home. Others go along if there's room. The Kraut are still looking for the crew."

"Okay. I won't ask for details. I'm just glad Werner got out all right. His mother lives in London. That makes it perfect. But why did you wait all afternoon to tell me? And not until I asked?" She is still sore.

"I couldn't with all the other people around. Anyway, good news is always welcome. Even if it has to wait. I heard you were caught in an air raid.

"Yes. Life depends on luck. Not smarts or hard work. Just plain luck. Like a lottery."

"Don't be sarcastic. If the fellow hadn't been smart, he wouldn't have taken the chance. It takes brains to get the right contacts and make things work. He was smart enough to find you!"

Hanne sighs. Luck plays the biggest part in life. Millions of smart people never have luck. Not to mention those who work hard at making it and never do. She is happy that Werner is safe in England. Another human being that slipped past the horror machine.

"It's a good feeling to have helped."

Chapter 14

The weeks drag on. Monotonous May has turned into monotonous June. Endless wait.

The girls shop for the Abram kitchen. For excitement they go to the Jewish Council downtown on North Keizersgracht. They want pocket money. They get it, reluctantly. Hanne suspects a catch somewhere. But who cares? She doesn't inquire into details but spends her wealth on food packages for her friends back in camp. Ruth does the same. Sibling disagreements are pushed aside in a kind of uneasy truce. They have the same goal. Home.

Sometimes they go sightseeing together. Witness the constant razzias in the streets. The window on the third floor makes a disengaged, comfortable distance to watch nightly roundups of Jews. The law of wearing the Jewish star does not apply to them. They ignore the law against using public transportation, against visiting public parks, other demeaning exclusions. No one challenges Hanne's interpretation. It's a new sensation of freedom that slowly wears off as she starts to take it for granted. Along with it grows her sense of being an outsider. Who is she? Where does she belong? The Nazis have divided society into two entities: Jew and Aryan. She may know who she is but she cannot show it. It's like playing musical chairs. What force is at work behind this exclusion? A game? Plain luck? Fate? Haunting thoughts. She is unable to resolve the matter.

"It's time we moved on."

* * *

Change finally arrives on a hot Monday afternoon. June 14, 1943. A messenger rings the doorbell. A sealed letter from Gestapo Headquarters on Adema van Scheltemaplein. Personal delivery for Hanne Kalter. She looks at it. Expectation mixed with dread. The name itself. The address even more. She thanks the boy. Then opens the envelope. Slowly, afraid of what it may contain.

The summons to pick up their Swedish passports with the *Sichtvermerk*. The gateway to real freedom. She is anxious to get it.

She finds Ruth in the kitchen stirring a pot of soup for Mr. Abram. His small frame disappears inside his huge apron, as usual.

"Well," Ruth says. She drops her spoon when she sees the letter.

"Our big appointment is tomorrow morning, June 15, at ten."

"I can hardly believe it."

"Yes. It feels strange."

"Congratulations," Mr. Abram says and looks up from his job stirring the steaming soup.

"Yes. Congratulations," Mrs. Abram calls from the pantry. She wipes her hands and shakes theirs.

Hanne senses jealousy vibrating in their voices. She cannot blame them.

The wait is over. Now they must meet the Gestapo. The very name conjures dark residual fears. One more hurdle to take with jittery gut.

* * *

They dress carefully for the meeting. Ruth is fussy.

"Shall I wear the light summer dress?"

"Sure, it's warm enough."

Hanne wears her usual skirt and blouse. She is no less nervous about the meeting. Imagine. Gestapo Headquarters wants to speak with her. She is ready. Edgy. The atmosphere in the bedroom chokes her. She needs to get out of the room.

"I'll wait for you downstairs. Perhaps they want us to get something from the bakery on our way back. Don't dawdle."

She enters the kitchen in high spirits. Only deep down inside her lurks an odd feeling of guilt. She can't explain it.

"We'll be passing by our favorite bakery. Want us to buy something on the way back?"

"We could use our extra coupons for some nice crumb cake. They're on the shelf by the door. Get the big sheet, enough for all of us," Mrs. Abram says.

Jacob Abram looks her over.

"You look stunning. Lord knows I hate the thought of losing you two helpers. We'll miss you."

Hanne has no answer. She looks at the small man before her and his wife by the sink. Running a boarding house these days presents special problems aside from the general worries Jews face. Heroes all, specializing in the heroics of survival. The survivors will be the real heroes. It's easy to be a gun-toting hero and shoot everyone dead around you if you have official power on your side. It takes special guts to survive. Cunning. Smarts. Some make it. Some don't. But heroes all. She wonders for the millionth time what fate has in store for her to have singled her out.

"I'm sure you'll manage." She is at a loss to say anything but banalities.

Ruth comes running down, two steps at a time. "I'm ready!"

"Another movie star," Mr. Abram teases.

"Trying to impress the Gestapo," Ruth calls into the kitchen before she pulls the front door shut behind her.

They walk the wide sidewalks of the affluent residential section that lies baking in the hot June sunshine. Housewives are out to shop for their daily dinner. Maids shake rugs and bedding through windows. Sparkling windowpanes, polished brass door-knockers and handles blind their eyes. The street is ready for its second morning cup of coffee.

"It's going to be a scorcher."

Pain and adversity hide behind the burgher façade. A light wind blows, ever so gently.

They know their way to Adema van Scheltemaplein. They have been there once before to report to the Gestapo that they arrived in Amsterdam from Westerbork. But that's all they did. No one special wanted to talk to them then.

They turn the corner into the main street. Two men on the other side of the street hold their briefcases up high against their chests.

"Try to hide the yellow star."

"A common sight these days".

"I'm sure glad to be done with this," Hanne mumbles.

Nazis know what they're doing. Wearing the star makes you feel inferior. It marks you, your very soul. With the star, inferiority invades your guts, no matter how much you fight it.

"You may tell yourself a thousand times who you are. That inferiority complex sticks with you. I wonder whether we'll ever get rid of it. Be like *the others*."

"Right. *Normal*."

"Yeah. There's a certain loyalty. Call it identification with our kind underneath it all."

"I think it's funny when I sit next to a moff in the streetcar. He doesn't know with whom he has the honor to sit. I always wonder what he would do if he knew."

"It's like playing a joke on them."

"All that because of a piece of paper."

"An official one, though, remember?"

"It's good to know that we can leave all this behind. It may sound selfish. But staying here wouldn't help anyone else."

Hanne muddles in thoughts. Years of insecurity have made her suspicious of the future. Take nothing for granted. Not until she has her passport will she believe in it. Not until she's safely outside German territory will she feel safe. If then. She pushes her doubts aside. Think positive. Things have gone well so far. What's she complaining about?

"A lot of wounded in the streets. Shows they're losing the war in the East. And now in North Africa."

"Yes. These are on leave to recuperate. Then return to the front."

"To defend the Thousand Year Reich."

Lately Hitler has been talking a lot about a secret weapon. Suppose he has one? What if he wins the war after all? Her whole being revolts against the idea. It mustn't be.

"Good God! Make an end to it before they destroy all the victims trapped inside! It's just that it's taking the Allies forever to win."

*　　*　　*

Only a handful of people are on the streetcar this time of day. A few civilians. On the rear platform a group of soldiers crack off-color jokes in their boisterous guttural tongue. She wonders whether the Dutch know what they're saying. Many of them speak German extremely well. The girls walk past the group and sit down inside the car.

"It must be me, or the summer heat. I still smell Westerbork on our clothes. It's less in the boarding house. But it's still there."

"Because that's all we smell in our room," Ruth explains.

"All my scrubbing doesn't help. It just clings."

Ruth nods. "Our clothes smell. We'll have to get rid of our stuff and get new things once we get to Sweden. There's plenty of everything there."

"Other people must smell it too."

Sweden is Shangri-La. Paradise. Heaven and safety all rolled into one.

"The smell lodges in our minds too. Mentally we're still in

Westerbork. It'll be different when we come home. Meanwhile I can keep my distance from other people."

"I wonder where Kurt Ehrlich went with his Nansen passport."

Now that she is about to separate from them she worries about her sibling friends. She looks forward to their letters telling her how much they appreciate the food packages. So far they're doing all right. As long as they can stay where they are. Bella's halo of red-gold ringlets around her pale freckled face surfaces in her mind. No. She is gone. The Nazis have no patience with mental cases.

"Time to get off," Ruth cuts into Hanne's ruminations.

They step out on the platform to wait for the next stop. The German soldiers bawl their off-color jokes. A pair of steel-blue eyes ogles Hanne. Invites her.

"*Fräulein, wollen Sie nicht ein Glas Bier mit mir trinken?*"

"*Nein, danke.*"

Hanne says it loudly. In German. She looks past him. Thankful that the streetcar has come to a halt. She jumps off. Ruth behind her.

"See what I mean? That's all I need. Drink beer with a Nazi. Can just picture telling him I'm a Jew!"

"That's what you get for not wearing the star." Ruth chuckles. "*Rassenschande*. What's the punishment for the crime? Five years in the slammer? Ten? Life? Death?"

They cross the plaza to Gestapo Headquarters. The Nazis have made themselves comfortable in the old theater.

"To requisition this beautiful building for their headquarters is a crime," Hanne mumbles. Master race. She stares at the imposing wide staircase leading up to the front entrance. It sports the customary sign these days. In thick black script.

Für Juden verboten.

"Do you think we should take the back entrance?" Ruth hesitates.

Hanne looks into her little sister's large eyes.

"Certainly not. Why should we walk through backdoors? We didn't do it when we were here the first time."

She has walked through enough backdoors. They are as good as anyone else entering the building.

Defiantly she pulls the heavy front door open. Her guts shakes but she smiles in defiance. "There."

They step into the wide foyer, dimly lit. Cavernous corridors wing out in both directions, lined with closed doors that hide surreptitious secrets. Uniforms stomp through the halls.

After the heat outside she feels goosebumps. An atmosphere of tension lies over the entire scene. Hanne straightens up. She pulls her sister forward to the dour girl behind the glass counter in the center.

"We have an appointment with Obersturmführer Pieffke."

"Your names?"

"Hanne and Ruth Kalter." She hands the girl the summons.

A barren smile collects around the narrow lips stained with blood-red lipstick. She rummages among the papers in front of her on the counter. Pale blond hair pulled back tightly in a knot, the invariable badge of German womanhood. Square jaws. She pulls one paper out and steps with it out of her cubicle.

"I'll check with him. Have a seat."

Hanne watches her sizeable round rump wobble down the corridor.

"Our name is neutral. But we are not Aryan." She mimics wagging her rump. They sit down on the bench along the wall and wait.

At the other end of the corridor a door releases a group of loudmouthed green Gestapo. Boots trample. The building echoes with unspoken threats. Hanne wishes the interview to be over so they can leave these surroundings. Gestapo Headquarters, a devil's brewery of heinous crimes against humanity. Gestapo, fiendish minds that concoct brutish laws for docile slaves á la Nietzsche. Madmen's utopia for a master race!

Behind them the back entrance door opens. Hanne cringes.

Several ss begin to herd a motley group of Jews into the building. New arrivals. Picked up during the night. Many flushed from no-longer-secret hiding places. More food for Barrack 66! Next week's trains! Hanne's heart bleeds. She knows their fate only too well. There is nothing she can do to help.

She argues with divine justice. Questions the whole concept. The unfairness of it all. Vati had it all wrong when he talked to her of a loving, caring, divine judge. Care about his world? Heavenly mercy? If this God exists, what is he doing? Where is he hiding? A partner in cahoots with an irresponsible, mead-slurping, drunken Wotan, both sacking it out on that bearskin in Valhall…? Or is he a chicken-footed demon *Ashmoday,* hiding his webbed feet in heavy leather boots polished to a shine? Take your pick!

Dad. Will he understand what has happened to her during these five long years of separation? He may praise his God. Thank Him for the rescue of his children, convinced that their return is a reward for good deeds by one of his forefathers. That makes no sense. Why save just two? Why just these two? Singled out of millions of others. More religious. More deserving.

The ss herd the new arrivals onto the floor. They huddle the way she once did, way back in a schoolhouse in Arnhem. Like these prisoners innocent all, huddling on the floor with their bundles. Apathetically they wait – for what? Their fate? An infant is crying in his mother's arm. She rocks her baby, back and forth, tries to feed it. Hush baby, hush, shh, shh.

"Good Lord, make an end to this, please. Please make an end to this," Hanne prays, unmindful of praying to the same deity whose existence she questioned a moment ago. "Good Lord, I don't mind being saved from all this. No. I don't mind. I'm grateful too. But why me? Why not the others? The millions of others?"

The receptionist comes clomping back from the depth of the corridor. She settles her weighty bottom laboriously on her stool behind the glass counter. Checks some papers again. Then she calls the girls.

"Obersturmführer Pieffke will see you now. Last door on the right."

Apprehensive, the two walk down the long corridor. Their steps echo hollow against the secrecy of closed doors. The last on the right. Hanne knocks.

"*Herein!*"

The polished brass handle of the carved oak door feels heavy in Hanne's hand. She pulls the door open. Huge dark tapestries over the windows keep the noonday heat out of the opulent interior. A crystal chandelier diffuses a million tiny glimmers across the room. Lights the paper-strewn walnut desk that overwhelms most of the inner space with its immensity. Huge oil paintings cover the walls. A thick Persian carpet absorbs every sound.

Hanne stares into the half-dark. It takes a while before she discerns the little man standing on the other side next to the desk. He is dressed in the odious green uniform. She feels his lynx eyes scanning them. Follow their every move. The girls stand still. Awestruck. His left chest hides behind a panel of colorful medals. A blood-red scar crosses his forehead from his right temple down to his left eye. Hanne cringes. *Cain.*

"*Guten Tag,*" he says into their silence, bows slightly and clicks his heels.

"*Bitte, nehmen Sie Platz.*"

A slight wave with his hand indicates where they are to sit. Two heavy upholstered chairs wait to be occupied.

How friendly! Not even the customary *Heil Hitler*! She is on guard.

"*Danke!*" They both mumble and sit down opposite his chair.

Obersturmführer Pieffke limps around the desk and sinks down. He almost disappears in his tremendous leather chair behind the desk. The scar shines blood-red. He smiles at the girls. Struts with self-importance.

"The Swedish Legation wrote about the Kalter *children.* We

expected two little girls. What a pleasant surprise to see two pretty young ladies. Hee-hee."

Smile. Dry cough.

Heavy silence. Hanne feels uncomfortable. Is he buttering them up? Whatever for? All right, the Allies are bombing Sicily and southern Italy and the Russians attacked Orel. No. They didn't come here to make cool conversation with a Gestapo. That's the last thing on her mind. She scans the desk. In front of him are two black passports with three golden crowns on the covers. The gold letters spell *S-V-E-R-I-G-E*. She faces him squarely.

He plays with his fountain pen. Coughs again. Responds to her gaze. Then comes to the point with a slight cough.

"Hm. Hm. Hrumph. The Swedish Legation in Berlin informs us that your parents in Gothenburg want you to come home as soon as possible. We have given you the *Sichtvermerk, which* permits you to leave German territory. If you will now sign your passports, I shall stamp it in. Then you're free to leave."

He picks up the two passports and heaves himself laboriously out of his leather armchair. Then limps around the desk. He puts a passport in front of each of them and hands her a pen.

"Sign here, please," he says.

Hanne shivers slightly. She signs while he watches over her shoulder. The pen scrapes across the paper.

"There," she says and hands him his fountain pen.

He repeats the procedure with Ruth. Hanne watches in the heavy silence, broken only by the scraping pen.

"Good," he says. He shuffles back, dragging his left foot. She watches him stamp the heavy green paper with his black stamp. Then he shoves the open passports across the desk. One for each. Hanne Kalter. Ruth Kalter.

She eyes the stamp with the onerous crooked cross, the Indian fertility symbol that has become the emblem of depraved bestiality. Pieffke pulls a large envelope out of his desk drawer. He opens it ceremoniously and shakes out its contents.

"The Swedish Legation sent us these tickets for your trip

Amsterdam-Berlin on June 16th. The Express leaves at 8:00 A M."
He reads from the letter in his hand. "They have booked reservation for you at Hotel Nordland in Berlin for that night. This is the
Legation's telephone number. They want you to contact them as
soon as you arrive in Berlin. They'll have the tickets for your trip
to Copenhagen and the ferry to Sweden from Hälsingör. They'll
give you the details once you arrive in Berlin."

Fastidiously he puts everything back into the manila envelope and winds the string closed around the button.

"Here," he says, gets up again, hobbles around the desk and
stops in front of Hanne, "here is everything," ceremoniously hand-
ing her the envelope.

Hanne takes the envelope. "Thank you."

The little green man with the medals clicks his heels.

"Good luck," he says.

Hanne ponders his misshapen left foot. "Devil incarnate,"
shoots through her head, "down to the clubfoot!"

He clears his throat. "*I hope you'll forget all the nasty things
you have seen here.*"

His words hang like deadweights in the ornate room. Leaden.
She sees his mouth flicker in an attempted smile.

"Forget?"

How can she forget? Her insides fight vehemently. She keeps
silent. No!

Then she gets up. Straightens out. Stuffs her precious papers
into her purse.

No. How can she ever forget? What they have done will always haunt her, for the rest of her life. *Forget?*

"*Auf Wiedersehen,*" she says.

"*Auf Wiedersehen,*" Ruth says.

"*Auf Wiedersehen,*" he says and clicks his heels again. They
turn to leave. Metallic sounds follow them as they walk to the
door.

"*Beelzebub,*" she thinks and clutches her purse tightly. She
walks out the door, Ruth close behind her.

Humanized by a piece of paper with an official stamp. They walk through the long, dark corridor. In a sudden hurry to get out. Hanne takes Ruth's hand and pulls her forward. "Come on. Let's get out of here!"

*   *   *

The universe, unhinged at its core. Vaporous fluid, roiling, boiling, broiling. Lightning spasms flash through the void from cosmos to cosmos, divide galaxies, inflame stars, ignite planets and hurl them on their way. They rollercoast, zigzag across planet earth. Spew through the Himalayas. Quake the Andes. Reel the Alps. Blast the Harz Mountains. Mount Brocken. Thunder rocks its foundations. Winds howl, unhinged, whip sheets of rain about open gorges. Hail crashes against craggy cliffs, tumbles through valleys, across plateaus. Knotty, knobbed trees bend stiffly in submission to their fury. Dare stand, get smashed to oblivion. Unleashed from restraints, Hell's furies reign on Walpurga night.

It is the annual witches' Sabbath on the mountain. The witching hour has arrived.

Hanne climbs the slopes. Step by step. Rocks crackle under her soles. Crack open. She holds on to cutting cliffs in her upward stride through the storm. Ancient evergreens with thousand-fingered limbs block her path, crooked digits that tear her garments. Weeds and thistles snare her legs. Prick her skin. Her feet slither forward. Sink into biting, brewing muck that glues them to ancient Earth. Her limbs strain, sore from pull and tug. Forward bent, labored breathing, she makes a last-ditch effort to overcome her odds. She heaves herself up and out, determined to face the forces of the night. Head-on.

A putrid smell hovers over the peak, a level plateau in the eye of the raging winds with orgies of their own. Busy night creatures float in the howling currents, serpents of indeterminate origin crawl, clutch, scratch. Opalescent vultures screech, argue, hack at each other with sharp crooked claws. Jackasses bay, pass her in nerve-racking gallop. Clop, clop, clop tap their hooves. Buzzards fight noisily for rotting prey. Three witches shriek bloody murder into the pandemonium. They swoosh around her on skinny broomsticks, on through the escarpments, hair flying in the upward draft. Bony fingers wag in dire warning.

"Beware! You're not one of us! Hie thee out of here!"

Their bleating ricochets through the mountain range in thousandfold echoes. "You don't belong! Not here! Not anywhere! Get out! Get out!"

The warning shatters, breaks up. A million fractures reverberate in the whining winds.

"Get out! Get out. Out. Out!" the syllables rupture.

Ashmoday flies off in disgust, webbed claws exposed for everyone to see.

Hordes of goat-bearded devils snort and hoof into the whirling winds, growling at her.

"What crazy notion! You don't belong here! Go home!"

"I'm a veget-ARYAN," Hanne screams at the winds.

Raucous laughter. Bellows. Bleats. The air stirs alive with mockery.

"Hip! Hip! Hurray! For us pure Aryans. Pure Cannibal-Aryans! We!!"

"I'll have me a juicy one tonight!"

"Crazy, crazy, crazy, crazed! Go, go, go on home…home, home!" The echo rebounds in a thousand layers from rupturing boulders, craggy cliffs.

"Crazy!… y… y…! Go… go… go… home… home… home…! I'll have me a juicy one tonight… night… night…"

Home! Where is *home*?

Hanne stands upright, frozen to the craggy cliff on which she stands. Surveys the scene before her. Witches, sorcerers, devils, a gathering of motley hellhounds from the four corners of the earth. Milling about. Single. In pairs. Groups. They gawk. Listen to their master, a goggle-eyed devil with horns and mustache. He screams his message down to the hordes of groveling specters before him. Hanne has seen this face before. Heard that voice with the foreign rolling R-s. *Führer* of the Cannibal-Aryans! Pieffke's master! His picture an icon on every wall. Every billboard. His utterances blare from every square, shout through all the loudspeakers in the plazas of his realm. For everyone to hear in every nook and cranny. Wild sweeping motions, flailing arms emphasize his every word.

The hellish audience bawls approval. Their eyes hang on his lips as in a trance. Hanne sees with all her pores. A hodgepodge of potbellied, overstuffed creatures in black, brown, green uniforms applauds. Hordes of hairy, half-naked hoboes with clubfeet, merit badges tattooed on their arms, mingle with hook-nosed, wrinkled, warty companions. Long lacquered fingernails stick through black shrouds. Dire persiflage. Vaporous toxins whirl up from the ground like loosened shrouds, spiral upward, bond with the sky, sputter outward with unchecked force. Congeal to shrines. A foul, gaseous smell blankets the putrid earth. Ashmoday shrugs, his wild bird claws ready for flight.

Transfixed, Hanne feels a strange lightheadedness overcome her. She tries to avoid the vapors. Turns away. In vain. They are everywhere. A tornado sweeps her upward. Chokes the lifeblood out of her. Her mind goes blank.

"A cyclone," she gasps.

"Ha ha ha… a… Zyklon B…B…B…B…," the mustache roars above the whirr.

"Ha ha ha. Zyklon B… Zyklon B… Zyklon B…," his drudges repeat.

"Zyklon B… Zyklon B… Zyklon B… Zyklon B," the echo reverberates a thousandfold.

Zyklon-drafts numb her brain. Souls float on gaseous matter, drift through chimneys into the universe. Coagulate in the mists. Homeless souls in infinity.

Cannibal-Aryans. Overhead the red clock ticks endless time relentlessly in the cosmic whirl. An inflamed blood-drenched orb on the western horizon sinks into swirling waters like a setting sun. Hanne watches the crowd dance in goose-step to the rhythm of the military band, the drummers, fiddlers and horn blowers naked except for the yellow star on their breasts where the heart used to sit, exposed, their hair and gold teeth in blinding shimmer heaped beside them. Red-tufted gnomes from the Rhine river basin guard the Lorelei on her mountain ledge, from where she beguiles the passing sailors with her chant. Fafner's fire-spewing exhalations shower the river bottom rim. His impenetrable scaly body guards the hoarded gold in eternity. The feast is in full swing. Headless dwarfs and red necked hobgoblins carry foaming beer steins from steaming cauldrons back and forth to serve the blond master race. Couples pair off into the bushes. Squeals, groans, moans. Uproarious laughter fills the poisonous air. The mustached leader whirls on in his madcap St. Vitus dance. His gyrations mimic the fury of the spinning top. Suddenly he hits the ground in an epileptic fit. Never to be subdued, he jerks upward and resumes his performance under the wild approval of the mad crowd. His savants grovel before him in the earth, their heads scrape the rough boulders. Unconcerned, the leader hoofs off, his tail an uncouth whip to lash out at his minions, around, above and beyond. A fiery explosion turns him into smelly smoke. Foul vapors persist. The brown woman follows him at a discreet distance. Into oblivion.

Ashmoday grimaces his malicious smile.

The crowd straightens out with a flash, the swastika-shaped Cain's mark branded into their foreheads. Reveals sealed, overstuffed cargo trains that groan under excess loads. Cattle trains roll in and out of center stage plateau in endless succession, their holds spill their cargo over the barren wasteland into eternity. Human wrecks no longer human. Anthropomorphic waste stripped of its human origin, sucked into the whirling funnel of the Zyklon. The evil eye of senseless murder fumes its fury. Flaming B. Inflamed. Dark-red blood drips from striped pajamas and brown-black uniforms. Collects in puddles. Coagulates in streamers. Stains the earth. Floats upward in smoke. Chimney escapees.

ss-men whip miles and miles of nakedness into lines of conformity – old, young, male, female. Skeletons inching forward mechanically on the way to their final cleaning. Zyklon paired with the second letter of the alphabet. Beta. Bath. Barbed wire. Barracks. Brick ovens. Bonfires. Burning brawn. Brick structures with smokestacks. Elongated. Electrified. Smoldering ringlets reek of flesh sacrifice. Brownish smoke shrouds rise. Bloodstained fingers. Wounded creation. Multi-layered cloaks of duty and cause. B for scarlet *Blotch* before C, the Cain's mark branded on the forehead of an indifferent creation, cosmos no longer, its conscience buried in the crags of convenience. Flaming, reeking chimney-digits. Flotsam souls accuse uncaring sky in a heedless universe.

The history. A rebellious Jewish prophet stretched to the Roman cross two thousand years ago. Symbol of suffering turns on his Jews who refute his divinity. The wandering Jew, symbol for a stubborn minority that clings to its belief. Stiff-necked foreigners in foreign lands. Convenient scapegoats. *Azazels*, a cure for indigent xenophobia. Ingenious brutality.

Crusaders. In the name of God hordes turn their swords against infidels, ghetto-dwellers devoted to study, single-minded scholars preoccupied with explicating their endless tomes. Books of wisdom and devotion interpreted *ad infinitum*. All the while devoted clergy teach deicide from pulpits in spired churches, grandiose medieval domes. Monks and friars in monasteries whip up nobles and simple peasants alike to a killing frenzy for their own glorious ends. *You killed Christ.* Preached the Popes. Tolled the bells. Performed the stage plays every year. *You crucified the Lord! You contaminated our wells! You killed our children! Made matzah with their blood!* Authority said so. And so get caught in the frenzy. *The Jews killed Christ!* Two thousand years ago. The eternal Jew!

The camp. Experimental station. Mengelenian doctrine reigns. Stark lights over the operating table where the doctor cuts into the brain of a woman.

"Testing, testing, testing," he dictates into the microphone.

Testing for the benefit of science. Human experiments under strict supervision give reliable results.

He jabs his scalpel further into her brain. Blood and gray matter gush over the table. Clot to a scarlet pool by the corpse. The nurse's aide cuts the long wavy hair from her scalp and tosses it lightly into the huge pile of human hair in the corner. Usable waste.

"Another one," she says.

"Next one for injection," the doctor orders.

His needle is ready.

"Murder," Hanne screams. A blue haze settles before her eyes. When she looks up the mustached leader stands in the room. Arranges lampshades in one corner, bars of soap in the other.

"Translucent! Without blemish! Beautiful, no? Just look!" He touches them with admiring pride.

"Nothing can compare with the skin of babies for the manufacture of shades. Jewish babes are made for this. Look at this perfection. This beauty. The skin of older humans won't do."

His Austrian R's roll from the deep funnel of his throat out into the operating room where the soap bars are stacked high in the corner.

"Made with the fats and oils of Jewish bodies. Methodical research wins high praise. No more shortages in the Third Reich. Thanks to German scientific ingenuity."

"You are deranged! A murderer! Cain killed for jealousy. You kill them for sick craving! For crazed politics!" Hanne screams, beside herself with rage. Her voice breaks.

"Vermin! Rats! Bloodsuckers! Unfit for Aryan society. The Final Solution will take care of you," he mocks.

"You're jealous! Envious because we have learned to live by our brains. You begrudge us our success. Our ancestors wrote books. Studied ancient texts and laws while yours still climbed trees!"

"Get her! She's dangerous!" the mustache rages. His finger

points at Hanne. "Get her this minute! She defends her own kind. She must be silenced!"

The mustache curls in red-rimmed laughs. Cruelty hangs dangerously low in the atmosphere. Whirls toward the horizon. The ss come running out of the thicket. Hanne runs for her life, around bushes, over stones, across boulders, between crags. Out of breath, she stumbles over a giant root. Scrambles up and runs on, the ss right at her heels, closing the gap. Her body is sore. Her limbs heavy. Her strength gives out. No, she can't give up. She mustn't. It's her life… she has to… she has to… she has a mission. She needs to… she has to tell… the truth…

"Quick. Don't give up. They're going to kill me… I must never give up," she gasps, at the end of her strength.

Hanne feels the back of her dress tear off.

"No." She screams at the top of her lungs. "No! You won't get me. I want my life! You hear me? I have a right to my life!" Suddenly Pieffke in full black regalia stands before her, the crimson scar on his forehead inflamed. His medals glitter across his left chest. The crooked cross burns vermilion on his left sleeve.

"*Forget all the bad things you've seen here.*" He smiles. It sounds like mockery.

"How can I?" Hanne waves refusal.

She feels herself slip downward. Disembodied. Weightless. She is falling… falling… sliding into the dark void. She gasps for air. How can I ever forget my past?

A cyanide combustion explosion. Valhalla blazing. Smoke-stacked ruins. Smoke ringlets dissolve upward. The götterdämmered apocalypse. The mustache expires. His brown woman with him. The ashes of burning hate run amok. They blaze their course.

Chapter 15

B erlin. Hanne draws out the two syllables between lips and tongue. Like all provincials awestruck with the capital's magnetic pull. Berlin, in her mind, exemplifies sophistication, culture. It is the center of the movie industry. Home of her idolized film stars. Trendsetters. Berliners are famous for their conceit. Snotty. Like citizens of capitals the world over. Provincials resent their verbal condescension. Accept it grudgingly with a good amount of secret envy. But Hanne likes their dialect. Their wit. She looks forward to seeing the city.

She opens the window as the train puffs into the airy station. The traffic on the platform overwhelms her. Busy humanity in action. Running, shouting, laughing, crying. Welcomes. Goodbyes. She feels lost.

The war is evident everywhere on this sunny seventeenth of June 1943. Uniforms in all colors dominate the scene: light blue air force, gray-green infantry, dark blue navy. All this intermingled with the ever-present dirty yellow of the SA and the ominous black SS, the red swastikas on white armbands around their left arms. Disturbing reminders of barbarity in human form. Hanne brushes aside the cringing fear they inspire. No weakness now. Please.

She looks at the soldiers. Hardly more than overgrown children, healthy, young, confident in too-big clothes. Their smooth faces disappear under their helmets. She knows the inevitable fanatical look in their eyes. Their conviction that might makes right. But there are other soldiers now too. Older, more sedate, less boisterous. Their weary looks belie their starched, officious uniforms and booted tread. Bandages and casts abound. Cripples on crutches. In wheelchairs. Veterans of service for a misguided Vaterland.

> *Lieb Vaterland magst ruhig sein,*
> *Fest steht und treu die Wacht, die Wacht am Rhein.*

"Serves them right!" Hanne has no compassion. How long will it take to defeat them all? The Russians in the East. The Allies in Africa, Italy. They need to start in the West. Storm *this watch on the Rhine River.*

She marvels at newcomers she has never seen before in the street picture. Where do these bland-faced Orientals fit in to this supposedly blond Aryan crowd that so prides itself on its purity? Odd. Aspiring blond-blue-eyed wannabe natives hate aliens with such self-righteous passion that calls for total extermination of anyone different. Japanese? Chinese? She cannot tell. What brings them here, these strangers? Strange bedfellows, these Axis cohorts. She watches a group of olive-skinned Italians arguing loudly, gesticulating hands and feet to emphasize a point. No Aryans, these Axis powers. A fact lost in necessity.

"It's exciting, despite all the uniforms around," Ruth babbles through her meditations. They pull their suitcases out of the nets. Hanne fishes in her pocketbook for the slip of paper with the name of the hotel and the telephone number of the Swedish Legation.

"Hotel Nordland," she mumbles, reassured.

The sign on the wall catches her eye. It's been with her on the train. She sees it everywhere outside.

Achtung! Feind hört mit!

Like an ever-present eye looking into a body's soul. Arousing suspicion throughout the country. A good reminder not to trust anyone. She has to be careful.

The train creaks to a halt. Its brakes shriek. The jolt throws her off balance. Then everything stops.

"Berlin Hauptbahnhof!" the trainmaster shouts on the platform outside. Doors open. Humanity rushing. Vendors and newspaper boys hawk their wares.

"Well. We've arrived." The girls stretch their stiff limbs, collect their luggage, push it forward as they move with the line. Down the steps. Off the train. They stand on the platform with their luggage.

"Horst Garnmann would be a big help now," Ruth says.

"We'll do it ourselves. Find a taxi," Hanne says.

Good old Horst. They had met him in Amsterdam several times during their stay. Like a big brother. When their home was broken up and converted to serve as offices for the Jewish Council, Horst could have returned to his parents in Germany. But they were afraid that the Wehrmacht would enlist him. Instead, he moved to Amsterdam on his own to stay out of the war.

Horst had come this morning to see them off at the railroad station and help them with their luggage. Their goodbye had been so final – it was unlikely that they would ever meet again. Like with Kurt Ehrlich, after they left Westerbork together a few weeks earlier. The thought saddens. It's like mourning close relatives.

"Holland is history now," she reflects out loud into the hubbub of the platform.

"Kalter! Kalter Kinder!" Has she heard correctly?

"Hanne, listen," Ruth says.

"Kalter Kinder!" They hear it again. It's not their imagination.

A tall blond fellow threads his way through the pandemonium of the platform carrying a sign with their name in huge letters. "There's the sign."

The girls wave and approach the tall blond man carrying it.

"We are the Kalters. Hanne and Ruth." They stand before him, ashiver with pleasant expectation. People rush around them.

"My name is Engström. From the Swedish Legation. I'm to find you and take you there."

"How nice of them to send you."

Hanne acts the lady of the world. She eyes the tall, blond, blue-eyed fellow who is here to help them.

"The car is waiting outside," he says with a friendly smile. Hanne's tense limbs relax.

"You don't know how much we appreciate this," Hanne assures him. She may act the lady, but inside her heart somersaults with childlike joy. Relieved to the core.

The chauffeur helps them load the luggage into the trunk. Hanne looks at the black limousine adorned with the Swedish crest. *Her* crest.

"A new chapter," she mumbles as she climbs into the leather seat.

The hustling big city glows red-gold-black in the afternoon sunshine. The traffic is overwhelming. The people here seem less worn, less frustrated, more determined, more self-assured than the Dutch. Ruth is right. Life is exciting, despite all its sad moments. She tells herself to relax. How many times will she have to remind herself that they are on their way to leaving the Nazis behind? Far behind. Including their war.

From the front seat Engström turns to make polite conversation. "Did you have a good trip?"

"Yes, thanks." She tries not to think of the signs everywhere. *Achtung! Feind hört mit!* They follow her. Make her cringe. Fill her with insecurity.

The car stops. The driver unloads their luggage. They stand in front of the building with the sign over the entrance bearing three golden crowns. It represents the country whose citizens they now are. Hanne is fascinated. She eyes the crest with a glow of pride. Her country has come to claim her. She suddenly feels uncommonly safe.

Engström rings the bell. "Here we are," he says.

"Yes?"

A blond girl about Hanne's age answers the door. She and Engström exchange a few words in a language Hanne has long been determined to learn. Soon. And well.

"These are the Kalter children," Engström introduces his charges.

"Welcome. Welcome. We've been expecting you," the girl smiles. All friendly charm, she steps aside to make room for the two new citizens to enter. His job done, Engström leaves them with her.

"Good afternoon," Hanne says. She floats on clouds of acceptance and steps across the threshold. Gawks at this creature from another world as they climb behind her up the thick-carpeted stairs.

Hanne feels her high spirits wane. The girl is gorgeous. Dimpled cheeks. Stark-blue eyes. Golden hair flowing long over her shoulders. Her well-cut, elegant outfit must have cost a fortune. She has good taste, for sure. That lilting accent, those singsong cadences, her rolling R's all enhance her looks. But it's not her speech, or her looks, or her taste that cloud Hanne's joy. It's the girl, her surroundings, what they stand for. They exude security, a sense of belonging, of knowing who you are – all the things Hanne lacks.

Hanne glances down at her dated dress, a hand-me-down from Mutti inherited by Hanne long ago, dragged through five years of refugee life, children's homes, the concentration camp. The smell of Westerbork hits her, an unwanted reminder of memories that she would rather let sleep. Her eyes fasten on her high-heeled pumps, borrowed this morning with extreme difficulty from her unwilling little sister to match her dress. The shoes are size eight, one whole size too large, but for the sake of style Hanne cramps her size-seven toes with every step she takes to keep the shoes from slipping off her heels. To wangle these shoes out of Ruth for even a day had been a feat. "Just for today," Ruth had insisted. Now Hanne examines the shoes.

I had to grovel, beg for them, swear not to ruin them, she reflects. Just because I want to make a good impression. They match my dress.

And after all that, she still looks like a pauper. Whatever possessed her to think that she belongs here? She'll never be good enough.

"In here," the girl says and opens a heavy door into the anteroom. Her voice is low, deferential, in the thick-carpeted hall upstairs. "Have a seat. Secretary Lind will be here presently."

Her elegance vanishes through another door. They are alone. Hanne's stomach growls.

"I'm hungry," she mumbles.

"Me too. We haven't eaten since breakfast in Amsterdam," Ruth says.

Hanne drops into one of the leather club chairs. She feels suddenly weak, tired, and famished. She would like to close her eyes. But excitement prevails. Numb, overwhelmed, struck dumb, she looks at the tasteful modern furnishings around her. I'd give my eyeteeth to belong here, really belong! Looks, accent, the works. Not just a belated newcomer, accepted as a citizen out of pity, with an accent that gives away my origins as soon as I open my mouth. I hate the constant question, "Where are you from?"

The door opens. A tall, thin, somewhat effeminate blond man enters with a large manila folder in his hands.

"Sven Lind," he introduces himself.

Blue eyes behind gold-rimmed specs scrutinize the two. They shake hands. Hanne recognizes the name from their correspondence. She tries to remember his title. Her mind draws a blank.

"Did you have a good trip?" he asks. He folds his long legs down onto one of these tremendous club chairs and opens his manila folder over his knees, then looks up with a grin. "We were expecting two little girls. All our correspondence was about the *Kalter children*. And here we meet two good-looking young ladies."

Sven Lind is amused. Hanne likes him. She loves his rolling R's and that peculiar Swedish singing lilt, just like the girl's.

"The ss in Amsterdam had the same problem. I guess to my parents we'll always be children. We haven't seen each other for five years." Hanne feels the necessity to explain.

Sven Lind smiles into his folder. Hanne's stomach growls for attention. Embarrassed, she hopes he does not hear it. Why do stupid things like that always interfere when you least want them to?

"Let's see. What have we here?" he says. Has he heard that growl or not?

He pulls out some colorful tickets. Looks at them.

She sits straight in her chair and sneaks a secret glance at her feet. Glad to have convinced Miss Greedy here that wearing decent outfits benefits them both. Never mind their size, the shoes match her dress. The high heels make her look grown-up and show off her ankles. Does Sven Lind notice?

He is busy investigating those tickets.

"Let's see what we have here," he repeats into the hush. "Your tickets for the Berlin-Copenhagen Express tomorrow morning at seven. Arrives in the Danish capital in time to catch the shuttle to Hälsingör. It goes right on the ferry to cross the Sund to Hälsingborg tomorrow evening. Your family will be waiting there for you."

He stuffs the tickets into one envelope and checks another.

"Ah yes. We thought that you would be hungry so we prepared a late luncheon for you here. But you have food coupons in here for your dinner tonight and for breakfast tomorrow morning. And, ah, yes, reservations for you tonight at *Hotel Nordland.*"

Hanne's stomach growls into a somersault. Food. She glances at Ruth. Isn't she hungry? She watches Sven Lind stuff the various envelopes back into the folder. Her tired bones swell with gratitude. The Swedes have thought of everything.

"Thank you," she says as she takes the folder from him. "You've really covered all the details."

"You received your passports in Amsterdam. Including your *Sichtvermerk*, is that correct?"

"Yes," the two nod in unison.

"Take good care of them. You'll need them at the borders."

Sven Lind straightens his legs into an upright position. Skinny and long. Hanne looks into blue eyes behind glasses.

"Mr. Vilhelm Ekman is on his way home from the Swedish Institute in Rome. He has kindly agreed to help you on the trip home. He'll contact you later at the hotel."

Hanne nods. No more a free agent but a parcel shipped off safely with the proper postage.

"This way, please." Sven Lind shows them the door to the dining room. "God speed. And a safe trip."

"Thanks again," she says, clutching the folder.

He bends in a correct, polite bow as they shake hands. Leaves and closes the door behind him. She can hear him walk into another room. They stare at the table set with all kinds of fish delicacies. Hanne's eyes pop. Herring in a thousand variations. Eel too. And shrimp! With her kosher parents she has never eaten that kind of seafood. All right. That's what she'll try first. Shrimp in mayonnaise sauce. The maid waits by the table to serve them hot soup from a tureen, German fashion. Real china. Silver flatware. Glass goblets. The white tablecloth crunches under her fingers.

"Oh boy, a real meal. The works." Her stomach dances a jig. Her mouth waters. It feels good to be Swedish. Strangely safe.

The maid's name is Marie. Speaks Berliner German.

Famished, they attack the food. Hanne chews shrimp with mayonnaise. "Yofel!"

"Forget that expression," Ruth says. "It belongs to a past we need to forget."

Hanne looks at her sister. Miss Proper. Forget your past?

"We'll have to learn that language in a hurry," Hanne counters with determined resolve. Advertise for a Swedish Julie? She reaches for the eel. Take the small fork. They have separate forks for fish. Etiquette. The eel tastes terrific. Small bites. Makes sure she chews like a lady. Those round fish balls? She'll skip those. They look too much like Mutti's gefilte fish.

Forget the past? How's she going to do that?

* * *

The dining room at Hotel Nordland is empty when they enter the lobby for dinner.

"It's too early. We'll stick out like sore thumbs," Ruth hesitates.

"We need to hit the sack early. It's been a long day. And another long one's ahead of us tomorrow. Besides, I'm hungry enough to eat now."

"After all that Swedish food? It was a real dinner," Ruth whispers in the formal hush of the posh surroundings.

Hanne shrugs. She could have eaten more. That intimidating maid with that funny Nazi look in her eyes.

"I was in a hurry to get to the hotel and rest," she says. No need to tell her that that woman was the real reason. "Weren't you?"

"Wasn't it neat to arrive at the hotel in an embassy car driven by a chauffeur?" Ruth's hazel eyes are dreamy. Flush with luxury.

They study the long dark silhouettes visible through the glass door of the dining room. They step through the etched-glass door. On the other side the waiters are lined up on call like a row of penguins in their formal black and white, their white napkins folded over their arms. Hanne and Ruth step formally past the penguins in frightened assertion and try to look like ladies. Hanne sniffs the mixture of draft beer, mustard, hot bouillon and white tablecloths, a smell particular to German restaurants that she hasn't smelled for years. The maître d' folds into a deep bow. His round crown ringed with black pomaded tufts shines tonsurelike for a second before her, then straightens into a face with a vacuous smile.

"This way, please."

She walks behind him. Wonders whether he is an escaped Catholic priest. Alwine once took her and Ruth to church on a Sunday morning and he reminds her of the genuflecting priests up front.

"Is this all right?"

With the aura of the seasoned traveler Hanne lets him push the chair under her as if she had never done it herself. Amused by the procedure, she watches him stalk around the table to seat Ruth.

The bartender, his face covered with pimples, arrives with his list. She shakes her head to his question. "No thank you. No drinks." She hadn't checked their coupons for alcohol. Probably none.

The waiter hands them the food-stained menu. Red for cabbage here too? Green? Spinach, perhaps. He leaves them and she studies the menu like an old pro. Ruth does the same.

"It's strange to hear German again."

Not just occasional German barks from soldiers. Regular. The atmosphere, the behavior of the people, their talk, even the smell of the hotel and the submissive arrogance of the waiters are unpleasant memories resurrected. The familiar has grown more loathsome with absence. Being in Germany, meeting Germans is not just uncomfortable. It's revolting. Disgusting.

The waiter comes with the bouillon and places it laboriously before them. Hanne contemplates the beady eyes of fat that stare back at her. She scatters them with her spoon and starts eating. She never liked Mutti's chicken soup. There was a time when she refused to eat soup. And Mutti sent her away from the table without food. Several times. Mutti was bossy. Hanne wonders whether she still is.

"Well, German is good for another few days. Then good riddance."

"It's funny to hear it spoken on the streets. Like regular, you know? I've become so used to Dutch. German is for close friends. Jongenshuis. Dr. Wolf." Ruth agrees.

"My stomach ties up in knots when I hear the Germans speak. I can't explain it. In my mind there's a distinct difference between the language of Germans and the German we refugees speak. It sounds different," Hanne confides.

"Never mind. We'll be done with all this by tomorrow night. I wonder whether Swedish is difficult to learn."

Hanne stares back at the fatty eyes in the bouillon in front of her. Disgusting. She slaps at them. Disperses them with her spoon.

"It's too salty."

Hanne pushes the soup aside. The waiter comes with the entrée. Servile in black and white. Behavior must come with the uniform a fellow dons. She eats in silence. Reflects on how difficult it was not to speak the Dutch language when she first came to Holland. The feeling of isolation when she could not communicate with others. Like a fog that settles around you, a veiled enclosure that separates you from everyone around you.

"Being in a country with a different language is like being deaf and dumb without being so," Hanne says.

"I always had the feeling they were talking about me," Ruth says without needing further explanation.

"Yes. Like a nasty cocoon you want to step out of. But you can't."

Up front people enter. Talk. Laugh. The penguins at the buffet get busy. Stalk from kitchen door to guests and back. Then return to their perch by the door. The maître d' leads two fellows to the table by the window at the far end of the room. A family of five dressed to the hilt, sequins and all, to another. The room fills with the subdued murmur of a public place.

"Dutch was fairly easy to manage after a while. Let's hope Swedish won't be more difficult."

"This time we have Mutti and Vati to help us."

"It's great to get out of here. Exciting to get to a new country. But not knowing the language is a sore handicap." They know this only too well, and dread it.

Ruth bends forward, exuding excitement. Whispers across the table.

"Don't look now, but one of those fellows over in the back has been staring at us since they came in."

"Oh?"

"I think that guy is watching you!"

Hanne throws a casual glance in their direction. Fellows who eye her deserve her attention. Dark-rimmed glasses. Rather good-looking. Brown hair combed backward. Charcoal business suit. He looks tall from where he sits. She hopes he is. She likes tall men. The busboy's arrival with his water pitcher gives her a chance at a second look. His companion is dark blond. Somewhat heavier. Good-looking strangers in a strange place – the idea tingles down her spine. First the Swedes. Now the hotel. Berlin sparkles with exciting possibilities.

"Of all the places," she says casually, glancing at Glasses in the back. Their eyes meet. Nonchalant, Hanne turns her attention to the chicken and boiled potatoes in front of her. Convinced the food is stolen from the farmers in Holland or Denmark. Or bought with money stolen from Jews. How else could the Nazis pay for their war and keep the soldiers happy, if they did not rob the territories blind. And Jews above all?

"Now, don't start anything foolish. This is Berlin," Ruth hisses across the table with sudden alarm. "Beware of strangers, especially in a big city. In a fancy hotel. Let's finish our supper and go up to bed. You said yourself we should turn in early. We've had enough excitement for today. Tomorrow is another day."

Hanne looks at this little sister of hers, going off like a siren sensing danger. Go upstairs? This is Berlin. The capital. When will we ever be in Berlin again? This is the chance of a lifetime! She eats her dinner. Mannerly. Conscious of the good-looking stranger ogling her. Let Ruth flash her beautiful eyes in anger. Absolute condemnation radiates from Ruth's side of the table.

"I shouldn't have told you. Can't you eat any faster? Hurry up. I'm ready for dessert."

Hanne's entire being balks. For as long as she can remember, this kid has policed her, reported her slightest trespass. These five years away from home were really a respite of sorts. Good Lord! She's gotten worse – a real pest. Careful! A red light blinks here. Hanne shrugs.

"There's nothing waiting for us upstairs, is there? We didn't even unpack. Let's just take it easy."

The waiter arrives and clears the dinner plates laboriously, then puts the plates with the dessert before them. Some fake-caramel pudding with that horrible ersatz whipped cream. But the hot chocolate drink is warm and not too sweet. It tastes like the good old stuff. She wonders where they got it.

"Coffee?" the waiter asks.

"Yes, please."

"How about our *Kirschkuchen*? Specialty of the house this time of year. Fresh from the oven."

"No, thank you. But make it a large pot of coffee."

"Yes, madam."

Hanne has plenty of time to linger.

Disapproval in Ruth's eyes glares black. A shadow crosses the table from behind. She looks up. Really. There stands *Glasses*. Quite tall. Handsome. An unexpected possibility materialized.

"Yes?" she looks up. Mimes worldwise sagacity.

"My name is Fritz Lohenfeld. I would like to make your acquaintance." He bows and clicks his heels. Dull pomposity personified. His voice resonates deep, melodious.

"German," flashes through her mind with healthy distrust. Her stomach leaps in singsong. Pleasure jitters uncoil from her spine out into her fingertips. She floats on a wave of excitement.

"I'm Hanne Kalter. My sister, Ruth." She gives him an offhand smile.

He takes her sweeping hand as an invitation. "May I join you?"

"By all means."

He sits down in the empty chair next to her. His smile has crooked front teeth. Impish crinkles in the corners of his eyes behind the glasses. It's as if meeting strangers in big city restaurants is the most natural thing in the world. She feels the kid's silent objection veer violently across the table. Hanne's gaze pleads tacit understanding, if not approval. It's just for this evening, please. But all she sees are the dark curls of Ruth's bent head preoccupied with her dessert. All right then. The eruption will be later. The waiter appears, almost a rescue, with the wine list. Fritz and she consult. Fritz orders champagne for all of them.

"Your face looks familiar. I'm trying to figure where we met before," Fritz resumes the conversation.

Indeed! Why can't he be more inventive than to give her this tired old line? Better set him straight. "I doubt it. This is my first day in Berlin. We arrived from Amsterdam this afternoon. Are you Berliner?"

"I am. I live in Wannsee. I met my business associate for dinner here. His train leaves shortly." They look over to his associate who nods at them on his way out.

"I'm going upstairs," Ruth announces, her voice a honed knife. The noisy push of her chair a deliberate show of disapproval.

"I'll pay our bill on my way out."

"Fine. I'll see you later." Good riddance. Hanne keeps her cool. She watches her sister leave. Her drawn back between the shoulder blades total denunciation. Exasperating kid trying to throw her weight around. Let her do what she wants.

Hanne turns to her present company with an indulgent smile. Shrugs.

"Fritz? I knew a Fritz Hohenstein. Son of our next-door neighbors when I was little. We lived at number 3, they at 5. Ilse Hohenstein and I were buddies. Playmates. Played marbles under the tree on the street. He was her older brother. Used to take me for a piggyback ride down Fuldastrasse, our street. My first secret love." Hanne muses half aloud and smiles in remembrance. "Childhood memories," she says.

The waiter sets the champagne with the glasses before them. They toast. She sips. Bubbles float through her, tickle her mouth. Down her throat.

Those piggyback rides. How can she forget them? He was her *Fitz*. She would throw her baby arms around his neck and hold tight while he horsed around. She atop, safe. Secure. Way back when. She smiles at old memories. *Fitz* her great secret love. Then the deep hurt later when *Fitz* became *Fritz*. When they ran into each other on the street and he pretended not to see her. Walked right past her. As if she didn't exist. Then she tried to avoid meeting him on the street. Especially when he started wearing his *Hitlerjugend* uniform. By that time Ilse and she had long stopped playing together. And Mutti had enrolled her in the Jewish school at Buchenbaum Street when it opened.

She gives this Fritz a searching look. How would he react if he knew my background? A Jew in this ritzy dining room? A decidedly unwanted Jewish presence in these Aryan surroundings?

"I hope this association is a pleasant one." Fritz's voice cuts through Hanne's memories. She feels old. Ancient. Almost wise.

"Oh. It's all so long ago. Way back when… I don't know where he is today." She shrugs a casual shrug. A soldier fighting for his Führer! In Russia? Italy? On leave? Wounded? Dead? A hero fallen for a madman who messes with the lives of people on this entire continent. Including my own.

"For someone just arrived from Amsterdam you speak an excellent German. Not a trace of an accent."

"Sure. I was born in Germany. Duisburg, to be exact." Does she detect some suspicion? How would she know? What is she to say? Unpack her history? Refugee? Jew? Better change the subject. "I'm leaving for Sweden tomorrow morning."

"So soon? What a shame. We just met."

His disappointment sounds almost genuine. He looks at his watch. His face brightens.

"The evening is young, you know. Why don't I show you Berlin at night. Perhaps take in a cabaret. How about a nightclub?"

Hanne has a fleeting vision of young girls kidnapped. Strangled. Dismembered. Sold into slavery. No. That's stuff for trashy novels. Tabloids. Ruth's warnings flash through her mind. Nonsense. She takes a deep breath. The fellow looks all right. She has never been to a nightclub. She's dying to see one from inside. Life owes her that much.

"Why not? It's not every day I travel through Berlin. Do you know a good show?" Why not grab the chance? She's not afraid!

"I know the owner. We don't need reservations."

"Let me just tell my sis so she won't worry. I'll call from the lobby."

Hanne walks out with Fritz, a strange man in the big city. Walking is an exercise in pain and frustration. Her matching shoes slip off with every step she takes. She cramps her toes to keep the shoes from falling off. Never mind. Deal with it. From the lobby she declares her message of independence through the telephone, easier than facing conscience-stricken little goody two-shoes in person.

Fritz takes her arm and they walk out of the hotel. The bellboys open and close. She the lady of the world. She tries her best to make her strange gait look natural. Outside, the setting sun floods golden streamers over the city. Promises one of those warm, mellow summer nights. Tall buildings stand stark against the gold flooded horizon tinged with a yellow-ochre-carmine-purple edge.

They take the streetcar. To sit down is a relief on her poor feet. Hanne glances down at her feet. It's worth the pain. High-heeled pumps make her feet look gorgeous.

Achtung! Feind hört mit! The same sign here too. All over the place. This one stares at her from inside the streetcar. These people are paranoid. See enemies lurking in every corner. She feels herself drawn into the net. Of course, she will have to be careful not to express her real thoughts. Her mind works in different directions. She is different from the rest.

She looks at the passengers. Mostly women. Not many children. The men are at the fronts in deadly combat. One old man in civilian clothes sticks out. An oddity. The rest are soldiers, in colors of the various forces. Out for a night of fun with overdressed, giggly dates. Expectant faces hungry for company. She studies her own escort from the side. Fritz. A stranger. Picked up in a fancy hotel. Who is he? Where is he taking me? her brain warns.

Indeed. Where were her brains when she agreed to this harebrained escapade? She should have listened to little sister's sane objections.

The big, strange city passing by outside the window makes her feel small, forlorn. Suspended in an unreal reality. Endless streets stretch from one unknown corner to the next. She pinches her thigh. Breathes deeply. Better stay alert. Remain on guard. This is Berlin!

"We get off at the next stop," Fritz motions into her thoughts.

They step off. Stand on the busy street. He takes her arm. A warm body, strange, in a bustling city. Darkened lights.

The sky is turning into dark blue velvet with orange purple stripes. A wide orange fringe frames the western horizon. The rest is black-blue dotted with glitter stars, starkly visible in the total darkness of war. Searchlights flash at regular intervals – white streaks sweeping across the dark expanse. Alert to enemy attack. Who is the enemy?

"You're awfully quiet. Meditating?" he says.

"There's so much to see. Even in the dark."

The shaded lights look ghostly.

"It's not far. Just around the corner," he reassures her.

She is grateful. Her calves hurt from the strain of keeping those stupid shoes on her feet.

"This way, please."

Even walking upstairs is a relief.

The owner himself leads them to a small table for two in the dimly lit, smoke filled room. Hanne sinks down on her chair. Her feet a burning hymn of gratitude. Finally she can throw off her shoes under the table. The threatening cramp in her toes may dissolve quietly on its own.

She looks around. Assesses. Posh. The expensive look reassures her. Again soldiers of all kinds, though Luftwaffe blue predominates. Their dates are flashy. Good looking. Dyed blondes, mostly. Dressed to the hilt. She feels sorely out of place for the second time today. Or is it the third? Her dumpy clothes prey on her. As if her background and lack of education, schoolyears spent in camps, weren't enough

"Cigarette?" Fritz holds his cigarette case under her nose. The faint smell of tobacco tickles.

"Thank you," she says and takes one. Tries to act worldly. Bends forward for Fritz to light it, glimmers in her eyes. Leans back in her chair. Puffs smoke. Then she inhales deeply the way she used to see movie stars do in American films long ago. Claudette Colbert. Greta Garbo. Bette... what was her name again?

Her first try at smoking flashes through her mind. Years ago, on the urine-smelly john in school where all the girls lined up to try. Fifth grade. After recess. One puff had made her throw up her entire lunch. She felt miserable long afterward and she wasn't the only one. They hardly made it back to class. She feels the nausea still.

Then there was the time at the Jewish social where a guy from Essen offered her one. He'd barely managed to light it when Vati appeared behind her. Made her snuff it out. Right in front of everybody. She was so embarrassed. And furious with her parents. After that she had smoked in secret a few times. Just to look grown-up. But she'd never really developed a taste for smoking. Though in her present situation she could hardly refuse. That would be admitting to a lack of sophistication. She stifles a cough as the tobacco hits her lungs. She feels lightheaded. Faint. Precious air drains out of her skull. She wants to exhale in a long stream of white smoke, à la Claudette Colbert. What was the name of that movie? Something with night... oh, yes, *It Happened One Night*. But her stomach is queasy. She turns limp. Nauseated. Stubs the cigarette against the ashtray with a silent prayer. Please. Not here. Not now. Her fingers grip the table leg under the white cloth. Opposite her Fritz smiles. Exhales with gusto, billows of gray ringlets, one after another. She doesn't want him to see her distress. His smile aggravates her.

"We smoke a Turkish brand here. It's hard to get any others. They're stronger than the American brands and have a sweetish taste." His eyes follow the upward dance of his smoke rings. "It's all we can get," he mumbles after them.

Her nausea subsides slowly. Ever so slowly. She waits. Takes a deep breath to let her stomach settle. There. Her brain starts functioning again. The cigarette on the ashtray suddenly bothers her. That smell. She pushes the burning cigarette out against the tray.

"Yes. They are different," she says with the aura of the expert.

The waiter appears at the table. Penguin lifesaver in black and white.

"Are you ready to order?"

They agree on a sparkling Rhinewine. Then settle back and listen to the dance band play the current hit, Der Wind hat mir ein Lied erzählt.

"Kurt Weill," she muses across the table, proud of her knowledge.

The singer has a deep voice.

"Almost as good as Zarah, who introduced it," she shows off.

He smiles good-naturedly across the table. "You're sure up on the latest hits."

"It's all over the radio. You can't help hearing it." She wants to add that Zarah is the propaganda minister's tart. But she holds her tongue in time.

After that they play a tango. Several couples walk out on the dance floor. She taps the rhythm with her stockinged foot. The wine arrives with the waiter. Bows here and there.

"Santé. And a good trip." Fritz lifts his glass to her.

"Santé," she says with a swing of her arm and takes a generous gulp. That should settle that obnoxious stomach of hers. The fizz courses in a warm wave through her body. It makes her dizzy and slightly drowsy. The day has been long and eventful.

Fritz leans across the table.

"You haven't told me what brings you to Berlin on such a short visit. Just one night! You're born in Germany, speak like a native. You came from Amsterdam today, you say?"

Despite her haze she can see how unbelievable her story sounds. Should she tell him the truth? Very iffy. Probably not. What else can she tell him? Never mind. She isn't about to lie. She's legit. There's nothing to hide.

"Why would you want to know?" The question hits her momentarily through her lazy fog. Is he just making conversation? Or is there more behind it? She is pleasurably tired with a warm glow. It makes her complacent.

"Just thought I'd ask," he says. He takes a nonchalant puff on his weed. Blows more rings. "You're an interesting person," he adds into the haze.

Indeed. What the hell. "I'm Jewish," she says. She stares with a gutsy smile at him, watching his face for the effect of her confession.

"You're what?" his mouth gapes slightly. His eyes narrow to slits behind glasses.

"Fritz. My sister and I escaped five years ago with a children's transport to Holland. January 1939. Before the war. The Germans came to Holland a little more than a year later and eventually we landed in a concentration camp. No. *Transitlager.* They let the two of us go because we're Swedish citizens. We're on our way to Sweden. Home." The last syllable is a singsong. A stone rolls off her chest. An unnecessary veil lifted. Her drowsiness is gone. Her senses have shifted into gear. Keen. Alert. With a proverbial sixth sense she watches him digest this information.

"We had Jewish neighbors when I was a kid. They kept their Sabbath on Saturday instead of Sunday. I don't know what happened to them. One day they weren't there anymore..."

"Oh, yeah?" She can't hide a definite tone of sarcasm. She could tell him what happened to the neighbors, if he doesn't know. Why do Gentiles always react to her Jewishness by associating her with some of their Jewish neighbors? Or roommates. People she has nothing to do with. Except that they belong to the same faith. They glance at each other across a growing distance. Better not discuss her feelings with him. Not tonight. It's not just that she isn't up to a discussion like that right now.

They glance at each other across their distances. Walls mount between them.

The sound of boots trample through the bar. Interruption of thoughts. He never answers. If he did she never hears it. Suddenly several ss-men appear out of nowhere. Demand everybody's full attention. Within minutes they block all the exits.

"Niemand verlässt das Lokal. Bitte bleiben Sie sitzen."

A razzia. Hanne's spirits drop to zero. She should never have confided in Fritz, a total stranger. So stupid of her, on top of her stupidity to go out with him. She knows about razzias. Why hadn't she thought of the possibility? All she can hope for now is for Fritz to keep his mouth shut. Well, never mind. Her passport and her ticket are in her handbag. They bear witness to the truth of her tale. She fumbles for them in her handbag under the table for reassurance. Her stomach tightens into that old familiar knot. Are they looking for someone in particular? Or are they on a routine search? Lots of Jews are caught in this manner. One never knows.

She watches the group of black robots disperse, post themselves in strategic spots – the exits, the toilets, along the walls. Their leader supervises from the bar. Two pairs begin to check people at tables, one pair from either end of the room.

"Ihren Ausweis, bitte."

People rummage in their pockets and handbags for their identification cards. Jews have a large *J* stamped on theirs, Poles a *P*. Easily identifiable. On the Nazi scale of ratings, Jews stand at the bottom rung. Poles one notch above. Both far below the master race of true-blooded Germanic Aryans.

Hanne fishes for her Swedish passport and places it on the table before her. That should do. Somewhere among her papers she has also her old ID with her religious affiliation. They never

took it back. Better keep that out of sight. She prays fervently to
the powers above to keep these menaces from investigating the
contents of her purse. No telling what they'll do if they find it.
Perhaps nothing, but you never know. Life is a matter of sheer luck.
She doesn't want her travel plans messed up. She has a vision of
Ruth gloating, "I told you so, didn't I? You never listen."

She feels herself trembling. Her fingers shake. Steady, she
tells herself. One may be tipsy, sleepy, bone tired, whatever. But
constant living in fear hones your mental acumen, snapping you
to full alert at the first hint of danger. Her head is clear. Lucid.
Keen. She steadies her hand. Concentrates. Wills it. There.

The four go about their business. The locale is quiet. Tension
crackles in the air. The only noise comes from boots trampling
from one table to the next, clipped demands for identifications.
Officious, stiff, alert, their companions watch from their various
posts. The music had stopped when they entered. In the tense lull,
the leader takes the mike.

"*Lassen Sie sich nicht stören. Spielen Sie ruhig weiter. Weiter-
machen*," he commands the band.

The players strike up again. The bandleader sings another
hit. *Vergiss mein nicht*! Hanne likes the song, but not the performance.

"That's Gigli's song from the movie," she says to Fritz.

He nods. The nerve to try to imitate his gorgeous voice. The
applause is accordingly lukewarm. Then a schmaltzy waltz. Small
talk begins here and there. The tension diffuses somewhat. People
relax. After all, these uniforms are not looking for them. They're
looking for criminals that belong in concentration camps to learn
respect for authority. Hanne glances at her escort. So dumb of her.
She could kick herself. Well, done is done. She'll have to get out of
this fix somehow. Fritz smiles at her from across the table. Probably satisfied with the little black passport sporting three golden
crowns in front of her.

The ss reaches the couple two tables away. Something is fishy
there. She watches anxiously. They have looked at the ID's. Now

they demand to see her handbag. The man stands up and empties his pockets. They search him quickly. Funny, all this junk that comes out of people's pockets. It's spread over the table. It looks odd. Misplaced between the wineglasses. Hanne breaks out in a cold sweat. Just suppose!

Her gaze follows the blue rings of smoke Fritz emits from his mouth. Round, widening as they float upward, they slowly diffuse in the dimness overhead. Fritz's smile unnerves her. Fate is unreliable. Nothing can stop these monsters from taking her away if they want to, probably not even the Swedes. She clasps her hands tightly. Prays.

"Dear God. Don't spoil everything now at the last moment. You can't do that to me! Please…"

The two move on. Apparently they found nothing incriminating on the couple. They are now only one table away. Dehumanizing, really, to have to submit to these punks. Stupid, arrogant clowns, hardly older than I. They have the guns. That allows them to play God. Hanne's mouth is dry. She fights to control her twitching body.

"Calm down, will you. Don't arouse suspicion. God, don't let them snoop through my purse!" Her mind demands.

The music stops between tunes. Someone hiccups noisily in the hush. Then the band strikes up again. The two finish a fast check of the four military at the adjoining table. They stand beside her.

"*Ihren Ausweis, bitte.*"

At least he is polite enough to add "please" to his demands. His words hang fatefully in the bluish haze of the locale that reeks of alcohol and smoke. Hanne hands him her passport. Her hand is steady. She wonders what his behavior would be like if he knew that she is Jewish. Fritz hands his ID over to the other fellow. That little Mephisto in Amsterdam had actually been pretty polite. But then, he knew of her Swedish protection. The two fellows study the papers thoroughly. Stare at them repeatedly. Compare the pictures with the originals.

"You're Swedish?"

Two pairs of eyes investigate her face. Time floats suspended in eternity. Hanne returns their stares.

"Yes." Is that the truth? Yes. Officially she is Swedish. Adopted. Dumb question anyway. The passport tells her place of birth.

"What are you doing in Berlin?"

"I'm traveling through from Amsterdam. I'm leaving tomorrow morning on the Berlin-Copenhagen Express."

"Oh."

The German language sticks in her throat. Her native tongue.

She holds up under his piercing stare. He flips more pages in her passport. Studies the Gestapo's *Sichtvermerk* for a long while. Another stare, haughty, supercilious. It penetrates the half dark of the nightclub like a physical affront. Stops outside her skin. He snaps the soft covers of the passport shut. With a metallic click of his heels and a slanted smile he returns the black passport with the three golden crowns into her hands.

"I hope you like our capital. Have a good trip."

Her stomach somersaults straight up into her throat. Tension gives way to exhaustion. She watches them turn their attention to Fritz while she places her prized possession carefully back into her purse. My lifesaver. She hums quietly along with the band as it repeats the refrain of *Lily Marlene*.

Hier wollen wir uns wiedersehn
An der Laterne woll'n wir stehn
Wie einst Lily Marlene
Wie einst Lily Marlene.

It's the current hit. She has no intention to see this place again.

Fritz passes the search with flying colors. They hardly look at his ID. Is that because he is her escort? Hardly. It must be another reason. She gives up wondering. Too tired to think straight. The two move on.

CHAPTER 15

"Fritz, do me a favor. Take me back to the hotel."

"I shall. As soon as they're through. There's just one more table left."

Hanne nods. Just don't let them think up another reason to keep us here, she prays. There's always that possibility.

She follows the inquiry at the next table. Passed, she sings inwardly, grateful, still on high alert. Nothing wrong over there. The two are satisfied. They nod at each other and look over to their leader at the bar.

"*Alles in Ordnung*," one shouts.

"*Ja, dann können wir ja gehn.*"

"*Fertig?*" the leader barks at the rest.

They are *fertig*. Done. The uniforms clomp noisily out of the nightclub. The echo of their boots resounds from the stairs to the tune of *Lily Marlene*.

Fritz waves for the waiter and pays. Then takes Hanne's arm. They walk out. The stupid shoes flop on her feet again.

"So you told me the truth. I thought it was a silly joke."

"No, Fritz, I'm not in the habit of making up stories about myself. My reality is confusing enough. I was just afraid they'd search my purse."

They leave the building to the last strains of *Lily Marlene*, the runaway hit of the season. The shoes are a nuisance, but she keeps it in proportion. They had slipped her mind entirely through the razzia.

"When you get to Sweden, could you arrange for me to come there too?"

That must be a joke, coming from a German. Hanne smiles wistfully through her fading anxiety. Why would an Aryan want to leave the country? They aren't persecuted. They don't even know what that means. Hanne hums the *Lily Marlene* refrain. She thinks of Bert. It would have been so nice to have him here next to her, walking with her to the hotel, instead of this stranger. If only these shoes weren't such a pain.

"Oh, I don't know. Why would you want to go to Sweden?"

But he just smiles an inscrutable smile in the dark. She cannot see his face properly. Who knows? The Allies are bombarding Sicily. The Russians are defeating the Nazis at Orel, near Stalingrad. There are rumors that the Allies are preparing for an invasion from the Mediterranean.

They stand in the lobby of Hotel Nordland. She is about to thank him for a wonderful evening. The unwelcome interruption was not his fault. She is exhausted and ready to roll into her bed upstairs.

Fritz has other ideas. "Hanne, I'd like to be with you tonight. I could get a room here."

He holds her hand with unexpected force. His voice urges. His eyes plead. She meditates into his crooked front teeth. Going to bed with him has never been in her plans.

"Thanks, Fritz. I thoroughly enjoyed meeting you and seeing your city in your company. But I'm tired, especially after that incident at the nightclub. And I have to catch an early train in the morning. Let's say goodbye here."

He keeps her hand in his grip. Hanne tries to twist it free.

"Hanne, please," he begs.

"No. It's too late."

She pulls her hand out of his with force and walks to the stairs. Her heels wobble under her feet.

"Don't be a spoilsport, Hanne."

She grips the banister. "No. Fritz, I'm exhausted. I've had enough commotion to last a lifetime. There's a tomorrow now. Goodnight. Thanks again for a pleasant evening."

She walks up the stairs. Slowly. Determined. She can feel his eyes bore into her back.

"Think about what I asked you," he mutters behind her, just loud enough for her to hear. She quickens her step. Why is he so intent on going to Sweden? He belongs here with all the other Nazis. This is his home. She has none and has to find one somewhere else, where she is not hunted like an animal. She turns halfway and looks down at him.

"Good night, Fritz."

She walks on. These shoes are impossible. She stoops and takes them off, then climbs the rest of the way to the fifth floor in her stocking feet, shoes in hand. No one is around to see her anyway.

* * *

"Where on earth have you been?" Ruth fumes from her bed when she enters the room, obviously concerned.

A flood of remorse wells up in Hanne, the older sister. She has failed in her responsibilities.

"We went to a nightclub. There was a razzia. I didn't realize you'd worry enough to wait up for me. You shouldn't have. Nothing is going to happen to me. I'm tough. A weed. Like the heather I had to pick."

Hanne plays cool. She begins to undress. Somehow, she believes in her toughness. She has gone through hell. Has been earmarked for death. Come out on the other side. Nonchalantly she whistles the refrain of *Lily Marlene*. It fills her head.

But Ruth isn't finished with her sermon by a long shot.

"Wait till Mutti hears about this. You run with the first stranger coming your way in a big city like Berlin. You're totally off your rocker."

Hanne whistles on. Ruth the police sergeant, always and forever. The same old story repeats again now that they are going home. That little nuisance bitching again. Pushing her around. She's gotten a lot worse these past five years. Hanne whistles on, trying not to worry. Just let her rant. Better get some sleep.

"A Vilhelm Ekman was here to see us. The Swedes sent him to help us. Of course, you had to shine with your absence. He's coming back to help us with our luggage at five-thirty in the morning. You'd better be ready."

"What? Who?"

Her own stupidity inflames her. Mr. Lind had mentioned this Ekman and she had forgotten in her excitement over Glasses. She should have been here to meet Ekman. If Ruth wants her to feel guilty, she has accomplished it.

"The Swedish fellow traveling home from Rome, remember?"

"Of course. I'm sorry I missed him. What does he look like?"

"He's a real looker. Blond, blue-eyed like the others. Medium height. Same cute accent they all have."

"All right. I'll see him in the morning. Did you set the alarm?"

"I did. And I asked the desk to call us at five, just to be sure."

"Fine. Let's hit the sack, then. We've been yakking for hours about getting a good night's sleep."

"Look who's talking!"

Brushing her teeth in the bathroom, Hanne assesses her reflection in the huge mirror. Brown hair, dark eyes that she wishes were larger. Straight, somewhat prominent nose. She looks down at her body. Good figure, though her hips tend to get too heavy if she's not careful. She'll never be a beauty queen. Too fat to be a movie star. But she is far from bad looking.

"Hanne Kalter," she smiles at her image in the mirror. Jewish, born in Germany. Swedish citizen.

The facts sound good. Solid. How else could she have managed to stand here and brush her teeth in the bathroom on the fifth floor of Hotel Nordland in Berlin, anno 1943. Three years into World War Two. After a visit to a nightclub, including a razzia, with a German stranger. Neat magic. All one has to do is to wave a black passport with three golden crowns under their stupid Aryan noses. How polite they can be all of a sudden!

I'd never have known how polite they can be had I remained in Westerbork. Pity! *Hope you like our capital*, she mimics into the mirror. That goes well with *forget all the bad things you've seen here*. Sure. Suuure. I should've told them that I'm a Jew, fresh out of the concentration camp. Then watched their reaction.

She sighs. That would've been to tempt fate. Who would dare before being done with all this?

"For goodness sake, stop dawdling. Come to bed so we can turn the lights off and get some sleep," Ruth calls from her pillow.

Without another word Hanne switches off the lights and tiptoes over to her bed. Crawls under the featherbed. An exciting day. Life is full of wonderful surprises.

"Sleep tight. And thanks for lending me the shoes," Hanne says into the dark. Then pulls the covers over her head.

The future is an open-ended marvel. I'm young and I've just been given a second chance. She smiles to herself in the dark.

Chapter 16

The black hand quivers forward on the white face of the huge station clock. One notch. A quarter to six. Hanne, Ruth and Vilhelm walk along the platform to the Berlin-Copenhagen Express. Its engine hisses billows of white cloud puffs into the airy glass enclosure of Berlin-Hauptbahnhof, patiently waiting to leave on its next trip north.

The three take it easy. Cover the nervousness they feel at the occasion. Their luggage is safely deposited in the net of their compartment. The long hours of sitting still on the previous day's journey are still in Hanne and Ruth's veins. Their seats saved, they wait outside and stretch their limbs in the short time remaining until the final departure. Hanne looks at the train – solid black steel, power pulsating through it. People coming and going, happy hellos, tearful goodbyes. Vendors shout their wares – newspapers, magazines, candy, toys. The exciting atmosphere of an important railroad junction.

Hanne has a fleeting vision of that other train, the vicious monster with the bottomless bowels on Boulevard de Misère in the Dutch Nowhere. The hungry reptile that devours its human cargo to digest it into oblivion. Where does it eliminate its human stuffing? She still doesn't know. It can't be a good place.

The disturbance fades. Better leave that behind for now. It's impossible to imagine that I was part of that only a few weeks ago her brain murmurs.

She feels a sudden urge to see her friends again: Eddie, Werner, Horsey, Ditta, Gerd, Jackie and all the others. Where are Klärchen Tepper and the Bettelheims? Still in hiding, she hopes. She feels a sudden pang of guilt for standing on this platform, in Berlin, on the way to freedom. Home. But why should she have to feel that way? She has a right to go home. People are not supposed to live herded into communal refugee centers. Concentration camps.

"You're a traitor," her brain insists.

Traitor? To what? To suffering? She hasn't done anything wrong. Neither have all the others. Hard to figure.

I'm too tired to figure all this out. I shouldn't look at trains. I've seen so many. Far too many.

That nagging feeling of guilt persists. Stubborn, it remains. Lodges in her brain. Settles with a gloat.

"We should board in a few minutes," Vilhelm says with a glance at the clock.

Hanne nods. He is a pleasant, intelligent travel companion. It just bothers her that he takes an obvious interest in that nitwit of a sister. Far more than in her. Rats. "I should've been at the hotel to welcome him last night instead of gallivanting around with a moff. A stranger with nothing more on his mind than to put me into a horizontal position. Oh well, can't win 'em all…" She shrugs.

Running footsteps echo on the concrete behind her. She turns. If it isn't…

"Hi there!"

It's Fritz. Out of breath. He gasps for air as he pushes a package into her hand. He smiles broadly into her face.

"Chocolates for the sweet. Something to munch on the train."

"Fritz. What a pleasant surprise." She is overwhelmed. Looks down at his present. "I never expected *you* here. This early." She gives him a grateful look.

"I almost didn't make it. Getting the chocolates and all."

They walk off to the side. He stands close to her. All urgency.

"Listen, Hanne. I have a selfish reason for coming. I asked you to help me get to Sweden. I meant it. Really. Here's my address." He hands her his card. "Please, don't lose it. And don't forget."

She is speechless. How can she promise him anything of the kind? Her own future is still more than unsettled.

"Look. I don't know whether I can help you. But I'll find out when I get there." She shrugs. Uncertain of the entire project. She to help him? That's a reversal of fate. She looks at him. "Sure appreciate your seeing me off. And thanks for the chocolates."

The stationmaster walks along the platform, holding his round red sign under his arm.

"All aboard!" he shouts as he moves forward toward the engine. Slams doors shut as he walks along. "All aboard!"

"Goodbye, Fritz."

"Goodbye, Hanne." Fritz reaches for her hand and kisses it. She climbs into the train. The stationmaster bangs the door shut behind her.

"Take care, Fritz," she mumbles through the open window down to him. Secretively she checks her hand. Does it show? The stationmaster reaches the front of the train. He lifts his round sign.

The train jerks to attention. Straightens out with a shrieking jolt. For a second it stands poised. Then it starts rolling. Out of the station. Slowly, steadily it gains speed.

Overwhelmed, speechless, Hanne sits down with her two companions. She gazes at her hand. Kissed! Does it look any different?

Ruth begins to unwrap the box of chocolates "Suchard," she

says, impressed. "At least he knows what's good. May I have one?" Without waiting for an answer Ruth stuffs a chocolate into her mouth, then offers the box to Vilhelm.

"They're expensive," Hanne says. "I wonder where he got Swiss chocolates."

"Black market," Vilhelm suggests.

Hanne looks at the card in her hand.

"Fritz Lohenfeld, Berlin-Wannsee, Kölnerstrasse 15," she reads out loud.

Her two companions look at her, both question marks. She slides the card into her purse.

"I never expected to see him at the station," she says, trying to explain Fritz and his sudden appearance, to herself and to the world around her. Both are quiet for a while. Meditate. Digest the information. Eventually she talks. Eases her conscience. As if compelled.

"He asked me to get him to Sweden. I just met him last night and now he wants me to help him get to Sweden. How can I? I'm not even there yet myself."

Crestfallen, she looks at Vilhelm. Then a light bulb ignites in her brain. Illumination has struck!

"I told him my background. Perhaps he wanted to make sure I was really leaving... But then, why the chocolates?"

"Who knows? Maybe he's a Gestapo agent. Assigned to supervise your stay in Berlin," Vilhelm offers.

Her face lights up. Of course. She should have thought of that. It makes sense. Hanne ponders for a while.

"That makes the adventure even more exciting, like a first-class detective story," she meditates.

"Then this morning he wanted to make certain that we left on the train. It does make sense," says Ruth.

"It still doesn't explain the candy. Or his wish to leave Germany."

"There could be a million reasons," Ruth spins further. "For one, Sweden's not in the war."

They sit in silence ruminating over the possibilities with the rhythm of the moving train. Fritz remains a puzzle.

"We'll never know what he was up to…"

They settle back in the compartment. Flensburg and the Danish border next.

"The chocolates are delicious. Have another."

Ruth has taken charge of the chocolates.

* * *

The sun disk hangs pale yellow over the Danish lowlands. It burnishes the graceful arching wheat and rye fields to a golden glow far into the horizon. Squares and rectangles of dark green, lush grass with black and white Holsteins break the golden cornfields at regular intervals. Lonely farms with their low thatched roofs dot the landscape. Life continues its steady, ancient rhythm on the other side of the border they have just crossed. A different mode of communication. Hanne listens intently to Vilhelm's animated conversation with a Danish woman who has just joined the three at Flensburg. It bothers her that she can't understand a word they're saying. She has a feeling that he is talking about them, his two charges. It's the same feeling she had when first coming to Holland, only more so. She promises herself not to remain deaf and dumb in her new country for long.

The train speeds on. In half an hour or so they'll be in Copenhagen, the Northern Venice, as the Danish capital is often called. With its harbor and canals and its old architecture it is said to be reminiscent of that grand old city. Hanne looks forward to walking its streets during the layover. Then on to the shuttle train to the ferry that takes them across the Sund overnight. Home.

Germany is behind them. For good.

Hanne sighs. A deep, grateful sigh of relief. She is tired. It's not only the long trip. It runs far deeper. The constant tension. She looks at Ruth and sees the same weariness. No wonder.

Shortly before Flensburg two German customs officials had boarded the train. Checked passports. Demanded of the passengers whether they had anything to declare. Orders barked with customary German supercilious gruffness. No, Hanne and Ruth have nothing to declare. Then the Germans order all passengers to leave the train while they search the luggage with characteristic German thoroughness. The passengers walk across to the other side of the platform to Danish customs. Show their passports. Another check, this time in a language she would give her eyeteeth to understand. All she can do is respond with a friendly nod when the official returns her passport. The relaxed atmosphere is new.

They watch German border police step off the train. Duly searched and inspected, the black iron tube rolls slowly across the border. The passengers may board it again.

Back in their compartment the girls look at each other. The train stretches. Creaks into gear with a heartfelt exhalation of *enough*. Rolls on into the Danish countryside. Fertile lowlands.

Vilhelm watches the two girls. His blue eyes light up. Relieved that his charges have safely crossed into Denmark. Then…How did it all happen? A fluke? A sudden inspiration? Hard to figure. But suddenly they are laughing. All three. An uncontrollable chuckle. A laugh unshackled from deep inside. A sudden release of overpowering tensions never acknowledged. Hard to explain. They laugh until their bodies ache. Relieved of a heavy burden.

Hanne's shoulders straighten in rhythm with the moving train.

There are several stops before Copenhagen. Passengers come and go. Danes. Vilhelm talks to them. Hanne listens to their animated conversation. Strange language. She has a feeling that they're talking about her and Ruth.

Of course, they're still in occupied territory.

"We're on our way. To freedom. Once we board the ferry this evening we'll be free. Free and safe," she says. She reels.

Freedom. There is magic in the word. The term is not in her experience. She only knows what it is not.

She has to relearn. To be able to speak out. Freely. Act according to her belief. Hold on to her convictions without fear.

She promises herself to make this freedom her own. To guard it zealously. Make certain that she'll never lose these rights again.

Hanne stretches her weary limbs.

"Tomorrow I'm going to write to Bert."

Tomorrow.

Photos

Hanne and Ruth, on vacation in Blankenberge, Belgium, 1926

Hanne's parents, Fanny Bindefeld Kalter and Max Kalter

Hanne Kalter

Hanne, Ruth and Sigfrid Kalter and Cilly Kalter, a distant relative, The Hague, 1939

Huis Cromvliet, Ryswyk, Spring 1939

Stuffing mattresses, Huis TenVijver with Zuster Haverkort, September 1939

Huis TenVijver in Scheveningen, Holland, 1940

Jongenshuis, Amsterdamscheweg 1, Arnhem, Holland

Hanne, Jongenshuis, Arnhem, Holland, 1941

١٩٤١ ,On our bikes through Holland from Arnhem

Jongenshuis, Arnhem, Holland, Winter 1942

Der Befehlshaber
der Sicherheitspolizei und des SD
für die besetzten niederl.Gebiete
Lager Westerbork.

Lager Westerbork, den .4.5.43. 194 .

E n t l a s s u n g s s c h e i n .

Die Jüdin   Henna   K A L T E R

geboren am   4.8.19__   in   Duisburg

ist am   5.5.1943.   entlassen.

Gründe: Auf Anordnung Sturmbannführer Zöpf

                      Ausreise Schweden .

Er / Sie ist verpflichtet sich unverzüglich bei der Zentralstelle für jüdische Auswan-
derung, Amsterdam - Zuid, Adama van Scholtemaplein 1, zu melden und diesen Entlassungs-
schein vorzulegen. Reisegenehmigung zur Fahrt nach Amsterdam ist erteilt.

Hat Erlaubnis sich am Entlassungstag
nach 8 Uhr abends auf der Strasse zu
bewegen.

Der Lagerkommandant:
J.F. Henne

Exit Permit